SIAM BECOMES THAILAND

JUDITH A. STOWE

Siam becomes Thailand

A Story of Intrigue

HURST & COMPANY, LONDON

First published in the United Kingdom by
C. Hurst & Co. (Publishers) Ltd.,
38 King Street, London WC2E 8JT
© Judith A. Stowe, 1991
Printed in Hong Kong
ISBN 1-85065-083-7

A catalogue record of this book is
available from the British Library

PREFACE

Many learned works have been written about the history and politics of Thailand, or Siam as it used to be called. Yet the actual course of events there during the past fifty years and more has tended to be glossed over in generalities. Political scientists are more interested in overall trends, whereas the Thai tradition still persists of writing history in terms of a formal chronology or a personal eulogy which eschews any criticism. Reverence for the dead has not yet yeilded ground in Thailand – as it has in many western countries – to the pursuit of objective historical analysis. The tendency has been compounded by the taboos surrounding the royal family. In fact, Thai history is often deliberately distorted to justify certain causes or individuals. As in many societies, established authority in Thailand rests on the assumption that anybody who dares to challenge it is automatically a rebel unless he succeeds in his endeavour. His legitimacy then has to be established by blackening the reputation and achievements of his predecessors in power. Modern Thai history is rife with such instances even to the point where official records have been suppressed or tampered with. Coupled with that, there is a tendency to blame external or alien influences for any problems which have occurred, particularly in the context of Thailand's international history.

This book was not, however, written with the intention of propounding an alternative thesis of Thai history. Rather, it emanated from a suggestion that it would be useful for observers of the current scene to refer to a straightforward account of what happened in the past and so avoid the false analogies which so frequently crop up when the course of Thai politics enters one of its more tortuous and sometimes even violent phases. Coups d'état might seem endemic in Thailand, but comparing one with another becomes invidious when knowledge of them is based on popular mythology rather than facts.

Yet to determine the facts has often proved difficult. First it has become apparent on the basis of the author's research that recent Thai history is far more complex than many existing accounts suggest. As a result, this volume covers a far shorter period than was originally envisaged. Moreover, as any journalist who has attempted to report on Thai affairs is well aware, official accounts rarely reflect the whole truth. Resort has therefore been made to a variety of sources, some Thai and others foreign. The Freedom of Information Act in the United States, and the subsequent decision of the British government to allow access to official records after thirty years have made much new material available. Even so, there are likely to be objections that this is a *farang** view of Thailand. In so far as the author is *farang*, that is inevitable, but many Thai students these days use the records available in London, Washington and Paris as a basis for research.

The current trend to resort to oral history is a different matter, especially when dealing with events which took place more than forty years ago. Many memories are bound to be tinged with the wisdom of hindsight. Still they have proved useful in cross-checking details, and in this context the author would like to thank A.C.S. Adams, Chundaeng Rintakul, Lieutenant-General Sir Geoffrey Evans, Sir Andrew Gilchrist, Konthi Suphamongkol, Pridi Banomyong and Thanpuying Poonsuk, Dr Puey Ungpakorn and family, Sirichai Narumet, Snoh Tanbunyuen, Dr Thanat Khoman, and Vivat na Pombejr. The many other people who have provided help and encouragement include Louis Allen, Apichart Chinwanamo, Authopol Wananuraks, Ian Brown, Chariwat Santabutr, Patrick Honey, Michael Leifer, Bryen Macmanus, Saneh Chamarik, Ralph Smith and Thongbai Hongviangchan.

Finally, this book would be incomplete without mention of Michael Stowe, who has grown up with it. Like it or not, he has had to cope with the fact that much of his mother's time, as well as very often the kitchen table, was pre-occupied with research for this book. In other words, it has been written in spare moments amid running a home single-handed and supporting it by working full-time in a profession which does not enjoy the benefit of academic vacations or research grants. That does not, however, excuse any mistakes or errors of judgement, for which the author accepts full responsibility.

London, November 1990   JUDITH A. STOWE

Farang was originally the Thai word for French, but it has long become the name commonly and often pejoratively applied to all people of European origin, including Americans.

CONTENTS

PORTRAITS

MAPS

THAILAND AND INDOCHINA

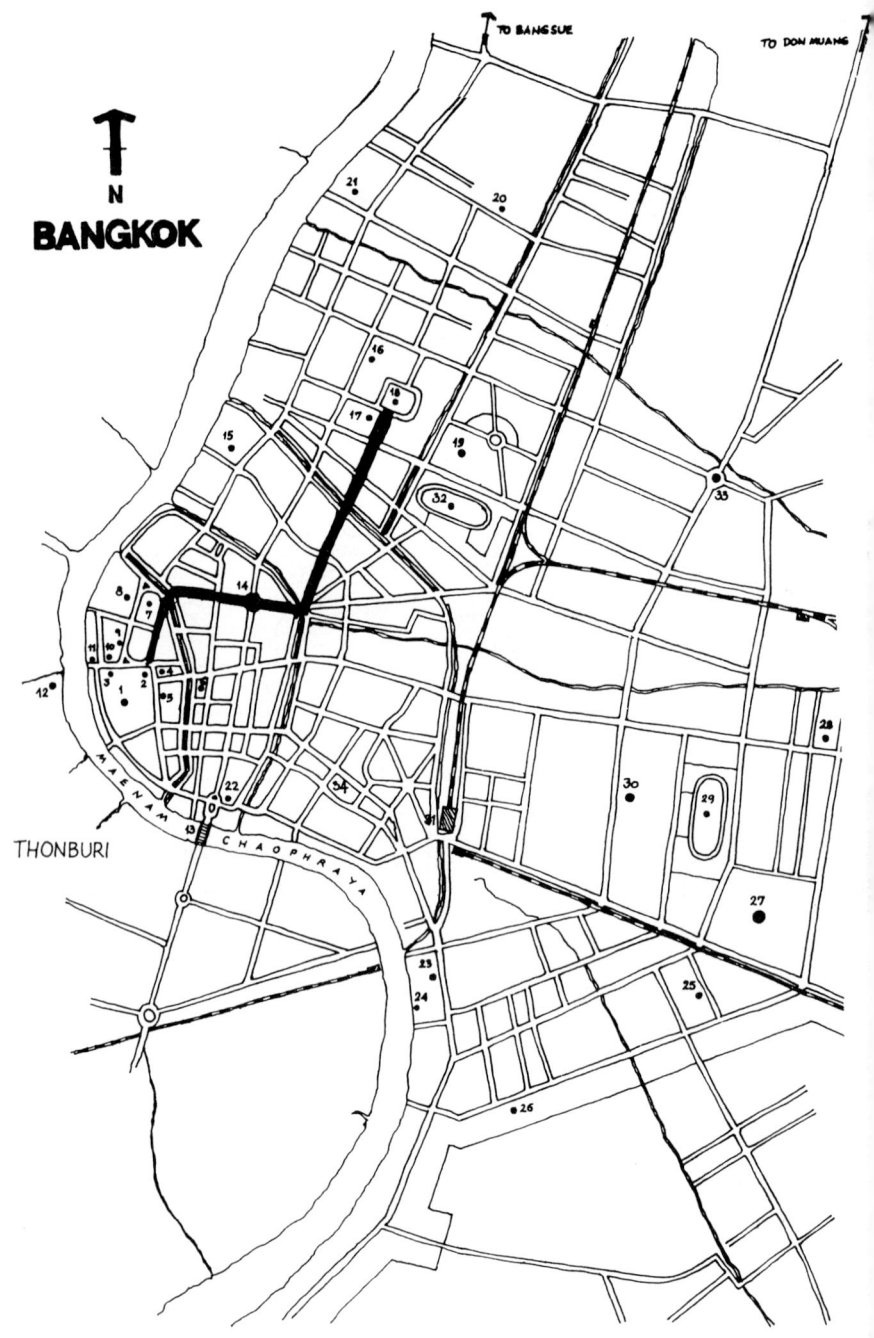

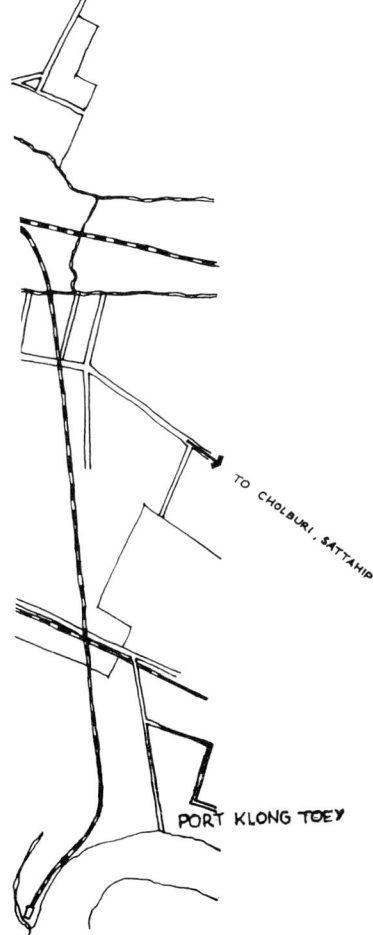

TO CHOLBURI, SATTAHIP

PORT KLONG TOEY

LEGEND

1 Grand Palace
2 Wat Phra Keow (Temple of Emerald Buddha)
3 Ministry of Finance
4 Ministry of Defence
5 Ministry of Foreign Affairs
6 Ministry of Interior
7 Sanam Lueng (Phramane Ground)
8 University of Moral and Political Sciences (Thamasat University)
9 Department of Fine Arts
10 Silpakorn University
11 Ta Chang and Pridi's Residence
12 Naval Headquarters
13 Chakri Memorial Bridge
14 Monument to Democracy
15 Prince Boripat's Palace
16 Suan Kulab Palace
17 Parusakavan Palace
18 Ananta Samakhom Throne Hall
19 Chitralada Palace
20 Prince Aditya's Residence (98 Setsiri Rd.)
21 Samsen E.G.A.T. Plant
22 Wat Lieb E.G.A.T. Plant
23 Post and Telegraph Service
24 French Legation
25 Japanese Legation
26 Chinese Chamber of Commerce (Japanese Military HQ)
27 Lumpini Park
28 British Embassy
29 Royal Bangkok Sport Club
30 Chulalongkorn University
31 Huaulumpong Railway Station
32 Royal Turf Club
33 Victory Monument
34 Chinese Quarter (Yaowarat Rd.)
▬▬ Rajdamnern Rd.

THAI TRANSLITERATION AND NAMES

Many systems exist for the transliteration of Thai into English and other foreign languages. None of them has been accepted as definitive. The Bangkok press and contemporary literature tend to be very pragmatic especially in the case of personal names. Hence the transliterations in this book follow those in common use rather than any specific system.

Thai names are, however, complex in themselves. It is customary for Thais to be referred to by their personal instead of their family names. That is the practice followed in this book. For instance Pridi Banomyong is known as Pridi rather than Banomyong. Moreover, under the absolute monarchy every official, whether civilian or military, was accorded an official title commensurate with his rank when it was customary for him to assume a new name. For example, Plaek Kittasangka, on being commissioned as a captain in the army became Luang Pibul Songkram and that is how he is usually known. Nonetheless since the system of official ranks was phased out after the introduction of constitutional government, they declined in importance and only the Chao Phya, Phya and Phra are referred to as such. Below that the lower ranks of Luang and Khun are largely ignored. But these ranks – just like the peerage in England during recent years – bore little more than symbolic meaning and are incapable of translation. Likewise the descending and sometimes changing orders of royal rank present a problem for the foreigner. Many Thais still prefer to refer to their kings by reign number rather than personal name, but the usual Western practice has been followed in this book as it has in the case of the princes. The more elaborate titles of those princes with the status of royal grandson or above have been omitted. Otherwise more junior members of the royal family are referred to simply by personal name in much the same way as official title-holders or commoners.

1
PRELUDE TO A REVOLUTION

Bangkok was tense on the morning of April 6, 1932. As so often happens, the city was rife with rumours, and strict security precautions were in force. What gave rise to these measures in 1932 was the 150th anniversary of the ruling Chakri dynasty, when the King was due to inaugurate a bridge constructed across the Chao Phya river not far from the royal palace.[1]

Usually the monarch's appearance in public did not cause any problems. The taboos constraining all subjects of the King of Siam to remain indoors and cover their faces when their sovereign lord travelled his domains had lapsed at least fifty years earlier.[2] The practice of full prostration in the royal presence was also being discouraged by the current incumbent of the throne. Yet old customs persisted. In the minds of the Siamese people their monarchs were imbued with divine attributes, although that belief too had been royally discarded.[3] Still the Kings of Siam remained absolute monarchs, theoretically enjoying the power of life and death over all their subjects. Consequently King Prajadhipok, who occupied the throne in 1932, was held in great awe. He could not even be referred to by his personal name. He was known as the seventh Chakri monarch.

Some people, however, regarded the celebrations to mark the Chakri anniversary unwise. They recalled a prophecy, said to have been made at the time the dynasty was founded in 1782, predicting that the Chakri family would reign over Siam for no more than 150 years. But despite stories of ghosts being seen near the Memorial Bridge the night before the King was due to preside over the inaugural ceremony, nothing untoward happened on the day itself. Instead, it was eleven weeks later that the absolute rule of the Chakri monarchs came to an abrupt end, which for many Siamese confirmed that the prophecy had been correct, if a little late in fulfilling itself.[4]

The security alert surrounding the inauguration of the bridge was not ordered simply on the basis of an ancient prediction. There had been talk of disaffection in Bangkok ever since the resignation the previous year of the Minister of War, Prince Bovoradet: ostensibly he had been protesting against decisions affecting the military ordained by the Supreme

1

Council set up by King Prajadhipok to help him rule Siam, but there were other suspicions as well.

Amid the polygamous complexities of the Chakri family, all princes were ranked in descending order depending on their lineal proximity to a monarch. The sons of a king were usually designated celestial highnesses, *Chao Fa*: this was the rank held by all members of the Supreme Council. They did not include Prince Bovoradet who, as a royal grandson, bore the lower rank of serene highness, *Mom Chao*. However, because ambition and jealousy are never far below the surface in Siamese society, there was a widespread belief that he resented not being appointed to the Supreme Council, and even more being over-ruled by it. This led to suspicions that Prince Bovoradet had resigned from the War Ministry in an attempt to curry support within the army to oust the senior princes and substitute his own rule in the name of the King.[5]

Adding weight to this thesis were other controversial moves made by the Supreme Council in early 1932 when trying to deal with an economic crisis stemming from the international recession and the decision of the British Empire, Siam's main trading partner, to abandon the gold standard. Rather than follow a similar course, the princes opted to introduce new taxes as well as cuts in official spending, including the military budget. The King foresaw that these policies might create discontent, especially in the army, and he therefore convened a special meeting of senior officers to explain why the cuts were necessary. In his address he also intimated that coping with the economic crisis was beyond his ability. No previous King of Siam had ever spoken in such terms. Many interpreted the speech not as the King apparently intended, namely as a frank appeal for understanding and cooperation. They saw it rather as a sign of his weakness and evidence that a system which perpetuated the rule of fallible autocrats should be abolished.[6] In other words, the King inadvertently provided fuel for a revolution.

This idea had already occurred to some people who regarded the absolute monarchy as an anachronism in a world where Siam was already sufficiently integrated into the prevailing international order to be affected by the recession. After all, in Asia alone China had thrown off the yoke of the Manchu dynasty and become a republic, while Japan, though retaining its Emperor, was making impressive progress in modernising itself. Even in the neighbouring colonies of South East Asia, there was a nationalist awakening prompted by contemporary political theories, none of which was permitted scope for expression in Siam. Despite moves to discard certain aspects of the divine monarchy, the concept of *lèse-majesté* still prevailed, and anybody who dared to criticise the King, let alone challenge his absolute authority, was liable to severe punishment.[7]

These taboos, while strictly applied to commoners, were more easily overlooked amid the prolific Chakri family where rival princes habitually vied for influence and power. As a result, some monarchs were more absolute than others, depending on the strength of their personalities and the extent to which they were able to impose their views on the royal court and the country at large.

The apparent weakness of King Prajadhipok seemed all the more pronounced in comparison with his father and grandfather. Both of them were credited with energy and vision in pushing through a series of reforms to modernise the country in order to prevent the Siamese monarchy from falling victim, like its neighbours in Burma and Annam, to the European powers expanding eastwards in search of trade and empire. However, King Mongkut was a venerated scholar when at the age of forty-eight he ascended the throne in 1851, and thus he had the authority to impose his will. His son Chulalongkorn, who succeeded him in 1868, initially had a much harder task because of his youth: he was only fifteen at the time. Indeed it was only towards the end of his forty-year reign that he managed to push through such significant reforms as the abolition of slavery and corvée labour.[8]

But perhaps the most important change advocated by both these monarchs was the introduction of new ideas on education, because these had a major impact on future generations. First, King Chulalongkorn, who had himself been taught by foreign tutors hired to teach within the confines of the royal court, sent all his many sons for long periods of education abroad. Then modern schools and a military cadet academy were set up in Bangkok to train an élite for the newly-established civil service and career armed forces. The system was expanded during the reign of King Vajiravudh, who succeeded his father in 1910, to include a university, where the most talented students, some of them even commoners, were granted scholarships to continue their education abroad.[9] Yet when they returned home they were often disillusioned by the lack of opportunity to use their newly-acquired knowledge. Traditional attitudes remained entrenched, and Siam still seemed very backward.[10] Therefore, in some eyes the country seemed in need of a revolution rather than reforms imposed from above in the name of the King.

Such perceptions became increasingly prevalent after King Prajadhipok succeeded to the throne in 1925. He was no less progressive in

outlook than his older brother Vajiravudh or their father Chulalongkorn; the three monarchs simply differed in the way they were able to
cope with entrenched court interests. King Chulalongkorn reigned for
long enough to impose his own views. By contrast, King Vajiravudh
positively outraged traditional circles by preferring the company of his
personal favourites, many of them commoners – albeit at great expense
to the Privy Purse and by extension the national budget.[11] As a result,
King Prajadhipok's inheritance was characterised by the senior princes as
"deplorable". Not only was Siam's financial standing in peril, but the
reputation of the Chakri family itself seemed to be at stake.

As the youngest of Chulalongkorn's thirty-two sons, Prajadhipok
had never expected to become king, and felt ill-equipped for the task. It
was one of the reasons which led him to establish the Supreme Council,
comprising five senior princes, most of them his elder half-brothers or
uncles. Gradually these princes arrogated increasing power by mono-
polising all the main ministerial positions. Perhaps they felt it their duty
to make amends for the mistakes of the previous reign, but if that was
so, it was not generally appreciated. Besides appearing to repress the
ambitions of able commoners to attain high office, the princes failed to
communicate to the public the purpose of the policies they were pursuing, first in trying to rectify the financial extravagances of the previous
reign and then in coping with the effects of the international economic
recession.[12] For example, Prince Purachatra, the Minister of Commerce
and Communications, in travelling abroad to seek new export markets
and buy equipment for the modernisation of Siam's railways, returned
home with films and expensive projectors to show how well he had been
received in other countries. Consequently, like other princes, he gave
the impression that he was enjoying and enriching himself at the expense
of the rest of the population.[13]

In the public mind, however, the person who really symbolised the
domination of the senior members of the royal family over the whole
administration was Prince Boripat, head of the Supreme Council and
Minister of the Interior. Educated in Germany in the Prussian military
tradition, he was regarded as a disciplinarian, and as such he was thought
to exert great influence over the King, to whom he was elder half-
brother. Furthermore, since the laws of succession in Siam did not
follow the rule of primogeniture, Prince Boripat was considered heir to
the throne.[14]

In establishing the Supreme Council, King Prajadhipok originally
envisaged it as a first step towards the introduction of a more broadly-

King Prajadhipok, Rama VII

based and ultimately more democratic form of government;[15] having been educated in England, he was familiar with the concept of constitutional monarchy, and throughout his reign he entertained the hope of introducing something similar in Siam. He indicated as much in a press interview given during a visit to the United States in 1931, where he also shook hands with several Siamese students, thus symbolically displaying his democratic attitude by breaking another formidable royal taboo:[16] this was the first time a Siamese had ever been seen to touch his monarch with impunity. On his return home, the King proposed the drafting of a constitution to be promulgated on the 150th anniversary of the Chakri dynasty, but he was dissuaded by the princes on the Supreme Council as well as by two advisers to the Foreign Ministry, one Siamese and the other American. They all argued that the people of Siam were insufficiently educated or politically conscious to cope with such a development.[17]

Short-sighted as that view proved to be in stifling rising hopes among the educated minority, it was nonetheless true that the mass of the people knew and cared little about the way they were governed. According to the 1929 census, Siam had a population of roughly 11.5 million, of whom about 90 per cent were peasant farmers. In most respects their way of life had barely changed over the centuries; the majority tilled their own land with traditional methods.[18] Buddhism, with an admixture of animism, was the prevailing religion. Royal authority was submitted to whenever it impinged sufficiently to make itself felt. The one innovation was the spread of a monetised economy after King Mongkut permitted the Western powers to trade with Siam in the 1850s; this also led to the substitution of local handicrafts such as weaving and metal-forging with manufactured goods. But if a peasant needed additional income to purchase such goods or feed an expanding family, there was usually extra land available which could be brought under cultivation. All these factors meant that, unlike the situation in other more populous ricelands of Asia such as parts of China and Tonkin, there was little actual starvation in Siam. There was also little impetus for change, let alone peasant revolt. On the contrary the whole national ethos militated against it. Theravada Buddhism taught submission and non-violence and, in addition, Siamese society was stratified according to Brahministic concepts with the King at the apex. Under him the only socially acceptable roles were those of court official, soldier, monk or peasant farmer, and consequently the entrepreneurial role in the Siamese economy was mostly left to aliens.[19]

Up till the reign of King Mongkut, all Siamese trade was a royal monopoly farmed out mostly to Chinese merchants.[20] When European traders were permitted to enter Siam, they simply extended the system without significantly changing it. The British in particular set up import-export houses and obtained concessions for the exploitation of Siam's natural resources such as teak and tin, but they usually employed aliens as clerks and labourers in these enterprises. At the same time, the Chinese moved into the expansion of retail trade. Their main role was that of middlemen in the rice trade, the basis of the Siamese economy and its major export commodity. Yet whereas the Europeans, Indians and other non-Buddhist Asians were always regarded as foreigners, the Chinese gradually became assimilated: during the nineteenth and early twentieth centuries, many immigrants to Siam were poor Chinese males in search of their fortunes. After establishing themselves, they often married Siamese women, yet even so they retained strong links with the land of their ancestors.[21]

This dual loyalty began to cause problems with the growth of the Chinese republican movement. In 1908 its leader Sun Yat-sen spent ten days in Bangkok, where his supporters had already set up a branch of the Chinese revolutionary alliance whose policy was to regard all Overseas Chinese as citizens of their ancestral homeland.[22] Under Siamese law, however, all people born in the country, including those of alien or mixed parentage, were entitled to Siamese nationality. Consequently a large number of Sino-Thais, in opting for the land of their birth, were unconsciously to have a significant impact on the future of Siam, not merely in the economic sphere. One of the first-ever outbreaks of popular political unrest in Bangkok occurred in 1910 when the Chinese community demonstrated against the poll-tax.

Although the Chakri family themselves had Chinese blood in their veins, King Vajiravudh decided to counter what he saw as an alien threat by promoting Siamese nationalism. He wrote plays designed to remind his subjects of Siam's rich cultural heritage. Using a pen-name, he also contributed articles to the press warning against alien influences, and especially the influence of the Chinese, whom he dubbed "the Jews of the East".[23]

At the same time, King Vajiravudh set up a new military organisation, called the Wild Tiger Corps, separate from the existing armed forces. The inspiration for it apparently stemmed from his personal experience while being educated in England. After studying law and history at Oxford, he completed a military staff training course at Sandhurst and was awarded a commission in the British army. As a result he came to appreciate the atmosphere of the regimental mess and sought to reproduce something similar in Siam. The Wild Tiger Corps was created, with an élite brigade of guards officered by the King's personal favourites and its own special mess which His Majesty frequented. That soon attracted the envy of the regular army and affected morale, particularly among junior officers stationed up-country far from the delights of life in Bangkok. In 1912, inspired possibly by the ousting of the Manchu dynasty in China, some of them hatched a plot to capture and depose the King. The conspiracy was uncovered before it could be realised, and twelve of its instigators were sentenced to long terms of imprisonment. Although the King later commuted the sentences, the incident constituted a lesson that was not lost on the monarchy. It stepped up its vigilance against any possible sources of opposition.[24]

Yet compared with what happened elsewhere in the world during the next twenty years, Siam remained an oasis of peace. Despite the precedent and reasons that existed for staging a revolution, the country continued to be stable and serene, priding itself that, alone among all the kingdoms and principalities of the region it had managed to maintain its independence in the face of European colonialism.

NOTES

1. M. Smith, *A Physician at the Court of Siam*, p. 154, and Landon, *Siam in Transition*, p. 10.
2. ibid., p. 52, and Thawatt Mokrapong, *The History of the Siamese Revolution*, p. 54.
3. M. Smith, p. 89.
4. Sivaram, *The New Siam in the Making*, p. 34.
5. Batson, *The End of the Absolute Monarchy in Siam*, p. 190, and Chula Chakrabongse, *Lords of Life*, p. 306.
6. Text of the King's speech in Batson, *Documents from the End of the Absolute Monarchy*, pp. 77ff, and Vella, *The Impact of the West on Government in Thailand*, p. 359.
7. Thawatt Mokrapong, p. 56.
8. Wyatt, *Thailand: A Short History*, pp. 192ff, and Riggs, *Thailand: The Modernisation of a Bureaucratic Polity*, pp. 56ff.
9. Landon, p. 96ff.
10. M. Smith, p. 86.
11. Vella, p. 359.
12. ibid., pp. 351ff; Batson (1974), pp. 2ff, and Sivaram, pp. 26ff.
13. Landon, p. 19.
14. Chula Chakrabongse, p. 307, and Sivaram, p. 21.

15. Text of King's memorandum in Batson (1974), pp. 13ff.
16. Thompson, *Thailand: The New Siam*, p. 57.
17. Texts of these exchanges in Batson (1974), pp. 82ff.
18. Ingram, *Economic Change in Thailand*, pp. 36ff.
19. ibid., p. 55, and Landon, *The Chinese in Thailand*, pp. 145ff.
20. Skinner, *Chinese Society in Thailand*, pp. 9ff.
21. ibid., p. 126ff.
22. Landon (1941), p. 283.
23. Text in ibid., pp. 33ff.
24. Chula Chakrabongse, pp. 274ff, and Vella, *Chaiyo*, pp. 27–54.

Part I
COUPS AND COUNTER-COUPS, 1932–1935

2

THE ABOLITION OF THE ABSOLUTE MONARCHY

The element in Siamese society which caused most concern to the monarchy was the relative handful of people who went abroad to study. The fear was they might become subject to alien political influences. For that reason King Chulalongkorn sent his sons to be educated only in European monarchies where they could be attached to the royal court. Later, when commoners won official scholarships to study abroad and it was appreciated that important republics such as France and the United States could not be ignored, Siamese diplomats were specially assigned to act as guardians of the overseas students. Their duty was to ensure the proper conduct of the students while abroad and that they would return home in due time to fulfil the terms of their scholarship by entering government service. Although this paternalistic system still exists, it proved of little avail when certain Siamese students experienced the heady political atmosphere of Paris just after the First World War.[1]

One such student was Pridi Banomyong, who arrived in France in 1920 to read law. That in itself was a considerable achievement for Pridi, who was born at the turn of the century in Ayuthya, a town in the agricultural heartland of the Chao Phya basin. However, he did not come from a traditional Thai peasant family; his great-grandfather on the paternal side had emigrated from China.[2] Therefore, as in most Sino-Thai families, the children were expected to go out into the world to expand the influence and fortune of their own family. For example, Pridi's eldest brother was sent back to China to learn banking, while he himself was destined to become a Siamese government official. Hence, after attending a local school in Ayuthya, Pridi was sent to Bangkok for further education, and at the age of nineteen graduated from the law school attached to the Ministry of Justice with the highest honours. That earned him an official scholarship to study at the Sorbonne where

9

he obtained not only a doctorate in law but also a diploma in political economy.

According to Pridi, his interest in politics dated from the time of the overthrow of the Manchu dynasty, when one of his teachers in Ayuthya pointed out its significance in both the Chinese and Siamese contexts. Later, while he was studying in Bangkok, the Bolshevik revolution also caused a stir. However, Marxist-Leninist theory waʳ a topic of much more intense debate in Paris where Pridi attended meetings with other Asians to discuss the implications of the Soviet revolution for their own part of the world.[3]

Apart from this, Pridi played a leading role in the association of Siamese students in France. In 1926 they mounted a petition to request an increase in allowances, because they believed they were receiving less than their compatriots elsewhere in Europe. The petition was presented by Pridi to Prince Charoonsak Kridakorn, the Siamese Minister in Paris. He was a typical autocrat, and even senior members of the royal family went in awe of him and his notoriously short temper.[4] His reaction to the petition was to demand that the government revoke Pridi's scholarship and recall him to Bangkok. According to Prince Charoon, Pridi was attempting to make revolutionaries of the students in Paris and was therefore "a danger to the throne". His career was only saved when his father appealed direct to the King, who ruled that Pridi should be allowed to complete his studies, which were then in the final year. Somewhat ironically, it was Prince Charoon who was subsequently recalled to Bangkok:[5] he was said to have conducted himself in a manner unbefitting a Siamese envoy, including allegedly embezzling money destined to pay student grants.[6]

Before this incident Prince Charoon had already clashed with the students in Paris when they applied for permission for two of them to attend a meeting in London. The request was turned down apparently because Prince Charoon had a strong personal dislike of the superintendent of Siamese students in Britain. Nevertheless, at least one of the students in Paris did manage to travel to London for the meeting: he was Prayoon Pamornmontri, who was able to evade Prince Charoon's ban because he had not gone to France directly on a government scholarship.[7]

There were other ways in which Prayoon differed from the rest of the students in Paris. He had been born in Berlin, the son of a junior official at the Siamese legation, married to a German woman. When the family returned to Siam during Prayoon's boyhood, he was presented as a page to the Crown Prince, later to become King Vajiravudh. Under this royal patronage, he attended the military cadet academy in Bangkok and obtained a commission in the Brigade of Guards. Later, he sought to broaden his horizons by obtaining permission and a royal allowance to travel to Europe, and spent several years there drifting around before ending up in Paris to enrol for a course in political science, which he apparently did not complete. However, during his variegated career in Europe he had made a lot of useful acquaintances.[8]

On Prayoon's arrival in France, there was already somebody to whom he felt closely attached. This was Plaek Kittasangka, a classmate from the cadet academy in Bangkok currently studying at the French artillery school at Fontainebleau. The extent of their previous friendship is open to question, but the link apparently served Prayoon well when Plaek was subsequently promoted captain in the Siamese army with the official rank of *Luang* and assumed the name Pibul Songkram, meaning literally "extensive warfare".

Unlike the majority of boys entering the cadet academy during the early years of the twentieth century, Pibul – as he is usually known – did not stem from an official background. His father derived a living from a durian* orchard in Nontaburi on the northern outskirts of Bangkok; Pibul had been born there in 1897.[9] One story often told of him is that his parents soon noticed that his eyes were higher than his ears, a feature considered so unusual that they called him *Plaek*, meaning "odd".[10] In later life Pibul regarded as a more significant omen, the fact that his birth-date was July 14, the anniversary of the French revolution. Still he had a conventional village upbringing until he came to the notice of a wealthy patron, who financed his training as a military cadet. On graduating in 1915, Pibul chose to become an artillery officer, more because of the colour of the uniform he would wear than for any other reason. He then spent several years in an up-country garrison before returning to Bangkok for a course in artillery training and another at military staff college, from which he emerged top of the class. It was this which earned him the official scholarship which took him to France.[11]

Given these differing backgrounds, Pridi, Prayoon and Pibul were, each in their own way, affected by their experience of France. Pridi was inspired by the political ideas he imbibed in Paris, Pibul was impressed by what he saw as the sophistication of French life in comparison to the backwardness of Siam, whereas Prayoon was ready to seize on to anything which would forward his own career prospects. As a result, the three of them agreed that changes were necessary in their own

*Durian is a large odoriferous fruit much prized by many Thais for its supposed aphrodisiac properties but shunned by most foreigners for its smell.

country, and the first essential was the abolition of the absolute monarchy. From there Pridi went on to advocate that the introduction of a constitutional form of government should be only the first step towards the reform of the entire economic and social system in Siam.[12] So persuasive was the way in which he argued his case that a small group of students, both civilian and military, gathered around him. Consequently Pridi came to be known as the mentor of those intent on promoting the end of the absolute monarchy. Within this group, Pibul then styled himself Captain while Prayoon readily assumed the role of organiser and contact-man.[13]

The first meeting of the promoters' group as such took place in February 1927 at the boarding-house where Prayoon was lodging in the rue de Sommerard on the Left Bank in Paris.[14] Seven people were present,[15] and at subsequent meetings the number never rose much higher, although membership of the group gradually expanded. One thing all the promoters shared was a desire to keep their intentions secret. Before asking anybody to join their discussions, the promoters first invited him to dinner to test his reactions to drinking and gambling; they thought it would provide a guide to his reliability. Every Siamese believed that if the authorities discovered that he was plotting against the monarchy, he would face immediate imprisonment.[16]

That being so, a significant recruit to the promoters' group was *Luang* Sindhu Songkramchai. He was a naval officer studying in Denmark, and like many other Siamese in Europe, he spent his vacations in Paris. Yet, unlike Pridi and Pibul, the family from which Sindhu stemmed had already distinguished itself in official service; for example, his elder brother was an admiral. This, possibly, was why it took a long time to persuade Sindhu to join the promoters,[17] but for them the effort was well worthwhile.

Early on, the promoters concluded – ironically, much as the King's advisers had done – that the Siamese people were politically immature. Not only did the majority of the population consist of illiterate peasants, but in Bangkok, the only urban centre of any consequence, the working class was small and consisted mainly of alien labourers. The incipient middle class also lacked any political or intellectual sense of initiative. With trade remaining largely in the hands of foreigners and particularly Chinese merchants, the Siamese bourgeoisie, such as it was, owed its position to the monarchy in the form of official appointments awarded more on the basis of royal patronage than merit. Hence, the promoters in Paris thought that it would be futile to try to arouse a mass movement aimed at curtailing the role of the monarchy. Rather, they sought to co-opt the support of individuals in positions of potential influence such as Sindhu in the navy. Consequently what they were planning was not so much a revolution as a *coup d'état* – an expression which did not then exist in the Siamese language.[18]

To this end Pridi, on his return home in 1927, gradually and secretly built up a group of about fifty civilian officials who wished to see an end to the absolute monarchy. The task was facilitated by his appointment as an official in the Ministry of Justice with a duty to lecture at its law school as well as at Chulalongkorn University. Furthermore, these positions qualified him for a title. Significantly he chose to call himself *Luang* Pradit Manutharm, literally ''exercise humanity''.

Pibul and Sindhu likewise returned home to positions of influence: they were assigned to teach at the military and naval academies. Pibul, however, was subject to certain distractions. The social polish he had cultivated in Paris led to his being appointed equerry to one of the princely members of the Supreme Council.[19] As a result it was left largely to *Luang* Tasnai Niyomsuk, another promoter from the original Paris nucleus, to spread its ideas within the army.

Tasnai, a cavalry officer, differed in character from Pibul. He was genuinely inspired by Pridi's ideas for establishing a new constitutional order in Siam. He also had a flair for inspiring others and, lacking any affectation, he was popular within the army among all ranks. Still, because of his marginal seniority, Pibul was credited with the leadership of the twenty or so junior army officers who agreed to promote the end of the absolute monarchy.[20]

But a group of civilian officials, with the addition of a few dozen junior army and navy officers, was clearly incapable of bringing about political change on its own. Its members realised that they needed the help of more senior officers. The economic crisis, coupled with the military retrenchments announced in early 1932, gave them reason to hope that they might obtain it. One senior officer who was thought to be unhappy, not merely over the retrenchments but also because of the way the princes dominated the armed forces, was Colonel Phya Phahol Pholpayuphasena, Deputy Inspector of Artillery. The problem for the promoters was how to sound out his views without arousing suspicion. Here Prayoon came up with a solution. His mother had given German lessons to Phya Phahol thirty years earlier before he had gone abroad to study; this old contact was reactivated, and indirectly it was discovered that Phya Phahol was thinking along the same lines as the promoters. From there the conspiracy rapidly expanded.[21]

In 1904, when Phya Phahol went to study in Germany, he was soon joined by another government scholarship winner, Phya Song Suradet, who by 1931 had also risen to the rank of colonel with the position of Director of Education at the Military Academy. There Phya Song enjoyed the respect of his students, being widely regarded as having the most brilliant military mind of his generation. For the same reason he commanded a personal following among older officers, whereas Phya Phahol enjoyed widespread popularity within the army because of his affable nature. The difference in character between these two men became apparent as soon as Phya Song was approached with the idea of joining a group to discuss the ending of the absolute monarchy: immediately he, rather than Phya Phahol, assumed charge of planning how the objective could be achieved.[22]

As a military tactician, Phya Song believed that to seize power in Siam the real necessity was to control Bangkok. The rest of the country did not matter. Another of his ideas was that if troops garrisoned in the capital rather than regiments from the provinces took over control, there was less likelihood of bloodshed, a factor that weighed heavily with Thai Buddhists. Phya Song was also mindful that most Siamese officers were intrinsically loyal to the monarch, and if they heard of a plot brewing, they were likely to report it to higher authority. Thus he insisted from the very beginning that knowledge of the promoters' aims should be restricted to the absolute minimum, despite objections from some of them that it might limit potential support.[23]

Clearly the first people from whom the conspiracy had to be concealed were the police, who, because of the rumours surrounding the 150th anniversary of the Chakri dynasty, as well as the manifest discontent in official circles prompted by the administration's economic measures, increased their vigilance in early 1932. Consequently, whenever the promoters met, there was always a pack of cards handy in case there should be a police raid. In addition Phya Phahol, who like most Thais was superstitious, insisted that there should never be more than eight people present at any of the promoters' meetings. For him eight was a lucky number.[24]

Perhaps the luckiest development for the promoters was an approach made to Phya Phahol by Prince Bovoradet. The former Minister of War wanted help in stirring up discontent within the military in order to oust the ruling princes, but the request was declined. Phya Phahol said that the idea was impractical because the princes were bound to take counter-action. Underlying his argument was Phya Phahol's reluctance to take part in a scheme which he thought would simply forward Prince Bovoradet's personal ambitions without touching the basic problem of curtailing royal power and princely privilege.[25] Instead, to divert police attention from their own conspiracy, the promoters deliberately spread rumours of Prince Bovoradet's disaffection. This also acted as a spur, since the promoters wanted to pre-empt any coup he might launch. However, it was not till June 1932 that Phya Song came up with a plan for overthrowing the monarchy.[26]

The basic problem confronting Phya Song was how to gain control of enough troops in Bangkok to carry out a coup. He, Phya Phahol and several other personal friends who agreed to join the conspiracy were all staff officers, and the same was true of the junior army and navy officers who had been building up their own factions independently. Hence Phya Song and Phya Phahol tried to win over those of their classmates from cadet days who had command of troops. Some declined, apparently out of fear of prejudicing their careers, but Colonel Phya Ritthi Akaney, commander of the First Artillery Regiment of the Royal Brigade of Guards based in Bangkok, was more amenable. He shared his friends' misgivings over the way the princes dominated the army, but was reluc-tant to take part in any action which might jeopardise the monarch's life.[27] The first plan conceived by Phya Song involved taking the King captive.[28] The problem was partly resolved in early June when the King departed for a holiday at Hua Hin, a seaside resort about 100 miles south-west of Bangkok where he had just had a summer palace con-structed. It was called Klai Kangwol – "Far From Worries".

Even with the King out of Bangkok, there remained the problem of the senior princes on the Supreme Council who had the power to thwart any coup with ease. Phya Song therefore tried to ensure that, if anything went wrong, as few people as possible would be held responsible. Most of the promoters were kept in the dark, and nothing was ever com-mitted to paper. Right up to the last moment, nobody except Phya Song and his close friends had any idea of what was about to happen, and even they were unsure whether their plans would succeed.[29]

Despite all these precautions, word reached the police that a plot was hatching. On the evening of June 23, its Director-General called on Prince Boripat, the Interior Minister, to request authorisation for the immediate arrest of several people suspected of conspiring against the throne. On perusing the list of those the police wanted to detain, Prince Boripat recognised the names of certain officials from well-known families. Hence he signified that the matter could wait till the next morning, when further enquiries should be made.[30] This delay proved to be crucial, for that same evening, soon after its senior officers went off duty, orders were circulated within the navy to move to suppress a Chinese uprising. Most of the junior officers remaining on watch were Sindhu's friends who knew that these orders were false in order to exonerate them if anything went wrong. They also knew what they had to do. One young naval promoter who was in command of a gunboat, slipped its moorings and manoeuvred it in the Chao Phya river to a position where its guns could be trained on Prince Boripat's palace. Sindhu himself mobilised 500 sailors to empty the naval arsenal in readiness for mounting an attack to capture the Ananta Samakhom Throne Hall at dawn the next morning. Well before then, other naval promoters took over the Posts and Telegraph Office with the help of Prayoon, who occupied an official position there.[31]

Also at the Post Office that night was Khuang Abhaiwongse. He had been a student in France at the same time as Pridi and Prayoon, but had not then been invited to join the promoters' group. He was regarded as too talkative; besides, his elder sister was married to Prince Charoon, the Siamese Minister in Paris. As a result, Khuang was only approached at the last minute to join the conspiracy since he had technical knowledge of the Post Office, and this was considered useful.[32] The plot required that all telephone lines to the palaces of the princes and other influential members of the administration should be disconnected. Once the navy seized the Post Office, the work proceeded apace with Khuang's assistance, although two officials became suspicious and slipped out in an attempt to warn the police.[33]

It was too late. Any action by the police needed the authorisation of Prince Boripat, and his palace was under surveillance not only from the gunboat in the river but also by a group of civilian promoters on land. Similar groups took up watch outside the homes of other senior members of the administration.[34] All the promoters clearly wanted to play some role that night. But where Phya Song was concerned, anything done by civilians was incidental to the main action, which had to be carried out by the military. It was due to start at 5 a.m., half an hour earlier than the normal time for reveille in the Bangkok garrisons.[35]

Just after 4 a.m., Tasnai and three other junior cavalry officers arrived at Phya Song's house to be given their final orders. From there they all moved off to the main meeting-point, where Phya Phahol and several of his friends were waiting; it was not far from the barracks of the First Cavalry Regiment of the Royal Guards, which served as a base for most of the armoured vehicles in Bangkok, and which for Phya Song was a crucial target. At 5 a.m. he led his small group of conspirators to the gates of these barracks where he reprimanded the officer on watch for sleeping while a Chinese uprising was taking place elsewhere in the city. The ruse worked. The regiment was roused by bugle call, the gates of the barracks opened, and Phya Song and the other promoters rushed in shouting about the alleged uprising. In the confusion Phya Phahol, armed with a pair of metal-cutters, made straight for the arsenal to break open its padlocks. Phra Prasat Pitthiyayuth, one of Phya Song's closest friends, took the commander of the regiment into custody. Pibul and his group, arriving late on the scene, were assigned to guard the rest of the barracks. Then Tasnai, as a cavalry officer, assumed charge of the troops: he ordered some into trucks to drive straight to the Throne Hall, while others were instructed to march to the barracks of the First Infantry Regiment. This was commanded by Phya Ritthi, who had finally agreed to join the promoters, once he knew that the vital first attack on the cavalry barracks had succeeded. To reassure him, the plot provided for Phya Ritthi to carry out practice manoeuvres early in the morning of June 24, thus ensuring that all the vehicles under his command were geared up and ready to move into action as soon as troops from the cavalry regiment arrived. If they did not arrive, nobody would be any the wiser, and Phya Ritthi would simply order his regiment back to barracks. As it happened, all went well and soldiers from the cavalry and infantry regiments, led by Phya Ritthi, moved off towards the Throne Hall.[36]

This destination had been carefully selected beforehand by Phya Song who, like other staff officers among the promoters, had been discreetly propagating constitutional ideas among his students. To bring all these cadets together, he arranged in advance for them to participate in a training exercise on the grounds in front of the Throne Hall at 6 a.m. For the same purpose, several military units based in Bangkok were ordered to send troops to provide practical demonstrations. Consequently, there was already a considerable throng assembled outside the Throne Hall when troops from the cavalry and artillery regiments arrived. Excitement mounted as news of the alleged Chinese uprising passed around. Confusion was further deliberately fanned by the promoters until Phya Phahol, as the senior officer present, suddenly climbed on to a tank to proclaim that the absolute monarchy had been abolished and replaced by a constitutional government. The promoters raised a cheer which was quickly echoed by the rest of the troops present, probably more out of a habit of deference than any comprehension of what was involved.[37]

In reality Phya Phahol was bluffing, and everything still depended on developments elsewhere in Bangkok. Using some of the vehicles taken from the cavalry regiment, Phra Prasat and several other senior military promoters had set off to arrest Prince Boripat and other leading members of the royal administration. It was a risky operation, since many of those to be detained were armed and well protected by personal bodyguards. In the event only one of them, the commander of the First Army Corps, offered any serious resistance, and he was the only person to be wounded during the coup.[38]

In all about forty people were taken into custody and detained under strict guard in the Throne Hall which had been secured by the navy. There was one notable absentee: Prince Purachatra managed to escape the promoters' net. As Minister of Communications he commandeered a railway engine and slipped out of Bangkok to go and warn the King at Hua Hin.[39] Bearing in mind other revolutions and particularly those in France and Russia, the Siamese royal family was fearful about its own fate. For instance, Prince Boripat's son fled with his family to seek asylum at the British Legation until he learned that the promoters considered him too insignificant to detain.[40]

The outcome of all these fears was that nobody offered any resistance to the coup. Apart from anything else, Siamese officials, no matter whether civilian or military, were unaccustomed to initiating collective action without prior orders from above, and possibly this was the greatest advantage enjoyed by the promoters, who scarcely numbered more than 100. By about 8 a.m. they had gained the day, even though they did not realise it at the time.

As planned beforehand, the next stage involved arousing popular support for the revolution. This propaganda work was assigned to the civilian promoters. To enhance their popular appeal, they decided to call themselves the Khana Ratsadorn, usually known in English as the People's Party.[41] During the morning of June 24, leaflets signed by the Khana Ratsadorn were distributed throughout Bangkok, and the text was broadcast on the radio.[42]

The Manifesto of the Khana Ratsadorn, as it was entitled, criticised the monarchy in very inflammatory terms. The King was accused of appointing his relatives and incompetent favourites to important positions without bothering to listen to the voice of the people. The royal administration was also attacked for treating the people as ''servants and slaves to sweat blood'' to finance the life of luxury led by the princes. Yet once it had abused the King for failing to introduce a constitution, the Manifesto stated the Khana Ratsadorn was prepared to allow him to remain on the throne provided he would act according to the will of a constitutional government. Otherwise, the Manifesto stated, ''if the King refuses or fails to reply within the time set, either because of his selfishness or his disapproval of the reduction of his power, he will be regarded as a traitor to the nation and the country will then have democratic rule: that is, the head of state will be a commoner elected by the Assembly for a limited period of time.'' In other words it was a threat to establish a republic.

The tone of a telegram sent to the King that afternoon was different. It stated that if he was not prepared to remain on the throne under a constitutional form of government, another royal prince would be appointed in his stead.[43] The telegram was signed by Phya Phahol, Phya Song and Phya Ritthi, the three full colonels among the promoters, who called themselves the Bangkok Military Command.

The contrast between the telegram to the King and the Manifesto of the Khana Ratsadorn has provoked much subsequent comment. There have been suggestions that it provides evidence that Pridi, who drafted the Manifesto, was bent on establishing a republic, whereas the senior military promoters remained royalists at heart. Alternatively, it can be argued that the two documents differed because of the audiences to which they were respectively addressed. While the Manifesto sought to evoke the support of the masses, the telegram to the King stated unequivocally: ''If members of the Khana Ratsadorn receive any injuries, the princes held hostage will suffer the consequences.''[44]

Even before the arrival of this telegram, the King was aware that something had happened in Bangkok. He was playing golf at Hua Hin that morning, and his party had reached the eighth hole when one of them, to his astonishment, saw a court official ''doing a sprint up the course'' with an urgent message for the King, who immediately withdrew from the game together with two princely ministers who were also present. Later in the day they were joined in discussion by Prince Purachatra following his precipitate escape from Bangkok on the railway engine. Apparently they considered various options for coping with the situation, ranging from fleeing the country or mounting a countercoup. The possibility of going into temporary exile across the border in

Malaya was also mentioned. Subsequently a *farang* who had been staying with the royal family at Hua Hin at the time commented that the King and his advisors appeared so taken aback that they would have been unlikely to follow through any of these ideas even if the need had arisen.[45]

In the event, once he received the telegram from Phya Phahol and his colleagues, the King cabled back his readiness to remain on the throne as a constitutional monarch, adding that it was a development he had always favoured. The one sticking-point came when a gunboat was sent to Hua Hin to fetch him. The King insisted on returning to Bangkok by train to prove that he was not a captive of the Khana Ratsadorn.[46]

Meanwhile in Bangkok those princes held in custody at the Throne Hall were not being treated in the manner to which they were accustomed. Although unharmed, they were confined to small rooms without servants to wait on their every need. According to Prayoon, one of the promoters assigned to watch over these hostages, Prince Boripat was very angry: he enquired scornfully whether those responsible for what he dubbed "this revolution" were aware of the history of the French Revolution and the fate of Robespierre, Danton and Marat.[47] Nonetheless, during the afternoon of June 24 the Prince agreed to sign a proclamation calling for peace, but only after deleting from the original draft presented to him an injunction to the people to obey the Khana Ratsadorn. Instead, Prince Boripat wrote in an appeal for everybody to avoid unnecessary bloodshed.[48]

It was not needed. As in so many subsequent coups, life in Bangkok was barely affected. One newspaper, published that same afternoon, commented: "Bangkok awoke this morning to find that the greatest political sensation in its 150 years of existence had taken place quietly and without forewarning in the early hours before dawn . . . Except for scattering crowds in the neighbourhood of the Throne Hall and the Grand Palace, there was not the slightest sign of excitement . . . Police were on duty as usual. Courts functioned. Mail collections and deliveries were as usual . . . Now and then a truckload of uniformed men with machine-guns mounted would appear from within the compound of the Throne Hall and as they passed the crowds outside, loud cheers arose which the soldiers returned vociferously. There was no hysteria, no bad feeling anywhere . . ."[49]

Still a few people noticed that the royal anthem usually played at the end of cinema performances in Bangkok was replaced by a new nationalist song. A similar change was made on the national radio station which had just started broadcasting in Siam. Indeed had it not been for the radio, most of the country would have known little of what had occurred in Bangkok and cared even less. As it was, the coup appears to have evoked almost no interest or reaction in the provinces.[50]

Anyhow, early in the evening of June 24 the promoters felt sufficiently confident to call a meeting of senior ministerial officials at the Throne Hall to try to persuade them to continue working as normal.[51] Addressing the gathering, Pridi acknowledged that the promoters themselves lacked administrative experience. If that caused problems, he suggested that reference should be made to Phya Phahol for guidance. Pridi stressed the need, above all else, to avoid any semblance of disarray which might tempt foreign powers to intervene as they had following revolutions in other countries.

What worried the promoters most was the attitude of Britain. Close and friendly relations existed between the Siamese and British royal families. Britain also had a major stake in the Siamese economy, as well as troops based in nearby Malaya and Burma. Indeed, many Siamese believed that the British had still not abandoned ambitions to expand their empire in Asia, and the promoters too thought that any breakdown of law and order might be seized upon by the British as a pretext to intervene – primarily to protect lives and property, but ultimately to take over Siam. With this in mind, Pridi asked officials from the Foreign Ministry to despatch an immediate circular note to all diplomatic representatives in Bangkok, containing assurances that the new administration would protect foreign lives and property in Siam as well as continue to honour the country's international treaty commitments.

The note was welcomed, even though there was little concern among the Western powers over the change of regime in Siam and certainly no intention of intervening. True, there may have been some fear in neighbouring British colonies that the Siamese revolution would act as a spur to latent nationalist movements elsewhere in the region. But it was the Foreign Office in London which was responsible for policy towards Siam and it greeted the news of the overthrow of the absolute monarchy in Siam with the comment ''So falls another autocracy''.

Yet in Bangkok, on the evening of June 24, the promoters were still apprehensive about whether their administration would be internationally recognised. A senior official from the Foreign Ministry pointed out that much would depend on the attitude of the King; if he agreed to remain on the throne and acknowledge the new administration, there was unlikely to be any problem. Similar thoughts occurred to the

monarch, and in the telegram he sent in reply to that from the promoters, he stated that the consequences of foreign powers refusing to
recognise the new administration was one of the factors which led him
to agree to remain on the throne.[52]

The King's telegram ended for the time being any thoughts the
promoters might have had of establishing a republic. His arrival back in
Bangkok on June 26 had the same effect. One of his first acts was to
receive some of the leading promoters in audience: as they entered the
room, the King greeted them with the words "I rise in honour of the
Khana Ratsadorn." It was a very significant gesture. According to
Siamese tradition, monarchs remain seated while their subjects make
obeisance.

By way of response, Pridi apologised for the defamation of the
monarchy in the Manifesto of the Khana Ratsadorn, and all copies were
withdrawn immediately from circulation. Also, the playing of the royal
anthem was resumed. The King quickly showed his gratitude, and
affixed his signature to a proclamation acknowledging the seizure of
power by the Khana Ratsadorn and exonerating those responsible since,
unlike many other revolutionaries, they had carried out the change of
regime without any bloodshed.[53]

Again the promoters responded. They agreed to release all their
hostages, and insisted only that Prince Boripat should leave the country;
he had been too powerful for the promoters to have felt easy if he had
remained in Siam. Hence he was escorted to the southern border from
where he went eventually to take up residence in Java. Later Prince
Purachatra and several other senior princes decided to go into exile elsewhere in South East Asia.[54]

Indeed, the transition from the absolute monarchy to the new
administration appeared to have taken place so smoothly that in London
an editorial in *The Times* referred to it as "a simple re-adjustment".[55]

NOTES

1. Vella (1955), p. 363, and M. Smith, p. 104.
2. Pridi in Pramote Pungsunthorn, *Bang Ruang Kiaokap Phraboromsanuwong nai Songkram Lok Ti Song*, p. 79.
3. Pridi Banomyong, *Ma Vie Mouvementee*, p. 27, and Duan Bunnag, *Tan Pridi Rataburut Awuso*, p. 38.
4. Chula Chakrabongse, *Brought Up in England*, p. 192.

5. Duan Bunnag, pp. 12ff, correspondence reproduced in *Bangkok Post*, Nov. 24, 1982, and Batson (1984), pp. 79ff.
6. Thawatt Mokrapong, pp. 79ff.
7. Duan Bunnag, pp. 9ff, and role of student associations in Batson (1974), p. 55.
8. Prayoon Pamornmontri, *Chiwit Ha Paendin*, first six chapters, and Thawatt Mokrapong, p. 6.
9. Ananta Pibulsongkram, *Chompol P. Pibulsongkram I*, p. 35.
10. Sripanon Singthong, *Sipsong Chompol Thai*, p. 2.
11. Ananta Pibulsongkram, pp. 38ff.
12. Pridi in Thak Chaloemtiarana (ed.), *Thai Politics 1932–57: Extracts and Documents*, pp. 52ff.
13. Thawee Bunyaket and La-iad Pibulsongkram in Ray, *Portraits of Thai Politics* pp. 63 and 192.
14. Prayon gives the date as 1924, but Pridi is more likely correct in Thak Chaloemtiarana (ed.), p. 38, compared with p. 51.
15. ibid., p. 38. Besides Pridi, Pibul and Prayoon, those present were Tasnai Niyomsuk; Naeb Phaholyothin, a student from Britain; Tua Lapanukrom, studying science in Switzerland; and Luang Siri Rajmaitri, a diplomat based in Paris.
16. Pridi in ibid., p. 53.
17. Thawatt Mokrapong, p. 9, and Thawee Bunyaket in Ray, p. 64.
18. Pridi in Thak Chaloemtiarana (ed.), p. 52. Inspiration derived from Kemal Atatürk's coup to end the Ottoman Empire, Prayoon in ibid., p. 39, and F5324/42/40 in FO 371/17175.
19. La-iad Pibulsongkram in Ray, p. 192, and Thawatt Mokrapong, p. 11.
20. ibid., p. 7.
21. Prayoon, p. 40, and Kularp Saipradit, *Buanglang Karnpatiwat 2475*, pp. 66ff.
22. Thawee Bunyaket in Ray, p. 66.
23. Phya Song in ibid., p. 75.
24. Kularb Saipradit, p. 87.
25. Thawatt Mokrapong, p. 98.
26. Phya Song in Thak Chaloemtiarana (ed.), pp. 77ff.
27. Kularb Saipradit, p. 87.
28. ibid., p. 102.
29. Phya Song in Thak Chaloemtiarana (ed.), p. 78.
30. Crosby, *Siam at the Crossroads*, p. 79; Chula Chakrabongse (1943), p. 171; and Prayoon, p. 69, giving names on list as Pibul, Pridi, Tua Lapanukrom and himself.
31. ibid., p. 159, and Thawatt Mokrapong, p. 31.
32. Khuang (sometimes referred to by official title Luang Kovit Abhaiwongse) in a speech to the Pedagogical Council in 1963, as published in *Chumnum Chulalongkorn* (1969), pp. 63ff, and Pridi in Pramote Pungsunthorn, p. 85.
33. Thawatt Mokrapong, p. 33.
34. Thawee Bunyaket in Ray, p. 67.
35. Phya Song in Thak Chaloemtiarana (ed.), pp. 79ff.
36. ibid. and Kularb Saipradit, pp. 118ff.
37. Phya Song in Thak Chaloemtiarana (ed.), pp. 81ff.
38. This was Phya Sena Songkram, ibid., p. 91, and Kularb Saipradit, pp. 120ff.

39. Landon (1939), p. 15; Sivaram, p. 23, suggesting Prince Purachatra suspected trouble and moved to a hotel near the railway station ready to flee.
40. This was Prince Chumpot, F5917/4260/40, in FO371/16261.
41. *Khana* is more properly translated "group" and is the term used by all subsequent coup groups, but never by political parties: Wilson, *Politics in Thailand*, pp. 248ff.
42. Text in Landon (1939), p. 11, and Sivaram, pp. 28ff.
43. Text in ibid. (1939), pp. 9ff.
44. Thompson, p. 63; Sivaram, pp. 49ff, and Thawatt Mokrapong, p. 112.
45. Queen Rambhai in Thak Chaloemtiarana (ed.), p. 9; F5547/4260/40 in FO371/16261 and Chula Chakrabongse (1960), p. §12.
46. Text in Landon (1939), p. 10; Thawatt Mokrapong p. 40.
47. Prayoon, p. 170.
48. Landon (1939), p. 13, and Sivaram, p. 22.
49. *Bangkok Daily Mail*, as quoted in Thawatt Mokrapong, p. 39.
50. Landon (1939), pp. 13ff, and Batson (1984), p. 239.
51. *Bangkok Times Weekly Mail* (BTWM), June 27, 1932.
52. F5180/4260/40 in FO371/16261, and Thawatt Mokrapong, pp. 106ff.
53. ibid., p. 41, and Sivaram, pp. 33ff.
54. Landon (1939), pp. 15ff, and Withet korani, *Hetkarn tang Karnmuang 43 Pi haeng Rabob Prachatipatai*, pp. 122ff.
55. *Times*, Aug. 2, 1932.

3
THE LEGITIMATION OF THE NEW ELITE

The Manifesto issued by the Khana Ratsadorn on June 24, as well as denouncing the absolute monarchy, enunciated six principles on which future government in Siam should be based. They were:

1. The independence of the country including its political, judicial and economic independence must be maintained.
2. Peace and security within the country must be preserved: efforts must be made to reduce crime.
3. A national economic plan must be drawn up to ensure the economic wellbeing of the people. The new government must provide work for every citizen, and will not allow people to starve.
4. Equal rights and privileges for everyone must be guaranteed. Royalty must not be allowed to have more privileges than the people, as was the case previously.
5. The people shall have freedom, provided that the exercise of that freedom is not in conflict with the above four points.
6. The people must be given the best education possible.[1]

Henceforth these principles were to serve as the creed for the promoters as well as their justification for seizing power. First however, their position had to be legitimised.

On June 26 when representatives of the promoters were received by the King, they presented him with a copy of a provisional constitution drafted in advance by Pridi. After perusing it, the King suggested several clarifications and amendments. They did not concern major matters of substance so his wishes were quickly met and the next day at 5 p.m. King Prajadhipok signed Siam's first constitution. It was promulgated immediately.[2]

The constitution started by announcing that "the highest power in the land belongs to all the people". After that democratic-sounding opening, it went on in effect to vest all authority in the hands of the promoters and strip the King of his power. Until a permanent constitution could be promulgated, Siam was to be ruled by a Peoples' Committee and a nominated Peoples' Assembly of seventy members. No enactment of the King was to be considered valid unless countersigned by a member of the Peoples' Committee. The monarch was also denied the right to veto any action taken by the Peoples' Committee. He could not even nominate his successor. Having thus reduced royal power to an absolute minimum without actually abolishing the monarchy, the constitution then set out rigid guidelines for the implementation of democracy. It was to be achieved in three stages. The first stage was the establishment of an Assembly nominated by the military controllers of the country – Phya Phahol, Phya Song and Phya Ritthi – who were said to be exercising power on behalf of the people. This first stage was to last six months or till such time as "the affairs of the country are in order". The second stage was described as a period when the people were to learn about democracy. During this period, the Assembly would consist of two categories of members, half of them officially nominated and the rest elected through a system of indirect representation. Even those standing for election would have to undergo examination by the Khana Ratsadorn before being allowed to put themselves forward as candidates. Finally, the provisional constitution stipulated that the third stage of full democratic representation in the Assembly could only be implemented at the end of ten years or when more than half the population had completed primary education, whichever was the sooner.[3]

Despite his Western education, Pridi apparently derived many of the ideas underlying this constitution from Sun Yat-sen's theory of a step-by-step approach to democracy.[4] As for all the high-sounding rhetoric about the people and their rights, Pridi clearly envisaged them in much the same way as did the monarchy. They were a concept to be invoked rather than individuals who could be expected to play any role in decision-making. Indeed, in advocating a lengthy period of political tutelage, Pridi was unwittingly echoing the views of royal advisers who had stated that the people were insufficiently educated or mature to cope with a more participatory form of government.

The innate conservatism of the promoters' approach to democracy was largely ignored. Instead fears were rife among the Bangkok élite that a group of rabid revolutionaries had seized power. The King may have given his formal approval to the constitution, but its use of the term "Peoples' Committee" sounded uncomfortably like Bolshevik terminology, and the establishment of what amounted to a one-party state only added to the impression.[5] The totalitarian image of the Khana Ratsadorn was compounded by the strict security measures with which its members surrounded themselves. But they too had their fears; they knew that they must have stirred up antagonism in certain quarters and were afraid of a counter-coup or acts of individual violence against themselves. After all, if they as a mere handful of people could seize power so easily, it would be just as possible for another group using similar tactics to oust them.[6]

In view of these mutual fears and suspicions, the promoters were cautious in their choice of an Assembly and cabinet. Anyway, they had agreed among themselves before mounting their coup that they had no wish to give the impression they were seizing power for their own benefit.[7] Hence the Peoples' Assembly, as nominated by the senior military commanders, was a judicious mix of promoters and distinguished officials from the previous administration. Out of the seventy representatives nominated, twenty-five were not members of the Khana Ratsadorn. These non-promoters included several prominent officials and judges, but all were commoners. In an even more symbolic gesture, two of the people who had been debarred from all public office after their involvement in the abortive 1912 revolution were appointed to this, the first Assembly in Siam's history.[8]

The convening of the Assembly on June 28 was an indication of how quickly the promoters were moving to establish the legitimacy of their new order. It was evidence too of how they ignored the rest of the country. In those days few up-country representatives, had they been nominated, could have reached Bangkok in time for the first session. The Assembly was opened by Phya Phahol: as the senior Military Controller, he formally handed over authority to the Assembly.

It proceeded first to elect a speaker, and the choice fell on a respected *ancien régime* official.[9] Phya Phahol then took the floor again to propose the appointment of Phya Manopakorn Nitthithada as Chairman of the Peoples' Committee.[10] Phya Mano, as he was known, appeared eminently suited to head Siam's new government. Having been educated in England as a lawyer, he was thought to be well grounded in the principles of democracy. In addition, on his return to Bangkok to become a judge in the court of appeal, he had been rebuked by the princes on the Supreme Council for suggesting cuts in the royal privy purse as against retrenchments in official expenditure to cope with the economic recession. More personal reasons for Phya Mano's discontent with the absolute monarchy later emerged. Although his wife had been lady-in-waiting to the Queen, his hopes of being appointed Minister of Justice had been thwarted by the princes.[11] Still, he was ostensibly as surprised as everyone else at being nominated to head the new government. His first reaction was to call for the temporary adjournment of the Assembly so that he could consult Phya Phahol and Pridi.[12] This did not last long. Phya Mano soon announced his acceptance of the position. In traditionally humble terms he said, "I still feel very heavy-hearted because since the day I was born, I never dreamed of taking such a position."

Even so Phya Mano had little say in choosing the members of the body over which he was to preside. As envisaged in the constitution, the Peoples' Committee was a sort of executive council or praesidium along vaguely Soviet lines controlled by the ruling party, in this case the Khana Ratsadorn. None of the promoters appointed to the Peoples' Committee was awarded a ministerial portfolio; they felt inhibited by their lack of experience. Instead the ministries were headed mostly by experienced officials who were not appointed to the Peoples' Committee. Clearly the system was devised to ensure that the promoters would retain overall control of the government while leaving day-to-day administration in capable hands.[13]

Among themselves the promoters also ensured that all their factions were represented within the Peoples' Committee. The point, however, was lost on the public at large, which still had little idea of who the promoters were or how they had come together. Nevertheless there was considerable relief when it was seen first that the Assembly and then that the government included some respected figures from the *ancien régime*.[14]

Another indication of caution on the part of the promoters was the absence of any move to get rid of the foreign advisers to the government, despite the possibility that they might put a brake on revolutionary policies. Nor was there an immediate purge of officials from the ministries. Instead the process was gradual with those removed from office being granted handsome pensions, at least to begin with. What is more, certain junior princes continued to work as government advisors and officials, although the more senior members of the royal family were specifically debarred from holding ministerial office or seats in the Assembly. It also became clear from appointments made by the new administration that the promoters intended to abandon what they considered as the feudal system of awarding titles to all officials. After 1932, nobody was appointed to the ranks of *Khun, Luang, Phra, Phya* or *Chao Phya*. Yet many of those who already held such titles – including some of the promoters – continued to enjoy them.

By comparison, reforms within the armed forces appeared far more drastic. Most of Siam's generals as well as high-ranking officers in the other armed forces and the police were dismissed or pensioned off.[15] Few of them were replaced. Some people thought that Siam had previously had too many generals.[16] Now Phya Phahol was appointed army commander with Phya Song as his deputy, and both retained their existing ranks as colonels. Such modesty dismayed some of the junior military promoters. Although they were all promoted one rank after the successful seizure of power, they foresaw that their higher aspirations might be blocked. The chief obstacle seemed to be Phya Song, because Phya Phahol was regarded merely as a figurehead.

Just as he had planned the coup, so Phya Song assumed charge of reforming the army. Following up his decision to rely solely on the Bangkok garrisons to seize power, he moved quickly to minimise any possible counteraction by troops stationed outside the capital. Orders went out for all ammunition held by up-country garrisons to be sent back to Bangkok on the pretext that it was obsolete.[17] It was neither returned nor replaced. Phya Song then proceeded to weaken the military in the provinces yet further by abolishing the regional command structure and making local garrisons responsive only to orders from Bangkok. Similarly, he reorganised military units within the capital, thus making a counter-coup even more unlikely. Another effect of these reforms was to concentrate power in Phya Song's own hands, yet the general impression was that in cutting out the defence hierarchy he was reorganising the army along republican lines.[18]

Few details of all these changes appeared in the press, which was not even allowed to report what happened at meetings of the Assembly. The promoters found it difficult to shake off their instinct for secrecy. Anyway Siamese newspapers only had a small circulation. What the promoters forgot was the potential of the press to influence the élite. Some newspapers, taking their cue from the Manifesto of the Khana Ratsadorn, started to publish stories about the princes and their alleged extravagance. Undoubtedly several princes were very rich, and the question of whether their wealth should be taxed had long been a major bone of contention within the Supreme Council until it was abolished together with the absolute monarchy. However, the subject had never till now been aired in print, and there was soon speculation that the new administration was about to confiscate the wealth of the Chakri family. This elicited a swift denial from Phya Mano who went on to warn that while his administration was in favour of press freedom in principle, it would not hesitate to take action against anybody who abused it.[19]

It does not seem to have occurred to the more liberal-minded civilian promoters that Phya Mano was starting to assert his authority, irrespective of what they might think; they were far more concerned about propagating the ideas underlying the change in regime. For example, one of Pridi's closest associates gave a series of public lectures to explain the virtues of a constitutional system of government and canvass for new members to join the Khana Ratsadorn.[20] During the next few months such proselytising was gradually expanded beyond Bangkok. Provincial officials were summoned to the capital to attend lectures on the constitution, while some civilian promoters travelled up-country for the same purpose. Consequently *The Times* in London commented: "Outwardly the new regime is democratic, but in practice so far it is a one-party government of a mildly fascist complexion."[21]

Such views had little impact in Bangkok. The tradition of authoritarianism was so deeply ingrained within the ruling classes that few questioned it. In any case, the promoters were evidently intent on strengthening their own support to ward off any attempt at a come-back by the royalists – a possibility that could not be dismissed. Rumours were circulating that Pridi had masterminded the revolution simply in a spirit of revenge against the royal family after his clashes in Paris with Prince Charoon. Differences of opinion between Phya Phahol and his princely senior officers were cited to a similar end. As for Prayoon, he was said to be in the pay of the Russians.[22]

Another disturbing factor for the promoters was the way their rhetoric was sometimes taken literally. There were those who believed that the Khana Ratsadorn was going to abolish all taxes and simply stopped paying them. They were unduly optimistic. True, economic prospects has now improved. Just before it was abolished, the Supreme Council finally decided that Siam should abandon the gold standard, and as a result trade was beginning to pick up and the outlook for rice exports was brighter. Even so, only the most unpopular taxes imposed by the Supreme Council during the economic crisis were abrogated. There was no move to do away with long-established levies like the poll-tax.[23]

Still, a new climate of opinion became manifest in a rash of petitions to the authorities, most of which concerned personal grievances against officials and employers. Similar complaints underlay various strikes in the latter half of 1932. But there was shocked surprise when pupils at one of Bangkok's leading high schools went on strike in protest at certain disciplinary measures.[24] Others, however, welcomed these indications that the public was at last awakening to demand its rights. Some workers, such as those operating Bangkok's trams, received official encouragement to set up an association,[25] and various individuals, possibly with an eye on their own future political careers, also began to talk about organising trade unions.

All such activities had previously been banned, and labour unrest was virtually unknown in Siam. Their advent simply reinforced diehard suspicions of the ultimate intentions of the Khana Ratsadorn. A message of congratulation, conveyed through diplomatic channels to the Khana from the Kuomintang, was transformed by rumour into a secret message of encouragement from the Comintern.[26] Then, on September 29, leaflets were scattered in Bangkok and five towns up-country calling on the people to rise up and establish a Soviet Siam.[27]

Security precautions were immediately reinforced and strict censorship was imposed on all political and military news, but these moves proved counterproductive: the re-appearance of armoured vehicles on the streets of Bangkok only heightened the atmosphere of tension, as did orders from Phya Song for guards to be placed on all arsenals. Having plotted the overthrow of the absolute monarchy and reformed the army along allegedly republican lines, the diehards thought Phya Song must be a communist as well. Rumour had it that to prevent him from installing such a regime, the foreign powers were preparing to intervene.[28] Another line of speculation was that Phya Song was applying pressure for a yet more radical constitution.[29]

The replacement of Pridi's provisional constitution by a permanent and more elaborate version was one of the first tasks to which the Assembly addressed itself. At the end of June, it nominated a drafting committee of six members; most of them were lawyers, with Pridi as the sole promoter.[30] They made little progress till October, when the increased tension in Bangkok resulted in the nomination of two more members to the committee.

One of the new appointees was the Foreign Minister, Phya Sri Visarn Vacha. Formerly he had been under-secretary in the Ministry, and in private had made no secret of his dislike and suspicion of the promoters, who, he claimed, had forced him at bayonet-point to take over the portfolio. Phya Sri Visarn also exploited his experience of foreign affairs to play on the promoters' fears by claiming that any manifestation of extremism on their part might court the intervention of the Western powers. The British, at least, quickly saw through that ploy. They regarded Phya Sri Visarn as a royalist diehard. Among other things, he was one of the people who in 1931 strongly advised the King against introducing a constitution. What is more, Phya Sri Visarn – who, despite his high position in the Foreign Ministry, was of Chinese origin

– retained a British passport to enable him to travel abroad easily in case of an emergency.[31]

The other new member of the constitutional committee was the Minister of Defence, Phya Radjwangsan. An admiral and former naval Chief of Staff, he too was not a promoter. Rather he owed his position to his younger brother Sindhu, the leader of the naval promoters. Other such family relationships existed between the promoters and officials working for the new administration. Still, fears persisted that the country had been taken over by a group of revolutionary hotheads.

Among those harbouring such views was the King. From the outset he had in reality been deeply apprehensive concerning the exact intentions of the promoters. For example, he had not raised any basic objections to the provisional constitution because he was unsure of the promoters' mood and anxious for the safety of his relatives held in custody.[32] But once they were released and he had had time to think, the King's attitude hardened.

In the first place, he disliked the revolutionary tone in which the constitution was couched. He would, in any case, have preferred to grant a constitution himself as a magnanimous gesture from on high, like all previous reforms in Siam; he felt he had lost face through having to act at the bidding of the promoters. At the end of June he gave an indication of his disquiet. At an audience granted to Phya Mano and several promoters, he intimated that he was considering abdication, and soon afterwards he began to make preparations for spending the rest of his life abroad.[33]

None of this was even hinted at in the press, but it gradually dawned on the public that the King had not appeared at any official functions since the change of regime and rumours spread that he was subject to some sort of house-arrest. In fact, extra guards were posted around his personal residence as soon as tension started to rise again in Bangkok during October. The situation also prompted Phya Mano to consult the King more frequently, and during one of these audiences he indicated that he would rather abdicate than approve a permanent constitution as radical as its precursor. This worried Phya Mano and others on the drafting committee, who saw themselves trapped between the wishes of the King and the extremist views of the promoters.

If such extremism existed, it was quickly modified after the communist leaflets distributed on September 29 attacked not only the monarchy but also the Khana Ratsadorn. The promoters were, after all, part of the bureaucratic élite, and now they were afraid that they might be challenged by a far more militant group of revolutionaries. Consequently, the Peoples' Committee retracted an announcement that the King's Birthday would be celebrated with a minimum of ceremony for reasons of economy. Instead royal pomp was fully reinstituted to rally popular support for the regime while for his part the King, believing he had made his point, once again appeared in public.[34]

As a result of these developments, the draft of the permanent constitution evoked some surprise when it was made public in mid-November. Its preamble described the monarch as "the greatest power in the world ... the great in the Sun's dynasty, who is God's beloved ... with incomparable power of merit ... an incarnation of God with widespread fame ..." He was stated to be commander-in-chief of the armed forces with the right to declare war and make peace. He was vested with the authority to issue decrees, proclaim martial law, grant pardons and conclude treaties with foreign states. He was also given the right to appoint members of the government and of the Assembly, which he could apparently convene and prorogue at will. These wide powers were questioned when the draft was submitted to the Assembly, but in reply a member of the constitutional committee explained that royal prerogatives had been acknowledged in order to honour the monarch, in the same way that theoretically the King of Denmark enjoyed various powers.

In reality the permanent constitution reiterated the provisions of its precursor that every law, royal rescript and decree must be countersigned by a cabinet member. The difference was that revolutionary rhetoric had been replaced by expressions of respect for the monarch while still depriving him and the rest of the royal family of any real power. It was politely put in a provision stating that since involvement in politics could entail blame as well as praise, it was inappropriate for princes of the rank of royal grandson and upwards to be members of the government or Assembly. On the other hand, the permanent constitution abandoned the principle that the Khana Ratsadorn was the ruling party.[35]

The Assembly was allowed less than two weeks in which to debate the draft before voting unanimously to approve it on November 29, 1932. The royal astrologers had already pronounced the most auspicious moment for promulgating the constitution to be somewhere between 2.53 and 3.05 on the afternoon of December 10. Provided that it was approved well before then, there was time for the text to be inscribed on strips of bamboo in the traditional manner of all royal decrees.[36]

While this process was underway, another symbolic ceremony took place. On December 7, Phya Mano led fifty members of the Assembly in an act of obeisance to the monarch. Flowers, candles and incense were proffered to the King by Phya Phahol. Then Pridi, as author of the Khana Ratsadorn's Manifesto, tendered profound apologies for its defamation of the royal family, and acknowledged that the Chakri dynasty had bestowed great benefits on the people of Siam. In reply the King complimented the promoters for admitting their past mistakes and gave his blessing to those present.[37]

Three days later, all the members of the Assembly were present in the Throne Hall when the King was revealed to them enshrined on high and wearing his crown for the first time since his coronation. In this majestic setting he appended his signature to the constitution submitted to him by Phya Mano. It was promulgated at precisely 3 p.m. to the accompaniment of beating gongs and blasts on a conch shell to signal the auspicious occasion.

What distinguished the ceremony from previous royal events was that those positioned closest to the throne were all commoners. The few princes invited to attend were relegated to the back of the hall with members of the diplomatic corps.[38] Yet the event aroused little public interest. Phya Song noted later that people had to be rounded up to cheer outside the Throne Hall, adding that perhaps they would have been more enthusiastic if the promoters had laid on entertainment and noodle soup. Still the promulgation of a new moderate constitution that was fully endorsed by the King appeared to put an end to the troubled period following the change of regime, and to usher in a new era of peace and stability.[39]

In fact the changes stemming from the new constitution were more cosmetic than real. Phya Mano and the rest of the Peoples' Committee duly resigned and reconstituted themselves as a State Council. There were no significant changes in its membership. The original balance between promoters and *ancien régime* officials continued.[40] Likewise, the composition of the Assembly remained the same, although it was due to be expanded once an electoral law had been passed and voting took place.

Such a prospect soon raised the question of whether political parties could be formed, but apparently the Khana Ratsadorn did not like the idea. Once it had lost its status as the ruling party, it transformed itself into an "association" with the stated aim of teaching the people about democracy and the constitution. In another gesture to modify its image, the Khana Ratsadorn Association was officially headed by a non-promoter. But at the inauguration of its headquarters, Phya Phahol stressed that the promoters would continue to play a guiding role in the affairs of Siam.[41]

On the other hand, some people considered it high time that opposition to the promoters was co-ordinated. In January 1933, a group calling itself the Khana Chart, or Nationalists, applied for official registration as a political party. Its members comprised mainly civilian officials and military officers, most of whom had lost influence or career prospects since the end of the absolute monarchy. At their head was Phya Sena Songkram, a retired major-general who had the distinction of being the only person to have been injured when the leaders of the old administration were detained by the promoters on the morning of June 24. Many other people listed as members of the Khana Chart, some of them the wives of formerly high-ranking officials, were also known for their royalist sympathies.[42] One exception in their midst appeared to be *Luang* Vichit Vadhakarn who, as a diplomat serving in Paris during the 1920s had known and sympathised with some of the students who were now leading promoters. Hence Vichit was disappointed at not being nominated to the Assembly, and the resulting sense of grievance was later compounded by a decision of the new regime to close down a newspaper with which he was closely associated. He protested by resigning from the Foreign Ministry.[43] Thus, it seemed, members of the Khana Chart were motivated above all by a spirit of vengeance, which was aggravated a few days after the Khana Chart announced its formation, when an attempt was made to assassinate its leader, Phya Sena. The atmosphere in Bangkok immediately became tense again.[44]

The government was faced with the dilemma of deciding what to do about the Khana Chart. To allow its registration could set a precedent, leading possibly to a proliferation of political parties. Alternatively, a refusal on the grounds of illegality might affect the Khana Ratsadorn, even in its newly-modified form, and necessitate its disbandment – which the promoters in fact suspected of being the basic aim of the Khana Chart's founders in proposing a rival grouping.[45] Consequently they were prepared to allow their opponents to register officially, but the decision was taken out of their hands.

Phya Mano, whom the promoters had expected to be a docile premier, was becoming increasingly assertive. Buoyed by his success in meeting the King's wishes over the constitution, he thought he had inflicted a considerable loss of face in leading Pridi and other prominent promoters in the act of obeisance to the monarch. After this, Phya Mano had no

compunction in consulting the King about the Khana Chart and accepting royal advice that it should not be allowed to register as a political
party. The King was quoted as saying that the people of Siam were not
sufficiently versed in the ways of democracy to cope with a multi-party
system. For Phya Mano this provided a cue to move against the Khana
Ratsadorn as well.[46]

Pridi does not seem to have realised how the balance of power was
shifting. In his youthful enthusiasm, he wanted to press ahead with
drafting a national economic plan, as envisaged in the six principles of
the Khana Ratsadorn. The aim of such a plan, Pridi explained at an
audience with the King, would be to improve agricultural production
and the living standards of farmers. It would also attempt to impose
greater Siamese control over the economy as a whole by eliminating the
role of the foreign entrepreneur. The King expressed great interest in
these ideas, and indicated he would like to read the plan as soon as it was
drafted and before its submission to the Assembly. His wishes were
complied with at the end of February 1933, when Pridi presented him
with a copy of a draft economic plan.[47]

It was a lengthy document with twelve sections and several
appendixes.[48] In a preamble Pridi explained how he had borrowed
elements from various economic systems in formulating the plan. This
was coupled with a warning that many people who talked about
economics had never studied the subject and were prepared to condemn
certain theories out of prejudice without giving due attention to what
they implied. Pridi requested readers of his draft to avoid these pitfalls
and consult him if any points were obscure. Still, he claimed that his
ideas were set out in simple terms in order to be comprehensible to those
who had no university education.

The plan began by citing the six principles of the Khana Ratsadorn
and appealing to the humanitarian instincts of readers by describing the
poverty and lack of security in the lives of peasant farmers throughout
Siam, as well as the urban masses in Bangkok. Consequently Pridi contended that they all wanted to work for the government in return for
regular salaries. Hence his basic idea was to make the entire population
state employees by introducing a system of social security, details of
which were outlined in an appendix to the plan. Pridi claimed that it was
not necessary to expropriate the property of the wealthy to finance this
scheme. Cooperative societies could be set up to exchange goods for
money, which the government would pay back to the people in the form
of monthly salaries.

Pridi reasoned that this system would obviate numerous problems which he saw as besetting Siamese economic development. For example, peasant farmers worked only six months in the year between planting and harvesting a single rice crop. If they were salaried employees of the government, cooperative and mechanised methods of agriculture could be introduced. So too could communal living, while surplus labour could be directed into other productive economic enterprises. The government would also be able to eliminate social parasites dependant on the labour of others. However, Pridi stated categorically that his scheme did not imply an intention on the government's part to destroy the wealthy classes. Those landowners who could never collect the full rents from their tenants, and yet had to pay taxes, would be glad to sell out. Alternatively the government could issue bonds to landowners to the full value of their property and take produce in payment.

Clearly Pridi realised that his proposals would arouse controversy and sought to defend himself in advance. Referring to the belief that peasants cease to care for and cultivate their land once it is transferred to public ownership, he pointed out that already many farmers in Siam did not own the land they tilled. For them there would be no difference between working for a landlord or for the government. Moreover, the government was more likely to introduce improvements such as better irrigation. Pridi also expressly denied that his proposals were intended to reduce everybody to the level of animals, make women common property or abolish family ties. Independent professionals such as doctors, lawyers and professors would be allowed to continue, as would private entrepreneurs if they chose to ignore the advantages of selling out to the government. In conclusion, he stated that if his economic plan was adopted, it would be the dawn of the age of Sri Ariya Mettraya – the next, ideal and final world age as conceived by Theravada Buddhists in South East Asia.[49] The Manifesto of the Khana Ratsadorn ended by stating: ''What everyone most desires, the greatest prosperity and happiness called Sri Ariya, will be realised by all the people.'' ''Utopian'' has in fact been a term often used in comments on Pridi's plan.[50]

The King had other ideas. He was quoted as saying: ''I do not know whether Stalin copied *Luang* Pradit [Pridi] or whether *Luang* Pradit copied Stalin . . . the only difference is that one is Russian, the other Thai . . . This is the same programme that has been used in Russia. If our government adopted it, we would be assisting the Third International to achieve the aim of world communism . . . Siam would become the second communist state after Russia . . .''[51] These comments were part of a detailed critique of Pridi's plan intended to be published under the King's name. No matter who was responsible, it was in clear breach of the principle usually observed in constitutional monarchies that the sovereign's opinion of the policies pursued by his ministers should not be made public.[52] Still, it was just the sort of ammunition the opponents of the Khana Ratsadorn had been looking for to destroy it once and for all.

One point seized on by Phya Mano was the likelihood of adverse foreign reaction to the plan. As drafted, it envisaged the nationalisation of foreign business concerns including European concessions to exploit Siam's natural resources.[53] British interests in particular would be affected, provoking fears that they might intervene militarily. At times it seemed as if that was what the Foreign Minister Phya Sri Visarn was hoping for. He frequently purveyed alarmist views of the promoters to the British minister in Bangkok. The Foreign Minister thought that the French too would be hostile to Pridi's plan, since they were trying to suppress communist activity in neighbouring Indo-China.

Instead Phya Sri Visarn could have argued that Britain and France would not dare to intervene in Siam because of the attitude of the League of Nations, which had just voted overwhelmingly to impose sanctions on Japan in protest against its intervention in Manchuria. Yet, rather than approving the resolution, Siam was the only member of the League of Nations to break ranks and abstain. Apparently Phya Sri Visarn made the decision on the grounds that Siam should continue to maintain its traditional policy of neutrality in all international disputes.[54] Others suggested that Siam was anxious not to antagonise Japan because it might prove a useful counterweight to British and French pressure. From there the rumour grew that Siam had offered to act as agent for Japan in avoiding the League of Nations sanctions. This the government in Bangkok denied.[55]

Meanwhile, in opposing Pridi's plan, Phya Mano had to assess how much support he enjoyed within the cabinet. He knew he could count on Phya Sri Visarn as well as the Minister of Defence, Phya Radjwang-san. Then there was Prayoon. As a reward for his role in 1932, he had been given a seat in the cabinet and appointed its secretary. This meant that he worked closely with Phya Mano, to whom he became increasingly attached.[56] Another crack in the promoters' solidarity centred around Phya Song, who resented the way Pridi was widely regarded as the intellectual leader of the Khana Ratsadorn; to Phya Song, this was a derogation of his own role in master-minding the seizure of power. Hence he was receptive to the view that Pridi's plan was communist-inspired.

To thrash out the problem the promoters held a special meeting where Phya Song received the backing of his own senior military clique in criticising Pridi. That led to a heated argument with a group of civilian promoters, which again appeared to Phya Song to be evidence of a lack of due respect. He reacted by calling another meeting, this time restricted to military promoters, but here too he was unable to command unequivocal support. Phya Phahol, who had been up-country during the preceding weeks, claimed he was out of touch and preferred to reserve judgement on Pridi's plan. Possibly, as overall leader of the Khana Ratsadorn, Phya Phahol was also worried by the split opening up in its ranks and anxious to avoid saying anything to make it worse. The junior military clique was equally reluctant to commit itself. Its leaders, Pibul and Tasnai, had special bonds of friendship with Pridi, dating back to their student days in Paris, and in addition they had their own reasons for resenting Phya Song. Soon after the seizure of power, he had tried to assert his authority over Pibul by relegating him to an insignificant staff position while assigning other members of the junior military clique abroad for training. Pibul was so angry that he appealed over Phya Song's head to Phya Phahol to get the appointments cancelled. The incident still rankled, and now once more it seemed as if Phya Song was trying to dictate policy.[57]

Formally it was the government which had to decide what to do about Pridi's plan. Its first step was to convene a special investigating committee; this consisted of fourteen members, representing a cross-section of opinion within the new administration, and included Princr Sakol Voravan, an adviser to the Ministry of the Interior who was regarded as one of the most liberal-minded members of the royal family as well as an economic expert. The committee met on March 12, and proceedings were opened by Pridi. He denied that his proposals were communist-inspired, and pointed out that he had left room for capitalist enterprise. During the discussion that ensued, most committee members appeared to agree with Pridi except for reservations on points of detail. Phya Mano was clearly irked, and turned to Phya Song for support. He responded with the argument that it would take fifty to 100 years to implement Pridi's plan successfully. In the mean time, Phya Song proposed the plan be kept secret while the public was gradually educated about what it involved. Pridi's instinctive response was that secrecy foments suspicion. As before he was supported by Prince Sakol. Here even Phya Song appeared to waver, and Phya Mano interposed once more to bring matters to what he considered an unsatisfactory close.

The report produced by the committee made two recommendations. A minority view, subscribed to by Phya Mano, Phya Song, Phya Sri Visarn and Phya Radjwangsan, proposed that economic reforms should be implemented gradually and without any specific plan being adopted. By contrast most members of the committee led by Pridi and Prince Sakol advocated the immediate promulgation of the plan, together with the establishment of a National Economic Council to discuss its implementation. Since the committee could not reach a unanimous view, it was agreed that if the plan was officially rejected, Pridi could publish it under his own name to continue the debate in public.[58]

Little indication of this controversy appeared in the press, but the public began to suspect that some sort of crisis was brewing. In early March, two of Pridi's friends in the Assembly enquired when a National Economic Plan was going to be debated, and were told that they would have to wait.[59] Simultaneously it was noticed the King had not appeared in public for over a month and at the last minute had cancelled his plans to attend ceremonies marking the anniversary of his coronation. Rumours that he had fled the country were denied by Phya Mano; the King, he said, was suffering from a slight indisposition and wished to stay at Hua Hin. At the same time the premier dismissed any suggestion of a split within the government.[60]

Phya Mano's credibility was strained a week later by an official announcement which in effect barred all government officials from membership of the Khana Ratsadorn.[61] It also applied to military officers. A statement issued in the name of Phya Phahol stipulated that it was inappropriate for military men to be involved in politics.[62] Since most of the Khana Ratsadorn's membership comprised government officials and military officers, a deliberate attempt seemed to be under way to emasculate it or force its complete disbandment.

In mid-March the matter was raised in the Assembly, when some members protested that the government was acting unconstitutionally. Phya Mano would have none of it; he re-affirmed that all officials must resign from the Khana Ratsadorn. He could not, however, prevent the calling of a full-scale debate on the issue. Before the Assembly went into recess on March 31, some representatives were equally anxious to debate Pridi's plan. Copies of it were already circulating unofficially in a binding which caused it to be referred to as the "Yellow Book".[63]

Towards the end of the month, the sense of crisis heightened. Once more, the King's movements provided the public with a clue. He returned to Bangkok to preside over ceremonies marking the Siamese New Year at the beginning of April, but it was suddenly announced that these arrangements had been cancelled and that the King was going back to Hua Hin.[64] His departure coincided with a cabinet meeting on March 28 to discuss Pridi's plan, which was rejected by a vote of 17 to 4.

Immediately afterwards, Phya Mano warned Pridi that stern measures would be taken to block any move by his friends in the Assembly to debate the plan or force a vote of no confidence in the government. Everybody entering the Assembly chamber would be searched for weapons, and indeed Phya Mano had reason to be afraid. Two civilian promoters owned a gunshop and before the coup had provided their friends with weapons, some of which continued to be carried for personal protection.[65]

Word was also passed around that if there was any trouble in the Assembly, it would be prorogued straight away. To back up the threat, Phya Mano, accompanied by his Defence Minister, travelled down to Hua Hin overnight to secure the King's signature on a decree proroguing the Assembly even before it next met on March 30.[66] As a result, some twenty representatives were too scared to attend the session, which degenerated into a heated but inconclusive debate on membership of the Khana Ratsadorn.

The next day's debate was far more crucial; it was the end of the financial year, and Phya Mano had left it till then to introduce the budget. He was concommitantly Minister of Finance, and had rejected a suggestion from the British financial adviser that, in line with parliamentary procedure elsewhere in the world, it would be reasonable to allow the Assembly several days to discuss such an important bill. Instead Phya Mano's idea was to get an official from the Finance Ministry to read out the budget and have it approved immediately without any debate. To ensure that this happened, not only were representatives searched by troops stationed outside the Assembly building, but sharpshooters were also posted within the chamber.[67]

Reaction was immediate. Members protested that it was not democracy but what they called "Manocracy", in other words an attempt by the premier to impose a dictatorship on Siam.[68] Most of this criticism emanated from civilian promoters within the Assembly. One of them, while acknowledging his own reputation for violence, stated openly: "If I wanted to shoot Phya Mano, Phya Sri Visarn or Prayoon, I would let them know in advance . . . I know that shooting in the Assembly is not a good thing . . . It seems to me, however, that the soldiers are not posted here as guards, but as a challenge . . . What is the real purpose of this? Do you want to use the soldiers to close the Assembly in order to prevent a vote of confidence?''[69]

Despite these strong words – but mindful of Phya Mano's warnings – there was no attempt to pass a vote of no confidence in the government. Instead some members pursued the tactic of challenging every clause in the budget, so prolonging the debate that it had to be adjourned without a vote being taken. In such circumstances, the constitution provided for the existing budget to remain in force for another year. For Phya Mano and his friends this was pretext enough. Even though technically the government had not been defeated, they decided to make use of the decree proroguing the Assembly.[70] It was promulgated on April 1, 1933, in the name of the King and his government.

The decree had in fact been countersigned by most of the cabinet including Phya Phahol and Pibul, despite their reluctance to commit themselves in the dispute surrounding Pridi's plan. Phya Phahol later excused himself by claiming that he had always realised the decree ran counter to the spirit of the constitution. He had only signed it because he had been out of Bangkok when the controversy first arose and so felt insufficiently briefed to argue with Phya Mano. As for Pibul, he appears to have weighed the strength of his friendship for Pridi against the consequences for himself of opposing the will of the majority.[71]

Issued together with the decree was an official statement disclaiming any intention to suspend the constitution. The Assembly was simply being prorogued until elections could be held. In the words of the statement, the move was necessary because, under its existing form, some members of the Assembly had attempted to impose on Siam ''for time immemorial'' a national economic plan ''by using undue pressure''. Such action was ''a menace to the state and the peoples' welfare''.[72]

So within a year of constitutional government being established in Siam, a precedent was created for dispensing with the Assembly on grounds which were to say the least dubious.

NOTES

1. Text in Thawatt Mokrapong, pp. 244ff, and Landon (1939), p. 11.
2. BTWM June 27, 1932, and F5197/4260/40 in FO371/16261.
3. Riggs, pp. 153ff, and Thawatt Mokrapong, pp. 111ff.
4. ibid., pp. 115ff, and Batson (1984), p. 241.
5. Prayoon, pp. 225ff.
6. F5920/4260/40 and file in FO371/16261.
7. Thawee Bunyaket in Ray, p. 69.
8. Thawatt Mokrapong, p. 127, and Sivaram, pp. 39ff.
9. This was Chao Phya Thammasak Montri.
10. Assembly record in BTWM, Oct. 19, 1932, and Withet Korani, pp. 111ff.
11. Thawatt Mokrapong, p. 132, and Chula Chakrabongse (1943), p. 127.
12. Withet Korani, p. 104, suggests Phya Mano already knew of his appointment.
13. Thawatt Mokrapong, pp. 118ff.
14. F5920/4260/40 in FO371/16261.
15. BTWM, July 7 and 9, 1932 and Withet Korani, p. 131.
16. Sivaram, p. 42.
17. Thawee Bunyaket in Ray, p. 69.
18. Prayoon, p. 202, and Sathuan Suphasophon, *Chiwit tang Karnmuang kong Pan Ek Phya Ritthi Akaney*, p. 113.
19. Thompson, p. 795; BTWM, July 6 and 13, 1932, and Batson (1984), pp. 238ff.
20. This was Sanguan Tularaks. BTWM, June 28, 1932.
21. ibid., Aug. 13, 1932.
22. Thawatt Mokrapong, p. 78; F7455/4260/40 in FO371/16262; and explanation of rumour in Prayoon, p. 88.
23. Thompson, p. 800, and Batson (1984), pp. 242ff.
24. BTWM, Sep. 9, 12 and 13, 1932.
25. ibid, Oct. 17 and 25, 1932. Inauguration of Tramway Workers' Association, presided over by Prince Sakol Voravan.
26. Compare BTWM, July 29, 1932, with Thompson, p. 67.
27. BTWM, Oct. 3 and 10, 1932.
28. ibid., Oct. 14, 1932, and F7290/4260/40 in FO371/16261.
29. F7172/4260/40 in ibid., and Thompson, p. 67.
30. Landon (1939), p. 17.
31. Prasert Patamasukhon, *Ratasapha nai Rop 42Pi*, p. 36, and F6563/4260/40 in FO371/16261.
32. ibid.
33. F6860/4260/40 in ibid., and Queen Rambhai in Thak Chaloemtiarana (ed.), pp. 25ff.
34. BTWM, Oct. 25 and 29, 1932, and F8279/4260/40 in FO371/16262.
35. Text in Thak Chaloemtiarana (ed.), pp. 96–108; BTWM, Nov. 17, 1932, and Thawatt Mokrapong, pp. 121ff.
36. BTWM, Nov. 13 and 30, 1932.
37. ibid., Dec. 3, 1932.
38. ibid., Dec. 12, 1932, and Sivaram, pp. 45ff.
39. Thompson, p. 68, and Thawatt Mokrapong, p. 85.
40. ibid., p. 136.

41. Fistie, *L'Evolution de la Thailande contemporaine*, pp. 134ff, and BTWM, Dec. 12, 1932.
42. ibid., Jan. 9, 1933.
43. ibid., Sept. 18, 1932, and Batson (1984), p. 80.
44. BTWM, Jan. 28, 1933, and Sivaram, pp. 54ff.
45. Thompson, p. 71, and Fistie, p. 136.
46. Thawatt Mokrapong, p. 200, and F1739/42/40 in FO371/17174.
47. Withet Korani, pp. 145ff; Thawatt Mokrapong, pp. 139ff; and p. 180, suggesting Pridi was lured into drafting the plan to destroy him.
48. Text in Landon (1939), pp. 260–302.
49. ibid., p. 186.
50. Fistie, *Sous-développement et utopie au Siam*, pp. 59ff.
51. Text in Duan Bunnag, pp. 183ff, and Thak Chaloemtiarana (ed.), pp. 193–236.
52. Chula Chakrabongse (1960), p. 318, and F3396/42/40 in FO371/17175.
53. Fistie (1967), pp. 144ff.
54. Record of League of Nations debate in *Documents on British Foreign Policy*, 2nd Series, XI, no. 473.
55. BTWM, Mar. 2, 1933.
56. Prayoon, pp. 206ff.
57. Thawatt Mokrapong, pp. 149 and 176ff.
58. Official report in Landon (1939), pp. 303–18.
59. Prasert Patamasukhon, p. 57.
60. BTWM, Feb. 21 and 22, 1933, and Sivaram, p. 53.
61. BTWM, Mar. 1, 1933.
62. ibid, Mar. 4, 1933.
63. Prasert Patamasukhon, p. 58, and Khuang Abhaiwongse, loc. cit., p. 67.
64. BTWM, Mar. 12, 26 and 27, 1933, and F2387/42/40 in FO371/17174.
65. Prayoon, p. 159.
66. Conversation of Mar. 28 with Phya Sri Visarn in F3109/42/40 in FO371/17175.
67. ibid., and Thawatt Mokrapong, p. 151.
68. ibid., p. 152.
69. This was Charoen Subsaeng, BTWM, Jan. 12, 1934.
70. F3109/42/40 in FO371/17175.
71. Thawatt Mokrapong, pp. 181ff.
72. Text in Landon (1939), p. 250, and BTWM, Apr. 3, 1933.

4

THE SPECTRE OF COMMUNISM

Phya Mano embarked on the prorogation of the Assembly with considerable anxiety for his personal safety. Before the decree was issued, he as well as Phya Sri Visarn and Prayoon moved into Paruskavan Palace, where the senior military promoters had set up their headquarters. In the event of any trouble, Phya Mano was obviously counting on the support of the army under Phya Song.[1] With Sindhu heading the naval promoters and his brother Phya Radjwangsan remaining as Minister of Defence, the navy too appeared to be firmly behind the government. Just to make sure, Phya Mano added another naval promoter[2] to the cabinet when he reshuffled it after proroguing the Assembly. The main purpose of the reshuffle, however, was to exclude Pridi and his friends from having any voice in government.[3] There remained the problem of how to silence them completely. Having branded them as communists, Phya Mano decided to pursue the idea. A strict anti-communist law was drafted and promulgated on April 2, 1933.

The Act concerning Communism, as it was called, was brief. It described communism as a theory which ''rests on the total or partial abolition of the rights of private property, actual ownership being ascribed to the community as a whole or the state''. In a parallel clause, the act stated that any doctrine advocating the nationalisation of industry, land, capital or labour was to be considered as communism.[4] On the basis of this slender definition, which was apparently derived in ignorance and haste from an old edition of the *Encyclopaedia Britannica*, the act proceeded to decree penalties. Anybody writing, publishing or otherwise disseminating communist ideas was liable to up to ten years' imprisonment and the payment of a substantial fine.[5]

The official founding date claimed by the Communist Party of Thailand is December 1, 1942. Only in recent years has it admitted that communists were active in the country before then;[6] they are believed to have started about 1927 when the attacks by the Kuomintang on Shanghai and Canton prompted many communists to flee to South East Asia – Nanyang or the South Seas, as the Chinese call the region – with instructions from Borodin, the Comintern liaison officer in the Far East, to report to a co-ordinating bureau set up in Singapore. In 1929 the bureau received a report from Bangkok claiming that a communist party had been established in Siam.[7]

Since most communists in Siam were initially immigrant Chinese, they faced numerous problems in expanding their political activities. Unlike the rest of South East Asia, there was no anti-colonialist, independence movement which they could exploit to rally support. Instead they had to contend with Siamese nationalism, which included a strong streak of anti-Chinese chauvinism.[8] But convinced internationalists were not deterred. They believed that once communism was established as a universal order, national chauvinism would disappear.

One such internationalist was Ho Chi Minh, who participated in some of the meetings of Asian revolutionaries frequented by Pridi in Paris. In 1921, when Pridi arrived there, Ho (or Nguyen Ai Quoc, as he was then known) was registered as a member of the French Communist Party through which he was trying to drum up support for the decolonisation of Indo-China. From Paris, he went on to Moscow for further studies before spending a period in China as secretary to Borodin. In Canton he also set up a revolutionary youth league providing political and military training for his compatriots, some of whom came from Siam where there were sizeable Vietnamese communities in Bangkok and several towns in the north-east. This proved useful in the wake of the conflict between the Kuomintang and the Communists, when the Vietnamese revolutionaries had to flee China and seek somewhere else close to their homeland where they could pursue their political activities.

Among those who made their way to north-eastern Siam was a man who called himself Thao Chin,[9] but some people recognised him as Nguyen Ai Quoc who, after fleeing Canton, had made another trip to Moscow before settling in Udorn. There he launched a newspaper and founded a school teaching both Vietnamese and Thai. He also visited Bangkok disguised as a Buddhist monk. His main concern was clearly to maintain contact with members of his original revolutionary youth league, which was in danger of splitting into rival factions. To sort out the problem well away from the reach of the French colonial police, a meeting was convened in Hong Kong in February 1930. Ho attended as a representative of the Comintern. The result was the founding of the party which later in the year was renamed the Communist Party of Indo-China. Shortly afterwards he was arrested by the British authorities in Hong Kong. Despite all his efforts to hide his whereabouts, he was followed more or less continuously by an officer of the French Sûreté. Consequently the latter spent some time in Bangkok with the acquiescence of the Siamese police, whom he kept informed of his investigations.[10]

At the same time, the police in Bangkok liaised with the British to intercept correspondence between communists in Siam and their head-quarters in Singapore.[11] These letters, almost invariably in Chinese, provided evidence of their ethnic origin as well as the difficulties they were encountering in expanding their influence. Yet they could not be entirely discounted. A Party document intercepted and submitted to the King in 1930 amounted to a perceptive analysis of Thai society and its need for revolution.[12] As such it differed from the tracts occasionally scattered through the streets of Bangkok. So too did the leaflets distributed under the name of the Communist Party of Siam and its youth wing on the night of September 29, 1932. They were duplicated texts in Thai, English and Chinese which began by proclaiming: "Peasants, workers and all oppressed people of Siam, the tyrannical government of Prajadhipok was overthrown in a night and replaced by a constitutional government. But this new government, is it a government of the people, for the people, by the people?" There followed criticism of several promoters, who were accused of pursuing their own personal interests. The leaflets ended: "Rise, people of Siam! The Khana Ratsadorn, the false revolutionaries, can never do us any good. The Russians are the only people in the world today who have any real freedom and happiness, for they have got rid of the Czar, the princes and the false revolutionaries and have taken their country into their own hands. People of Siam, let us follow in the footsteps of our brothers in Russia. Unite in the struggle against the King, the princes and the Khana Ratsadorn, the false revolutionaries, and imperialism. Establish a Soviet government of Siam so that we can have real independence and liberty!"[13]

A few days after these leaflets were distributed, a French Sûreté official in Bangkok notified the Siamese police that an Annamite who was a leading member of the Third International had just passed through the city on his way north. The French did not think it was the man they knew as Nguyen Ai Quoc[14]. As far they were aware, he was still in prison in Hong Kong, but they were wrong. His lawyer subsequently revealed that he was quietly released in July 1932 before eventually making his way to the Soviet Union again.[15] Yet whoever the author of the leaflets was, one significant factor about them was their criticism of Pridi by name for pursuing his own personal interests to the detriment of the general public.

This communist attack on Pridi was completely ignored in the official campaign against him. In an atmosphere where even Phya Song could be rumoured to be a communist, only to emerge a few months later as the chief protagonist of a conservative military faction, nobody was likely to rationalise his opinions about Pridi on the basis of evidence contained in a communist leaflet.[16] Even so, some newspapers were criticising Phya Mano for using Pridi's plan as a pretext to prorogue the Assembly. And to prosecute him under the anti-communist act might prove even more counter-productive. It was therefore decided, in the words of an official announcement, that Pridi was going "to continue his studies abroad" on a scholarship – or, as rumour had it, a pension – amounting to £1,000 a year, a handsome sum in those days.

Pridi left for France with his wife in mid-April 1933. The degree of public support he still enjoyed was evident in the large crowd which assembled to bid him farewell. It included many prominent promoters and most notably Phya Phahol and Pibul.[17] Others were even more demonstrative. Pridi was accompanied to Singapore by several civilian promoters and Tasnai, the cavalry officer among the original group of Paris promoters, who played an important role in the seizure of power. After that, however, he declined a seat in the cabinet or the Assembly. He said he was a soldier and not a politician. Yet such was Tasnai's devotion to Pridi and his ideas that, when they came under criticism, he was ready to move to his friend's defence with troops. He was dissuaded by Pibul, who claimed that the moment was not opportune because Phya Song and his clique controlled the balance of power in Bangkok. Two months later, Tasnai died of a heart attack. But there was speculation that his death was hastened by Pibul who was jealous of his popularity within the army.[18]

These developments still did not put an end to Phya Mano's problems. Facing continuing criticism in the press, he ordered the closure of one of the most outspoken newspapers, and in a statement denouncing Pridi's plan threatened anybody else who expressed support for it with prosecution under the anti-communist act.[19] When this warning was ignored by another influential newspaper, it too was barred from publishing.[20] Finally, towards the end of April, a total ban was imposed on all comment about Pridi's plan, whether for or against.[21]

This affected the publication of the King's critique as well as an attempt by Pridi's friends to get his original draft into print so that the debate could be continued in his absence. Indeed the full text of Pridi's plan was not published in Siam till after the Second World War, and the campaign against it was based mostly on rumour. Naturally Pridi felt hurt. As soon as he reached Singapore, he denied categorically that he was a communist. It was the first time since the beginning of the crisis that he had spoken to the press. His remarks were republished in Bangkok and the controversy continued.[22]

Phya Mano reacted by setting up a special committee including two foreign advisers. Their task was to prove the government was not totally opposed to economic reform by recommending ways of raising the living standards of the people.[23] The committee soon came up with the idea of establishing a series of agricultural collectives as well as state-owned rice mills and storage facilities – ironically, much as Pridi had done. Yet these proposals were swiftly accepted as government policy.[24]

By then the promoters had other pre-occupations. They had noticed that Pridi's farewells were boycotted by Phya Song, who indeed was rumoured to have gone to see the King with an offer to shoot Pridi. That further antagonised the junior military promoters who, as Tasnai had shown, were devoted to Pridi's cause.[25] It also placed Phya Phahol in an increasingly uncomfortable position as head of the Khana Ratsadorn trying to bridge the split between its factions. Phya Mano too, with Prayoon ever more closely ensconced at his elbow, could scarcely fail to be aware of the dangers inherent in the situation. In an effort to placate the junior military faction, a special gazette was issued in mid-April promoting eighty-two junior officers. Pibul, for instance, was made a lieutenant-colonel, only one rank below Phya Song.[26]

On the other hand the diehards and royalists interpreted Phya Mano's victory over Pridi as reason to hope that there might after all be a return to the absolute monarchy.[27] Many of them, finding the atmosphere in Bangkok increasingly uncongenial, removed to Hua Hin where the growing sojourns of the King created an illusion of life as it was "in the good old days". There was one significant difference. After the departure abroad of several senior princes, the court came to be dominated by Prince Svasti, who was both father-in-law and uncle to the King.

Marriage between cousins, far from being considered detrimental to the royal stock, had often been encouraged within the Chakri family to strengthen the cohesion of the dynasty. What was unusual in this case was that when Prince Svasti's daughter married him, Prajadhipok was not expected to become King. He was the fifth son of Queen Saowabha, sister to Prince Svasti. Among themselves, the senior princes tried to ensure that only the most able of them attained positions of influence. Prince Svasti's career had not been very distinguished until his son-in-law ascended the throne in 1925. He then assumed control of the royal privy purse, but his influence on the King only became noticeable after the change in regime – to which he was bitterly opposed, as was apparent from the columns of a Bangkok newspaper he controlled.[28]

Few people would go as far as one writer, who characterised Prince Svasti as "tyrannical, dipsomaniacal, unscrupulous, cruel and narrow-minded".[29] Even so, he came to be regarded in some quarters as the King's evil genius, and was held responsible for actively dissuading the monarch from returning to Bangkok to carry out his ceremonial duties. However, the official reason given for the King's protracted absence from the capital was that he was unwell and that the climate in Hua Hin suited him better.[30] The reactionary atmosphere there was also making its mark. The King thought Phya Mano should have acted more decisively to curb the power and influence of the promoters. That, at least, was the view expressed in a letter to Phya Mano from the King's secretary describing the ousting of Pridi as "merely a strike at the snake's tail".[31]

As things turned out, Phya Mano was spared from reacting to this hint. On June 10, 1933, the "four tigers" of the Khana Ratsadorn – as Phya Phahol, Phya Song, Phya Ritthi and Phra Prasat were known – suddenly announced their joint resignation from both their government and military positions to take effect from June 24, the first anniversary of their seizure of power. In a statement explaining their decision, they claimed that the government was now strong and stable, whereas they were in poor health and needed a rest.[32]

Military leaders in Bangkok often seem to think that the public will believe whatever they say, no matter how implausible. Instead they simply give rise to a lot of speculation as in this case. Some people, unaware of what had gone on behind the scenes, saw the resignations as the outcome of a straight power struggle between Phya Mano and the leaders of the Khana Ratsadorn, with the losers simply bowing out.[33] Another story current at the time attributed the decision to Phya Phahol. He was said to be angry with Phya Song for pursuing his vendetta with Pridi to the point where it would destroy the unity of the promoters. As their leader, Phya Phahol therefore tried to check and discipline Phya Song by proposing that the "four tigers" resign.[34] Allegedly to eliminate rivalry among themselves, they had previously made a secret vow always to act in concert.

Later Phya Phahol claimed it was not he but Phya Song who first suggested the joint resignations following an argument they had about whether or not Pridi should be reinstated.[35] That too was the version believed by Phya Mano and his friends.[36] They were therefore worried about the eventual outcome of this tactical manoeuvring among the "four tigers". To deprive them of their power, it was quickly announced that their resignation had been accepted by the government and the King. The prime minister then sought further reassurance from Phya Radjwangsan, Phya Sri Visarn and Prayoon, the three people he trusted most. Together they were reported to have had a secret meeting with Pibul in a field on the outskirts of Bangkok. Apparently the intention was to ensure that the junior military promoters would continue to support the government irrespective of any action instigated by the "four tigers". Afterwards Phya Visarn at least was certain there would be no problem.[37]

Such confidence was also manifest in the way a military reshuffle was announced several days before the "four tigers" were officially due to relinquish their positions. More significantly still, they were not replaced by promoters.[38] On the contrary the key appointments in the army were awarded to bitter opponents of the Khana Ratsadorn with Pibul promoted to serve under them in the prestigious but – in the circumstances – powerless position as deputy army commander.[39] Unfortunately for Phya Mano and his friends, the manoeuvre was too transparent.

Pibul soon realised that his own position was in effect a sinecure. That led him to suspect that it was part of a plan by the enemies of the Khana Ratsadorn to restore the absolute monarchy. Another ominous sign was increased police surveillance around Phya Phahol's home. Then Luang Suphachalasai, one of the leading naval promoters who was beginning to rival Sindhu for influence, was suddenly ordered to go to sea with all the gunboats under his command. Supha too was suspicious and first went to see Pibul. They decided that to save the situation they would have to act quickly before the resignation of the "four tigers" became effective. The only solution which occurred to them was to stage a coup.[40]

In contrast to the previous year, the junior promoters in both the army and navy now had troops under their direct command, but they still did not feel confident enough to mount a coup without the backing of a senior military figurehead. In the eyes of Pibul and Supha, that person could only be Phya Phahol. Reluctant to approach him directly on such an important matter, they sent two carefully-chosen envoys. One was an elderly personal friend of Phya Phahol,[41] and the other was Luang Thamrong Nawasawat, a naval promoter turned lawyer whose powers of persuasion later earned him the nickname "Lin Thong" (golden tongue). This time it was to no avail. Despite several hours of pleading, Phya Phahol declined to withdraw his resignation and lead a coup. He felt bound by the oath he had sworn with the other three "tigers" to remain united.

Nevertheless Phya Phahol had agreed to join his colleagues in submitting his resignation only very reluctantly. Having headed the move to install a constitutional government, he believed he had a duty to remain in office to protect it. In that frame of mind he was dismayed that the King had accepted his resignation without granting him the customary courtesy of an audience.[42] On the other hand some of the public were far more demonstrative in expressing their appreciation of the role he had played. For example, members of the Tramway Workers' Association called formally at Phya Phahol's home to present him with a copy of a petition they were submitting to the King, requesting the reinstatement of the four "tigers".[43] The two envoys sent by the junior promoters did not seem to realise the impact all this had on Phya Phahol, but his wife knew better. She was of Chinese descent and related to the family which played host to Sun Yat-sen during his visit to Bangkok in 1908. That appears to have given her an added motive for ensuring that the fruits of the Siamese revolution were not negated. In any event, she prevailed in persuading Phya Phahol to change his mind, where the junior promoters had failed.[44]

As soon as Phya Phahol agreed to lead the coup, it was carried out quickly and easily. On the morning of June 20, 1933, tanks again rolled through the streets of Bangkok, while armed soldiers and sailors seized various strategic buildings such as the Defence Ministry, the main barracks and the Throne Hall. Conveniently for Thai coup-makers, these buildings all lie within about a mile of one another in what is otherwise a very sprawling city.[45] This time, too, there were fewer figureheads to detain than the previous year. Several junior military promoters soon took Phya Mano, Phya Sri Visarn and Prayoon into custody where they were politely requested to relinquish their positions. The statement encompassing this demand explained that the army, navy and civilian bureaucracy, as well as the public, disapproved of various – albeit unspecified – policies of the government which henceforth would be placed under the charge of Phya Phahol. He was one of the signatories of the statement, together with Pibul and Supha.[46] Confronted with such a coalition, Phya Mano took the easy way out. He is said to have resigned with the somewhat ingenuous remark, "Had they told me about this before, there would have been no need to seize power like this. I have only a pen in my hand.''[47]

To suggest that the deposition of Siam's first prime minister set a precedent for the fate of many of those who succeeded him would be an over-simplification. But certain patterns were beginning to emerge. Just as after the seizure of power a year earlier, the coup-promoters in 1933 first despatched a telegram to the King – he was, as usual, residing at Hua Hin – requesting him to remain on the throne and recognise the legality of their action. This time, they stressed in addition that they had no intention of establishing a communist regime; they simply wanted to revert to constitutional government. These assurances were accepted by the King, who also agreed to the reconvening of the Assembly if the promoters insisted.[48]

Next, as ever, the coup-promoters were worried about foreign reaction. Their chief concern in 1933 was that the British and French would intervene on the pretext that Siam had been taken over by communists. To pre-empt any such Western move, resort was quickly made to the Japanese. Within a few hours of assuming power, Phya Phahol asked the Japanese Minister in Bangkok to pay an unofficial and, by implication, secret call at Paruskavan Palace. The invitation was swiftly accepted. The Japanese were well aware that Phya Phahol was the only leading promoter who had visited their country – during the 1920s on a year's attachment to the Japanese army. To reinforce this contact, Pibul paid a call on the Japanese Legation shortly before the coup, but it was hardly necessary. The Japanese were anxious to exploit any foothold of influence in Siam to rival and replace all other foreign entrepreneurs in the country's economy. On arrival at Paruskavan Palace, the Japanese Minister was therefore very receptive to pleas from Phya Phahol and Pibul for help. In reply he stressed that Siam should help itself by breaking the British grip on its economy and turning to Japan for investment and technical expertise. Phya Phahol agreed and the meeting concluded, with the understanding that both sides would keep it strictly secret.[49]

After that, reverting to the procedure adopted in the previous year, notes were sent to all the other diplomatic missions in Bangkok with assurances that existing treaty commitments as well as foreign lives and property would be respected by the new administration which – as was additionally stressed this time – was not communist-inspired.[50] The same point was made at a press conference given by Phya Phahol. He denied heading the coup in order to rehabilitate Pridi and his national economic plan. Rumours were already circulating that Pridi had been asked to return immediately from Europe by air to assume power.[51]

Unintentionally this speculation was aggravated by Phya Phahol. As soon as the Assembly reconvened, he announced he would only head the government for fourteen days. That made it look as if he was acting as caretaker till Pridi's return. Instead Phya Phahol explained that he was simply a soldier, lacked administrative experience, and above all wanted to avoid giving the impression that a military dictatorship was being installed.[52]

Given that two consecutive regimes had now been ousted by force of arms within the space of a year, it was clear that no government in Siam could afford to ignore the military, and certainly after their experience with Phya Mano the promoters were not going to nominate another premier from outside their own ranks. That left them with little alternative except Phya Phahol. As the only person acceptable to all the factions within the Khana Ratsadorn, he had to take over the premiership on a long-term basis, like it or not. The King too accepted the situation. Returning briefly to Bangkok, he made his first-ever broadcast to signify his approval of a new government headed by Phya Phahol.[53]

Apart from the change at the top, the composition of the government remained much the same. Naturally Phya Mano's close friends were dropped, but *ancien régime* officials continued to hold all the ministerial positions. The promoters were still very conscious of their own lack of administrative experience, as Phya Phahol was quite ready to admit. He attached to himself as personal adviser Prince Wan Waityakorn Voravarn, younger brother to Pridi's friend Prince Sakol and owner of one of the newspapers closed down for criticising Phya Mano. There were other reasons for this choice. Prince Wan enjoyed the reputation of having one of the most astute political brains in Siam. Educated in England, he had risen through the Siamese diplomatic service to become Minister in Paris before his career was interrupted by a divorce and remarriage which alienated him from much of the royal family. Now there was another snag. As a grandson of King Mongkut, he ranked among those princes debarred from holding cabinet office. He was therefore appointed adviser to the Foreign Ministry, although in reality he assisted the Prime Minister. Special permission was also sought for Prince Wan to participate in Assembly debates, despite the ban on his membership of it.[54]

Phya Phahol needed all the help he could get to keep the country on an even keel after the controversial events of the recent past. A group of students called for the impeachment of Phya Mano on the grounds that he had contravened the constitution in proroguing the Assembly. Similar demands were voiced within the Assembly itself. They were all quietly side-stepped by Phya Phahol.[55] He clearly wanted to avoid any further polarisation of the political scene which might result from raking over past events. Besides, it could prove awkward. Apart from Phya Mano, the prorogation decree had been signed by the King as well as several prominent promoters including Phya Phahol himself. Consequently no action was taken against Phya Mano, and several months later he disappeared to exile in Penang. Before he left, however, some of his decisions were vindicated on July 27 when the Assembly voted to approve all the measures decreed following its prorogation, including the anti-communist act.[56]

The continuation in force of this act had little effect on the rumour-mills. There was further speculation that Phya Phahol's government would soon show its true colours by recalling Pridi to head a communist regime. When he did not reappear, it was attributed to pressure from the British. They were said to be threatening to intervene if Pridi rejoined the government.[57] Such rumours were completely unfounded and apparently emanated from diehards who were becoming almost paranoid in their fears. Some of them even suggested that since the King had proved so weak in caving in and acknowledging the outcome of the coups, he should be replaced by Prince Boripat, the former Minister of the Interior and heir to the throne.[58]

The promoters' anxiety was increased by what was happening in their own ranks. Of the "three tigers" who resigned together with Phya Phahol, only Phya Ritthi requested reinstatement. Phya Song and Phra Prasat simply let their resignations stand and departed up-country. Prayoon too, through his overt cooperation with Phya Mano was regarded as a traitor.[59] Worse still, some promoters suspected that their renegade colleagues might team up with the royalists.

Such thoughts clearly occurred to Pibul and Supha. In mid-July, they addressed a circular letter to several people they believed were planning a coup. Among the recipients were Prayoon and Prince Bovoradet, the former Minister of War. One of them was so indignant at receiving such a communication that he sent a copy to the press which duly published it. It read:

Both times the Khana Ratsadorn seized power, it acted in an orderly fashion for the sake of peace and the freedom of the people. It appears from our investigations that you are trying to destroy that peace by attempting to overthrow the present government. Such a move would interfere with the orderly progress of the nation. In our position as guardians of the peace, we advise you to desist. If you insist on causing trouble, our group will use strong measures to assure the peace. This is not a threat we signed to intimidate you, but is advice hopefully given.[60]

The publication of this letter created a furore, with Pibul and Supha coming under criticism from numerous quarters. They tried to defend themselves by claiming they had written the letter as private individuals and not in an official capacity. In that case, the press retorted they had no right to threaten strong measures.[61] Indeed, rather than averting a counter-coup, they made it more likely. Plots and rumours of plots abounded, prompting increasing signs of nervousness on the part of the government. In August it ordered the temporary closure of the newspaper controlled by Prince Svasti.[62] It also denied speculation that Japan had agreed to come to the rescue of Siam, should the Western powers intervene to put an end to the continuing internal unrest.[63]

Given such obsessive concern over foreign intervention, the King had not felt free since June 1932 to receive any of his Western friends, fearing that such meetings would be misconstrued by the promoters. His self-restraint finally snapped after fourteen months. In identical letters addressed to at least two of the British advisers attached to the government, the King showed just how pessimistic he had become. Although he conceded that a few diehards ''out of touch with reality'' wanted to see the return of the absolute monarchy, there were far more monarchists who were prepared to accept the constitution. The problem was that they had been betrayed by Phya Mano. In a scathing criticism of his previous Prime Minister, the King complained that he had failed to listen to advice or pay any attention to popular feeling, thus precipitating his own downfall by unwisely proroguing the Assembly. As a result those people who were politically conscious had no alternative but to team up with the communists. In propounding this thesis the King discounted the military, except in so far as they had guns. Those who supported Pridi were far more dangerous, because he wanted to establish a republic yet was clever enough to realise that such an objective could not be achieved overnight. Hence the King claimed that Pridi's followers had embarked on a scabrous campaign to discredit the royal family, and the only way to stop it was to use the bogey of foreign intervention, the one thing of which Pridi and his friends were afraid. The King therefore concluded his letter by suggesting that all foreign advisers attached to the government should resign as a warning against the forthcoming establishment of a communist regime.[64]

The recipients of the King's letter did not respond to his appeal. They considered his views unduly alarmist. Apparently, too, the monarch had little idea how foreign advisers continued to exercise considerable influence over the administration. For example, despite the upheavals of the past year, Siam's financial position remained stable and its economy was steadily recovering. Rather, the real threat to the country came from the military which, though anxious to acquire modern Western equipment, had never brooked the presence in its midst of foreign advisers who might have instilled a greater sense of professional discipline.

The problem arose again in August 1933 when part of the navy, acting ostensibly at the instigation of the former Minister of Defence Phya Radjwangsan, showed signs of mounting another coup. As a result the naval commander was abruptly replaced and Supha was appointed deputy commander on a par with Pibul in the army. The main loser seemed to be Sindhu, the original leader of the naval promoters. He had been deliberately omitted from the planning of the June 1933 coup because it was directed against his elder brother among others. Yet since he had taken no overt action against the Khana Ratsadorn, Sindhu was shunted aside into what appeared to be a desk job as naval chief of staff.[65]

Another source of tension was Pridi. He was quoted in Paris as saying that he favoured the idea of nationalising some industries and services. In the same interview he denied being a communist or a member of the Third International. Instead he equated his views with the Labour Party in Britain. Pridi also stated that he had no intention of returning to Siam unless or until invited by the government.[66]

After the turmoil of the previous few months, it was a measure of Phya Phahol's devotion to Pridi that such an invitation was issued. The premier was apparently prepared to take such a political risk in the hope that Pridi's return would help cement the loyalty of the civilian promoters. First, however, the ground had to be prepared with the public. In early September it was announced that the King had authorised the return home of Pridi after he had signed a declaration agreeing to abide by the basic economic principles drawn up by the committee established by Phya Mano in April.[67] To ensure there was no public misunderstanding of what was entailed, Phya Phahol's government stressed that if agricultural cooperatives were set up or official assistance was given to industry, all existing property rights would be fully respected.

At least in some quarters, this statement had the desired effect. One

Bangkok newspaper commented: "It is only reasonable that before Luang Pradit [Pridi] was summoned to return the government had to come to a clear and definite arrangement with him. But outside government circles some of us are somewhat timid and presumably it was to reassure us that this very full statement was issued . . . a full profession of faith with nothing objectionable in it . . . before the expected arrival."[68]

Not everybody viewed Pridi's return in the same light. Phya Song, who had disappeared from public view when his resignation became effective, suddenly arrived back in Bangkok. He was said to have been offered the Ministry of the Interior to keep an eye on Pridi and his followers. Instead it was announced that Phya Song and his close friend Phra Prasat were leaving on a "study tour" of Europe with full pay plus a daily travel allowance. That was even more generous than the sum granted to Pridi when he was sent abroad. To the public it was equally obvious that the departure of Phya Song and Phra Prasat was directly related to the return of Pridi, although they denied it and said they were leaving because they were tired of politics.[69]

Pridi arrived back in Bangkok on September 29, 1933. A large crowd went to the port to welcome him including 400 law students who had previously called for the impeachment of Phya Mano. Pridi did not meet this enthusiastic welcome committee. His steamer was met at the bar of the river by a naval gunboat which transported him rapidly to a landing stage in the centre of the city, and from there he was whisked to the safety of Paruskavan Palace, which the promoters had fortified and transformed into Government House. Two days later came another indication of how far Phya Phahol was prepared to go in reintegrating Pridi: it was announced that he had been reappointed to the cabinet as a minister without portfolio.[70]

To many people, communism no longer looked like a vague threat on the horizon. They were convinced that a communist had entered the government.

NOTES

1. F3113/42/40 in FO371/17175 and Withet Korani, p. 217.
2. This was Luang Supha Chalasai.
3. Thawatt Mokrapong, p. 155, and Sivaram, pp. 57ff.
4. Text in Landon (1939), p. 251.
5. F5574/42/40 in FO371/17175.
6. Text of new Party history as broadcast by "Voice of People of Thailand", Dec. 9, 1977, in Turton (ed.), *Thailand: Roots of Conflict*, pp. 158–68.
7. Kennedy, *Communism in Asia*, p. 200, and Brimmel, *Communism in South East Asia*, pp. 112ff.
8. Batson (1974), p. 61.
9. Huynh Kim Khanh, *Vietnamese Communism, 1923–45*, pp. 60ff, and Lacouture, *Ho Chi Minh*, p. 39. The alias suggests he posed as a Lao dignitary of Chinese origin.
10. ibid., p. 45, and F7839/4260/40 in FO371/16262.
11. For example, F1738/42/40 in FO371/17174.
12. Text in Batson (1974), pp. 66–71.
13. BTWM, Oct. 3, 7 and 13, 1932. Apart from Bangkok, leaflets were distributed in Pichit, Udorn, Nongkai, Sakol Nakorn and Nakron Panom, all towns with Vietnamese communities.
14. The French believed that he was Le Hong Phong, another Moscow-trained Vietnamese F7839/42/40 in FO371/16262 and despatch of Jan. 25, 1933, in FO371/17178.
15. Duncanson, *China Quarterly*, no. 57 (Jan.–Mar. 1977), pp. 98ff.
16. In May 1934, the Comintern also mistakenly referred to Pridi as "a Siamese prince who has studied in London and imbibed socialist ideas". Quoted in Maclane, *Soviet Strategies in South East Asia*, p. 198.
17. BTWM, Apr. 13, 1933, and Thawatt Mokrapong, p. 156.
18. ibid., p. 8, and Thawee Bunyaket in Ray, p. 71.
19. Text in Thawatt Mokrapong, p. 156; BTWM, Apr. 13, 1933; Sivaram, pp. 64ff.
20. BTWM, May 15, 1933.
21. ibid., Apr. 19 and 21, 1933, and Sivaram, pp. 60ff.
22. BTWM, Apr. 24, 1933.
23. ibid., Apr. 17, 1933.
24. Thompson, p. 74.
25. F3396/42/40 in FO371/17175.
26. Thawatt Mokrapong, p. 161.
27. Vella (1955), p. 369.
28. Thompson, pp. 795ff, and *Bangkok Daily Mail* in Landon (1939), p. 35.
29. Vella (1955), p. 359, quoting Phra Sarasat Pholkand. Also M. Smith, p. 125.
30. F4143/42/40 in FO371/17175.
31. Thawatt Mokrapong, p. 188.
32. BTWM, June 13, 1933.
33. Landon (1939), p. 32, and Thompson, p. 76.
34. F5574/42/40 in FO371/17175.
35. Thawatt Mokrapong, p. 241.

36. F4439/42/40 in FO371/17175 and Prayoon, p. 241.
37. Landon (1939), p. 31, and Phya Sri Visarn's account in F4150/42/40 in FO371/17175.
38. BTWM, June 19, 1933, and Sivaram, p. 64.
39. The army commander-designate was Maj.–Gen. Phya Pichai Songkram while Col. Phya Srisith Songkram, who had rejected appeals from the promoters to join them before they seized power, was appointed Director of Military Operations. Kularb Saipradit, p. 63, and Thawatt Mokrapong, pp. 161 and 197.
40. ibid., pp. 192ff, and F5574/42/40 in FO371/17175.
41. This was Phya Suriya Nuwat, father to Prachuap Bunnag, a civilian promoter.
42. Thawatt Mokrapong, p. 194.
43. BTWM, June 19, 1933.
44. Thawatt Mokrapong, p. 194.
45. According to Khuang, Pibul asked him to cut the telephones again. He refused. Instead the Post Office failed to put through any calls while the coup was under-way. Khuang, loc. cit., p. 72.
46. BTWM, June 20, 1933.
47. Thawatt Mokrapong, p. 164.
48. Sivaram, p. 68; Prasert Patamasukhon, pp. 70ff; F5327/42/40 in FO371/17175.
49. Flood, *Japan's Relations with Thailand, 1928–41*, pp. 51 and 58ff, quoting Miyazaki memorandum of June 15, 1940, in Gaimusho Kiroku files. Miyazaki was inter-preter to Japanese Minister Yatabe Yasuhichi. But Flood errs in referring to Pridi's exclusion from this meeting. He was abroad.
50. Text in F4412/42/40 in FO371/17175.
51. F4097/42/40 in ibid.; BTWM, June 21, 1933; Sivaram, p. 69.
52. BTWM, June 23, 1933, and Prasert Patamasukhon, pp. 73.
53. BTWM, July 4, 5, 6 and 12, 1933; Sivaram, p. 75; Prasert Patamasukhon, pp. 80ff.
54. ibid., p. 79; BTWM, July 17, 1933; F5574/42/40 in FO371/17175.
55. BTWM, July 21 and 27, 1939, and Sivaram, pp. 77ff.
56. Thompson, p. 77.
57. F4194/42/40 in FO371/17175.
58. F6035/42/40 in ibid.
59. ibid.
60. Text in BTWM, July 20, 1933, and Landon (1939), p. 37.
61. Thompson, p. 78, and Sivaram, p. 84.
62. BTWM, Aug. 8, 1933.
63. ibid., Aug. 9, 1933.
64. F7061 and F7281/42/40 in FO371/17176.
65. F6338/42/40 in FO371/17175.
66. Reuter interview of July 31 in BTWM, Aug. 28, 1933.
67. ibid., Sep. 1, 1933; Thawee Bunyaket in Ray, p. 72; Sivaram, p. 79.
68. BTWM Sep. 22, 1933, and Landon (1939), p. 62.
69. BTWM Sep. 23, 1933, and Thawatt Mokrapong, p. 169.
70. BTWM Sep. 30, 1933, and Prasert Patamasukhon, p. 95.

5
THE BACKLASH

Whenever tension runs high in Bangkok, even the most innocuous-seeming reports can be significant. Certainly that was the case following Pridi's return. A lot of attention focused on an item in the press about a visit by Prince Bovoradet, the former Minister of War, to Korat, the main garrison town in the north-east. He was said to be indisposed and receiving calls from various old friends, many of them military officers.[1]

Since his resignation in 1931, Prince Bovoradet had kept out of the public eye, despite his reputation for being ambitious. As a result some people initially believed him to be the hidden force – or the third hand, as the Thais say – behind the promoters.[2] The opposite proved to be true. Before selecting Phya Mano as Siam's first Prime Minister, they did give some thought to offering the position to Prince Bovoradet. The idea was rejected on the grounds that he was likely to exploit the premiership to forward his own personal ambitions. Possibly, too, the Paris promoters were swayed by his being the younger brother of Prince Charoon, the minister with whom they had clashed so bitterly during their student days.[3] Indeed, when it came to allocating positions in the new regime, Prince Bovoradet was completely ignored and not offered even an advisory role, as might have been expected. Still he did not show any overt hostility until approached by opponents of the Khana Ratsadorn to join a move to oust the government. There was then no hesitation. Asserting his rank, Prince Bovoradet immediately arrogated the role of leading a coup.[4]

His basic plan was apparently to rally army units in the provinces, surround Bangkok and force the government to surrender. First he set out to gain the support of military officers in Korat and other north-eastern garrisons. More important still was the cooperation of troops based in Ayuthya, just to the north of Bangkok: they had become disaffected under the influence of Phya Srisith Songkram, a retired colonel whose career prospects had twice been thwarted by the promoters. Consequently he was planning his own coup before agreeing to join forces with Prince Bovoradet.[5] Vengeance likewise motivated Phya Sena Songkram, leader of the aborted attempt to set up the Khana Chart. He readily undertook to rally the garrison at Nakorn Sawan to the north of the central plains in a move against the promoters.

Despite such promises of support, Prince Bovoradet remained doubtful of success. He wanted the garrisons at Ratburi to the west of Bangkok and Prachinburi to the east to cooperate in closing the ring around the capital. With that in mind he sent a personal envoy on a flying mission to Ratburi on October 11. It turned out to be a fateful move.

That same day Phya Phahol happened to be in Ratburi and soon realised what was in the wind. He immediately rushed back to Bangkok, proclaimed martial law and ordered reinforcements to Ratburi to secure the loyalty of the garrison there.[6] Other troops were moved to Bangsue in the northern suburbs of Bangkok where the artillery arsenal was situated. It was thought likely to be one of the main targets of provincial forces who had not been resupplied with ammunition since 1932.

Bangsue is also the junction where the main railway lines running into Bangkok converge, and in 1933 rail was the only means of transporting large numbers of troops rapidly around the country. There were few roads outside the capital and even the airfield at Don Muang just north of Bangkok, which was used as a landing-ground for international flights to Siam, was only linked to the city by an unmetalled track.[7] Moreover, October marks the height of the rainy season when only railway embankments stood out above the inundated paddy fields of the Chao Phya basin.

Instead of waiting for more propitious weather, Prince Bovoradet decided to advance his attack as soon as he realised his plotting was known to the government. On the evening of October 11, troops from Korat were ordered to move in the direction of Bangkok. Travelling by rail, it was only a few hours before they linked up with soldiers from Ayuthya and other central plains garrisons who were already advancing on the capital under the command of Phya Srisith. By noon the next day, they captured Don Muang and with it Siam's infant air force, so enabling Prince Bovoradet to fly in and establish his headquarters there.[8]

To the amazement of many military experts, the opponents of the government did not exploit their aerial advantage. Instead there was a lull in all activity, while Phya Srisith who was encamped near Bangsue, addressed an ultimatum to Phya Phahol.[9] It demanded the resignation of the government within an hour on the grounds that the promoters had incited the people to despise the monarchy. Apparently Phya Srisith was referring to the leader of the Tramway Workers' Association who had caused public outrage by announcing his intention to sue the King for libel over some allegedly derogatory remarks about labour activists made during the controversy over Pridi's plan. Although the man in question had already been detained,[10] Phya Srisith's ultimatum went on to claim that Pridi's reinstatement proved the government was moving towards the installation of a communist regime.

No response, either political or military, was made to the ultimatum, and when it expired, Prince Bovoradet still did not order his forces into action. Rather he sent another ultimatum. It differed considerably from the first. It requested the revision of military policy in order to restore a measure of power to the provincial garrisons. It also proposed that official appointments be made on the basis of ability and experience rather than political considerations. More surprisingly, the ultimatum expressed respect for the constitution and ended by requesting that everybody who had taken up arms against the government be pardoned.[11] None of them subsequently explained precisely what their intentions were, but the terms of the second ultimatum in particular and Prince Bovoradet's reluctance to launch an immediate attack on Bangkok would seem to suggest he might have preferred a compromise.[12] The promoters thought otherwise.

After an official communiqué was issued reaffirming the government's loyalty to the King and denying that Pridi was a communist, resort was made to the premise that anybody challenging the authority of those in power must be a rebel. To discredit their opponents even more, the promoters claimed that an attempt was underway to restore the absolute monarchy by force.[13] Rewards were offered for the capture of the rebel leaders, certain army reservists were called up, and the public was asked to rally to the support of the government. Similar appeals were voiced on the radio by Phya Phahol, leading many workers, students and boy scouts to volunteer their services.

What concerned the promoters far more was the attitude of the King. As usual he was at Hua Hin where Phya Phahol addressed several telegrams stressing his loyalty to the throne and proposing that the monarch return to Bangkok for his own safety. In reply the King cabled back: "That Prince Bovoradet contemplates disturbing the peace is contrary to His Majesty's wishes for he is constantly warning members of the royal family not to do so. But when there is somebody not heeding his wishes in this matter, His Majesty can only regret it."[14]

This somewhat ambivalent response provided little comfort for the government. It suspected Hua Hin of being the nerve-centre if not the actual headquarters of the rebellion. Its apprehension was increased by the poor state of communications throughout Siam. The promoters were unable to determine how many provincial garrisons had marched against Bangkok. Judging by the strong wording of Phya Srisith's ultimatum, the rebels had mustered a powerful force. There was also some doubt about the loyalty of certain elements in Bangkok. Phya Ritthi, one of the "four tigers" who had resumed charge of the artillery, showed reluctance to become involved in any armed conflict.[15] Likewise the navy declared its neutrality, and to emphasise the point its newly-appointed commander removed himself and several gunboats downriver to the mouth of the Chao Phya.

As this small flotilla passed under the Chakri Memorial Bridge, it was involved in an exchange of gunfire which left several dead and wounded.[16] Although it was not clear whether the military guarding the bridge had orders to deter the navy from leaving Bangkok, Sindhu and his elder brother Phya Radjwangsan intervened. They proposed that the Supreme Patriarch of the Buddhist Sangka should be asked to mediate between the government and its opponents.[17] The suggestion went unheeded since Pibul had already assumed control of the troops in Bangkok and ordered battle to commence.[18]

An artillery officer by training, Pibul's idea was to bombard rebel positions to the north of Bangkok. This gun barrage lasted several days until Don Muang was finally recaptured on the evening of October 16 at the cost of many dead and injured, civilians included.[19] Fighting continued as the rebels retreated reluctantly along the railway line. Soon the odds turned against Prince Bovoradet. The morale of several garrisons which had promised to march on Bangkok was wavering. The troops were told they were going to the capital to suppress a communist takeover, but some were apparently reluctant to fight under such a commander as Prince Bovoradet.[20] Phya Phahol's broadcasts appealing for national unity were also making their mark. For this reason, listening to the radio was banned in areas controlled by forces opposed to the government.[21]

Apart from that, Prince Bovoradet had already been deprived of one major source of support. Phya Sena, having rallied the garrison at Nakorn Sawan, found his southward move blocked at Lopburi where his troop-train was deliberately derailed. As a result, the men under his command fled back home, leaving him to make his way alone and ignominiously to Don Muang.[22] A somewhat similar incident occurred west of Bangkok. Troops from Petburi attempting to make their way towards the capital were repulsed by the newly-reinforced garrison at Ratburi.[23]

Phya Phahol did not let any opportunity slip. Once Don Muang was recaptured, he sent another message to the King appealing to him to return to Bangkok. What resulted was just the opposite. Alarmed by the clash between the Petburi and Ratburi garrisons not far north of Hua Hin, the court panicked, commandeered a train and fled eventually to Songkla not far from the border with Malaya. The King and his consort meanwhile put to sea in a small boat which soon ran out of fuel on its way south and had to be helped out of difficulty by a passing foreign cargo ship. Some hours later the freighter took the royal couple on board when two warships were sighted off Songkla. The alarm was short-lived. Aboard one of the warships was the commander of the navy who had decided to offer the monarch protection.[24]

To the north of Bangkok, the government still did not have everything going its own way. In order to impede the advance of troops under Pibul's command, the rebels launched an unmanned railway engine down the track. It crashed headlong into a train carrying government troops, causing numerous deaths and injuries.[25] The incident made Pibul all the more determined to inflict a stinging defeat on his enemies, and the battle along the railway line was pursued with greater vigour. Events were swayed by developments in Korat which had been reinforced by troops moving up from Ubol. Suddenly they mutinied and fled. At that, Prince Bovoradet split the forces remaining loyal to him. Some units, placed under the command of Phya Sena, were ordered to attack the turncoats from Ubol and resecure Korat. On the other front, Phya Srisith was assigned to stop government troops advancing from Bangkok.[26] The result was a major battle which took place on October 23 at Hin Lap on the fringes of the north-east plateau. During this action, Phya Srisith was killed together with many of his troops.

The defeat so disheartened Prince Bovoradet that he abandoned the defence of Korat and fled by plane to Indo-China. News of his flight inspired Phya Sena to do likewise. He simply left his troops who were still battling to reach Ubol and rode off through the jungle also in the direction of Indo-China.[27] That marked the end of the fighting as such. The government later claimed that the whole episode, which is usually known as the Bovoradet rebellion, cost the lives of fifteen government soldiers and two police officers, with a further fifty-eight wounded.[28] No figures were given to indicate the much larger number of rebel forces or civilians dead and injured. The instinctive reaction of the authorities has always been to hush up the true extent of any violence, especially when it is the result of political unrest.

Still, even before the fighting ceased, the government moved to round up those it suspected of sympathising with the rebel cause. They included many of the people involved in the abortive attempt to establish the Khana Chart, some of them women.[29] Another casualty of the political purge was the newspaper in which the King's father-in-law, Prince Svasti, held a controlling interest. It was closed down and its editor and proprietor were eventually arrested on charges that their offices were the Bangkok headquarters of the rebel movement.[30] With strict censorship imposed on the rest of the press, rumours soon spread that the prisons were packed to overflowing. They prompted an official communiqué which stated simply: "His Majesty's Government wishes to make it known that it is preferable to possess a silent tongue."[31] When the government finally got round to issuing details of the arrests, it claimed that only 300 people had been detained, almost half of whom had already been released for lack of evidence.[32]

To deal with those remaining in custody, legislation was hastily enacted to establish special courts. In effect they were military tribunals where the accused, both military and civilian, had little right to legal representation or appeal of any sort. Shortly afterwards, an Act for the Protection of the Constitution was also promulgated. It provided for prison sentences of up to twenty years for anyone found guilty of challenging the constitution, although it was very vague in defining the crime. The drafting of this legislation was widely attributed to Pridi since he was appointed head of a commission set up by the Assembly 'to protect the constitution'.[33] These moves not only dismayed those directly affected; there was also widespread disillusion among people who had hoped the promoters would live up to their proclaimed ideals of creating a more just society. Yet although the government chose to subject those it had detained to such an arbitrary system of justice, little was done to press for the extradition from Indo-China of the figureheads of the rebellion who had fled there.[34]

It was not so easy for the government to ignore the problem of the royal family remaining at Songkla. With little news reaching Bangkok of what was happening there, speculation grew that it had become the new centre for the pursuit of the rebellion,[35] a theory given added credence by the continuing presence in Songkla of two warships and the commander of the navy. Alternatively there were rumours that the royal family was preparing to flee *en masse* to Singapore.[36] To sort out the situation, Phya Phahol sent his Minister of Justice to Songkla,[37] but initially it only made matters worse. Songkla buzzed with rumours that the government was determined to arrest certain key figures in the royal family including Prince Svasti and his sons.[38]

This situation lasted for over a month, during which envoys travelled regularly between Bangkok and Songkla on the twice-weekly express train to negotiate with the King. They included Prince Wan in his capacity as adviser to Phya Phahol.[39] On one occasion they took with them the Tramway Workers' leader to apologise in person to the King for the attempt to sue him.[40] Eventually, after many false alarms, the crisis was resolved in early December. The two warships returned to Bangkok where the naval commander was instructed to report in person to the Defence Ministry.[41] Simultaneously Prince Svasti and his sons departed to Penang, as did several other members of the royal family and the King's secretary.[42] These developments paved the way for the King to return to Bangkok to resume his duties as constitutional monarch. Before that, Siam had experienced its first-ever elections, and martial law had been lifted.

The electoral process was already underway when the rebellion broke out, and it was decided that it should continue in order to prove that the government was still in control and not wavering in its resolve to pursue the path of democracy. An electoral law passed in February 1933 laid down a complex formula of indirect representation designed, according to the official explanation, to overcome the political immaturity of the people. In each *tambon* (the secondary level of local administration, grouping several villages) the residents were supposed to select a suitable person to vote on their behalf. On election day, these *tambon* representatives were required to attend provincial meetings where aspiring parliamentary candidates presented themselves and their policies in short speeches. As political parties were non-existent, it was the only form of electioneering envisaged in 1933. Once they had heard the speeches, the *tambon* representatives were allowed several hours in which to reflect before casting their votes. The count was soon completed, since there were rarely more than 100 voters in any one constituency.[43]

In practice, what happened varied widely. Some *tambons* failed to send anyone to represent them. By contrast the elections in Songkla turned into a grand occasion when the King decided to observe them in person. He also took an interest in the outcome in Bangkok by discreetly encouraging a candidate influential enough to stand up to the promoters. This was Major-General Phya Thephatsadin, who had led the Siamese military contingent which fought alongside the French and British during the First World War. As such he was a well-known

figure whose reputation had been enhanced by pioneering aerial transport in Siam.[44] That apparently made him suspect in the eyes of the promoters, and he was one of the first people to be detained, albeit temporarily, during the rebellion. He referred to this in his vote-canvassing
speech, and it did him no harm. He was elected to represent Bangkok,
together with two prominent lawyers.[45] This result mirrored the
general trend throughout the country. Most of the successful candidates
were respected local figures. For the more remote provinces, it was a
matter of prestige because for the first time ever they were choosing a
voice to represent them in the centre of affairs. The two members elected
to represent the northern province of Chiengmai, for example, were
conveyed by a traditional procession of elephants through crowded
streets to the railway station to embark on the journey to Bangkok to
take up their seats in the Assembly.[46]

The date selected for the opening of the new Assembly was December
10, the first anniversary of the permanent constitution, when all 180
representatives – half of them elected, the others nominated by the
government – gathered at the Ananta Samakhom Throne Hall. Having
been established as the home of Siam's parliament, it again provided the
setting for a ceremony conducted with traditional pomp. Once the
members of the Assembly had convened, curtains were drawn back to
reveal the King enshrined on the throne in full regalia. Also, as had happened exactly a year earlier, the occasion seemed to symbolise a reconciliation between the monarch and the government. In his speech from the
throne, the King deplored the prorogation of the Assembly and the subsequent rebellion. He went on to express the hope that constitutional
government would flourish in future.[47]

Again the King's stay in Bangkok was short. He insisted on leaving
for Europe in January 1934 because he was suffering from cataracts and
needed medical treatment.[48] Phya Phahol was dismayed; he feared that
the monarch's departure so soon after the rebellion would create the
impression that he was going into exile. The government even proposed
to pay for any eye-surgeon the King cared to name to travel to Siam at
official expense but the offer was rejected. The King said he was tired
and needed a complete rest away from affairs of state.[49]

In private, he explained his attitude more frankly to two British
advisers to the government. Quoting the saying once prevalent in
England that the King could do no wrong, he said that in Siam it seemed
the King could do no right. Every move he had made had been either
misinterpreted or criticised. He had advised Phya Mano against pro-

roguing the Assembly, but was blamed for authorising it. He had condemned Prince Bovoradet's rebellion, yet continued to be suspected of supporting it. At the height of the fighting he had gone to Songkla to avoid becoming a hostage to political fortune, but had been accused of equivocation, and even his offers to mediate between the two sides had been ignored by the government. After all the crises of the previous eighteen months, the King hoped that by going abroad he would contribute to calming and stabilising the situation.[50] He attempted to convey the same message in a radio broadcast expressing full confidence in the government and its ability to administer the country in his absence under the regency of one of his uncles.[51]

Nonetheless, even after his departure, the King continued to arouse controversy. On his way to Europe he spent two days at Medan in Sumatra where various people assembled to greet him. These included Prince Boripat, Prince Purachatra and Prince Svasti as well as several other prominent personages who had gone into exile in South East Asia. According to the Bangkok press, it was the first opportunity the senior Chakri princes had had to meet and discuss family matters since the revolution.[52] But it was easy to put a very different interpretation on such a gathering taking place so close to Siam and so soon after the rebellion.[53]

Anyway, people in Bangkok viewed the conduct of the royal family as unhelpful to those accused of participating in the rebellion. The first trials under the Special Courts Act took place in December 1933 when two retired major-generals were found guilty and sentenced to death.[54] A separate trial was accorded to Prince Bovoradet's younger brother, Sitthiporn. He was sentenced to life imprisonment.[55] The verdict was the more surprising since Prince Sitthiporn was one of the few members of the royal family who openly favoured the idea of constitutional government and continued to work with dedication under the new regime. He was Director-General of Agricultural Research – his main interest in life.[56] Yet, for one reason or another, he went to Don Muang when his elder brother seized the airfield at the start of the rebellion. Afterwards he made no attempt to flee the country and was promptly arrested. It was totally unprecedented for a prince of Chakri blood to be imprisoned. Previously, no matter what crimes they had committed, they were regarded as above the law and could only be punished on the express instructions of the monarch. But what really shocked the public was that Prince Sitthiporn was shackled like any common criminal.[57]

The treatment of political prisoners became a subject of so much

adverse comment that the government issued a special statement in justification of its policy.[58] Another controversial issue was whether those
sentenced to death would be executed. Workers' organisations which
had supported the government during the rebellion petitioned for
clemency.[59] Letters to the press suggested that executions would only
add to the number of the government's opponents. Within the Assembly these views were echoed by Phya Thephatsadin – who, as the King
had hoped, was influential enough to attract the support of many representatives and be chosen as deputy speaker. He was bitterly opposed by
several military promoters just nominated to become members of the
Assembly; they argued that those who dared rebel against the government, causing the death and injury of numerous soldiers, deserved the
punishment meted out to them.[60]

To register their feelings, the promoters organised a special cremation
in February 1934 for their supporters killed during the rebellion. Significantly and unprecedentedly, the ceremony took place on the open space
in front of the Grand Palace in Bangkok reserved for royal cremations.
But the execution of those sentenced to death – widely expected to coincide with the event – did not take place.[62] The government had reason
to be mindful of its popularity.

It was having to cope with a new spate of labour unrest, first in the
ricemills and then in the railway workshops.[62] In addition, some people
detained during the Bovoradet rebellion were suing certain ministers for
wrongful arrest, and a special act of indemnity had to be rushed through
the Assembly to protect them.[63] In its attempts to reform the structure
of local government, the government was also accused of carrying out
an anti-royalist purge.[64] As a result there was renewed speculation about
the possibility of foreign intervention. It was even suggested in Bangkok
that this was why the British had just decided to strengthen their naval
base at Singapore.[65] Instead the only threat to Siam came once more from
within its own armed forces. The navy was on the brink of mutiny.

The decision by the naval commander to remain neutral during the
rebellion had provoked a deep factional split. Even his resignation when
ordered to return from Songkla did not satisfy some young naval promoters led by Supha. Having given their full support to the government, they wanted a purge of all naval officers who followed a neutralist
line during the rebellion. In January 1934, one of Supha's friends published a call for twenty-three officers to be discharged for disloyalty, a
demand backed up with threatening action by a group of naval ratings.[66]
The crisis was most acute in the cabinet. There Supha, in supporting

the call for the purge, was at odds with its only other naval member, Sindhu, who had gone along with the neutralist line. Eventually, in March, a compromise was reached. The former naval commander was taken into custody while Supha was removed from his position as deputy commander to a sinecure in the Ministry of Public Instruction. However, he remained a member of the cabinet despite his alleged involvement in another conspiracy which led to the arrest of over 100 people at the end of March. Among them was a leader of the Bangkok Taxi Drivers' Association, but few details of the plot – if such it was – emerged.[67] Rather, the navy as a whole was made to suffer. For several years its financial needs were almost completely ignored when the defence budget came to be allocated. That enabled the army to benefit from the funds available to purchase arms and strengthen its power base, so sowing the seeds for future antagonism between the two armed services.[68]

Another contentious issue which continued to rumble on was the question of whether or not Pridi was a communist. After the elections, he resigned from the cabinet and demanded that a commission be set up to investigate the charges made against him.[69] It was chaired by Prince Wan who first asked two foreign advisers, one French the other British, to draw up a joint memorandum outlining what communism entailed. This provided a basis for questioning Pridi on various aspects of communist doctrine such as the establishment of soviets, the nationalisation of private banks and property, the repudiation of foreign debts, the abolition of marriage and religious practices, the advocacy of class war and the dictatorship of the proletariat, and the use of compulsory labour. On each point Pridi replied that he was opposed to such practices. Likewise when asked specifically whether he was a member of the Communist International or in any way associated with it, his answer was negative. He also repudiated the idea that Siam should be joined to the Soviet Union in a communist world economic order. Instead he claimed that the main source of inspiration for his draft economic plan was not communist or, for that matter, Nazi concepts but rather the social work of the League of Nations. Consequently the commission came to the conclusion that Pridi was not a communist.[70]

This view has been shared by others who have subsequently studied Pridi's plan. For instance, they have pointed out that his proposal to set up a social insurance and pension plan to cover the whole population differed little from the programmes being put forward by socialist parties and trade unions in Western Europe during the 1930s. Indeed many foreigners would agree with Pridi's own definition of himself as an agrarian socialist, albeit an extremely idealistic one.[71]

It was significant that the report of the commission investigating Pridi was published. It provided the public with the first detailed explanation in Siamese of what communism entailed. Yet there was a major outcry several months later when a school textbook included a brief history of the Bolshevik Revolution.[72] Diehard opinion was also alarmed when Pridi re-entered the cabinet and Phra Sarasat Pholkand was appointed Minister of Economic Affairs.[73] The two men were believed to be close friends. Phra Sarasat boasted of having helped Pridi financially in Paris during the 1920s and stimulated his ideas and those of other young promoters by circulating revolutionary tracts among them. In Bangkok Phra Sarasat was also known to be the author, under the pen-name "555", of outspoken articles advocating the transfer of the economy to Siamese hands.[74] It appeared to be the policy he intended to pursue at the Ministry of Economic Affairs and soon led to rumours that he was going to revive Pridi's plan, nationalise all foreign business interests and spend vast sums in the process. All such speculation was denied by a government spokesman. But Phra Sarasat continued to issue statements about the wide-ranging plans he was drawing up. Moreover he exhorted his staff to work harder, and recruited more including another well-known economic nationalist, Chote Khumband as Director of Commerce.[75]

Chote's tenure of office did not last long. He was the leader of an ultra-nationalist group which had already been officially warned against using patriotic slogans to drum up popular support. Some promoters feared that the movement was intended to challenge their own power. But when Chote's group started to use the fascist salute, he and seven of his leading supporters were arrested on charges of contravening the Act for the Protection of the Constitution.[76] Their trial took place in secret, and the report subsequently issued referred to the charges only in vague terms. Public resentment increased when the defendants, many of them well-known figures in Bangkok, were sentenced to spend at least five years in what was termed "restricted residence in the interior", which turned out to be banishment to a penal colony established at Mae Hong Sorn near the north-western border with Burma.[77]

By contrast, a separate group of thirteen people, most of them army sergeants, were arrested in August 1934 and placed on trial in open court where they were accused of plotting to install a new government under the leadership of Phya Thephatsadin,[78] who immediately denied all knowledge of the plot. However, a couple of days later the police searched his house and took away several documents; he claimed that they amounted to little more than the text of a speech he had made criticising the allegedly communist school textbook plus a plea addressed to him by several political prisoners requesting help in alleviating their conditions of detention. To prove his innocence, he demanded a commission be set up to enquire into his political beliefs in the same way that Pridi had been investigated. It was not merely a call for parallel justice: Pridi had just been appointed Minister of the Interior and as such was responsible for the police. However, he dodged the issue by asserting that political beliefs were not involved in Phya Thephatsadin's case, and that nothing could be done until the police had completed their investigations.[79]

These exchanges took place in the Assembly where theoretically Phya Thephatsadin enjoyed parliamentary privilege, but once it was adjourned he was arrested and charged with conspiring to overthrow the government.[80] Yet when the case came to court the only evidence presented by the prosecution was the draft of a resolution Phya Thephatsadin intended to present to the Assembly about the treatment of political prisoners based on complaints from his constituents. The defence was far better prepared. Phya Thephatsadin had engaged a British lawyer working for a local legal firm,[81] who contended that his client's action was considered normal practice under a constitutional, let alone a democratic form of government. After that the rest of the trial was held in secret and Phya Thephatsadin was sentenced to two years' imprisonment but later acquitted on appeal.[82]

Compared with many other people arrested and tried for political offences during 1934, Phya Thephatsadin was fortunate. With long terms of imprisonment or banishment up-country being imposed in numerous cases, the impression grew, especially among the Bangkok élite, that the promoters were engaged in a witch-hunt against all their potential opponents. Hence there was considerable surprise in October when the government suddenly resigned. True, it had been defeated in the Assembly but not on an issue which seemed important. During a debate about ratifying an international rubber agreement establishing Siam's export quota, Phra Sarasat's ministry – which was responsible in this case – showed such ignorance of the subject that a vote of no-confidence in the government as a whole was approved.[83]

The crisis turned out to be short-lived. Since there was no alternative premier acceptable to all the promoters, Phya Phahol was soon persuaded to head a new cabinet, which differed little from its predecessor except for the appointment of Pibul as Defence Minister. That put him on a par with Pridi, the first of the young promoters to achieve a ministerial portfolio. On the other hand the main casualty was Phra Sarasat. He lost his cabinet seat and later claimed that the whole incident was rigged simply to oust him from his ministry.[84]

Other decisions taken by the Assembly in 1934 had more wide-ranging repercussions. In March it approved a bill to levy an estates tax, including a provision to impose the payment of death duties on royal properties following the demise of a monarch. The King, who according to the constitution had to append his signature to all legislation before it became law, warned privately that he would rather abdicate than approve such a bill.[85] The gambit proved successful until later in the year when the Assembly voted in favour of amending the civil and military penal codes. One change was a stipulation that in future death sentences could be implemented without first having to secure royal approval.[86] Again the King protested, and in two letters submitted by the Regent to the Assembly claimed the abrogation of such a time-honoured custom would be contrary to the will of the people, who would think that the government had arrogated the right to sign death-warrants in order to deal with political prisoners more swiftly. As a compromise the King proposed holding a national referendum on the issue.[87]

Phya Phahol was dismayed. He thought he was doing a favour to the King, who had previously indicated that as a Buddhist his conscience was troubled by having to sign death warrants.[88] Some Assembly members took a different view. They believed that in proposing a referendum, the King was implying that the Assembly did not represent the will of the people. Hence they voted in a resentful mood to re-affirm the amendments to the penal codes.[89]

Before the King left Siam, it was announced that he was going to the south of France for a rest, followed by several months touring Europe, after which he intended to travel to the United States for eye surgery before returning home in October.[90] The governments of the countries on his itinerary were also informed that he did not wish to be formally entertained because he was travelling privately and as far as possible incognito.[91]

Yet soon after his arrival in Europe, he proceeded to Rome where he was officially received by King Victor Emmanuel, Mussolini and the

Pope. From there he went on to visit Paris, London, Copenhagen, Berlin, Budapest and Prague. In each capital the King of Siam and his entourage were formally entertained by heads of state and government. He also attended many social functions as well as carrying out an extensive programme of visits to modern industrial and agricultural projects. Throughout the tour, the King was reported to be in good health and in June he had an operation performed on one eye in London. But when he returned to England in September 1934, his doctors doubted whether he was strong enough for further treatment. It was then announced the King had taken a lease of six months on a house in Surrey, and no mention was made of his previous plan to return to Siam before the end of the year.[92] Coming on top of the controversy over amending the penal codes, the public soon realised that relations between the monarch and the government were seriously strained. Behind the scenes they were more than that. On October 14, the Regent informed the government that the King intended to abdicate immediately.[93]

If the Khana Ratsadorn or any of its factions had wished to pursue the threat in its Manifesto to establish a republic, there was now a good pretext. However, that option does not appear to have been considered. On the contrary, Phya Phahol and his colleagues were far more concerned that the King's abdication would cause further instability. So they started to consider the royal succession.

Prince Boripat, who had previously been regarded as heir to the throne since King Prajadhipok had no children, was now obviously ruled out for political reasons. Reference was therefore made to the law of 1924 governing the succession, which comprised a complex series of provisions designed to cope with the polygamous tradition of the Chakri family and the perpetuation of its supremacy. For instance there was a ban on all princes not born of pure Chakri blood ascending the throne. It was applied in 1925 when Prajadhipok became king. Two sons of his elder brothers were passed over because their mothers were either commoners or foreign.[94] If these two princes were again to be discounted on those grounds, other problems would arise. One of the strongest candidates for the throne was considered to be the young Prince Ananda Mahidol, whose late father was the son of one of King Chulalongkorn's senior queens. However, his mother was a commoner. Phya Phahol was well aware of these problems. He still depended heavily on the advice of Prince Wan, who was believed to have his own

ambitions. However, Prince Wan claimed that his main aim was a constitutional amendment removing the ban on high-ranking princes holding cabinet positions.[95]

Still, the government wanted if possible to dissuade the King from
abdicating, and proposed sending a delegation to England to discuss
with him a way of overcoming his objections to the amendment of the
penal codes.[96] But even that suggestion created alarm. The King,
worried possibly by the recent assassination of King Alexander of
Yugoslavia, sought special protection from Scotland Yard against what
he claimed was a delegation being sent from Siam to murder him.[97] In a
letter to the Regent, he also made it clear that no matter what concessions the government was prepared to make to meet his objections, he
would never return to Siam to be confronted by the man he described as
his worst enemy.[98] The person concerned was thought to be Pridi, who
wanted to go to England to reassure the King personally that he was not
hostile towards the monarchy. But when the nature of the King's
feelings became apparent, it was decided that the delegation should be as
uncontroversial as possible. Led by a respected *ancien régime* official,[99] it
consisted of Thamrong ("the golden tongue") and a young civilian
promoter from the Foreign Ministry.[100] They left Bangkok in early
November 1934.

Although the possibility of the King's abdication was the main topic
of conversation in Bangkok from mid-October onwards, the Siamese
press and radio made little reference to it.[101] But, just as in England
during the crisis in 1936 leading to the abdication of Edward VIII, all
sorts of rumours emanating from abroad were current. Many originated
from Singapore where the press, prompted perhaps by some of the high-
ranking Siamese exiles resident in Malaya, frequently speculated on the
instability of the government in Bangkok. One story was that the
King's lavish expenditue on his European tour had bankrupted Siam, so
leading to a dispute with the government.[102]

To counter such rumours, the government proclaimed its loyalty
to the King by celebrating his birthday on November 6 with great
display.[103] All public buildings were illuminated for the occasion, while
the Bangkok press carried special messages of congratulation. Particularly noticeable was one editorial, signed "Radical", which amounted
to a plea to the King to ignore the advice of his entourage and return
home.[104] Likewise, in contrast to most buildings in Bangkok which
displayed portraits of the monarch outlined in coloured lights, the
University of Moral and Political Sciences – newly-established on Pridi's

initiative – chose to carry the symbol of the constitution. The University was already attracting a reputation as a hotbed of radicalism.[105]

Meanwhile the delegation sent to England, having overcome the King's initial suspicions as to its motives, appeared to be making some progress. Agreement was soon reached on a formula which would remove the King's objections to amending the penal codes, but he then indicated that he was not willing to return home before certain guarantees were forthcoming for his personal safety, and the constitution was amended to eliminate the nominated members of the Assembly and make it an entirely elective body. Each time the delegation, after referring back to the cabinet, tried to meet these demands or calm the fears underlying them, the King seemed to equivocate.[106] As a result, those people with inside knowledge of the negotiations gained the impression that the King's poor health was affecting his judgement. It was recalled too that ten years earlier, on ascending the throne, he had claimed to be too inexperienced to rule alone.[107] By 1935 all the princes on whom he had relied for guidance were gone. Instead the most influential member of his entourage appeared to be Queen Rambhai's brother. Like his father Prince Svasti, he was regarded as a diehard who would have been tried for complicity in the Bovoradet rebellion had he remained in Siam.[108]

This situation eventually culminated in London on March 4, 1935, when *The Times* published a statement by the King announcing and explaining his decision to abdicate. He said he had always been in favour of a constitutional monarchy and had agreed to remain on the throne in June 1932 in the hope of contributing to the change. But the promoters had been determined to monopolise power. Referring to his attempts to modify the constitution, the King stated that he had only agreed to one half of the Assembly being nominated on the understanding that he himself would be allowed to choose its members. It had not happened. The promoters had selected their own men irrespective of merit and the country had lurched from one crisis to another. "I consider," the King continued, "that the government and its party employ methods of administration incompatible with individual freedoms and the principles of justice . . . I am willing to surrender the powers I formerly exercised in favour of the people as a whole, but I am not willing to turn them over to any individual or party to use in an autocratic way . . . and since I feel I can no longer assist or protect the people, I therefore desire to abdicate." The King also renounced his right to nominate his successor, and expressed the hope nobody would use his abdication as a pretext for creating unrest. His statement ended with an apology for being unable to serve Siam as preceding monarchs had done.[109]

The government was determined that there should be no more problems with the monarchy. News of the abdication was suppressed in Siam until the Assembly met in secret session on March 7 and agreed to offer the throne to Prince Ananda Mahidol. There were many factors militating in his favour as far as the promoters were concerned: he was only nine years old and thus unlikely to be imbued with the prejudices and fears prevalent among the older generation of the royal family. More important, his late father had been a friend to some of the Paris promoters during their student days and was regarded by them as being the most democratic member of the Chakri family.[110]

At one time regarded as a possible heir to the throne, Prince Mahidol was passed over in favour of his half-brothers Vajiravudh and Prajadhipok, the sons of another of Chulalongkorn's senior queens. He then chose to become a doctor, but that was impossible in Siam because of the taboo on royal personages coming into intimate personal contact with the common people. So Prince Mahidol went abroad and while studying in the United States married Sangwalya Chakramol, a nurse from Siam. During the first years of their married life, they travelled frequently between America and Europe where their three children were born: the first a girl in London, the future King Ananda in Germany, and a second son Bhumipol in Boston, Massachusetts. Eventually, in 1927, the whole family returned home where Prince Mahidol, frustrated by the bureaucratic positions offered him in the Department of Public Health, went to work at the American hospital in Chiengmai and the nearby leper colony. His wife and children did not accompany him north. They stayed in Bangkok in the care of his mother, the somewhat formidable dowager Queen Sawang, the sole surviving royal consort of King Chulalongkorn.

Inspite of being a commoner, Mom Sangwalya as she was known, was no stranger to court practice, or to Queen Sawang, by whom she had been adopted as a child. Sadly, however, she was soon deprived of the support of her husband when Prince Mahidol died in 1929 from an abcess of the liver. After that, Mom Sangwalya continued to reside with her mother-in-law, and when the children were old enough they were sent to Bangkok's leading private schools. However, this was not for long: in 1933 Prince Mahidol's widow sought and obtained from the King permission to take her children to Switzerland for the sake of their health and education. It has also been suggested that she felt ill at ease in

Queen Sawang's household and believed she would be fulfilling her late husband's wishes by bringing up their children in a more democratic atmosphere.[111]

Thus it was in Lausanne that Prince Ananda learnt he had been proclaimed King of Siam. In some eyes, the youth of the King – he could not legally ascend the throne until he was twenty – and his absence from the country were seen as the main reasons for his selection by the promoters. Meanwhile, until he could assume his full duties, the government, having appointed a Council of Regents thought to be docile to its wishes, would have a free rein over the destiny of Siam. All this led some people to believe that the abdication of King Prajadhipok marked the real end of the rule of the House of Chakri.[112]

NOTES

1. BTWM, Oct. 11, 1933.
2. Prince Boripat as quoted in Prayoon, p. 168, and Batson (1984), p. 240.
3. Withet Korani, p. 102, and Thawatt Mokrapong, p. 132.
4. Chai-anant Samutwanich, *Khana Ratsadorn kap Kabot Bovoradet*, p. 49.
5. Prayoon, p. 272.
6. BTWM, Oct. 12, 1933, and F7213/42/40 in FO371/17176.
7. Landon (1939), p. 139.
8. Sivaram, p. 86, and F7425/42/40 in FO371/17176.
9. BTWM, Oct. 13, 1933.
10. ibid., Sep. 28 and Oct. 2, 1933, and Prasert Patamasukhon, p. 102.
11. Text in BTWM, Oct. 17, 1933.
12. Chai-anant Samutwanich, pp. 35ff.
13. BTWM, Oct. 13, 1933.
14. Text in F7213/42/40 in FO371/17176.
15. Chai-anant Samutwanich, p. 35.
16. BTWM, Oct. 14, 1933.
17. Thawatt Mokrapong, pp. 210ff.
18. BTWM, Oct. 14, 1933.
19. ibid., Oct. 17, 1933, and Sivaram, p. 91.
20. F7592/42/40 in FO371/17176.
21. BTWM, Oct. 20 and 21, 1933.
22. ibid., Oct. 14, 1933.
23. ibid., Oct. 17, 1933.
24. F7296/42/40 in FO371/17176. Queen Rambhai in Thak Chaloemtiarana (ed.), p. 16, and Sivaram, pp. 92ff.
25. Among the injured was Luang Kad Songkram, a junior military promoter. BTWM, Oct. 17, 1933.
26. ibid., Oct. 20, 1933, and Thawatt Mokrapong, p. 212.

27. BTWM, Nov. 1, 1933, and eye-witness account in ibid., July 11, 1936.
28. BTWM, Dec. 1, 1933.
29. ibid., Oct. 14, 1933, and Sivaram, p. 96.
30. BTWM, Sep. 6, 1934, and Thompson, pp. 793ff.
31. BTWM, Oct. 19 and Nov. 2, 1933.
32. ibid., Dec. 6, 1933.
33. ibid., Oct. 30, Nov. 13 and 23, 1933, and Chai-anant Samutwanich, pp. 43ff.
34. F563/21/40 in FO371/18206.
35. Chula Chakrabongse (1943), p. 187.
36. BTWM, Oct. 27, 1933.
37. This was Phya Nitthisart Paisal: ibid., Nov. 1, 1933.
38. Queen Rambhai in Thak Chaloemtiarana (ed.), p. 18, and F7534/42/40 in FO371/17176.
39. F7589/42/40 in ibid.
40. BTWM, Dec. 2, 1933.
41. F279/21/40 in FO371/18206.
42. F551/21/40 in ibid., and BTWM, Nov. 29, 1933.
43. Landon (1939), p. 35, and Thompson, p. 83.
44. F4143/42/40 in FO371/17175.
45. BTWM, Nov. 27, 1933.
46. ibid., Dec. 11, 1933.
47. ibid.
48. Sivaram, pp. 101ff.
49. Queen Rambhai in Thak Chaloemtiarana (ed.), p. 18, and government statement in ibid., p. 328. An operation performed on one eye in the United States in 1931 was only partly successful, and Japan secretly offered to send a top eye-surgeon to Bangkok. Flood, p. 72, quoting telegrams in GKR file A600, no. 1–27.
50. F1194/21/40 in FO371/18206.
51. BTWM, Jan. 12, 1934.
52. ibid., Jan. 27, 1934, and Landon (1939), p. 39.
53. Report of family arguments centering around Prince Svasti in F886/115/40 in FO371/18207.
54. BTWM, Dec. 7, 1933.
55. ibid., Feb. 13, 1934.
56. Batson (1974), pp. 7 and 45.
57. F2264/21/40 in FO371/18206.
58. Text in Landon (1939), p. 252; Sivaram, p. 109; BTWM, Jan. 23, 1934.
59. ibid., Feb. 7, 1934.
60. ibid., Jan. 12, 1934, *passim*.
61. F1695/21/40 in FO371/18206.
62. BTWM, Jan. 31, and Apr. 27, 1934, and Skinner, p. 279.
63. BTWM, Dec. 23, 1933, and Jan. 4, 1934.
64. Landon (1939), p. 45, and Vella (1955), p. 379.
65. BTWM, Mar. 30, 1934.
66. ibid., Dec. 16 and 26, 1933, Jan. 17 and May 24, 1934, and Prasert Patama-sukhon, p. 129.
67. BTWM, Mar. 9, Apr. 4, 5, 7 and 18, 1934, and F3067/21/40 in FO371/18207.

68. F3240/21/40 in FO371/18206 and Sangworn Suwannachip (Luang Sangworn Yutthakit) *Anusorn Pol Rua Tri Sangworn Suwannachip*, p. 59.
69. BTWM, Dec. 26, 1933.
70. Commission report in ibid., Mar. 12, 1934, and Landon (1939), pp. 319–23.
71. Vella (1955), p. 377, and F6016/123/40 in FO37/18208.
72. BTWM, Aug. 10, 14 and 23, Sep. 4, 1934.
73. Official denial of leftward trend in government, ibid., Aug. 8, 1934.
74. Phra Sarasat Pholakand, *My Country Thailand*, p. 151.
75. BTWM, July 3, 9, 18 and 21, 1934; Thompson, p. 82; F6014/21/40 in FO371/18207.
76. F6886/21/40 in ibid.; BTWM, July 24, 1934.
77. Ibid., Oct. 8, 1934, and Chai-anant Samutwanich, p. 125. Another of those sentenced was Thamanoon Thien-ngern, later a prominent Bangkok politician.
78. BTWM, Sep. 3, 1934. Among the defendants was Tha-ngai Suwannathat, later a prominent Bangkok politician.
79. ibid., Sep. 4, 8, 10 and 22, 1934.
80. ibid., Oct. 1, 1934, and Prasert Patamasukhon, p. 161.
81. This was Victor Jacques.
82. BTWM, Oct. 6, 10 and 18, 1934, and Jan. 31, 1935, and F597/296/40 in FO371/19377, suggesting that Phya Thephatsadin was involved in a more serious plot with Phya Song, which the government dared not reveal.
83. BTWM, Sep. 12 and 13, 1934, and Khuang Abhaiwongse, loc. cit., p. 70.
84. Chula Chakrabongse (1943), p. 259, and F598/296/40 in FO371/19377, suggesting the British financial adviser's involvement.
85. F6014/21/40 in FO371/18207.
86. Thompson, p. 86, and BTWM, Aug. 22, 1934.
87. Prasert Patamasukhon, p. 155, and Sivaram, pp. 110ff.
88. F7144/21/40 in FO371/18208.
89. BTWM, Oct. 1, 1934.
90. ibid., Dec. 30, 1933.
91. F3870/42/40 in FO371/17174.
92. BTWM, Nov. 5, 1934.
93. Text in Thak Chaloemtiarana (ed.), p. 24.
94. These were Prince Chula Chakrabongse and Prince Varanand.
95. Pridi in Pramote Pungsunthorn, pp. 42ff, and F7145/115/40 in FO371/18208.
96. F7144/115/40 in ibid.
97. F6349/115/40 in ibid.
98. F7456/115/40 in ibid. Text of King's letter to the Regent in Siri Premchit, *Chiwit Lae Ngarn kong Pol Rua Tri Thawat Thamrong Nawasawat*, pp. 178ff.
99. This was Chao Phya Sri Thammathibet, speaker of the Assembly.
100. This was Direk Chaiyanam.
101. Thompson, p. 87.
102. BTWM, Oct. 31, and Nov. 7, 1934.
103. ibid., Nov. 3, 1934.
104. Reprinted from *Le Démocrate* in ibid., Nov. 12, 1934.
105. Founding of University in February 1934 in Prasert Patamasukhon, p. 133, F3068/21/40 in FO371/18201.

106. Thawatt Mokrapong, pp. 221ff; record of discussions in Siri Premchit, pp 123ff.
107. F142/42/40 in FO371/19376.
108. This was Prince Subha Svasti (Tan Chin). Queen Rambhai in Thak Chaloemtiarana (ed.), p. 27; Sivaram, p. 111.
109. Text in Batson (1974), p. 101.
110. Pridi in Pramote Pungsunthorn, pp. 42ff, and Queen Rambhai in Thak Chaloemtiarana (ed.), p. 28.
111. Chula Chakrabongse (1960), p. 304; Rayne Kruger, *The Devil'. Discus*, pp. 38ff; Princess Galyani Wattana, *Chao Nai Lek: Yuvaksatri*, pp. 11–132.
112. Thompson, p. 88.

Part II
CONSOLIDATION OF POWER, 1935-1940

6
THE RISE OF THE MILITARY

Reaction to the abdication was muted. Everybody was afraid of what might happen next. The government refrained from challenging any assertions in the King's abdication statement for fear of arousing further controversy. Opponents of the régime kept quiet because they felt intimidated and forsaken by the King whom they regarded as the only person capable of standing up to the promoters. In other words, the absolutism of the monarchy had been replaced by that of the Khana Ratsadorn with the military looming in the wings as the ultimate arbiter of power.

The irony of the situation does not seem to have occurred to the promoters. Even Pridi, the most idealistic among them, had demonstrated by advocating a one-party state in his original constitution that his views were far removed from Western democratic concepts. Nor had the intervention of the King in the drafting of the permanent constitution made much difference. His negative attitude towards a multi-party system during the controversy over the Khana Chart had a far more crucial effect. With no organised opposition to face, the promoters disdained to compete in the elections. Rather, they considered it their right to be nominated to the Assembly and to dominate it.

Yet, as head of this autocratic system, Phya Phahol lacked public charisma, and his personal ability to head a government was also open to question. Doubt was likewise felt about how far he could control the contending factions among the promoters. According to customary deference, Phya Song and his senior clique should have played a leading role, but instead the junior military promoters, by showing their mettle in the June 1933 coup and the subsequent rebellion, had asserted their dominance with their leader Pibul being acclaimed as a national hero.[1]

For a man only thirty-six years old, it was a remarkable if controversial achievement. Pibul had clearly taken advantage of his somewhat fortuitous appointment as deputy army commander in 1933 plus the fact that his nominal superior Phya Phahol was preoccupied with affairs of state. Many of the far more senior and experienced officers coming under Pibul's command also thought he had usurped power from Phya Song, and there was no doubt as to the continuing antagonism between the two men. After Phya Song and Phra Prasat returned from their "study tour" of Europe in June 1934, Pibul absented himself from cabinet meetings and threatened to resign until eventually appeased in October by being appointed Defence Minister.[2]

To register the event, Pibul made a major speech very different in tone from the promoters' usual rhetoric. Harking back to the reign of King Vajiravudh, when all true patriots were exhorted to manifest their loyalty to King, country and the Buddhist faith, Pibul redefined the idea. He claimed that Siam had four basic institutions – the monarchy, the Assembly, the government and the armed forces – of which only the armed forces were "abiding and permanent". He went on to explain that the monarch could die, the government might be reshuffled, and the Assembly "abolished through various events and causes". What is more, Pibul specifically rejected any suggestion that the military was obsolete and certain to be defeated if ever the country was again involved in war with its neighbours.

In fact Siam had not fought any external enemies since an army was sent to Luang Prabang in the 1880s. After that the country was bordered on all sides by British and French colonies which, if the need arose, could clearly muster the strength to overwhelm the Thai military. Instead, under the absolute monarchy and even more following the Bovoradet rebellion, the Siamese armed forces, comprising some 30,000 men in 1934, had come to regard themselves as the main pillar of governmental power. That was basically what Pibul meant when he said that without its armed forces Siam would be "effaced from the world". His speech ended with an appeal to the public to donate funds for the country's defence needs.

Again the idea was not new. King Vajiravudh had urged the public to contribute to the purchase of a new warship.[3] By contrast the emphasis and expenditure on defence was considerably reduced during King Prajadhipok's reign, a trend Pibul was now obviously trying to reverse. As well as soliciting funds from the public, he wanted a far larger share of the national budget allocated to the military. Here he enjoyed the support of Sindhu who, having restored discipline in the navy, hoped that its funding would be reinstated and augmented.

Colonel Phya Phahol Pholpayuphasena

The first major policy clash on this issue occurred in January 1935 when the next annual budget was being discussed in the cabinet, and it became apparent that money was available due to cutbacks in spending on the royal household, a move long advocated by successive British financial advisers. In this situation, Pridi as Minister of the Interior put in a competing bid for more expenditure on local government to supplement what was already underway in the field of education, where the amount spent was doubled in the first few years of constitutional government in order to promote literacy and popular participation in the democratic process.[4] With the same aim in mind, Pridi wanted to speed up the reform of local government by sending out into the provinces officials well versed in constitutional theory. Obvious candidates for such jobs were students undergoing rapid courses of instruction at his newly-created University of Moral and Political Sciences.[5] As well as enrolling them in the conventional way, the University embarked on a system of tuition by correspondence for those unable for any reason to attend full-time courses.

From the very outset, Pibul indicated his concern at the nationwide influence Pridi might achieve through this scheme. All army personnel were barred from enrolling for such courses, the reason given being one that has frequently been echoed ever since: the military should not be involved in politics.[6] Even in 1935, it had a hollow ring because of the way the junior army promoters were intervening in government and getting themselves nominated to seats in the Assembly.

On the other hand, Pibul sought to make his own mark on the expanding educational scene. For example, in late 1934, he inaugurated a display of tanks and other weaponry at one of Bangkok's leading high schools where pupils were invited to try their hand at rifle practice.[7] Within a few months this turned out to be a pilot experiment for a new youth movement called Yuvachon, apparently modelled – at least, to begin with – on the officer training corps in certain British and American high schools.[8] Even then one Bangkok newspaper, which tried to raise the alarm by commenting that such militaristic trends ran contrary to the Buddhist faith, promptly had its licence to publish suspended. But in the Assembly it was more difficult to stifle such criticism voiced by several of Pridi's personal supporters.[9] As for the dispute in the cabinet between the rival budget bids from Pibul and Pridi, it proved to be so serious a problem for Phya Phahol that he referred the whole matter to the British financial adviser.

James Baxter, who held this position in 1935, was, like all his predecessors, a stern advocate of the balanced budget. He also regarded Pridi as a wild idealist, whereas he thought Pibul's plans to purchase more guns and ships would at least produce tangible results. This advice counted with Phya Phahol, who finally managed to persuade the Assembly to approve increased defence expenditure despite vocal opposition from Pridi's friends.[10]

In the midst of this controversy, an attempt was made to assassinate Pibul. He had presented prizes at a military football match in Bangkok and was getting into a car to leave when three shots rang out. One bullet missed completely but the other two just grazed his neck causing him minor flesh wounds.[11] The would-be assassin was detained in the ensuing turmoil, and turned out to be a hired gunman; however, he refused to reveal the identity of his employer. The immediate presumption, given the surrounding events, was that Pridi or his friends were responsible, but later enquiries concerning the gunman's movements suggested that he had links with royalists involved in the Bovoradet rebellion.[12]

The investigation was carried out by Luang Adul Detcharat, one of Pibul's close friends. As classmates at the military academy and fellow artillery officers, Adul had stayed in Pibul's house while helping to carry out the June 1932 coup. Subsequently at Pibul's request, Adul somewhat reluctantly relinquished his military career to take charge of the police with the special task of protecting the promoters from all conspiracies.[13]

By contrast, Adul took little interest in what became a major scandal involving the payment of a large sum of public money for the seizure of nine tons of opium as it was being transported across the border from the Shan States in Burma. Instead, the matter was raised by Baxter. As the government's financial watchdog, he alleged in a heated exchange of letters that an illicit deal had been arranged with the connivance of the head of the Excise Department, who happened to be an influential civilian promoter.[14] Baxter also accused Pridi of failing to investigate the case as was expected of a Minister of the Interior. These charges were rejected by the government, prompting Baxter to resign in protest and leave Bangkok on July 31, 1935, when his farewell was attended by Pibul.[15] Within the next week, Pridi also suddenly departed abroad after a cabinet reshuffle in which the head of the Excise Department was dismissed.

Phya Phahol had been expected to resign and reshuffle his cabinet in deference to the King's abdication in March, but the move was delayed for fear of causing further instability in what Phya Phahol thought might be an already volatile situation. Another complicating factor was renewed lobbying for Phya Song to be given a ministerial portfolio; neither Pibul nor Pridi would countenance the idea, especially if it meant forfeiting their own positions.[16] By August, Phya Phahol was subject to different pressure. Pibul wanted to get more seats of influence in the cabinet for his friends such as Sindhu, who was awarded the education portfolio despite being preoccupied with reorganising the navy.[17]

Coinciding with the cabinet reshuffle, it was announced that another anti-government conspiracy had been uncovered leading to the arrest of several army sergeants.[18] To deal with them, the Assembly quickly approved a Special Courts Act providing for the reconvening of a military tribunal similar to that which had tried those involved in the Bovoradet rebellion. However, there was a new provision that those sentenced to death were to be given the right to appeal to the throne for clemency. If it was not granted within forty-eight hours, they were to be executed immediately. During the minority of the King, that placed the burden of decision on the regents.[19]

When new regents were appointed in March 1935, the promoters' choice fell on three seemingly uncontroversial figures, none of whom had played any significant role during the previous reign.[20] The senior regent was Prince Oscar Anuvatana, a grandson of King Mongkut, who like many of the Chakri princes suffered from poor health. However, his death a few days after the new Special Courts Act came into force was a shock, and there was speculation that he had taken his own life to avoid his added responsibilities. This prompted the government to submit a police report to the Assembly confirming that Prince Oscar had committed suicide but attributing it to problems concerning the administration of royal property following the abdication plus the abolition of the Bureau of the Royal Household.[21] Many people remained incredulous; given the aura of semi-divinity surrounding the monarchy, they refused to believe that princes could haggle over money matters, let alone violate a sacred taboo as the senior regent had apparently done in taking his own life. But at least the government was given credit in some quarters for stopping the proliferation of rumour by trying to hush up the matter completely.[22]

In contrast, rumour ran riot when no official reason was given for Pridi's precipitate departure abroad on August 7. Even though he was seen off by Phya Phahol and Pibul as well as a large crowd of enthusiastic supporters,[23] Pridi was said to be once again under a political cloud and to have been forced into exile. Among the reasons cited for his disgrace was the opium scandal or alternatively his implication in plotting against the government. In fact he left the country with Phra Sarasat, who had been criticising the régime ever since losing his seat in the cabinet.

The two travelled together only as far as Singapore.[24] From there Phra Sarasat went on to Japan, while Pridi travelled to Europe where he carried out various official duties. First he paid a formal call on the young King in Lausanne, before going on to London to discuss with the Bank of England the appointment of a new financial adviser to replace Baxter. He also wanted to negotiate a reduction in the rate of interest paid on British loans to Siam.

The successful outcome of Pridi's visit came as a relief both to him and to the British. They thought, rightly as it turned out, that the Japanese were applying pressure to take over the key position of influence vacated by Baxter, who was continuing to cause trouble: in a letter published in Singapore on October 30, explaining at length the reasons for his resignation, he condemned the Siamese government as "morally bankrupt", and expressed the hope Pibul would soon assume power.[25] In Bangkok the British Minister immediately tendered apologies that a foreign adviser should intervene so directly in the affairs of Siam. Pibul too was embarrassed because Baxter was obviously encouraging him to stage a coup.[26]

Talk of such a coup had been widespread since the departure of Pridi and a subsequent application by Phya Phahol for sick leave, which was progressively extended until January 1936.[27] During this period Pibul was said to have ordered a quantity of new guns which were assigned to military units controlled by his friends. The question was whether they were strong enough to stage a coup. Many of the tanks and provincial garrisons remained under the command of more senior officers who supported Phya Song and were dismayed by Pibul's appointment as Defence Minister. As for Phya Song himself, he was so disgruntled at his rival's promotion that he officially retired from the army and departed up-country.[28]

Tension therefore rose rapidly in late 1935 when Phya Song suddenly returned to Bangkok to stay with one of his clique members, a colonel who was in command of the capital military district.[29] In the absence of Phya Phahol, they seemed determined to force a showdown with Pibul.[30] But nothing happened except for a few cryptic news items in the press reporting the departure of Phya Song on another foreign trip while one of his friends left even more hastily for what turned out to be forced exile in Indo-China.[31] Later Pibul alleged that he had foiled an attempt by Phya Song's clique to force him to resign at gunpoint.[32]

This sequence of events seemed to confirm an increasingly prevalent belief that the Khana Ratsadorn had evolved into some sort of secret society with its own rules. After 1933, no further attempts were made to broaden it into a nationwide political movement; rather, the promoters appeared to cherish their exclusivity. They referred to themselves as Dee Nung – "Number One Good". It also emerged that a secret oath they swore before assuming power included a provision precluding them from taking up arms against one another. That explained why Phya Song was reluctant to use force against Pibul – equally it accounted for the lack of any action against Phya Song's clique beyond sending some of them abroad. It looked as if whenever a crisis was brewing within the ruling circle, the promoters met in secret conclave to thrash out a compromise with the top leadership working out the details.

By 1936, the leadership of the promoters had crystallised into "the big five": Phya Phahol, Pridi, Pibul, Sindhu and Thamrong. It was they who finally resolved the crisis provoked by Phya Song's clique with another cabinet reshuffle worked out at a party held at Pibul's home in February 1936. Despite his poor health, Phya Phahol agreed to stay on as premier; apparently, nobody else was considered capable of maintaining the stability of the government and the promoters. Moreover, because of their internal rules, factional rivalry could not be eliminated. Pridi, who had just returned flushed with success from his foreign tour, re-asserted his right to a leading position in government. Likewise Pibul still had to contend with Phya Song's clique. Several of its members retained their cabinet seats and Phya Ritthi, irrespective of his qualifications, was even rewarded with the agricultural portfolio. The need to maintain the solidarity of the promoters apparently overrode all other factors.[33]

The extent to which the original guiding principles of the Khana Ratsadorn were being ignored was again demonstrated by Pibul during the 1936/7 budget debate. Following the practice observed under the absolute monarchy, he insisted that defence expenditure be approved as a global figure without any indication of how it was to be spent, despite objections from some members of the Assembly that the new adminis-tration should be more accountable to the people.[34]

Several months later, Pibul caused another outcry by contributing an article to the press claiming that the security and prosperity of the country could only be guaranteed if the administration were vested with dictatorial powers. Eventually matters were only smoothed over by the excuse frequently used by controversial Thai generals, namely that there had been a misunderstanding.[35]

The statement to this effect was issued by a naval secretary,[36] who was part of a large personal entourage Pibul was building up. The purpose behind this was obvious: Pibul wanted to be surrounded by men whose prime loyalty was to him rather than to the government or the Khana Ratsadorn. This also applied to Prayoon, whom Pibul rescued from the political wilderness in 1936 to serve as his military secretary.

Prayoon's fall from grace was not simply due to his close associa-tion with Phya Mano. He was also suspected of involvement in the Bovoradet rebellion as well as another plot several months later when he was temporarily detained.[37] Thereafter his disgrace seemed complete. He was sent off to Saigon as consul,[38] but Prayoon was not the sort of person who could be content to stay away for long from the centre of affairs, and in 1936 Pibul needed somebody to help him deal once more with the problem of Phya Song. The latter returned to Bangkok after only a short stay abroad, and again there were rumours of lobbying for him to be given a seat in the cabinet;[39] instead he was given command of a new military school set up in Chiengmai to keep him occupied well away from Bangkok.[40]

Pibul's obvious ambition, plus the new spirit of militarism with which he was trying to imbue the country, did not only cause disquiet in Bangkok; the Western powers were particularly worried about articles appearing in Siam's military journals referring to what were called "the lost territories". These were areas which, it was claimed, Siam had been forced to cede to Indo-China, Burma and Malaya around the turn of the century under Western pressure. Maps showing these territories in the same colour as Siam were being used in high schools and military colleges. This was much to the dismay of the British and French, who lodged official protests, but in reply they were told the maps were simply part of a history course covering those areas over which Siam had previously exercised sovereignty.[41]

The concept of national sovereignty and frontiers was however only introduced in South East Asia by the Western powers towards the end of the nineteenth century. Before then, much of the region had com-prised small local fiefdoms which paid tribute to Bangkok, Hue or else-where as and when the need arose. But such considerations were easily overlooked by Siamese nationalists, especially when they found a cham-pion of irredentism in Pibul; in June 1936, to mark the fourth anniver-sary of the end of the absolute monarchy, he broadcast a rousing call to the armed forces to remember "the obligatory cession of what was once our territory" by standing ready to repel any foreign invasion.[42] In particular, the irredentists made great play of the fact that Siam had been forced to abandon its claim to large areas of northern Indo-China in 1893 when French gunboats sailed up the Chao Phya to threaten Bangkok. That in turn led to talk of the capital being moved to a more inaccessible site up-country.[43]

Such speculation, which was quickly denied by Phya Phahol, had been sparked off by Pibul, who had ordered the construction of a new military base at Lopburi about 100 miles north of Bangkok. He justified the move by claiming that the terrain near Lopburi was more suitable for military manoeuvres and artillery practice than the populous and frequently inundated ricelands around Bangkok. Others suspected that he wanted to set up his own independent power-base. Still, Pibul continued to keep some heavy weaponry in the capital for his own political purposes as well as to meet any threat similar to that posed by the Bovoradet rebellion. In that context, too, Pibul pursued a policy of denying military equipment to the provincial garrisons, although his hold over them was gradually expanding as senior officers were pensioned off and replaced by his protégés.[44] Yet even his close friends were unhappy about being posted to Lopburi: conceived as a model garrison town on a grandiose scale, for many years it lacked basic amenities such as a regular supply of water.[45]

Not to be outdone, the navy also planned to construct a new base. Sindhu argued that it was necessary because the navy was being re-equipped. After the re-instatement of its budget in 1935, he received an invitation to visit Japan, where he was lavishly entertained and given an extensive tour of the shipyards; this hospitality he repaid by placing orders for several warships and submarines. The decision was justified on the grounds that Japanese prices were far lower than those in Europe, although a couple of gunboats were commissioned from Italy. As the site for a new base for these ships once they were delivered, Sindhu chose Sattahip on the coast south-east of Bangkok.[46]

To the French the move seemed ominous since Sattahip was within easy sailing distance of Indo-Chinese waters. The British were concerned too, since they feared that the upsurge in Siamese militarism was inspired by the German takeover of the Rhineland and the Italian conquest of Abyssinia.[47] For many Siamese, however, what was much more relevant was the example set by Japan, the only other country in East Asia which had remained totally independent of the Western powers. After ignoring the sanctions imposed by the League of Nations over their action in Manchuria, the Japanese in early 1936 renounced a treaty with Britain and the United States limiting their naval power, and then aligned themselves with Germany in the anti-Comintern pact.[48]

Long before this, the Japanese had recognised the importance of Siam as the only country in South East Asia where they could in theory compete on equal terms with the European colonial powers for trade and influence. As a result of a great deal of effort, the Japanese share of Siam's imports rose from 3 per cent in 1928 to over a quarter ten years later.[49] More significant still in Japanese eyes was Siam's decision to abstain in the League of Nations vote on the Manchuria issue in 1933, which they interpreted as a gesture of friendship and Asian solidarity.[50] After this, Japan began to woo Siam in earnest: several Japanese friendship delegations descended on Bangkok, while a growing number of Siamese were invited to Tokyo. Particular stress was laid on the fact that both countries were Buddhist. To promote and expand these links, special bilateral organisations were set up in both Bangkok and Tokyo.[51] What is more, by 1937 over 200 Thai students were being educated in Japan, more than in any other foreign country except the Philippines.[52] In reply to Western expressions of concern at this trend, an official spokesman pointed out that the cost of maintaining students in Japan or for that matter the Philippines was less than for Europe. At the same time, the Foreign Ministry rebutted a claim that Siam had agreed to join an Asian League.[53]

At the receiving end of Western protests at the allegedly pro-Japanese trend in Siamese policy, as well as its growing irredentism, was Pridi who became Foreign Minister on his return home in 1936 – with a distinct project in mind. During his travels, which took him on from Europe to the United States and Japan, he had broached the idea of revising all Siam's foreign treaties. It involved the renegotiation of formal relations with thirteen countries to remove once and for all any lingering traces of Western domination which originally imbued them. For the Siamese it was a major matter of prestige.[54] On the other hand, their treaty partners were more concerned to protect their own interests. Britain, for instance, was anxious to maintain its predominant trading position in Siam as well as to provide for the rights of its many colonial subjects living and working in the country. France too had its neighbouring colonial interests at heart, whereas the Scandinavian countries wanted to preserve their extensive shipping and trading links with Siam. As for the Japanese, they discovered to their dismay that they had to renegotiate their bilateral treaty along the same lines as the Europeans and Americans without being accorded any special privileges.[55]

All the complex work on these treaties kept Pridi occupied for several years. He was aided by Prince Wan, who also continued to act as adviser to the Prime Minister when required. Phya Phahol's departures from Bangkok on sick leave were becoming increasingly frequent and in early 1937 he announced his intention to retire from the premiership after elections to be held later in the year. He also indicated that his successor was likely to be Pibul, despite the controversy and possible split it might cause among the promoters.[56] Apparently Phya Phahol was not referring only to the reaction of Phya Song's clique.

In an obvious attempt to rival and outshine Pridi's standing as the intellectual leader of the Khana Ratsadorn and Rector of the University of Moral and Political Sciences, Pibul accepted nomination as Rector of the older and more prestigious Chulalongkorn University.[57] Yet there seemed to be little he could do to dent the reputation Pridi was acquiring as a skilful diplomat in his treaty negotiations with the foreign powers. As a result, the impression of Pridi as a wild revolutionary was fading and he was coming to be regarded as one of the more moderate and stabilising influences in the cabinet as well as a staunch upholder of democratic values in the face of Pibul's evident dictatorial ambitions. In public, however, it was Phya Phahol who appeared to be keeping Pibul and his clique in check. In 1936, for instance, when Pibul made his incautious remarks about dictatorship, Phya Phahol issued a firm but tactful public reprimand.[58] Likewise he poured cold water on the irredentist campaign by pointing out that Siam had enough territory of its own, which it found hard enough to develop without seeking to acquire more.[59]

None of Phya Phahol's strictures seemed to have much effect on Pibul's clique. In March 1937, Prayoon created a furore by threatening those members of the Assembly who had once more been carping during the annual budget debate at the ever-increasing allocations to defence expenditure. The most persistent critic was proving to be Thong-in Buripat, one of three members elected to represent Ubol, a large province in the north-east. This time he made his mark by forcing Phya Phahol to concede at the end of a stormy debate that Prayoon's threats to the Assembly were ill-advised.[60] Soon afterwards, Prayoon departed to spend a year in Germany "to study military science", as the official announcement put it, but according to rumour, Prayoon had gone at Pibul's behest to study how Hitler had set up his dictatorship.[61]

Already Pibul appreciated the potential of radio. A broadcast he addressed in April 1937 to the youth movement, the Yuvachon, exhorted its members to serve their country, which he claimed had once been "weak and trampled on" and was still subject to bullying. In this context he cited a ban imposed on the export of Siamese livestock. He then called on the entire country to arm itself in self-defence because its security and independence were threatened by the conflict about to break out between Britain and Japan in their struggle to impose their own domination over the whole of South East Asia. To this end he claimed that the Japanese were busy infiltrating subversive agents into Singapore.[62]

Although this speech was made almost five years before the outbreak of the Pacific war, Pibul was saying nothing new. Given Japan's growing power in East Asia and Britain's strengthening of its naval base in Singapore, talk of a conflict in the region was already quite widespread. Yet both the Japanese and the British lodged official protests at Pibul's speech. Each of them stressed that they were committed to respect Siam's neutrality, and denied any intention of going to war with one another. What really dismayed the Japanese, however, was that Pibul, of all people, should have made such a speech. They had discreetly been courting his friendship and understanding ever since his approach to the Japanese Minister during the 1933 coup.[63] As for the British, they especially resented what they saw as Pibul's gratuitous remarks about the ban on the export of livestock, which had been imposed to prevent an outbreak of rinderpest in southern Siam spreading to Malaya.

However, there was more to it than that. Since 1934, the British Minister to Siam had been Sir Josiah Crosby, who had spent most of his career in the country and spoke the language fluently. He considered it his task to uphold and expand Britain's predominant influence in Siam by actively cultivating the friendship of those in power whoever they happened to be. Consequently he was on close personal terms with the leading promoters. Another of Crosby's preoccupations was to counter and outflank what he saw as the Japanese threat to British influence in Siam, as was evident in his reaction to Pibul's speech. Besides lodging an official protest, Crosby pointed out to Pridi that Pibul's derogatory remarks about foreign intentions would not help the revision of Siam's treaties; on the contrary, he warned that unless Pibul was removed from office, Britain might refuse to sign a new treaty with Siam. This threat alarmed Pridi. He had previously indicated to diplomats in Bangkok his hope that the new treaties could be concluded before the end of 1937 so that his democratically-minded friends could cite them as an achievement to win votes in the forthcoming elections. Now Pibul was apparently trying to sabotage the process as well as Pridi's reputation by making such an outrageous speech. To save the situation, Pridi begged the British to conclude their treaty with Siam; but he added privately that he would sympathise if, in the event of Pibul seizing power, ratification were withheld.[64] Meanwhile, at the express wish of the Japanese, Pibul agreed to make another broadcast retracting his allegations about them. It involved a considerable loss of face for him personally and for the military as a whole.[65]

In the eyes of some of the military, one of the main obstacles in the way of their ambitions was Prince Wan. Besides his official duties at the Foreign Ministry and as adviser to Phya Phahol, he controlled the newspaper which had come to be regarded as the main exponent of government views. There was therefore considerable public surprise in mid-1937 when this newspaper was subjected to official censorship.[66] What happened was that it had taken the part of some *samlor** men in a clash they had had with army lorry-drivers.[67] It was a minor incident but the military was offended and took the law into its own hands. After failing to find Prince Wan at his newspaper office, a group of soldiers marched to his home, and it was said that only his disappearance into a nearby paddy field saved him from being beaten up. A month later it was announced that Prince Wan had been awarded a high decoration, obviously in an attempt to salve his damaged pride.[68]

The public was paying increasing attention to the way some promoters were enjoying and abusing their power, in marked contrast to the note of high moral probity with which they put an end to the absolute monarchy. At first, for instance, the new regime had eschewed awarding decorations, but now it was even handing out a medal marking the King's accession, which was traditionally the monarch's own personal gift after his coronation.[69]

The usurpation of royal prerogative was also evident in other directions. In March 1937, two years after the abolition of the Bureau of the Royal Household, the Assembly assigned the Ministry of Finance to take over the administration of the privy purse and crown lands. However, this legislation was not gazetted until July.[70] In the mean time some Assemblymen noticed signs of unusual activity among the Council

---

*The *samlor* is a three-wheeled pedalled trishaw, known as the *cyclo* in Indo-China and the *bechak* in Indonesia.

of Regents and at the Ministry of Agriculture, both of which had previously been responsible for royal property. Eventually the issue was
brought out into the open by Liang Chaiyakal who, like Thong-in
Buripat, represented Ubol. Liang, a lawyer, claimed in the Assembly
that he had discovered through a family misfortune that crown land in
Bangkok was being sold off clandestinely at ridiculously low prices,
which enabled the purchasers to make a quick profit by renting out or
reselling the property at far higher prices on the open market. Liang
named thirty-four people, many of them government ministers and promoters implicated in this illegal dealing. Most corrupt of all, he alleged,
were the regents.[71]

During the heated debate which ensued in the Assembly, it emerged
that one of the key figures under suspicion was the senior regent, Prince
Aditya Dib-abha. He immediately tendered his resignation, which was
followed by that of the other two regents. Simultaneously, Pridi and
several other ministers announced they were resigning from a government so publicly tainted with corruption; the rest of the cabinet quickly
followed suit. This meant that in effect Siam no longer had a head of
state or government. The only remaining constitutional body was the
Assembly. Tension rose. Various prominent figures busied themselves
in whitewashing their part in what came to be known as the Crown
Lands scandal. Pibul was among them. A statement broadcast on his
behalf claimed that as soon as he realised he had acquired land illegally,
he returned it. Others alleged to be involved were Adul the police chief,
Phya Phahol's wife, several naval promoters and the Minister of Agriculture, Phya Ritthi. As for Liang, having exposed the scandal he was
placed under police surveillance, allegedly for his own protection.[72]

The crisis soon assumed a new dimension. Meeting in secret session
on July 29, the Assembly selected a new Council of Regents. The next
day the old regents announced that they were withdrawing their resignations "as a result of anxiety expressed by the armed forces".[73] In other
words, as it later transpired, they had been forced at gunpoint to issue
the statement. Similar threats were made to the new regents to deter
them from assuming office. At first the Assembly was not prepared to
accept such coercion, and continued to meet in secret session, even over a
weekend, to debate which of the two sets of regents should be recognised. Significantly absent from these deliberations were numerous
nominated members, most of them military officers. They obviously
wanted to make it clear to the Assembly that if it did not comply with
the wishes of the military, it might be prorogued as in 1933, or suffer an

even worse fate. The threat worked.[74] The Assembly eventually agreed to reconfirm the former regents in office.[75]

The question remained who would head the next government, since Phya Phahol had indicated that he could not continue as premier because the scandal involved his wife. Again the Assembly convened in secret. What could not be concealed was that it was a very acrimonious session which apparently centred around the continuing tension between the cliques headed respectively by Pibul and Phya Song. The outcome was the seemingly inevitable compromise. Phya Phahol was asked to remain in office. Initially he made a show of reluctance because, as he put it, he was not "devoid of all blemish", but that was soon overcome. Seventy members of the Assembly called at his residence with a petition requesting him to continue as Prime Minister. Even so, it emerged not long afterwards that Phya Phahol had divorced his wife, although this was apparently more because of her personal rather than pecuniary affairs.[76]

In reconstituting a government, Phya Phahol dropped those immediately responsible for the scandal such as Phya Ritthi, the Minister of Agriculture. Otherwise, the scandal had little impact in the longer term. The press published a list of those who had returned property to the privy purse. The Assembly voted to set up a commission of enquiry into the whole matter,[77] and three months later it published its report. In it the commission noted the return of all property, and everybody was officially absolved from blame.[78]

Even so, the reputation of the regents looked somewhat dented; they were seen to be little more than the creatures of the Khana Ratsadorn or, at least, of its more unscrupulous members.[79] The main target of such criticism was the senior regent, Prince Aditya. He had been a student in Europe at the same time as Pibul and Pridi, and they had struck up an acquaintance, after which their paths diverged for a while. On his return home, Prince Aditya was entitled to a provincial governorship, yet he soon remembered his friends when they overthrew the absolute monarchy. He was one of the first high-ranking princes to make public his support for the Khana Ratsadorn,[80] and this apparently earned him his position on the Council of Regents. He then became increasingly friendly with Pibul, and rumour had it that Prince Aditya wanted to play Victor Emmanuel to Pibul's Mussolini. Anyway, the Crown Lands scandal left little room for doubt about the independence – or, to be more specific, the lack of it – shown by the regents and especially Prince Aditya in representing the interests of the monarchy. It was considered a serious disadvantage if another crisis were to arise involving the monarchy; there are precedents in Siamese history for dynastic upsets taking place at the instigation of regents during the minority of young monarchs.[81]

Soon after the accession of King Ananda, the government made preparations for him to return to Siam in late 1935 to be formally presented to his people. These arrangements were cancelled when the King's mother and grandmother decided that he was too young and frail in health to undergo the journey and all the ceremonies involved.[82] This prompted rumours that the King was about to abdicate, but these were emphatically denied by Phya Phahol.[83] Proposals for the young monarch to return in 1936 also came to nothing. Meanwhile, the public noticed what appeared to be tactical manoeuvring within the Chakri family which had become seriously split by the events of the previous few years.

Apart from Prince Aditya's transparent attempts to ingratiate himself with the promoters, one of his more senior half-cousins, Prince Chula Chakrabongse, expressed his confidence in the new regime by buying government bonds issued to raise capital for new state enterprises being set up.[84] It was considered significant, because both in 1925 and ten years later Prince Chula was regarded as a serious contender for the throne, despite his Russian mother.[85] He himself assumed a disinterested pose. He continued to reside in England where part of his fortune provided financial backing for the motor-racing career of a distant cousin, Prince Bira, who became the first Siamese to make a mark in the international sporting world. As a result, when these two young men returned to Siam for a brief visit in the latter half of 1937 they were acclaimed virtually as public heroes. The fact they were both princes only seemed to add to the warmth of their welcome.[86]

Reactions were mixed. In some quarters, there were misgivings tinged with jealousy about the motives underlying Prince Chula's visit, but these were soon dispelled by the prince himself when he announced his intention to marry an Englishwoman and so ruled out any possibility of succeeding to the throne. But the visit of the two princes, in providing evidence of the continuing popularity of the royal family, led some to suggest that the unknown King Ananda should abdicate and Prajadhipok be restored to the throne. One of the main proponents of this view was rumoured to be Phya Song, who was said to believe that the ex-King would be the most effective person to contain Pibul's ambitions. On the other hand, the opinion of Phya Phahol and many other Siamese appears to have been that the sooner King Ananda returned home to show himself to his subjects, the better it would be for the country and the government. Thus there was considerable disappointment when once again in 1937 the King's proposed visit to Siam was postponed, this time on the grounds that the elections scheduled for November might give rise to political instability.[87]

In the event the elections were peaceful and orderly, although they were the first in which the electorate was able to vote directly for the candidate of its choice. In contrast to the procedure used in 1933, the franchise had been extended to all men and women over the age of twenty regardless of whether they were literate or not.[88] Still, the government refused to allow the formation of political parties as urged by some Assembly members, most notably Thong-in Buripat.[89] The promoters, so it seemed, felt so comfortably entrenched in power that they were reluctant to meet any concerted challenge. None of them stood as candidates, and the 1937 elections turned out to be a free-for-all.

More than 500 candidates put forward their names independently to contest the ninety seats to be filled, but the voters proved far less enthusiastic. Under half the electorate exercised its right to vote and in Bangkok the turnout was even lower. Nonetheless, the results showed a remarkably uniform trend throughout the country. Most of the successful candidates were lawyers or retired civil servants, and only eleven of the previous members of the Assembly were re-elected. Significantly, they included the two outspoken representatives from Ubol: Thong-in and Liang. In Bangkok Phya Thephatsadin, who complained of police harassment during the election campaign, was narrowly defeated. In most other constituencies the tendency was to elect candidates who strongly supported constitutional democracy as opposed to military rule. Consequently there was much speculation over who would be the next Prime Minister when Phya Phahol reiterated his intention of retiring from office.[90]

As usual when there was a major decision to be taken, the promoters convened in secret conclave. Significantly, on this occasion Phya Phahol absented himself to leave the field clear for the rest of the top leadership to thrash out the issue of the premiership among themselves. By that stage their "inner caucus" had expanded to nine. Besides the original "big five", other promoters had grown in influence. One was Adul the police chief, who – as if to demonstrate his importance – announced the discovery of another anti-government plot while the conclave was in session. By contrast, Khuang Abhaiwongse, the promoter responsible for disconnecting telephone lines during the seizure of power in 1932, had staked a claim to a place in the top leadership by subsequently building up a reputation in certain quarters as a staunch proponent of democracy. Then there was Supha who, after going into eclipse in 1934, was beginning to re-assert himself as the leader of a growing faction within the navy opposed to the policies of Sindhu. Nor could Phya Song's clique be overlooked. His friend Luang Chamnan Yutthasilp still commanded the all-important Bangkok military district.

Unfortunately for Pibul among this top leadership, only two people – Adul and Sindhu – were positively identifiable as his supporters. As a result, the deliberations of the promoters took much longer than expected. The new Assembly convened on December 10, 1937, and it was twelve days before an announcement of the composition of the new government emerged. This revealed the usual compromise. Phya Phahol was to continue as head of a cabinet that was basically unchanged except for the return of several previously disgraced promoters such as Phya Ritthi. Yet despite such blatant disregard for performance in office, the crucial finance portfolio remained securely in the hands of an experienced *ancien régime* official.[91]

After this setback to his ambitions, Pibul appeared somewhat chastened. In the Assembly he actually apologised for his inability to reduce military expenditure and promised that he would try to avoid any further increases. He also refrained from making controversial speeches.[92] Yet his friends were as active as ever. Prayoon, on his return from Germany, took charge of the Yuvachon and proceeded to expand it along the lines of the Hitler Youth movement. The amalgamation of Germany and Austria on ethnic grounds in March 1938 also sparked off a renewed spate of articles in army and navy journals lamenting the fate of Siam's "lost territories". For most Siamese, however, the most significant development was the Japanese take-over of Peking and the intensifying war in northern China. It polarised opinion in Bangkok between those sympathetic to the Chinese and those who admired Japanese military might or saw it as a useful counter to the spread of Chinese influence in South East Asia.

To Pridi such views seemed ominous, and he gave several interviews stressing Siam's commitment to a policy of strict neutrality in all international disputes. At the same time he denied speculation that Siam was about to join the Anti-Comintern Pact between Germany and Japan.[93] But there was little Pridi could do to calm French fears that the Siamese were clandestinely colluding with the Japanese in preparing to attack Indo-China and divide the spoils between them. There were rumours that a secret clause to this effect was attached to the bilateral treaty Pridi had negotiated with Japan in 1937.[94] In reality there was far more interest in Tokyo in the idea of using southern Siam as its springboard for attacking Malaya. In March 1938 even this proposal received a setback: the Emperor quietly indicated that he would not countenance any military plans which involved the infringement of Siamese neutrality unless the government in Bangkok first acquiesced. Despite the growth in Siamese militarism, this still looked very unlikely in Japanese eyes.[95]

The British were not so sure. Unaware of the decisions taken in Tokyo, they secretly conducted a survey of southern Siam to determine whether it was militarily feasible for the Japanese to launch an attack from there into northern Malaya. The results were inconclusive, but even so the British kept a wary eye on persistent stories that the Japanese had secretly obtained agreement to construct a shipping canal across the Kra Isthmus in order to by-pass Singapore.[96]

Throughout this period of growing international tension, Pibul appeared to do nothing even though he was acting Premier for most of the time. Once more Phya Phahol had withdrawn from the public scene. Similarly, in July 1938, Pridi and Thamrong departed on sick leave largely due to overwork in their respective portfolios. More surprisingly Pibul also disappeared, leaving the government apparently leaderless.[97] Yet there was little danger of anybody exploiting the vacuum. For all its irredentist bluster, Pibul's clique was not strong enough on its own to seize power, and the navy too was less powerful than it outwardly seemed. Sindhu's decision to place most contracts for its re-equipment with Japanese shipyards was causing dissatisfaction. The new ships did not come up to expectation. For instance, when the first Japanese-built submarines arrived in the Chao Phya river, the navy turned a deaf ear to suggestions that it should demonstrate the ability of its new acquisitions to submerge. There were widespread fears about safety.[98]

Such demoralisation led many young naval promoters to follow the example already set by Thamrong and Supha in retiring from active service to move into comfortable governmental positions. With similar trends prevalent among the rest of the promoters, they were thus expanding their influence in the higher levels of the administration. Sometimes this was beneficial. Several civilian promoters were appointed to positions where their qualifications helped to speed up the government's proposed reforms, but in the case of the military promoters it was more often a matter of "jobs for the boys". The nominated category of the Assembly was packed with them as more and more *ancien régime* officials either retired or resigned.[99] A new field of lucrative positions was opening up as a result of the government's policy of trying to eliminate foreign entrepreneurs by setting up state enterprises. Individual ministries were also going into business on their own account: the Ministry of Defence set up a factory to make uniforms and, later, a vegetable oil factory next door to it.[100] All these new enterprises needed directors. Some of them were functional, others not. In the final analysis, however, effective management was usually to be found in the hands of people of Chinese origin, although the main objective of the policy was to promote Siamese participation in business and industry.[101]

The birth of Siamese nationalism is usually attributed to King Vajiravudh who, as well as reviving traditional dances and dramas, composed new ones. Yet because of the reputation he acquired among the senior princes of being a misguided spendthrift, his achievements were largely ignored during the succeeding reign. That in itself was reason enough for some promoters such as Pibul to take a fresh look at Vajiravudh's record.[102] The process of resurrecting his writing was pursued most vigorously at the Department of Fine Arts which since 1935 had been headed by Luang Vichit Vadhakarn who, after his early quarrel with the promoters, was appeased with a seat in the Assembly and became one of the new regime's most ardent proponents. As a writer and versifier, Vichit appeared to model himself increasingly on King Vajiravudh, producing up-dated versions of traditional dance-dramas. These were published by his department for circulation to schools.[103] A recurrent theme in his plays was the rich cultural heritage shared by the vast family of T'ai peoples.[104] In Vichit's eyes, they included not only the modern Siamese and Lao but also the many hill-tribes inhabiting the belt of mountains extending south-east from Tibet through Burma and Yunnan into northern Tonkin.

Embroidering on this pan-Thai theme in an article written in 1938, Vichit suggested that the Austrian *Anschluss* provided an example for a new division of the world on the basis of race, language and culture. He went on to cite the work of Dr Goebbels, the Nazi Minister of Propaganda, as an outstanding model of what could be achieved. The natural corollary to this line of thinking emerged in a lecture Vichit gave at Chulalongkorn University in July 1938. Quoting from King Vajiravudh's writings, he claimed that the Chinese were the Jews of the East, and to prove the contemporary relevance of his theory, he drew attention to part of an official financial report referring to the large amount of money remitted annually by the Chinese living and working in Siam to their families in China.[105]

Reaction to Vichit's speech was instantaneous. The cry went up that the Chinese must be stopped from exploiting Siam. Many people, including a large youth delegation, called at the Department of Fine Arts to express support for Vichit's views. Naturally the Chinese community in Bangkok was alarmed,[106] and leaflets were circulated demanding Vichit's resignation. Other leaflets countered with praise for his speech – these turned out to be publications of the Fine Arts Department when the police raided its offices at the instigation of several Assembly members who had forced a debate on the issue.[107] Vichit did not attend, let alone apologise. Since he himself was of Chinese origin, he has been compared to a religious convert whose views are stronger than those of one born in the faith.[108]

Some Assembly members were so incensed that they refused to let the matter drop. Again the most heated protagonist was Liang Chaiyakal who had made a reputation and many enemies for himself in his exposure of the Crown Lands scandal. This time retribution came swiftly. He was seized and manhandled out of the Assembly and into a nearby pond. The leader of Liang's assailants, a junior military promoter, later claimed that it was a joke which misfired because the original intention had been to duck Vichit as well. However, as a cabinet minister he could not be submitted to such an indignity.[109] The explanation did not satisfy many elected representatives, who boycotted the Assembly until the matter was somehow smoothed over by Pibul, at least for the time being.[110]

A month later another conflict erupted in the Assembly. Again it involved the public accountability of the government, which was suddenly confronted with a demand for full details of all official budget allocations. Again too it was rejected on the grounds – so often repeated in Thai parliamentary history – that politicians were acting irresponsibly in seeking to challenge the government's authority. But Phya Phahol's warnings to this effect were of no avail; the government was defeated by 45 votes to 31. What happened was that a young Assemblyman, who like Thong-in and Liang represented a north-eastern constituency, waited until the tea interval on a Friday evening, when most people had left for the weekend, to challenge the government.[111] Phya Phahol reacted immediately by announcing the dissolution of the Assembly and the holding of new elections.[112]

This development was inopportune in many respects. The elected representatives had to face the expense of contesting their seats for a second time within the space of one year. In addition, fears were again voiced that elections would lead to political unrest. The international situation made matters more uncertain still. The crisis in Europe following the German move into Czechoslovakia remained unresolved, while nearer home the Japanese were threatening to attack Canton. Even so, all such considerations paled into insignificance when agreement was finally reached between the government and the royal family that the King would arrive in Bangkok on November 15. Public enthusiasm at this prospect was running so high that no government, no matter how secure, would have risked cancelling these arrangements at the last moment.[113] And at that juncture the government was by no means secure. Behind the scenes a major political and military crisis was brewing.

Despite his apparent public moderation, Pibul had been working since June 1938 on a major reorganisation of the military command structure. The details emerged gradually. A general staff headquarters was established, as was a new Defence Advisory Board. Appointed to the latter body were several senior military officers including Phya Song and his close friend Phra Prasat. The other influential member of their clique, Chamnan, was also finally dislodged from command of the Bangkok military district pending his transfer abroad for "advanced studies". These moves, coupled with a reshuffle of most of the regional military commanders, made it apparent that Pibul was shunting his potential rivals into sinecures and replacing them with his own brood of junior promoters and personal adherents.[114]

Phya Song's first reaction was to comment sarcastically that it was a pity Siam had no genius like Hitler or Mussolini. And when he travelled down to Bangkok to attend the first meeting of the Defence Advisory Board, he told the press that the secret oath sworn by the promoters in 1932 specifically rejected any idea of creating a dictatorship or vesting power in a clique "whose practice is to find jobs in the administration for themselves or their friends".[115] After that, Phya Song returned to Chiengmai and announced his resignation from the Defence Advisory Board on the grounds that he did not feel competent to do the job.

As if to counter this public rebuff to Pibul, the rumour spread that Phya Song was suffering from leprosy.[116] Here his fellow clique member Phra Prasat stepped into the fray by stating that he too was resigning from the Defence Advisory Board. The government tried to cover up the dissension, but Phra Prasat was undaunted in publicising his support for Phya Song's views.

Then came the turn of Phya Ritthi, another of the "four tigers" within the promoters' original leadership. After several official denials, it was finally conceded that he had resigned from the Ministry of Agriculture and departed for Penang following his arrest and a confrontation with several leading promoters. The government went on to deny that a further twenty or more high-ranking officers had been detained after the discovery of a conspiracy to restore King Prajadhipok to the throne.[117] Eventually Pibul felt it necessary to issue a statement claiming that the army was as united as ever and ridiculing suggestions that he was carrying out a purge similar to that just instigated by Stalin in the Soviet Union.[118]

Public interest in this power struggle waned quickly. Allegations of plots against the government had become commonplace. In any case, the impending arrival of the King was a far more exciting prospect. It also usurped attention from the elections hastily arranged to take place on November 12, three days before the King was due to arrive.[119]

Amid these developments, Pibul arranged to host a dinner party on the evening of November 9 to bid farewell to a senior officer whom he was shunting off to London as military attaché. For the purpose of such occasions, he had instituted a new dress uniform for officers of the armed forces, but this was unpopular, being considered excessively ornamental and unsuitable for a climate such as that of Bangkok. For instance, it necessitated the wearing of tight fitting boots. As Pibul, still in a state of semi-undress before the dinner-party, was being helped into his boots, his valet pulled a pistol and started firing. Accounts of what happened next vary. Some say that Pibul ducked and grabbed his assailant by the knees. A shot is alleged to have been fired in the direction of Pibul's wife in an adjoining room. According to Pibul's own story, he fled but, being unable to lock a door behind him, was shot at again. In any event, all the bullets missed and Pibul, together with his wife, appeared at the party half an hour late with profound apologies but no explanation for the delay.

One of the guests at the dinner was Crosby, the British Minister, who heard the subsequent announcement of an assassination attempt with surprise. However, unlike other people in Bangkok he did not believe that the story was contrived to further Pibul's ambitions.[120] Yet two days later, it was reported that Pibul appeared with a pronounced limp to greet a mass rally of soldiers, railway workers and members of the

Yuvachon who gathered outside the Defence Ministry to express support for him.[121] After that, Pibul's public appearances became much rarer than they had been following the first attempt on his life in 1935, and he was conspicuously absent when the rest of the government assembled to greet the King on November 15.

King Ananda was thirteen when he returned to Siam for the first time as its monarch. Since he had spent most of his life abroad, even his knowledge of Siam was rudimentary and he had to be specially rehearsed to make the formal speeches expected of him. Yet public opinion was delighted with the air of dignity with which he performed the many ceremonies pertaining to both state and religious affairs that marked his two-month visit. Only in private did the King compensate for the restraints imposed by the full official programme on his natural high spirits.[122] According to the foreign press, which was less constrained than that of Bangkok in reporting on the personality of the young monarch, he was much like any other boy brought up in Europe. He liked making model aeroplanes and wanted to become a train driver or otherwise a racing driver like his distant cousin Prince Bira. Eventually, even the Bangkok press got round to reporting that the King and his younger brother Prince Bhumiphol, when not fulfilling their official duties, spent their time riding around the palace grounds on bicycles or in a toy electric car.[123]

The very presence of a monarch resident in Bangkok appears to have been a welcome reassurance for many Siamese that all was well with the country after five uncertain years under the rule of the promoters. The only people unable to participate in the general rejoicing were the remaining political prisoners, by then numbering less than 100. Despite frequent rumours to the contrary, the government did not announce an amnesty to mark the King's arrival.[124] It had other preoccupations.

In the elections, about half the previous representatives, most of them outspoken critics of the government, were re-elected. The situation was made even more uncertain by Phya Phahol, who said nothing about his political intentions and concentrated on his duties as prime minister in attendance on the monarch. As a result the press assumed that he had decided to continue in office.[125] The impression was reinforced when the premier made his customary Constitution Day speech again without referring to the future composition of the government.[126]

At this juncture, attention once more had to be paid to Pibul. Another attempt was said to have been made on his life: allegedly it had taken place as he was lunching at home in the heavily guarded artillery compound in Bangsue with his family and members of his personal entourage, who suddenly, one after another, collapsed with stomach pains and were rushed to hospital. Some accounts have it that Pibul was on the brink of death because the family cook had put strychnine in the food.[127] Again doubts were expressed about the truth of such stories, although some people who met Pibul shortly afterwards said he appeared to be genuinely ill.[128] Anyway it did not harm his career.

On December 16, 1938, it was announced that Pibul had been appointed Prime Minister. The next day Phya Phahol broadcast a brief statement saying that he was resigning because of poor health. He added that, under a democratic system of government, a change in the premiership was a normal occurrence and not one to be feared.[129] These remarks were seen as confirmation of rumours that Pibul forced Phya Phahol to resign. They have been subsequently denied by some of those close to the event, but other accounts describe how Phya Phahol was urged by a group of military promoters to make way for Pibul. In any event, to reassure the public that Phya Phahol had not lost face as well as office, the first act of the new premier was to grant him the special rank of Elder Statesman with Paruskavan Palace as his permanent residence for life.[130]

NOTES

1. Sivaram, p. 128.
2. F4005/21/40 in FO371/18207.
3. BTWM, Nov. 14, 1934, and Vella (1978), pp. 95ff.
4. Batson (1984), pp. 91ff, and Landon (1939), p. 55.
5. Thompson, p. 785, and F3587/25/40 in FO371/19375.
6. BTWM, July 19, 1934.
7. ibid., Nov. 13 and 20, 1934.
8. Prayoon, p. 345, and Thompson, p. 308.
9. F2979/21/40 in FO371/19374.
10. F1936/296/40 in FO371/19377.
11. BTWM, Feb. 26, 1935, and Ananta Pibulsongkram, I, p. 255.
12. F1571/296/40 in FO371/19377, and testimony of Police General Adul on Dec. 13, 1945, in Suphote Dantrakul, *Pol Thamruat Ek Adul Aduldetcharat*, p. 68.
13. Ananta Pibulsongkram, I, pp. 39 and 53.
14. This was Luang Narubet Manit (Sanguan Chutatemi), who led an important sub-clique among the civilian promoters.
15. F4128/25/40 in FO371/19375, containing an acrimonious exchange of correspondence between Baxter and Phya Phahol.
16. F2986/296/40 in FO371/19377.
17. F5260/296/40 in ibid.

18. BTWM, Aug. 2, 1935.
19. ibid., Aug. 8, 1935.
20. ibid., Mar. 8, 1935, and Pridi in Pramote Pungsunthorn, pp. 50ff.
21. BTWM, Aug. 21, 1935, and Sivaram, pp. 128ff.
22. F5566/296/40 in FO371/19377.
23. Sivaram, p. 130. Little was reported about the tour, and its purpose continued to arouse speculation. *Straits Times*, Feb. 11, 1936.
24. Later Pridi claimed that Phra Sarasat accompanied him out of panic, Thak Chaloemtiarana (ed.), p. 385, but Phra Sarasat told the Japanese that Pridi was involved in a bitter factional struggle with the military, Flood, pp. 114ff, quoting a report of Sep. 3, 1935. Singapore to Tokyo in GKR A6-0-0.
25. Pridi, pp. 37ff. For the Japanese view of Pridi's visit and their efforts to court his friendship, see Flood, pp. 130ff, quoting file GKR L3-0-0 and F6825/25/40 in FO371/19375.
26. *Straits Times*, Oct. 31, 1935, and F6961/25/40 in FO371/19375, including Pibul's statement about Baxter in *Krungthep Varasab*, Nov. 30, 1935.
27. BTWM, Nov. 11, 1935.
28. F3875/296/40 in FO371/19377.
29. This was Luang Chamnan Yutthasilp.
30. F281/216/40 in FO371/20299.
31. This was Luang Ronnasith Pichai. BTWM, Jan. 27, 1936.
32. F1919/216/40 in FO371/20299.
33. F1072/216/40 in ibid., and Satuan Suphasophon, p. 237.
34. F3502/216/40 in FO371/20299.
35. This was Luang Yutthasat Kosol.
36. BTWM, June 16, 1936, and Thompson, pp. 92 and 306.
37. BTWM, Nov. 13, 1933.
38. ibid., Apr. 4 and 10, and June 10, 1934.
39. ibid., Mar. 10, 1936.
40. Thompson, p. 91, and Thawee Bunyaket in Ray, p. 72.
41. Crosby, pp. 113ff.
42. BTWM, June 22, 1936.
43. F6775/216/40 in FO371/20300.
44. F2569/1068/40 in FO371/21053, and Chula Chakrabongse (1943), p. 265.
45. Prayoon, p. 347, and Netr Khemayothin, *Chiwit Nai Pol*, p. 58.
46. Flood, p. 99, quoting correspondence of Aug. 1935 in GKR L3-0-0 No. 8–12; Thompson, p. 303; and Sanguan Suwannachip, pp. 84ff. Ironically, Baxter was persuaded in Jan. 1935 of the need to re-equip the navy by allegations of Japanese espionage: F983/394/61 in FO371/19341.
47. F2247/1494/40 in FO371/19341.
48. Vella (1955), p. 382, and Jones, *Japan's New Order in East Asia 1937–45*, pp. 23ff.
49. Landon (1939), p. 59, and Flood, pp. 15ff., detailing Japanese efforts to increase trade with Siam after the "Tsinan Incident" in 1928, when Chinese traders in Bangkok imposed a boycott on Japanese goods.
50. ibid., p. 53, and Netr Khemayothin, p. 151.
51. Sivaram, pp. 139ff. For British suspicions about these organisations, see Roberton, *The Japanese File*, pp. 11ff.
52. Flood, pp. 104ff, and Thompson, p. 134.

53. BTWM, Mar. 3 and 10, 1936, and *Foreign Relations of the United States* (FRUS), 1935, III, pp. 155, 170 and 315.
54. Countries involved were Belgium, Britain, Denmark, France, Germany, Italy, Japan, the Netherlands, Norway, Portugal, Sweden, Switzerland and the United States. Bilateral treaties with all these countries were concluded in late 1937. Details in Chariwat Santaputra, *Thai Foreign Policy 1932-46*, pp. 127ff.
55. Flood, p. 183.
56. BTWM, Jan. 27 and Mar. 11, 1937, and F2239/1494/40 in FO371/21053.
57. BTWM, Jan. 28 and 29, 1937.
58. ibid., Aug. 21, 1936.
59. ibid., Mar. 11, 1937.
60. ibid., Mar. 20, 23 and 24, 1937, and Thompson, p. 304.
61. F2142/164/40 in FO371/21052 and Prayoon, pp. 351ff, detailing a year he spent in Germany mainly in conventional military training.
62. BTWM, Apr. 3, 1937.
63. Flood, pp. 172ff, quoting a report of Apr. 20, 1937, in GKR 6-0-0. Pibul's main contact was the Japanese Military Attache, Capt. Tamura Hiroshi. For his role in coordinating Japanese military intelligence, see Robertson p. 161.
64. F2286/164/40 in FO371/21052, F6054/4837/40 in FO371/20301, and Adul in Suphote Dantrakul, p. 68.
65. Text in BTWM, Apr. 15, 1937.
66. ibid., June 4, 1937.
67. Prachachart report in ibid., May 31, 1937.
68. ibid., July 13, 1937. For Adul's temporary resignation from the cabinet in protest at the military usurpation of police power, see Suphote Dantrakul, p. 66.
69. Chula Chakrabongse (1943), p. 294.
70. BTWM, July 20, 1937.
71. ibid., July 28, 1937; Thompson, pp. 93ff; Withet Korani, pp. 497ff.
72. BTWM, July 29, 1937; F4290/1494/40 in FO371/21053; Prasert Patamasukhon, p. 235.
73. BTWM, July 31, 1937.
74. Thompson, p. 94, and Chula Chakrabongse (1943), p. 255.
75. BTWM, Aug. 6, 1937.
76. Prasert Patamasukhon, p. 238; F5040/1494/40; file in FO371/21053.
77. BTWM, Aug. 12 and 13, 1937.
78. ibid., Dec. 9, 1937.
80. BTWM, Jul. 2, 1932, and Sivaram, p. 42.
81. F5561/1494/40 in FO371/21053.
82. BTWM, Aug. 22, 1935.
83. ibid., Aug. 21, 1936; Sivaram, p. 126; Princess Galyani, pp. 137-52.
84. Prince Chula studied at Cambridge, where one of his friends was Anthony Blunt, much later revealed as a Soviet agent. See Boyle, *The Climate of Treason*, pp. 68ff, and Chula Chakrabongse, *The Twain Have Met*, p. 146.
85. Chula Chakrabongse (1943), pp. 118 and 176, disclaiming ulterior motives for financially supporting the government, and p. 190 on the succession.
86. ibid., pp. 265ff.
87. BTWM, Sep. 18, 1937, and F5030/216/40 in FO371/20300.
88. Thompson, p. 96.

89. BTWM, Mar. 25, 1937.
90. ibid., Oct. 9, Nov. 3 and 27, 1937.
91. ibid., Dec. 11, 16, 20, 21 and 22, 1937.
92. F113/113/40 in FO371/22207.
93. BTWM, Apr. 25, June 8 and 28, 1938; *New York Times* (NYT), May 8, 1938.
94. BTWM, Jun. 15, 1938; F7178/113/40 in FO371/22207; Decoux, *A la Barre de Indo-Chine,*, p. 125.
95. Flood, pp. 191ff, quoting from documents in War History Division, Tokyo.
96. Allen, *Singapore, 1941–1942*, pp. 46ff; Thompson, pp. 130ff, and Sivaram, pp. 134ff.
97. BTWM, June 4 and July 6, 1938.
98. ibid., July 1, 1938, and Macdonald, *Bangkok Editor*, p. 131, on submarines still not submerged in 1946.
99. F10432/1321/40 in FO371/22214, and Thompson, p. 305.
100. ibid., p. 309.
101. Crosby, p. 97ff.
102. Vella (1978), pp. 269ff and Pibul's statement in BTWM, Dec. 20, 1935.
103. Charnvit Kasetsiri in *Journal of Siam Society* (JSS), July 1974, vol. 62, pt. 2, p. 39. Translation of songs in Thak Chaloemtiarana (ed.), pp. 317–22.
104. *T'ai* is the spelling used by ethnologists, but *Thai* became popular usage because, according to an official explanation, "*Thai* with an H is like a sophisticated girl with her hair set, her lips touched with lipstick and her brows arched with eyebrow pencil, while *T'ai* without an H is like a girl who is naturally beautiful without any added beautification." *Bangkok Post* (article by Thamsook Numnonda), July 30, 1977.
105. F6382/113/40 in FO371/22207; BTWM, July 22, 1938; and Landon (1941), pp. 165ff.
106. BTWM, July 22, and 25, 1938.
107. ibid., July 27, Aug. 15, 16 and 17, 1938, and Landon (1941), p. 167.
108. Skinner, p. 246.
109. This was Khun Nirandonchai, officially deputy secretary to the Throne. Others involved included Prayoon and Luang Prom Yothi. Prayoon, p. 377.
110. BTWM, Aug. 8, 9 and 13, 1938; Charnvit Kasetsiri, loc. cit., p. 33; F10004/113/40 in FO371/22207.
111. This was Thawil Udol, representative for Roi Et. BTWM, Sep. 12, 1938.
112. Withet Korani, p. 537, and Thompson, p. 99.
113. F7435/113/40 in FO371/22207.
114. BTWM, June 23, and 25, July 11, 1938, and F8526/113/40 in FO371/22207.
115. BTWM, July 1 and Aug. 12, 1938.
116. F10001/714/40 in FO371/22213.
117. BTWM, Oct. 1, 5 and 7, 1938; F10755/113/40 in FO371/22207, Sathuan Suphasophon, pp. 365ff, quoting Phya Ritthi on his interrogation at Paruskavan Palace.
118. Text in ibid. and BTWM, Oct. 14, 1938.
119. ibid., Nov. 11, 1938.
120. Chula Chakrabongse (1943), p. 292; Ananta Pibulsongkram, I, pp. 261ff; Prayoon, p. 339; F12317/714/40 in FO371/22213; F254/254/40 in FO371/23593.

121. BTWM, Nov. 11, 1938.
122. Chula Chakrabongse (1943), p. 294.
123. Singapore and European press comment in BTWM, Nov. 16, 21 and 24, 1938.
124. ibid., Nov. 16, 1938.
125. Reports from Tai Mai and Sri Krung in ibid., Dec. 7 and 8, 1938.
126. ibid., Dec. 12, 1938.
127. ibid., Dec. 10, 1938; Prayoon, p. 380; Ananta Pibulsongkram, I, p. 265; Sriphanon Singthong, p. 176.
128. Chula Chakrabongse (1943), p. 294.
129. BTWM, Dec. 17, 1938.
130. Thawee Bunyaket and La-iad Pibulsongkram in Ray, pp. 75 and 196, as compared with Adul in Suphote Dantrakul, p. 67; Prince Aditya's testimony of Oct. 19, 1945, alleging that Luang Prom Yothi and Luang Kad Songkram were the main instigators. Prayoon, p. 302, also claims a part, whereas Sangworn Suwannachip, p. 95, says that he reluctantly represented the navy.

7

THE PURSUIT OF NATIONALISM

Pibul's assumption of the premiership seemed to be in tune with the times. It was not simply a matter of emulating Hitler and Mussolini. The international situation appeared to stress the need for a strongman at the helm. In Siamese eyes, the Munich crisis in September had been followed by an even more significant development: the fall of Canton to the Japanese in October. For Pibul's clique it was a striking example of what could be achieved by military might. Others saw it differently. Previous Japanese campaigns in China had been limited to the north of the country and the Yangtse basin. The attack on Canton brought the echoes of war much closer to Siam and there seemed to be little to stop the Japanese continuing further south. Neither the British in Hong Kong nor the French in Indo-China looked like having the will or the means to protect even their own colonies.[1] Another worrying factor for the Siamese was the reaction of the Overseas Chinese. Most of those residing in Siam stemmed from the southern coastal provinces near Canton. As the Japanese threat to their ancestral homes became obvious, they started in earnest to mount a boycott of imported Japanese goods as well as the export of Siamese rice to Japan.[2] Since the Chinese still controlled some 80 per cent of the Siamese economy, their attempt to halt trade with Japan was a matter no government in Bangkok could afford to ignore.[3]

Even so, Pibul – just like many subsequent Thai leaders – appeared to be magnifying the dangers facing the country for his own political purposes. Shortly before he became premier, he ordered the first ever air-raid practice to be held in Bangkok. A blackout was imposed and people venturing on to the streets were challenged by the security forces.[4] They included the Yuvachon, who were assuming an increasingly military air as well as expanding to include girls.[5] To enhance the standing of the youth movement, it was announced that the King had agreed to become its official patron, and together with Prince Bhumipol he was invested with the uniform and insignia of the Yuvachon by Pibul personally.[6] As head of the movement, Prayoon sounded another note. In a special broadcast, he warned the public to be wary of alien traders who sought to profit from international tension, as he claimed the Jews had done in Germany during the First World War.[7]

On becoming premier, Pibul continued to betray the anxiety of an ambitious strongman. His first concern was apparently for his personal safety. Even though the latest attempts on his life were said to have been made by servants within his own household, he proceeded to select and fortify a new government house to replace Paruskavan Palace, which the promoters had always used for the purpose.

The same besieged state of mind pervaded Pibul's first broadcast as prime minister. He claimed that he had accepted the position only with great reluctance "in the face of cruel actions by political cranks who adopt dirty methods". Then, switching to the attack, he made it clear that he would not allow his premiership to be disrupted by the Assembly. If some representatives persisted in challenging the government, Pibul warned, the next stage of democracy as envisaged in the constitution, namely the phasing-out of nominated members, would be delayed.[8]

Ten days later, only two representatives voted against a resolution expressing confidence in the new government which Pibul headed. Neither of them was a prominent opponent of the military, as was subsequently claimed.[9] Still, over thirty Assembly members abstained in the vote, despite some complex bargaining behind the scenes.

Pibul was obviously worried about how Phya Song's clique would react to his assumption of the premiership. Hence he tried to secure support from other sources, including the civilian promoters. The price he had to pay emerged in his speech to the Assembly outlining the policies his government intended to follow. Contrary to earlier indications, Pibul pledged to uphold democracy and the six principles of the Khana Ratsadorn.[10] Furthermore, he promised to abolish the poll tax, considered by many Siamese to be a feudal anachronism because it was levied on everybody irrespective of means and standing. Yet it raised 7 million baht yearly, a substantial sum given the government's total annual revenue of only 100 million baht.

One consequence was that the *ancien régime* official who had long served as Minister of Finance resigned in protest,[11] and his departure enabled Pibul to offer the portfolio to Pridi. Other civilian promoters were similarly flattered with influential positions in the new government. But Pibul also rewarded several members of his own army clique, as well as a couple of naval promoters, with seats in the cabinet for the first time. Indeed, in the final analysis it was clear that power was vested firmly in his own hands. Besides becoming Prime Minister, Pibul retained the defence portfolio and took over the Ministry of the Interior.

Subsequently, when Phya Phahol formally resigned command of the army, Pibul further expanded his list of titles.[12]

One of the first issues which the new cabinet had to resolve concerned the education of the King. Now that he had begun to assume his official duties, the private school he had been attending in Lausanne was no longer deemed adequate to equip him for his future role. The choice of an alternative proved difficult. In the past, the Chakri family had diversified the education of its numerous offspring; still, the overall tendency was for the princes to go to England where a public school education would lead on to either military staff college or university. That was what was proposed for King Ananda, albeit with certain reservations. Fears were expressed that in England he might come under the influence of ex-King Prajadhipok, who continued to reside there. Another problem was the need to avoid showing international bias at a time of growing world tension. The point was stressed in particular by Sindhu,[13] but here he came up against the views of the Queen Grandmother.

Reputedly, the Dowager Queen Sawang was determined to exercise her influence over the throne after what many people considered to be the loss of face she had suffered in earlier years when the line of royal descent was transferred from her children to Vajiravudh and Prajadhipok, the sons of another of King Chulalongkorn's senior queens.[14] By the time Queen Sawang came into her own again as the proud royal grandmother of King Ananda, she was in her seventies and in poor health. But she was not to be denied her hour of glory. When the steamship bringing her royal grandson from Europe anchored at the bar of the Chao Phya to await a naval escort to accompany it up-river, one of the first to go on board to pay homage was Queen Sawang. Thereafter the young King's daily routine included a call on his august grandmother who was reported to be much improved in health and spirits as a result of all the honour at last accorded her family. Hence once the Dowager Queen had decided that her grandson should be educated in England, she would brook no opposition from a mere cabinet minister.[15] At least, that was the idea when the King and his immediate family returned to Switzerland in mid-January 1939, after what was widely acclaimed as a very successful visit.[16]

Significantly, neither Sindhu nor Pibul was among the dignitaries who assembled to bid farewell to their monarch. Sindhu absented himself by joining the fleet in naval manoeuvres in the Gulf of Siam, while Pibul took two weeks' official sick leave.[17] With doubts still being expressed as to whether the reported assassination attempts were genuine or not, many attributed Pibul's absence from the ceremonies marking the King's departure to feelings of jealousy that someone else could so easily attract the loyalty and affection of the people.[18] The impression was reinforced soon after the King left: in a series of moves, Pibul demonstrated who was now going to be master in Siam.

The first indication came towards the end of January in an army order stripping Phya Song of his rank, salary and pension rights. Some newspapers added that he had been taken under escort to the border with Indo-China and forced into exile. At the same time, two army officers died up-country while reportedly resisting arrest on charges of conspiring to overthrow the government and restore the absolute monarchy, with either King Prajadhipok or Prince Boripat as its head. The public was officially asked to remain calm, not to believe in "sinful rumours", and to await further government communiqués.[19] None emerged for the next four days.

Meanwhile the health of the Queen Grandmother aroused concern. She was said to be distressed by the arrest of some of her "favourites".[20] More sensationally, the foreign press claimed a royal purge was taking place in Siam. Journalists rushed to interview ex-King Prajadhipok, who was visiting Cairo at the time, allegedly on his way home to Siam. His reaction was to deny any knowledge of a plot to reinstate him on the throne. Instead he stated that the discovery of anti-government intrigue was a regular occurrence in Siam because the regime did not permit the formation of political parties through which the public could legitimately air its grievances.[21]

The next official indication of what Pibul intended came during a session of the Assembly on February 2. A bill was introduced to set up special courts following the precedent created after the Bovoradet rebellion. The legislation was shepherded through the Assembly by Thamrong, who had just taken over as Minister of Justice; but he made it clear that responsibility for the special courts rested with the Ministry of Defence. In other words, the detainees were to be tried under martial law conditions. The re-establishment of such an arbitrary judicial procedure was challenged in the Assembly. Several new representatives queried why a special tribunal had to be set up when Siam already had an adequate and equitable three-tier system of justice;[22] they claimed that the public would begin to think such courts useless if the government persisted in by-passing them for all important trials. These and other objections were brushed aside by Thamrong. Using his "golden tongue", he succeeded in getting the Special Courts Act passed through all its stages in a single afternoon.[23]

Pibul did not attend this session of the Assembly, nor did three other members whose detention was announced by the Speaker.[24] One of these was a young and active politician, just elected to represent Bangkok.[25] The other two were nominated members, including a senior military officer who had accompanied Phya Song on many of his travels abroad.[26]

Clearly Pibul intended to teach a lesson to all his opponents whether real, imagined or potential. However, the timing of his move seems to have been dictated by Phya Song. Towards the end of January, he and some of his students travelled down from Chiengmai to stay with the commander of the garrison at Ratburi west of Bangkok. In the eyes of Pibul, who was still not sure of the loyalty of various other garrisons around Bangkok, this looked suspiciously like the build-up to the Bovoradet rebellion. In any case, Adul and the police commanded by him went into action. Dawn raids were carried out on homes and palaces throughout the country. Casting the net far wider than Phya Song and his clique, the police arrested Phya Thephatsadin and others involved in earlier political trials. Another target was the royal family. One of the first places to be raided was the Bangkok home of Prince Rangsit. He was away in Chiengmai at the time, but on hearing what had happened, he rushed back to Bangkok. He was arrested at the main railway station in full public view.

The shock caused by the detention of Prince Rangsit – one of King Chulalongkorn's few surviving sons – was all the greater because he had never been associated with politics; instead, he was well-known as a collector of Siamese antiquities. His other main concern was the well-being of the Queen Grandmother by whom he had been adopted as a child. After the death of her son Prince Mahidol, this responsibility expanded. Prince Rangsit acted as guardian to the young monarch and when the police raided his home, it was correspondence about the King's education that was seized upon as incriminating evidence. Some of the letters came from ex-King Prajadhipok. Naturally Prince Rangsit's arrest caused great distress among the royal family, and it was said to be the reason for the Queen Grandmother's ill-health. He was detained like a common criminal without any special privileges.[27] Pibul was not the only person to be blamed; as senior regent, Prince Aditya appeared to do nothing to alleviate the plight of his relations. He excused himself by claiming that any intervention on his part might jeopardise the position of the royal family as a whole.[28]

In Pibul's eyes, the Chakri princes were not all equally suspect. He continued to make use of the services of Prince Wan, as Phya Phahol had done. One of Prince Wan's first tasks, as instructed by Pibul, was to protest to the British about the activities of ex-King Prajadhipok – who, according to Pibul, was exerting an unhealthy influence on Siamese students abroad.[29] A stir had been created in Bangkok by an article critical of the lack of democracy in Siam published in the journal of the association of Thai students in Britain.[30] Pibul was also worried by a letter he had just received from his eldest son, Prasong, who had gone to Britain for naval training. He wrote home alleging that Prajadhipok was actively whipping up anti-government feelings among the students. On behalf of Pibul, Prince Wan told the British that unless they expelled the ex-King, all Siamese students would be prohibited from studying in Britain. He hinted that this meant first and foremost King Ananda. However, these threats were not carried through; after receiving assurances from London and from the ex-King himself that he would refrain from any further contact with the students, Pibul modified his line.[31] He decided to take direct action by stopping all official allowances to the former monarch.[32]

While Pibul was thus preoccupied in neutralising potential opposition to his rule, he appeared little in public. After addressing the opening meeting of the Assembly in December, he did not appear there again before it was adjourned at the end of March, 1939. Yet this was the most intensive and productive session the Assembly had ever held, due mainly to the energy of Pridi.

Just as he launched into a full-scale reform of local government on becoming Minister of the Interior, and undertook the revision of all Siam's treaties when transferred to the Foreign Ministry, so Pridi on taking over the finance portfolio embarked on a massive project to reform the country's entire fiscal system. His plans included the formulation of a totally new revenue code. In part this was necessitated by the pledge to abolish the poll tax. Alternative sources of revenue clearly had to be found. But Pridi complicated matters by deciding to abolish the paddy land and other agricultural taxes which yielded another 5 million baht a year. His idea was to help peasant farmers who still constituted the bulk of the population.[33]

In some quarters, these plans aroused fears about the resurrection of Pridi's 1933 economic plan.[34] The anxiety was shared by William

Doll, the British financial adviser, but he soon changed his mind. Pridi quickly showed he had learnt a great deal during his subsequent years in high office about the importance of maintaining Siam's international economic and financial standing. Likewise he was alive to the danger of the military eating away at the treasury reserves for capital expenditure. To Doll's surprise and admiration, Pridi also managed to track down large sums of money allocated to government departments in previous budgets and still lying idle due to bureaucratic delay. What is more, he was well aware that after the revision of the foreign treaties, Siam was free to adjust its tariffs as it wished.

In drawing up a new code of tariffs, Pridi was careful to minimise the duty paid on the import of agricultural equipment, fertilisers and other goods likely to boost the welfare of the peasants. Instead the burden of the new tariffs was designed to fall mainly on the entrepreneurial class.[35] Given the structure of society in Siam, the first people affected were alien traders rather than Siamese. A new tax on incomes and business premises had a similar outcome.[36] But when Pridi introduced a tax on commercial signboards, the effect was positively discriminatory. There was a basic scale of taxes according to the size of signboards written in Thai and what amounted to a penalty tax for those in Chinese.[37]

Still, what struck the Chinese most was the contrast between the abolition of the poll tax for Siamese and the introduction of a new annual registration fee for aliens. The press made matters worse by leaking news of the fee the day before a secret debate in the Assembly to decide how large it should be.[38] Indeed the practice during this Assembly session of introducing a large amount of legislation which had to be debated in haste and in secret led the Chinese community to suspect that it was the object of a vast and deliberate conspiracy hatched by the government.[39] However, the many Indian traders in Siam were also affected as were some Western business interests. For instance, Pridi acknowledged that in hastily drawing up a bill to curb and tax Chinese cigarette manufacturers, he had overlooked its effect on a major international company which had just embarked on a project to encourage local tobacco-growers.[40] Likewise the passing of a Liquid Fuel Act threatened the commercial activities in Siam of two of the world's leading oil companies.[41]

The drafting of the petroleum legislation was attributed not to Pridi but to Vanich Pananond, an ambitious Sino-Thai businessman who in 1935 had persuaded Pibul that in time of war the Siamese armed forces needed their own source of oil supplies independent of any controls applied by international companies. The idea stemmed from Japan's move to set up a monopoly over oil supplies in Manchukuo. Hence, when Vanich was appointed head of a new Fuel Oil Department established under the Ministry of Defence, he duly commissioned Japanese business interests to construct oil storage facilities for the Siamese armed forces.[42] Later he expanded his horizons to a refinery with the contract again being awarded to the Japanese.

Vanich also had a personal interest in the Thai Rice Company, a state enterprise set up to by-pass Chinese middlemen and millers in the trade. Its business received a boost in March 1939 when the Ministry of Defence and other government agencies were ordered to procure rice solely from state enterprises.[43] At the same time Vanich suggested to the Japanese that they circumvent the boycott the Chinese were trying to impose by transferring all their business to the Thai Rice Company.[44]

In pursuing these aims Vanich prevailed upon the Ministry of Economic Affairs, which was in any case responsible for a great deal of discriminatory legislation. For instance, it got an act passed establishing a government monopoly over the slaughter of all livestock. Previously the task had always been carried out by Chinese because the Thais as Buddhists were averse to taking life for whatever purpose.[45] More petty was a ban on aliens collecting birds' nests: the soup made from them was essentially a Chinese delicacy. A lot more people were inconvenienced by a ban on alien food vendors peddling their wares in the grounds of government establishments, including schools. Because most food vendors were Chinese, many Thais were deprived, at least temporarily, of the snacks and soft drinks they are in the habit of taking at all times of day.[45] Another discriminatory measure was a law reserving the driving of taxis exclusively for Siamese citizens.[46]

In principle, all these restrictions affected only immigrants and not second-generation Chinese born in Siam who were entitled to local nationality. One of the basic aims of government policy was to encourage such Chinese to become assimilated in the land of their birth. With the same aim in mind, the education authorities ordered Thai to be used as the language of tuition in all Chinese schools while restricting the teaching of Chinese to a couple of hours a week.[47]

Resentment among the Chinese was increased by the police stepping up their vigilance against the boycott on Japanese goods, which was being enforced by means of threats to life and property. The Thais attributed such acts to Chinese secret societies, including the Kuomintang which could not function openly in Siam because of the ban on all

political parties. It was also specifically prohibited in Siam – unlike elsewhere in South East Asia – from collecting donations to fund the
Chinese war effort against the Japanese.[48] In fact, to the Siamese authorities the Kuomintang now seemed to constitute more of a threat than the
communists. After reaching a peak in 1933, the incidence of leaflet distribution and politically-inspired labour unrest noticeably diminished.
The Comintern had decided in 1936 to switch to a policy of united front
tactics to fight against fascism, which in East Asia meant the struggle
against Japanese militarism. In Siam there was an added dimension.
Most Chinese became united in opposing what they saw as the threat of
Siamese economic nationalism.[49]

Although the spate of enactments affecting the Chinese emanated
from various government departments, some people held Pridi responsible for master-minding the whole campaign. Since he was half-
Chinese, he was equated with Vichit in seeking to deny his ancestry by
proving himself ultra-Siamese in loyalty.[50] However, Pridi's friends
disagree, claiming that he was motivated more by a desire to help the
poor and stop them from being exploited by Chinese traders.[51] But he
was too hasty. Many of his bills were badly drafted and proved impracticable to implement. For instance, legislation to impose a tax on gambling had to be rapidly amended when it was found to involve the
stamping of over 40 million playing-cards.[52] Nor was the Assembly
given the opportunity to eliminate some of these anomalies, even
though the session was extended and meetings were held daily (including weekends) to cope with all the legislation pending.[53]

After several weeks of such pressure, with at times as many as fifteen
bills a day being introduced in the Assembly, it looked as if some
members were preparing a revolt. At that juncture, a secret session was
suddenly convened.[54] The outcome was the expulsion of one of the most
outspoken representatives under a hitherto unused provision in the
constitution ruling against disorderly behaviour in the Assembly. The
effect was instantaneous.[55] The next day all the remaining legislation
was approved, so that the Assembly could be adjourned as planned. For
Pridi it was a notable triumph. Within the space of a couple of months
he had got the Assembly to approve a thoroughgoing reform of Siam's
entire financial system. His achievement was acknowledged when he
presided on behalf of the government over the adjournment of the
Assembly, since Pibul once again did not deign to attend.[56]

During his first few months as premier, Pibul was busy elsewhere
burnishing a new image for himself as leader of the nation by receiving a

string of foreign visitors. At the end of January, when the police were arresting his potential rivals, he distanced himself from events by entertaining the Governor of the Straits Settlements.[57] As soon as the Governor had left for Singapore, the admiral commanding the French naval squadron in the Far East arrived in Bangkok, to be followed in quick succession by a French military mission from Indo-China and ships from the British and American fleets. The officers involved in these visits were personally entertained by Pibul and his wife, now comfortably installed in the elegant Rose Garden or Suan Kularb Palace. There they enjoyed holding tea-dances which were regarded in those days as a fashionable form of entertainment.[58]

To all his guests Pibul appeared a charming host, far removed from the dictator he had been expected to become on assuming the premiership.[59] Moreover, he was so flattered by the attention and compliments showered on him by this procession of Western visitors that he discarded his sympathy for the totalitarian states and suggested that Siam conclude an alliance with Britain. He was dissuaded by Prince Wan, who said such an alliance would violate Siam's traditional policy of neutrality. It would also offend the Japanese,[60] who were already disappointed with Pibul. After all the effort they had put into cultivating his friendship, they had expected him on becoming premier to pursue overtly pro-Japanese policies, as advocated by a section of the Bangkok press. Some Thai newspapers which received subsidies from Tokyo were pressing for Siam to join the anti-Comintern pact, thus openly aligning itself with Japan and Germany.[61] The idea was firmly rejected by government spokesmen. Even so, Japan's advocacy of pan-Asian and anti-Western policies was making its mark. One of the more impartial Bangkok newspapers commented that if war broke out in Europe, Japan was bound to take advantage of the situation to offer support to the colonial peoples of South East Asia in their struggle for independence. As the only sovereign state in the region, Siam would have to support the anti-colonialist cause and side with Japan to the detriment of the friendly relations it had always sought to maintain with the European powers.[62]

Such thinking aroused doubts about Pibul's wisdom in playing host to so many Western military visitors. Here the Japanese had a ready explanation. They saw these visits as part of a vast and deliberate Western plot to exert pressure on Pibul.[63] As a counter they decided to resort to flattery by awarding him a prestigious decoration,[64] a gesture clearly calculated to exploit one of Pibul's susceptibilities. He had just shown a penchant for high honours by having himself promoted major-general, a rank to which no appointments had been made since June 1932. To allay any criticism of this departure from previous policy, Sindhu was simultaneously appointed rear-admiral and Prince Aditya and Phya Phahol were also awarded honorary promotions.[65]

The occasion for these promotions was the traditional Siamese New Year on April 1, when Pibul made a broadcast disclaiming any intention of discriminating against aliens or depriving them of their livelihoods. Rather, the purpose of all the legislation just passed by the Assembly was to encourage Thais to move into such occupations as food-vending and taxi-driving. Above all, Pibul stressed that everybody should pro-mote the virtues of democracy and patriotism.[66]

The main proponent of Thai nationalism remained Vichit, who raised the question of what the Thais called their country. He claimed that Siam was a name invented by the rulers of Angkor, from whom the Chinese and later the Europeans had adopted its use. Vichit argued that a name of such alien provenance was no longer fitting, since the Thais were one of the greatest nations on earth comprising not only the 13 million people within the country but also a further 23 millions scattered through southern China, French Indo-China and British Burma. To unite them all and focus their loyalty, Vichit asserted that the name of the country had to be changed.[67]

This speech proved to be just as controversial as his earlier pan-Thai and anti-Chinese outpourings. During the next few weeks the Bangkok press was full of letters both for and against the change,[68] which has remained a subject of controversy ever since. In 1939 many people argued that Siam was only just beginning to establish its identity in the world at large, and there would be confusion if it suddenly became something else.[69] There was also the question of what alternative to use. Thais usually refer to their country as Muang Thai or more formally Prathet Thai. Both were considered too much of a mouthful for foreigners. Even Pibul wavered. At first he said Prathet Thai should be adopted except in communication with foreign countries, when Siam would continue to be used. On June 23, he changed his mind and decreed that henceforth Siam was to be known as Thailand.[70] The date of the change was important. Pibul had quietly dropped the practice of celebrating the King's birthday as the National Day. From now on the National Day was to be June 24, the anniversary of the end of the absolute monarchy.[71]

Clearly Pibul intended the first celebration of this new national day to be a grand event. On the previous evening, he and his wife held a ball at Suan Kularb Palace for everyone they considered of importance in Bangkok. The next morning, units of the three armed forces and the Yuvachon paraded through the streets of Bangkok while the entire air force staged a fly-past overhead.[72] It was an impressive display. Early in 1939, military analysts assessing the balance of power in East Asia noted that the Siamese air force now numbered more planes than either the British or French had based in the area. Likewise Siam was estimated to have the second largest navy in Asia, exceeded only by Japan and equal in size to that of Australia.[73] Thus Pibul had reason to be proud. He also had cause for concern. Several days before the celebration of the National Day in Bangkok, the Japanese captured Swatow, the home of the Teochiew who were the dominant community among the Chinese in Siam. Pibul referred to the fate of Swatow in an hour-long speech broadcast on the evening of June 24, but he claimed there was nothing to worry about. Aliens and all other foreigners would learn to fear the Thai people because of the strength of their defence forces.

Originally Pibul envisaged a very different theme for the new National Day. In April property-owners along Rajadamnern, the road leading to the open ground in front of the royal palace compound, were ordered to vacate their premises within sixty days to make way for a prestigious new government construction project. Pibul, inspired possibly by the Champs Elysées in Paris, wanted Bangkok to have a processional avenue suitable for holding large-scale parades. The centrepiece of the development was planned as a monument to democracy to commemorate the promoters' feat in establishing constitutional government. On the morning of June 24, watched by large crowds, Pibul laid the first stone of the monument followed by Pridi, Sindhu, Thamrong and other prominent members of the Khana Ratsadorn. Few of them could have imagined at the time the role it was to play in the later history of Thailand, or the oft-repeated quip that monuments are usually only constructed after the subject of their veneration is well and truly dead. Pibul in his speech that evening had much to say about the virtues of democracy and the constitution. He contrasted the progress achieved since 1932 with the situation under the absolute monarchy, when power was vested in the hands of a single individual and was subject to that person's whims and fancies.

Another theme in Pibul's speech was the need to re-awaken the spirit of Thai patriotism as first conceived by King Vajiravudh. He said that his government intended to introduce *Rattaniyom*, a newly-coined word in the Thai language which Pibul explained as a concept "similar to the proper type of etiquette observed by all civilised people". To illustrate his point, he cited the case of a man "who ill-treats a member of the weaker sex in a public place". *Rattaniyom* would require such a person be punished by the people with no need to resort to the courts. Similarly, he said, bullies should be thrashed on the spot by the public.[74]

The source of inspiration for this new doctrine emerged a few days later. Vichit was appointed head of a committee to advise on *Rattaniyom*, which he laid down should be translated into English as "State Convention". He explained that it was a modernised version of an ancient concept known as *Rajaniyom* whereby former monarchs gave their opinions on the conduct of their subjects. By contrast, *Rattaniyom* was intended as an expression of public opinion.[75] The first was declared in retrospect to be the adoption of Thailand as the name for the country. The second was more broad-ranging, and amounted to a patriotic code of behaviour for the Thai people "to prevent danger and discredit falling on their nation". The *Rattaniyom* decreed that they were not to reveal any information to foreigners, act as "agents or mouthpieces of aliens" (for example, in land purchases), or carry out any other action deemed dishonourable or treacherous to their own race. In conclusion, the *Rattaniyom* stated that it was the duty of all Thais to "suppress" anybody considered guilty of violating these norms.[76]

This code was issued in the name of Pibul and never debated in the Assembly. Methods for its implementation were nonetheless discussed in the press.[77] Vichit was known to favour public lynching, and wanted it authorised as part of the *Rattaniyom*. Fortunately nothing came of the idea, because in pushing patriotism to the fore Pibul, as urged on by Vichit and other like-minded people, struck a responsive chord from the public.[78]

In mid-1939 the main target of patriotic opinion was the foreign oil companies. They were teetering on the brink of ending their operations in Thailand with the entry into force of the Liquid Fuel Act. During last minute negotiations on the subject, the Bangkok press mounted a campaign of abuse against those companies who were alleged to be exploiting Thailand and motivated only by their own profit levels.[79] It was a one-sided exercise. The companies refrained from replying publicly and putting their own case. They knew, for instance, that Vanich had long been involved in secret dealings with the Japanese to enable them to become the sole suppliers or rather middlemen in providing Thailand's oil requirements. As for the refinery they were constructing in Bangkok, it would not be completed before 1940. Till then, the Fuel Oil Department was incapable of complying with one of the main provisions of the Act requiring anybody trading in oil in Thailand to keep six months' stocks in reserve. Consequently, when the foreign oil companies finally pulled out in July and the department run by Vanich became responsible for distribution and sales, Thailand was virtually bereft of petrol and kerosene. The situation was made worse by local speculation and hoarding. More unfortunate still, Thailand had to embark on purchasing oil for itself on the world market at a time of rising prices and shortages because the major world powers were stockpiling in anticipation of the possible outbreak of war.[80]

As well as the renewal of tension in Europe during the summer of 1939, the Japanese were expanding their campaign in China to apply pressure on the Western concessions, most notably the British at Tientsin. These developments seemed to increase the likelihood of Japan taking advantage of a war in Europe to attack the colonial territories in South East Asia. In such circumstances, most informed people in the region believed that it would be months before the British and French could build up their strength sufficiently to counter such a move. Politicians in London tended to take a different view: they regarded the threat from Japan as illusory because its military potential seemed to be already exhausted in vainly trying to subjugate the whole of China.[81]

Nonetheless, an Anglo-French defence conference was convened in Singapore at the end of June to discuss the situation. Here the French again propounded their long-held view that Siam had secretly agreed with Japan to collaborate in seizing Indo-China. Despite repeated official denials in Bangkok, the French also suspected the Thais of clandestinely building up their military strength along the border with Laos.[82] Such fears were not even laid to rest when arrangements were made for the French military delegation which visited Siam in early 1939 to tour the border area. Pibul wanted the French to see for themselves that Siam continued to respect the 25 km. demilitarised zone as stipulated in the 1907 border treaty between the two countries.[83]

The British tended to regard the French as unduly alarmist and subject to the influence of Thai political exiles resident in Saigon like Prince Bovoradet and Phya Song, who had every reason to try to discredit Pibul.[84] Hence there was little concord at the Singapore conference. Basically, what the French wanted was a guarantee of benevolent neutrality from Siam, including a pledge that in the event of a Japanese attack on Indo-China the Thais would grant transit rights to French and

British reinforcements. Such a proposal, the British argued, was bound to be rejected as a matter of principle by any government in Bangkok, and in the case of Pibul it would simply propel him straight into the embrace of the Japanese. Eventually all that the British and French could agree was that because Pibul was undoubtedly subject to growing Japanese pressure, Siam had to be regarded as a very volatile element in the situation in South East Asia. Hence the Western powers decided to step up their defences in the region as soon as possible.[85]

The deliberations of this conference were kept secret, but inevitably knowledge that it had taken place led to widespread speculation. One London newspaper reported that Britain and France had offered to guarantee the security of Siam.[86] Alternatively it was suggested that Thailand had approached the European powers with a request for such a guarantee and had offered military facilities in return. As for the Japanese, they thought a Thai representative had secretly attended the Singapore conference.[87] All such speculation was officially denied in Bangkok.[88] Still, Pibul was clearly worried, and Crosby tried to reassure him, as well as Sindhu, that the Europeans were not colluding to seal the destiny of Thailand behind its back.

The French adopted a different line. Their Minister in Bangkok proposed that France and Thailand should conclude a non-aggression pact. There was no immediate Thai response to this;[89] Pibul was irked that the French apparently still suspected him of conspiring with the Japanese. The Thai premier pointed out that with one son already studying in Britain and another in Belgium, both on military training courses, he was just about to commit yet another hostage to fortune by sending his daughter to a school in Paris.[90]

The education of Pibul's children was a sore point with the Japanese who hoped at least one of them would go to Tokyo.[91] Since Pibul's attitude seemed to be coloured by his own experience in France, the Japanese sought to impress members of his entourage who were not European-educated. One point they stressed in particular was that they had inflicted a considerable defeat on the British at Tientsin; what is more, they compared it with the victory Vanich was said to have achieved in forcing the Western oil companies out of Thailand.[92] In other words, Asians were capable of defeating Europeans and would soon be able to free their part of the world from all Western domination.

The effect of such arguments was noticeable. Pibul started to consider whether Thailand's international position should be re-aligned to take advantage of the prevailing current. Here Pridi warned that the country could not afford to alienate Britain because most Thai gold and foreign currency reserves were held in London. Pibul seemed to appreciate the point, but not for long.[93] In mid-July he decided to ease out his Foreign Minister, a British-educated *ancien régime* official,[94] and add the portfolio to all those he already held himself. The Japanese were delighted. As soon as Pibul became Foreign Minister, he proceeded to expound to his cabinet colleagues the need for Thailand to depend exclusively on Japan because the Western powers were so patently weak by comparison.[95]

The move came as no surprise to the Chinese, who had concluded long since that Pibul was basically pro-Japanese. Despite assurances from the Thai government that it was not anti-Chinese as such, and that only those who broke the law were being penalised, the Overseas Chinese thought otherwise. More and more Chinese schools in Thailand were closed down for violating government instructions on language tuition. When some Chinese newspapers attempted to protest, they had their licences to publish withdrawn. But what really stunned the Chinese community in Bangkok was the arrest in July of two prominent bankers, accused of remitting funds to the anti-Japanese war chest in Chungking. As it turned out, they were both British citizens domiciled in Malaya where such activities were permitted.[96] Consequently there was a considerable anti-Thai outcry in the British colony, much to the dismay of Pibul.

In August Pibul's daughter, who was to study in France, embarked on a steamer at Penang together with two children of Adul, the police chief. To see them safely aboard, they were accompanied to Penang by their mothers, who went on from there to make a private visit to Singapore. There the Thai consul was so worried about the personal safety of two such prominent ladies that he requested special police protection for them. Alarming rumours soon reached Bangkok about the dangers they were supposed to be facing, and Pibul ordered them to return home immediately.[97]

Apparently the Thai premier had not realised up till then that he was widely regarded in Malaya as master-minding an anti-Chinese campaign, while Adul, as his loyal henchman, was held responsible for all the arrests and alleged harassment involved. In fact, however, Adul and the police under him acted strictly according to the law in handling the case of the two bankers whose detention caused such an outcry. They were quickly brought to court and sentenced to be deported to Malaya. Other less prominent Chinese, similarly indicted for soliciting funds for the Kuomintang's war effort, did not get off so lightly: if they could not claim another nationality, they were often sentenced to deportation to their ancestral villages in China and sometimes handed straight over to the Japanese.[98]

Such actions only contributed to Adul's reputation for harshness. Many Thais also regarded him as a sinister figure. The son of a British subject who had arrived in Siam from Ceylon, he was unusually tall and dark in complexion. He shunned appearing in public and had a habit of prowling the streets of Bangkok at night. Hence he came to be equated in the public mind with Himmler, the head of the Nazi Gestapo.[99] Above all he was blamed for the round-up in January of those accused of conspiring against the government. The trial of these detainees by special tribunal started in April.[100] All the proceedings were held in secret and little information was divulged to the public about what was at stake. Even so, it became increasingly clear that members of Phya Song's clique were emerging as the chief suspects.[101]

Another target of continuing official hostility was the former monarch. His portrait was removed from all official buildings in July,[102] shortly before the government sued him and his consort for over 6 million baht, which they were charged with having transferred abroad illegally in 1933. Although Prajadhipok had still been on the throne at that time, there was no provision in the constitution specifying the legal immunity of the monarch. The case against the royal couple was heard quickly before the ex-King could despatch a lawyer from London to plead his case.[103] In August, as soon as the Court of Appeal upheld a verdict of guilty, the government took possession of Sukhotai Palace, the ex-King's private residence, and all its contents. Simultaneously three boxes of royal jewels and other valuables were seized from a Bangkok bank where they had been placed in safe-deposit.[104]

Besides affording proof of just how anti-royalist the government had become under Pibul, these developments led many people to conclude that certain promoters were simply bent on self-enrichment. In Malaya, where several prominent Thai royalist exiles continued to reside, there were suggestions that public outrage against the Khana Ratsadorn would lead to a situation similar to that in 1933 when an attempt to sue the monarch had been one of the pretexts for launching the Bovoradet rebellion. Instead, reaction in Thailand was muted; by mid-1939 Pibul, as he himself acknowledged, had virtually succeeded in his aim of stifling any potential opposition to his rule. The confiscation of royal wealth was an extra bonus: Pibul believed that it had been used to finance the plots against him.[105]

In any case, Pibul was becoming adept at courting support from other influential groupings besides the military. He instituted monthly press conferences when journalists were invited to Suan Kularb to hear at first hand how the premier was concerned about the welfare of the nation.[106] Members of the Assembly were flattered with similar invitations, plus promises from Pibul of being allowed greater participation in Assembly deliberations and the award of a pay rise.[107] Likewise he set out to ingratiate himself with the civilian promoters. One of them was appointed Deputy Foreign Minister when Pibul took over the ministerial portfolio.[108] Another became cabinet secretary, albeit with considerable misgivings, realising how Pibul tried to manipulate people for his own ends.[109] Indeed, in some eyes these appointments were seen as an attempt by Pibul to wean Pridi's friends away from him.

After his burst of legislative activity in early 1939, Pridi himself acknowledged that he was being eclipsed. He attributed this partly to his obvious bias towards the democratic powers, in contrast to the military who believed that Thailand should side with the totalitarian states.[110] Yet Pridi continued to carry out his duties as Finance Minister conscientiously; with Europe apparently on the brink of war, he managed skilfully, and without causing any harm to Thailand's international financial standing, to transfer part of its foreign currency reserves from London to New York.[111]

In 1939 the United States did not loom very large in Thai thinking. Compared with the European powers and Japan, its trading interests in Thailand were small. Nor did the American adviser to the Ministry of Foreign Affairs seem to exercise much influence after Prince Wan appeared on the scene. Rather Crosby and his French counterpart were left, as they saw it, as the champions of the democratic world competing with the totalitarian states for the sympathy of the Thai government. Only in August, when it became evident that war in Europe was virtually inevitable, did the American position change. Through diplomatic channels, the United States quietly reminded Thailand that it had an interest in maintaining the existing balance of power and stability in East Asia.[112]

Germany too had far less influence in Thailand than Britain, Japan or France, but it did have contacts in high places. Apart from Prayoon's continuing links with the land of his birth, several members of the senior military clique had studied there. They included Phya Phahol and Phra Prasat who, it transpired, had been classmates of Goering, one of Hitler's leading henchmen. In moving against Phya Song's clique, Pibul attempted to take advantage of these old bonds. Phra Prasat was banished to Berlin as Siamese Minister with express orders to re-establish contact with Goering and cultivate his friendship.[113] One Bangkok newspaper soon got wind of the ploy and reported that Hitler was about to invite Pibul to visit Berlin. Its licence to publish was immediately suspended.[114]

Despite such sensitivity, Prayoon flew off to Germany at the end of August apparently to find out why Germany had just surprised the world by concluding a non-aggression pact with the Soviet Union, which Pibul realised significantly changed the international situation. The main effect, as far as he was concerned, was the collapse of the anti-Comintern pact and the end of pressure on Thailand to join it. Looking further ahead, Prince Wan expressed the hope this re-alignment in the international balance of power would lead to a rapprochement between the Western democracies and Japan, thus further easing the pressure on Thailand.[115]

Anyway, the outbreak of war in Europe on September 3 caused Pibul far less anxiety than it would have done a month earlier. Thailand duly proclaimed its neutrality, and the belligerent powers pledged to respect it.[116] Here Crosby was very pleased that the British got in first before the Germans or anyone else in acknowledging Thai neutrality. So intense was the sense of rivalry between the great powers that such things were thought to count, especially with Pibul. Crosby regarded him as a human weather-vane ready to turn towards whomsoever flattered him most.[117]

For most Thais, however, the war in Europe meant little. Still Pibul took full advantage of the opportunity to build on his image as father of the nation. In a broadcast he reassured the people that there was nothing to worry about. All the same, he urged them to help themselves, their families and the fatherland by developing economic self-reliance.[118] To set an example, he personally supervised the passing through the Assembly of a Kitchen Garden Act,[119] and at his next press conference he distributed eggs from ducks being reared in the compound at Suan Kularb Palace.[120] At the same time, the hoarding of commodities was forbidden, stricter price controls were promised, an Air Raid Precautions Act was promulgated, and betel nut chewing among the armed forces was discouraged. Some military reserves were called up, and it was announced that naval patrols in the Gulf of Thailand were being increased as a deterrent to the belligerent powers taking action against each other's shipping there.[121]

Of far more immediate concern to the Bangkok élite was the plight of their relatives and friends in Europe. Pibul proved the exception. He requested that his son Prasong be allowed to continue his naval training in Britain and if possible participate in operations at sea, despite the war.[122] Above all, his attitude was in marked contrast to anxiety expressed about the safety of the King.[123] Although Switzerland's neutrality never seemed in doubt, it was officially suggested in Bangkok that the King should return to Thailand. The response of the King's mother (now formally designated the Princess Mother) was that her family would prefer to go to the United States, a country she knew well and which seemed unlikely to be involved in the war. The fact was that relations between the Princess Mother and the government in Bangkok were tense: she had protested in strong terms at the detention of Prince Rangsit, prompting renewed speculation about the abdication of the King. It was reinforced by Prince Aditya, who claimed in private that Pibul had offered him the throne, but that he had replied he would only accept if it were the will of the people.[124]

Another idea which struck Pibul at that juncture was that if Germany could change the course of history in Europe by concluding a non-aggression pact with the Soviet Union, Thailand might be able to do the same in South East Asia. He therefore proposed to Britain and France that they should enter into non-aggression pacts with Thailand. The French, who were still awaiting a reply to the similar proposal they had put forward in July, responded enthusiastically, but then Pibul appeared to have second thoughts and indicated that it would be a deviation from the traditional Thai policy of neutrality. Behind the scenes, the influence of Prince Wan was at work; it occurred to this subtle-minded diplomat that since the French were so eager, Thailand should make the most of the opportunity. Consequently he told them that Thailand would be only too happy to sign such a pact, provided they first agreed to amend the treaties dating back to the beginning of the twentieth century defining the border with Indo-China.

No similar pre-conditions were attached to the non-aggression pacts which Prince Wan simultaneously proposed to the British and the Japanese. It transpired too that the Thais simply wanted France to agree to adjust the border where it coincided with the Mekong river, so that the main navigational channel should be recognised as the frontier of Indo-China according to the internationally accepted Thalweg principle. France had previously insisted on a demarcation line placing all the islands and sandbars in the river under Indo-Chinese sovereignty, no matter how close they might be to the Thai bank. Apart from anything else, it affected Thai river traffic. To stress the reasonableness of the Thai proposals, Prince Wan pointed out to the French that Britain had on several occasions, and most recently in 1939, agreed to readjust Burma's borders with Thailand when the rivers which served as a demarcation line changed course.

Britain's basic attitude towards the Thais had however long been very different from that of France. The reaction of the French colonial authorities, both on the ground in Indo-China and in Paris, to the proposed adjustment of the Mekong frontier was that if the Thais were given an inch, they would seek to take a mile. On the other hand, the French Foreign Ministry thought that a few islands and sandbars in the Mekong were a small price to pay for a non-aggression pact of lasting value. These contrasting views gave rise to a prolonged inter-ministerial dispute in Paris, and the British, realising what was happening, declined a request from Pibul to intervene with the French on Thailand's behalf.[125]

The British were also asked to intervene in China's dispute with Thailand. Since Pibul was adamantly opposed to the idea of the Chinese establishing any sort of consular representation in Bangkok, the government in Chungking asked the British to act on its behalf. In other words, the British Legation in Bangkok would be required to assume responsibility for the 3 million or more people of Chinese origin living in Siam, all of whom the Kuomintang regarded as Chinese citizens. The request was refused because of the obvious problems involved.[126]

In the latter half of 1939, the Thais were becoming increasingly angry with the Overseas Chinese; they resented what they saw as the continuing milking of the Thai economy by the remittance of funds to the war chest in Chungking. Violence, too, was often involved: one prominent Bangkok Chinese, murdered in September, was alleged to have headed a secret death squad engaged in political intimidation.[127] Broadcasts from Chungking, however, claimed that it was the Thai authorities who were harassing and persecuting the Chinese in Bangkok. The Thais countered by starting their own broadcasts in Chinese. Eventually matters became so heated that Chiang Kai-shek sent a personal message to Pibul requesting an end to what he called the molestation of the Chinese community in Thailand. Instead of reacting angrily, as might have been expected, Pibul replied in courteous terms with assurances that the entire Chinese community in Thailand enjoyed the full protection of the law, and that only those who broke it had action taken against them.[128]

Pibul was in fact preoccupied by a very different problem. Verdicts on those people arrested in January were ready to be made public. To avoid any awkward questions on the subject, the Assembly was adjourned for at least six months but not before its members had been invited to a party at Suan Kularb where Pibul thanked them personally for their cooperation with the government.[129] After these precautionary moves, it was announced on November 24 that twenty-one people had been condemned to death by the Special Tribunal and a similar number sentenced to life imprisonment. The press was allowed to publish their names but not the grounds on which they had been convicted, pending the publication of another official statement. It emerged a couple of days later in the shape of a 300-page book containing the judgement of the Special Tribunal, which the press was enjoined to publish in its entirety or not at all. No extracts were allowed and comment was equally discouraged. In compliance with these instructions, the government-controlled radio broadcast the whole judgement and then a speech by Pibul. Assuming that his listeners had heard the judgement, he launched into a justification of the record of the promoters and their attitude towards the monarchy.[130]

Pibul had good reason to be worried about popular reaction to the judgement. After giving a detailed account of anti-government conspiracies since 1932, the blame for all of them was attributed to Phya Song's clique acting in collusion with the royal family. These plots allegedly culminated in the two attempts to assassinate Pibul just before he became premier. While much of the evidence cited to prove this thesis was of doubtful value, one of the most striking features about the judgement was the insight it provided into the internal history of the Khana Ratsadorn and Pibul's struggle to dominate it. As a result its verdict seemed all the more harsh. At the end of November the press published a petition for clemency by those sentenced to death, but with three exceptions it was rejected by the Council of Regents. No further official statements on the subject were issued. Instead it was left to word-of-mouth to circulate the news that eighteen people were executed at the beginning of December, the first time in modern Thai history that anybody had suffered such a fate on political grounds.[131]

Apart from the valet who actually shot at Pibul, those executed were mostly military officers who at one stage or other in their careers had been associated with Phya Song. One exception in their midst was an outspoken young politician elected to represent Bangkok in 1938.[132] He died because he was found guilty of conspiring against the government by having his election campaign financed by royalist interests including allegedly ex-King Prajadhipok and Prince Boripat.

Despite what many people considered to be the outrageous nature of such charges, the Special Tribunal was not completely indiscriminate in meting out its sentences. For instance, although Phya Song emerged from the judgement as the arch-conspirator in all the plots, no move was made to sentence him *in absentia* or have him extradited from Indo-China. Furthermore, one of his close friends, who had returned to Thailand voluntarily, had his death sentence commuted to life imprisonment.[133] By contrast, there was no compunction about executing another senior officer and former cabinet minister who had accompanied Phya Song on most of his trips abroad. Since the man who was spared was a promoter, it seemed that their secret oath vowing to respect each other's lives still held good.[134]

Different criteria prevailed in the case of the other two people who had their death sentences commuted to life imprisonment. One was Phya Thephatsadin: while two of his sons were executed, his own life was spared because, according to an official statement, he had rendered valuable service in leading the Siamese military contingent to Europe during the Great War. However, the real reason was Pibul's anxiety about public reaction to the execution of such a prominent figure. The same was even more true of Prince Rangsit; despite Pibul's efforts to undermine the standing of the Chakri family, he clearly thought that it would be going too far to execute the King's favourite uncle and guardian. Even so, Prince Rangsit was stripped of his royal rank and titles on being imprisoned for life.

The Princess Mother immediately wrote from Switzerland in the name of her son appealing for his uncle to be banished from Thailand rather than serving his sentence, but notwithstanding the action taken against Phya Song and other political exiles, the appeal was rejected on the grounds that no Thai citizen could be forced to leave his own country. Pibul also categorically denied at one of his press conferences that the royal family had attempted to intercede on behalf of Prince Rangsit.[135] Again there was speculation about the King abdicating, but the Queen Grandmother was apparently determined that the throne should remain in her personal line of descent.[136]

Underlying the anxiety over the fate of Prince Rangsit was, as ever, the question of how political prisoners were treated. The government had recently established a new penal colony at Terutao island in the Andaman Sea, just north of the Malayan coast.[137] Some of the political prisoners sentenced following the Bovoradet rebellion had already been transferred there, and it was beginning to acquire a reputation similar to that of Devil's Island, the French penal colony off the coast of Guiana, and Poulo Condore, its notorious counterpart in Indo-China.[138]

Another cause for concern was that in its judgement the Special Tribunal had appeared to inculpate various people who had not been detained. One person who was anxious on this score was Phra Sarasat, the former Minister of Economic Affairs. Soon after the judgement was published he once more fled to Japan, where his political sympathies lay. Since leaving the cabinet in 1934, Phra Sarasat had frequently written articles advocating the need for closer economic cooperation between Japan and Siam.[139] Nonetheless he also continued to stress his long-standing friendship with Pridi who thought that he too might come under suspicion.[140]

Anyway, Pridi shared the public dismay at the verdict of the Special Tribunal. In his eyes, it was glaring evidence of how Pibul and his clique abused power to their own advantage. Already Pridi felt that he was fighting a losing battle at the Ministry of Finance against increasing military expenditure, which was relentlessly diminishing the treasury reserves. Furthermore, he was in a position to appreciate how state enterprises were being mismanaged for the personal benefit of their directors, many of them promoters. Consequently, Pridi applied in January 1940 for sick leave and tendered his resignation. It was rejected. Apparently Pibul was not prepared to countenance the departure of such an important figurehead from his cabinet, where there were other rumblings of discontent. Yet nobody dared challenge Pibul openly. The proceedings of the Special Tribunal had achieved their evident objective. Everybody, including the press, had been cowed into silence.[141]

Ostensibly the only thing Pibul now had to worry about was the international situation, and early in 1940 it did not look as if it would cause many problems for Thailand. After the initial outburst of warfare in Europe the "phoney war" followed, and in the absence of any more major battles most Thais completely forgot about it. Yet behind the scenes work was continuing on non-aggression pacts to be concluded with the major powers. Besides Prince Wan, the main Thai negotiator was Direk Chaiyanam, who had been appointed Deputy Foreign Minister when Pibul took over the portfolio. Direk seemed eminently suitable for this job: trained as a lawyer, he was one of the most diligent of the civilian promoters. He had served ably as cabinet secretary under Phya Phahol and been a member of the delegation which went to England in 1934 to negotiate with King Prajadhipok before his abdication. But perhaps Direk's greatest asset was that he spoke English fluently and had a reputation for getting on well with Europeans.

Indeed, with Direk in charge of the negotiations a pact was quickly agreed with Britain and could have been signed in early 1940. A delay was deliberately imposed by the British. They did not want to disadvantage the French in their much more arduous negotiations involving the Thai demand for the adjustment of the Mekong frontier. Eventually, after much heated discussion within the French administration, it was agreed that this demand should be met in the interest of securing a long-term guarantee of Indo-China's sovereignty against any broader Thai aspirations. Accordingly, in April, France signified its readiness to redelineate the Mekong frontier later in the year following the conclusion of a non-aggression pact and the despatch of a high-ranking official from Paris to participate in a joint survey team with the Thais to determine the new borderline on the spot.[142]

No similar progress was made on the pact simultaneously proposed to the Japanese, who did not even bother to reply to Prince Wan's original démarche in October. The view in Tokyo was that, rather than concluding a Western-style non-aggression pact, what Japan really needed was "a special political understanding" with Thailand. The idea was elaborated in a policy paper drawn up in December 1939 when the Japanese Foreign Ministry, which was increasingly subject to militarist influence, first acknowledged the strategic importance of Thailand in a southward drive to seize control of Singapore. In other words, the "special understanding" the Japanese wanted with the Thais was envisaged as the basis for future political and military cooperation between them.[143] The problem was how to broach the question.

The time was clearly not ripe in April when Direk, on Pibul's instructions, pressed the Japanese for a reply on the proposed non-aggression pact. Hence they equivocated by claiming that such a pact was unnecessary because Japan and Thailand had no common border. The Japanese Minister in Bangkok also suggested that in concluding pacts with Britain and France the Thais might offend the Germans and Italians. Pibul reacted by telling Direk to consult the two Axis powers and the United States as well for good measure. None of them saw any reason why Thailand should not sign non-aggression treaties with countries with which it had the most contiguous relations;[144] it made little difference. On perusing the texts of the treaties agreed with Britain and France, the Japanese became convinced that there was some sort of devious Western plot afoot to undermine Thailand's freedom to conclude agreements with other countries. Still, the Japanese felt that they could hardly insist that the Thais renegotiate their treaties with the European powers at that late stage. Rather, they changed tactics. Stating that some of the Western-style phraseology in the Thai draft of the proposed pact violated certain hallowed Japanese precepts, the Foreign Ministry in Tokyo offered to sign a treaty of friendship and mutual cooperation. It included a guarantee of territorial integrity as well as a provision for an exchange of information and a mutual pledge not to assist enemy states in time of war. Eventually the Thai cabinet agreed to these terms, only to find that the Japanese were anxious to conclude such a treaty before the British and French signed their non-aggression pacts.[145]

During the weeks that Direk was negotiating with the Japanese, the situation in Europe changed dramatically, and for the first time the war began to have a direct impact on Thailand. Many Thai exports had regularly been shipped by Scandinavian freighters, whose services were now impaired by the German invasion of Denmark and Norway.[146] The German move into the Netherlands had an even more direct bearing on South East Asia, since it apparently made the oil-rich Netherlands East Indies vulnerable to Japanese attack. Pibul immediately rushed off on an inspection of southern Thailand which he had long thought the Japanese might want to use for mounting an attack on Singapore and thence the Dutch colony. In his absence the cabinet felt powerless to act in dealing first with the shipping crisis and then with the even greater problems looming with the German invasion of France and the British evacuation from Dunkirk.

These developments made Crosby and his French counterpart all the more frustrated at the delay caused by Japan to the signing of the non-aggression pacts; they were apprehensive lest Pibul, judging the collapse of France and Britain to be inevitable, should decide to cancel the pacts altogether.[147] In the event, he did not change his mind; rather, it was the Japanese who caused a last-minute hitch. Reluctant to be seen acting in concert with the Western powers, they insisted that their treaty with Thailand be signed in Tokyo, whereas the British and French formalised the conclusion of their non-aggression pacts in Bangkok. Here the Europeans gained some advantage as the pacts were signed by Pibul himself.

Indeed, the personal prestige accruing from this ceremony was probably the main reason why Pibul decided to go ahead with the signing on June 12, 1940. He was building up his achievements for another spectacular celebration of Thailand's national day later in the month.[148]

In 1940 the first item on the National Day programme was the inauguration of the monument to democracy of which the foundation stone had been laid the previous year. It was unfortunate that during the ceremony the balloons which were supposed to lift the Thai flag from the monument's centrepiece (symbolising the constitution) failed to ascend at the crucial moment and had to be prodded aloft with bamboo poles. Some of the assembled gathering, both Thai and foreign, remarked that it did not seem a good omen for the future of democracy in Thailand.[149] The same could have been said of the military parade which followed. It was the largest ever witnessed in Bangkok, and Pibul proudly took the salute from the steps to the monument to democracy. Later in the day, other ceremonies were held to inaugurate a National Bank, the oil refinery and a new headquarters for the Post Office, as well as a scheme promoted by Pibul to build a nationwide road network. The first major long-distance road in Thailand was constructed between Bangkok and Lopburi, Pibul's new garrison town. He formally opened the highway by driving to broadcast his National Day speech from Lopburi.[150]

In contrast to the previous year, when his main theme was democracy, Pibul concentrated on how civilised a country Thailand was becoming, and as evidence he cited all his government's tangible achievements which had been inaugurated that day. He also referred with pride to the agreements signed with France, Britain and Japan, claiming that they had brought lasting peace and security to Thailand. Above all, Pibul boasted about his government's feat in persuading the French to agree to adjust the border with Indo-China.[151]

NOTES

1. F12115/12115/40 in FO371/22214.
2. Landon (1941), pp. 150ff, and BTWM, Dec. 6, 1938.
3. Charnvit Kasetsiri, loc. cit., p. 44.
4. Flood, p. 204, and BTWM, Nov. 2, 1938.
5. ibid., Sep. 29, 1938.
6. ibid., Nov. 18, 1938.
7. ibid., Oct. 14, 1938.

8. ibid., Dec. 19 and 23, 1938, and Chula Chakrabongse (1943), p. 304.
9. BTWM, Dec. 27, 1938. They were not Liang Chaiyakal and Chamlong Daoruang, as claimed in Ananta Pibulsongkram, II, p. 47.
10. BTWM, Jan. 27, 1939.
11. This was Phya Chaiyos Sombat.
12. BTWM, Jan. 3, 1939, and F64/43/40 in FO371/23586.
13. 112114/9692/40 in FO371/22214.
14. M. Smith, pp. 72 and 133.
15. F3402/3402/40 in FO371/23579.
16. BTWM, Jan. 15, 1939.
17. ibid., Jan. 13 and 14, 1939.
18. Chula Chakrabongse (1943), p. 300.
19. BTWM, Jan. 30 and Feb. 1, 1939, and Sathuan Suphasophon, p. 416.
20. BTWM, Feb. 3, 1939.
21. BTWM, Feb. 2, 1939; Daily Mail (London), Jan. 31, 1939; Queen Rambhai in Thak Chaloemtiarana (ed.), p. 20.
22. Criticism led by Chamlong Daoruang, Assemblyman for Mahasarakham.
23. Pibul allegedly threatened to prorogue the Assembly if it rejected the Special Courts Act. Sripanon Singthong, p. 27.
24. BTWM, Feb. 3, 1939.
25. This was Nawnen Talalakshana.
26. This was Phra Sitthi Ruangdetphol. The third parliamentary detainee was Mangkorn Sansen, later released without standing trial.
27. BTWM, Feb. 16, 1939, and F1658/43/40 in FO371/23586.
28. F6697/43/40 in ibid. and Chula Chakrabongse (1943), pp. 303ff.
29. F2695/61/40 in FO371/23586.
30. Article in *Samakhi Sarn* written by Chamkad Balankura and reprinted in BTWM, Jan. 23, 1939.
31. F4062/61/40 in FO371/23586.
32. F8059/61/40 in ibid.
33. BTWM, Mar. 3, 1939.
34. Landon (1941), pp. 169ff.
35. F352/242/40 and file in FO371/23590 and BTWM, Feb. 20, 1939.
36. ibid., Mar. 13, 1939.
37. ibid., Mar. 4 and 28, 1939, and Landon (1941), pp. 229ff.
38. ibid., pp. 210ff, and BTWM, Mar. 15, 1939.
39. Landon (1941), p. 225.
40. This was British American Tobacco Company, which had extensive plans for developing tobacco-growing in Siam. F3622/3622/40 in FO371/23579, and BTWM, Mar. 24, 1939.
41. ibid. Companies involved with Standard Vacuum of New Jersey and Royal Dutch Shell, which supplied Siam from refineries in Sumatra and Borneo, trading as Asian Petroleum Co.
42. F6864/6060/40 in FO371/20301, and FRUS (1937), IV, pp. 893ff, and F204/204/40 in FO371/23589.
43. BTWM, Mar. 17, 1939, and Landon (1941), p. 245.
44. BTWM, Mar. 9, 1939; F251/251/40 in FO371/23592; Flood, p. 214.
45. BTWM, Mar. 24, 1939, and Landon (1941), pp. 219 and 245.

46. ibid., p. 247, and BTWM, Apr. 11, 1939.
47. ibid., Apr. 8, 1939.
48. ibid., May 27 and June 3, 1939; Flood, pp. 209ff; Landon (1941), p. 152.
49. ibid., p. 283, and Brimmel, p. 115.
50. Skinner, pp. 244ff.
51. Thawee Bunyaket in Ray, p. 76.
52. F4113/242/40 in FO371/23590, and BTWM, Mar. 9, 1939.
53. ibid., Mar. 22, 1939.
54. ibid., Mar. 28, 1939, describing the Revolt against the supplementary budget drawn up by Pridi on changing the financial year to start from October 1 for climatic reasons.
55. ibid., Mar. 29, 1939. The Assemblyman expelled was Inthorn Singhanetr (representative for Chiengmai), later a persistent critic of government.
56. ibid., Mar. 31, 1939, and Prasert Patamasukhon, pp. 286ff.
57. BTWM, Jan. 30, 1939.
58. ibid., Feb. 6, 8, 13, 14 and Mar. 24, 1939.
59. F2803/2130/40 in FO371/23595.
60. F1860/1860/40 in ibid.
61. BTWM, Feb. 18 and 24, Mar. 3 and Apr. 13, 1939, and F2339/1860/40 in FO371/25395.
62. Tai Mai editorial reprinted in BTWM, Apr. 21, 1939.
63. Flood, p. 218, quoting reports in *Asahi Shimbun*, Mar. 31 and Apr. 8, 1939.
64. BTWM, Apr. 24, 1939.
65. ibid., Apr. 4, 1939.
66. Text in ibid., Apr. 3, 1939.
67. ibid., May 29, 1939, and Vichit Vadhakarn, *Thailand's Case*, pp. 121ff.
68. BTWM, June 2, 1939ff.
69. E.g. Winston Churchill, *History of the Second World War*, III, pp. 642 and 748.
70. BTWM, June 12 and 23, 1939.
71. ibid., Mar. 18, 1939.
72. ibid., June 26, 1939.
73. *United Services Review*, quoted in ibid., Feb. 6 and July 5, 1939.
74. ibid., June 26, 1939.
75. ibid., June 30 and July 4, 1939, and Landon (1941), p. 188.
76. Text in Thak Chaloemtiarana (ed.), p. 245, and BTWM, July 4, 1939.
77. ibid., July 15, 1939.
78. F7786/43/40 in FO371/23586.
79. BTWM, July 3, 1939.
80. ibid., Aug. 7, 8 and 10, 1939; F8060/204/40 in FO371/23589; Flood, p. 223; Landon (1941), p. 240.
81. F4802/1860/40 in FO371/23595, and Churchill, e.g. as quoted in Thorne, *Allies of a Kind*, pp. 18ff.
82. BTWM, Jan. 5, Mar. 3 and Apr. 13, 1939.
83. ibid., Feb. 15, 1939.
84. F8969/1860/40 in FO371/23595.
85. Official British record of conference in F7285/2742/40 in FO371/23549, and French account in Decoux, *A la barre de l'Indo-Chine*, pp. 22ff.

86. *Daily Telegraph*, June 26, 1939.
87. Flood, p. 220, quoting report of July 29, 1939, in GKR A–6–0–0.
88. BTWM, June 27, 1939.
89. F7486/1860/40 in FO371/23595.
90. F8969/1860/40 in ibid.
91. Crosby, p. 102.
92. F6123/46/40 in FO371/23592.
93. F7011/1860/40 in FO371/23595.
94. Chao Phya Sri Thammathibet resigned on health grounds, BTWM, July 14, 1939, but it was a diplomatic illness. F7825/43/40 in FO371/23586.
95. Flood, pp. 221ff, quoting July 29 report to Tokyo in GKR A–6–0–0.
96. Landon (1941), pp. 277ff, and BTWM, July 28 and 31, Aug. 2, 5, 7, 16 and 21, 1939.
97. ibid., Aug. 14 and 28, 1939.
98. F11603/4784/40 in FO371/23597.
99. Thawee Bunyaket in Ray, p. 75, and Coast, *Some Aspects of Siamese Politics*, p. 11. Adul was arrested one night as a suspect criminal. He reacted by reprimanding the policeman responsible for failing to recognise his commanding officer and later promoting him for efficiency on duty. Story in Suphote Dantrakul, p. 29.
100. BTWM, Apr. 24, 1939. Full list of detainees in Withet Korani, pp. 564ff.
101. Luang Chamnan Yuthasilp, former commander of the Bangkok Military District, sent abroad in late 1938, was stripped of his foreign allowance, military rank and pension rights, so forcing him to return home to face immediate arrest. Another member of Phya Song's clique (Luang Ronnasith Pichai), exiled to Indo-China in 1935, ignored orders to return. BTWM, Feb. 3 and 20, Mar. 1 and 25, Apr. 21, May 18 and 25, 1939. Accounts of proceedings of Special Tribunal as described by two of accused in *Buangraek Prachatipathai*, pp. 240ff.
102. BTWM, July 11, 1939.
103. ibid., July 18 and 19, 1939; Queen Rambhai in Thak Chaloemtiarana (ed.), p. 19; and F8059/61/40 in FO371/23586.
104. BTWM, Aug. 24 and 25, 1939.
105. Malay press comment in ibid., Aug. 30 and Sep. 5, 1939, and F4792/403/40 in FO371/23593.
106. BTWM, Aug. 19 and Sep. 7, 1939.
107. ibid., Oct. 6, 1939, and Prasert Patamasukhon, p. 305.
108. This was Direk Chaiyanam.
109. Thawee Bunyaket in Ray, p. 84.
110. F9346/1860/40 in FO371/23595.
111. F9468/242/40 in FO371/23590, and BTWM, Aug. 29, 1939.
112. In 1935 the American foreign affairs adviser Raymond Stevens resigned because of Prince Wan's attitude, and his successor Frederick Dolbeare had his role reduced. F1611/296/40 in FO371/19377; Darling, *Thailand and the United States*, pp. 32ff, and FRUS (1939), III, p. 119.
113. Prayoon, p. 345, and F4111/1830/40 in FO371/23594.
114. BTWM, Aug. 24 and 26, 1939.
115. F10059/1860/40 in FO371/23595. Prince Wan thought that the Nomonhan

Incident in August 1939, involving hostilities between Soviet and Japanese troops along the Manchurian border, would lead to a wider war, with Japan attacking the Soviet Union.

116. BTWM, Sep. 6, 12, 21 and 22, 1939.
117. F10320/1860/40 in FO371/23595.
118. BTWM, Sept. 6, 1939.
119. ibid., Sep. 9 and 11, 1939.
120. ibid., Nov. 3, 1939.
121. ibid., Sep. 6, 7 and 9, 1939.
122. ibid., Sep. 5, 1939, and F10466/192/40 in FO371/23587.
123. BTWM, Aug. 28 and 31, 1939.
124. F9925/43/40 in FO371/23586.
125. F10316/1860/40 and file in FO371/23595; Direk Chaiyanam, *Siam and World War II*, p. 14; Decoux, p. 130.
126. F9027/4784/40 in FO371/23597.
127. BTWM, Oct. 10, 17 and 19, Nov. 22 and Dec. 8, 1939, and Landon (1941), p. 153. Another cause of friction was the growing split within the Kuomintang between pro-Chiang Kai-shek and pro-Wang Ching-wei factions. Flood, p. 124.
128. Texts in BTWM, Nov. 20, and Dec. 7, 1939, and Landon (1941), pp. 192ff.
129. BTWM, Oct. 13, 1939, and Prasert Patamasukhon. p. 308.
130. BTWM, Nov. 24 and 29, 1939.
131. ibid., Nov. 30 and Dec. 2, 1939. Pibul later blamed Adul for the executions. Sriphanon Singthong, p. 30, and Coast, p. 11. Anonymous eye-witness account of executions in *Buangraek Prachatipatai*, pp. 284ff.
132. This was Lieut. Nawnen Talalakshana.
133. This was Luang Chamnan Yutthasilp, former commander of Bangkok Military District.
134. This was Luang Sitthi Ruangdetphol.
135. BTWM, Jan. 18, 1940.
136. F12638/43/40 in FO371/23586, and Prayoon, p. 382.
137. BTWM, Apr. 21, June 12 and Sep. 20, 1939.
138. *Bangkok Post*, July 31, 1977.
139. BTWM, Jan. 5, 1940, and Thak Chaloemtiarana (ed.), p. 387.
140. F2802/246/40 in FO371/23592.
141. BTWM, Jan. 12 and Mar. 12, 1940; F1080/123/40 in FO371/24753; report of Feb. 7, 1940, in 892.00/201 in RG59.
142. F710/19/40 and file in FO371/24750, and Direk, p. 15.
143. Flood, pp. 239ff, quoting Nov. 1939 policy report in GKR A6–0–0.
144. Direk, p. 15, quoting conversations of Apr. 11 and 13, 1940.
145. ibid.; Flood, pp. 253ff; F3205/19/40 in FO371/24751.
146. BTWM, Apr. 16, 17 and 22, 1940, and F3286/3286/40 in FO371/24756.
147. F3326/19/40 in FO371/24751.
148. Direk, p. 17, and pp. 271–6. For texts of treaties, BTWM, June 12, 1940.
149. F4723/3286/40 in FO371/24756, and Prayoon, p. 388.
150. Schedule of events, BTWM, June 25, 1940.
151. Text in ibid., June 29, 1940.

Part III
INTERNATIONAL PRESSURES, 1940–1941

8
THE TRIUMPH OF IRREDENTISM

For all his ambition and vanity, Pibul was not blind to the possibility that the rapidly changing international situation might place his achievements in jeopardy. Even when he made his National Day speech in 1940, he was concerned about the capitulation of France to the Germans. Yet characteristically his first reaction was emotional. Recalling his military training at Fontainebleau, Pibul expressed sympathy for the fall of Paris, a gesture acknowledged with gratitude by Saigon Radio.[1]

The French in Indo-China were beginning to feel very isolated and in need of all the sympathy they could get. As the colonial administration hesitated between expressing loyalty to the new collaborationist regime in Vichy or coming out in favour of the Free French under De Gaulle, the Japanese started to apply pressure on Indo-China.

Immediately Prince Wan noted the arrogance with which Japan demanded the closure of the railway between Haiphong and Yunnan to prevent the transit of western supplies to Chiang Kai-shek's forces. Direk was dismayed by French alacrity in complying with the demand.[2] Pibul's attitude was more ambivalent. He knew the defeat of the European colonial powers at the hands of the Germans was viewed in certain quarters in Tokyo as an opportune pretext for asserting the doctrine of Asia for the Asians with the backing of Japanese military might. His friend, the Japanese military attaché in Bangkok had often talked in such terms.[3] At the end of June, this policy appeared to receive high level endorsement. A speech by the Japanese Foreign Minister referred openly to the expansion of the "New Order in East Asia" to encompass the whole of South East Asia.[4]

Pibul was already aware that the Japanese were grooming a pretender to take over the throne in Annam and set up a puppet state along the same lines as in Manchukuo. He also believed that local communists would try to exploit any opportunity to seize power in Indo-China.

Pibul told Crosby he had rejected a demand from them for arms because any such unrest was bound to affect Thailand adversely. In particular he was worried about what might happen in Laos and Cambodia, where his hope was that the French would remain firmly in control.[5] Pibul did not relish the prospect of a Japanese military presence in territory directly bordering on Thailand. His fears were intensified in July. Thousands of refugees were reported to be flooding across the border from Indo-China bringing with them rumours of imminent war. To stem the influx, Pibul quickly ordered reinforcements to be sent to the north-eastern border provinces. At the same time he sought to reassure the public that the country was in no danger because its neutrality had been guaranteed by all the major powers.[6]

Some Thais saw these developments in a different light. Several Bangkok newspapers took pleasure in publishing travellers' tales about the obvious joy of the people of Indo-China at the collapse of the French in Europe.[7] Such reports fostered a widespread belief in Thailand that French rule in Indo-China would soon collapse too, so providing a golden opportunity for the "lost territories" to be regained. Pibul knew he could not afford to ignore such views. Since 1939, Vichit had built up a lot of popular acclaim for his pan-Thai doctrine, which included a strong streak of irredentism; in fact, his plays were temporarily banned in order not to imperil the negotiation of the non-aggression pacts with France and Britain.[8] Now Pibul feared that he would lose support if he let slip the opportunity to avenge what many Thais saw as the humiliations which the French had heaped on Siam in the past. Equally, it dawned on him that his personal prestige would receive an enormous boost if he could succeed in regaining some of the "lost territories". The question was how much of Indo-China Thailand should claim.

Despite Vichit's assertions concerning ethnic kinship, the Kings of Siam had never enjoyed complete sovereignty over all the territory inhabited by the Lao people. Instead they had vied with the Emperors of Annam for suzerainty over several princely fiefdoms, which the French later grouped together to form Laos. Likewise, the Siamese throne had at various periods exercised suzerainty over the Kings of Cambodia and helped them to repel the Annamites. Yet only the three north-western provinces of Cambodia had ever been directly ruled from Bangkok. In his writings, however, Vichit made no distinction between sovereignty and suzerainty. Moreover, it might no longer be a matter of regaining territory from the French. Pibul realised that he would now have to take

Japanese views into account, especially after a new and apparently more militant government assumed power in Tokyo in July 1940.[9]

A couple of days later, Vanich Pananond quietly departed for Tokyo. The purpose of his visit was ostensibly to discuss the export of Thai rice, since he had just been appointed Director of Commerce. On arrival in Tokyo, he also claimed to be a secret envoy sent by Pibul to sound out the views of the new Japanese government regarding South East Asia.[10]

The trip probably came as a personal relief to Vanich, whose moves to place responsibility for Thailand's oil supplies in Japanese hands had gone seriously awry. The affairs of the Fuel Oil Department had been so badly mismanaged that Vanich and several members of his staff were arrested in April 1940. For Pridi it was a pretext to persuade Pibul to agree to negotiations for the return of the Western oil companies to Thailand, but Vanich did not remain in custody for long.[11] Although he was regarded as something of an upstart among the ruling élite in Bangkok, he had an influential connexion in his brother-in-law Sindhu – not that it was of much help to Thailand in obtaining oil.[12] Their friends in Japan were experiencing similar problems. The war in Europe and its possible implications for South East Asia had led the authorities in the Netherlands East Indies to limit Japanese oil purchases. And at the end of July, the United States imposed restrictions on the sale of aviation fuel to Japan.[13]

One factor underlying the American move was the pressure being applied to Indo-China by the Japanese, who were demanding troop transit rights along the railway from Haiphong to Yunnan as well as the establishment of military airfields in Tonkin. Since the French felt too weak to reject these demands outright, they tried to bargain. In negotiations held in Tokyo, they sought in return from Japan a guarantee of French sovereignty over Indo-China. Besides blocking any further Japanese inroads, it would serve as a deterrent to Thai irredentist claims.[14]

For the same reason, the government newly installed in Vichy was anxious to get the non-aggression pact with Thailand ratified as soon as possible. The problem was that before such formalities could take place, the two governments had agreed to adjust the Mekong border according to the findings of a joint Franco-Thai commission. But it could not start work until November at the earliest, when the level of the river fell at the end of the rainy season. What is more, because of wartime difficulties in sending out anybody from Vichy, the French indicated that they would be represented on the commission by their Minister in Bangkok, assisted by officials from Indo-China.[15]

Vichy's attitude aroused the suspicion of Pibul and his advisers. They jumped to the conclusion that France was going back on its previous commitment and trying to wriggle out of the border readjustment. Pibul also argued that Thailand had agreed to conclude a non-aggression pact with France, specifically in order to protect its eastern borders, but now, he claimed, the French through their own weakness were about to allow Japan to station troops in Indo-China, thus threatening Thailand's security. From there Pibul and Prince Wan went on to reason that rather than pressing for ratification of the pact, it would be more appropriate for France to acknowledge that it had damaged Thailand's strategic interests and provide some sort of compensation. For example, Pibul thought that it would be only fair for the French to cede the two provinces of Laos situated on the west bank of the Mekong, so enabling Thailand to use the river as a natural defence line if the Japanese took over the rest of Laos. Prince Wan suggested that the principle be extended to Cambodia as well.[16]

Before reaching any final decision, Pibul received and accepted an invitation to send a Thai goodwill mission to Japan. Sindhu added an extra gloss. In a secret visit to the Japanese legation in Bangkok, he suggested that the delegation going to Tokyo would be happy to discuss military cooperation in the context of Indo-China as long as Thailand's territorial interests were taken into account.[17]

Sindhu's proposal aroused great interest in Tokyo, where a military staff conference on August 7 discussed how to exploit Thai irredentist claims. As a first step, it decided to expand the staff of the military attaché in Bangkok.[18] Three days later, instructions were also sent to the senior Japanese diplomat in Bangkok to put a series of proposals to Pibul in order to strengthen ties between the two countries. First, the Japanese wanted to set up a joint commission to discuss matters of mutual interest. Pibul unexpectedly replied that since 1932 Thailand had suffered from a lack of competent diplomats and that apart from himself, he could name only Sindhu, Prayoon, Vanich and Direk. Nor did he give any direct response to Japan's other proposals. He said he was interested in concluding a cultural agreement, strengthening economic links and according recognition to the government in Manchukuo, as well as that just installed by Japan in Nanking under Wang Ching-wei to counter Chiang Kai-shek. Only first, Pibul indicated that he would have to consider the impact of all these developments on the Chinese community in Thailand.[19]

Underlying his obvious equivocation was Pibul's uncertainty about

Field-Marshal Luang Pibul Songkram

how the international situation was going to develop. Consequently, he proposed that *en route* to Tokyo the Thai goodwill mission should visit Indo-China to ascertain at first hand the attitude of French colonial officials. Pibul also announced that Sindhu would soon head another goodwill mission to investigate the situation in "the new Europe" – apparently meaning German-occupied Europe, which Hitler had boasted would extend to London by the end of August.[20] Crosby immediately insisted that Sindhu must visit Britain as well to prove that Thailand was still remaining neutral in the war.[21]

Amid all this manoeuvring, Pibul clearly wanted to find out what the major powers thought about Indo-China. He told Direk to ask the Germans and Italians how they would view a move by Thailand to recover its lost territory, including the whole of Cambodia. As Pibul had expected, the immediate response of diplomats representing the two Axis powers in Bangkok was encouraging. He believed that the Germans and Italians would be happy to support any move contributing to the collapse of the French and British colonial empires in Asia.[22] Nonetheless, he still wanted to preserve the appearance of Thai neutrality, and instructed Direk to sound out the views of the Americans and British as well.

For his pains, Direk received a lecture from the American Minister, Howard Grant, about the unwisdom of Thailand disturbing the *status quo* in Indo-China.[23] The British response was more diplomatic: Crosby tended to sympathise with Pibul's desire to secure the Mekong as Thailand's natural line of defence. Moreover, Crosby said that if French rule in Indo-China collapsed, he would prefer to see Thailand take over those territories to which it had a valid claim than letting them fall into the hands of the Japanese. But, he told Direk, the French were doing their best in the circumstances to resist Japanese pressure, and Thailand should avoid undermining these efforts. In other words, Thailand should only reclaim its "lost territories" if and when the French bowed out of Indo-China. Even then, Crosby warned against regaining any territory with Japanese help because they were likely to take advantage of the situation to make Thailand a vassal state similar to Manchukuo within the context of their "New Order" in East Asia.[24]

Direk's activities angered the Japanese, who considered themselves to be the natural leaders in East Asia, and resented not being formally consulted before Thailand started to moot its claims on Indo-China. In particular, they chided Direk for consulting the Americans and British about Indo-China, "a country which is no concern of theirs".[25] Direk was hurt since he had been expressly forbidden from making such a démarche to the Japanese. Pibul said they were to be dealt with through separate channels, meaning presumably himself and the mission soon going to Tokyo.[26]

The French were even more annoyed. It looked to them as if Japan was talking in Tokyo about guaranteeing the sovereignty of Indo-China, while secretly egging on the Thais to press their territorial claims.[27] At the same time, Direk protested about French planes violating Thai airspace on flights from Saigon to Vientiane.[28]

French rule in Indo-China was clearly not collapsing as quickly as many Thais originally thought; nor was the war in Europe proceeding as Pibul expected. Since the British were still showing no signs of capitulating to the Germans, he had second thoughts about the missions he was sending abroad. Sindhu did not depart for Germany, and Pibul accepted an invitation for another goodwill mission headed by Thamrong to visit various British dominions in Asia and Australasia.[29]

In the public eye, Thamrong still enjoyed respect as Minister of Justice. But he also played an important role in a secret committee set up to orchestrate popular support for the return of the ''lost territories''. Despite the care with which the government tried to conceal its hand, the British at least were well aware that the growing wave of irredentist demands in the press and the Assembly was not as spontaneous as it seemed on the surface. On August 21 Crosby received an assurance from Pibul that irredentist activity would not be allowed to extend to those territories Thailand had ''lost'' to the British.[30]

To ensure that Pibul did not change his mind, Crosby stepped up British efforts to retain Thailand's friendship. The ratification of their non-aggression pact was rushed through parliament in London so that documents could be exchanged in Bangkok before either France or, more important, Japan completed these formalities. Churchill, too, spared a moment amid the grim struggle for the defence of Britain to stress, in a personal message addressed to Pibul, the value of Anglo-Thai relations. It also expressed confidence in Pibul's leadership and ability to maintain Thailand as ''a bulwark of peace'' in South East Asia.[31]

At the same time the British urged the Americans to show more interest in Thailand, where they had the means to exert some influence. Despite the pro-Japanese manoeuvring of Vanich, Thailand was now having to purchase oil direct from the United States. Pridi was also hoping to raise a loan on the American market to finance Thai economic development. Once he realised this, Pibul decided that Khuang, who was already in America on Post Office business, should have his trip elevated to the status of a goodwill mission so that he could pay official calls in Washington.[32]

Of all the Thai missions travelling abroad, that going to Tokyo was clearly the most crucial. Even so – as Pibul pointed out to Crosby – it was headed by Colonel Luang Prom Yothi, the deputy Minister of Defence, rather than by Sindhu or anybody else regarded as pro-Japanese. The choice was welcomed by the more democratic elements in the government. True, Prom Yothi had graduated from military academy in the same class as Pibul and Adul, which explained why he was a junior military promoter enjoying ministerial preferment, and why he had presided over the Special Tribunal set up in 1939 to deal with Pibul's opponents. However, in other respects Prom Yothi was different from the rabid nationalists and militarists with whom Pibul normally associated. For instance, he had protested openly about an unsubtle attempt by the pro-Japanese faction to bring pressure to bear on him.[33] The incident created such a stir that Pibul became suspicious. Remembering that Prom Yothi had spent longer than himself in Europe at military staff college, he surmised that his hitherto trusted lieutenant was trying to build up a pro-Western faction to seize power. Hence he suggested to the Japanese that Prom Yothi's visit to Tokyo would provide a useful opportunity to wean him away from his European bias.[34]

First, however, Prom Yothi and his mission toured Indo-China. The timing could scarcely have been more unfortunate. They arrived in Hanoi on September 4 when the French were involved in desperate negotiations with Japanese military envoys to try to stop them moving troops into Tonkin in force.[35] Pre-occupied by these developments, Admiral Decoux, the Governor-General of Indo-China newly appointed by the collaborationist Vichy government, had little time to spare for Prom Yothi. In any case Decoux had long harboured a deep mistrust of all Thais and was convinced that they were acting in collusion with the Japanese – an impression which Prom Yothi's visit did nothing to dispel. Although he spoke fluent French and gave other indications of his Western military training, Decoux considered it "a superficial varnish fabricated to mask his devious oriental nature". Consequently he did not take Prom Yothi seriously when he stated that Thailand would cooperate with France in opposing Japan if only the two Lao provinces on the west bank of the Mekong were restored to Thai sovereignty. Possibly, in proposing the deal, Prom Yothi was acting on his own initiative without the approval of Pibul, but in any case Decoux temporised by replying that Vichy would first have to be consulted.[36]

The French Foreign Ministry was far more interested in an agreement concluded in Toyko on August 30 whereby Japan guaranteed to respect the sovereignty of Indo-China. The hope in Vichy was that the Japanese would restrain Thai irredentist claims as well. On the strength of this premise, Paul Lepissier, the French Minister in Bangkok, was instructed to apply pressure on the Thais by demanding the entry into force without further ado of the non-aggression pact between the two countries.[37] The proposal simply reinforced Pibul's suspicions that France was trying to go back on its previous commitment to readjust the Mekong frontier. He reacted by summoning Lepissier to set out Thailand's counter-demands for the first time in full. Before the non-aggression pact could be ratified, not only would the French have to redelineate the border along the Mekong, but they would also have to cede to Thailand the province of Sayaburi in northern Laos opposite Luang Prabang as well as the Bassac or Champassac region of southern Laos where it borders on Cambodia. Pibul further demanded a written guarantee from France that in the event of its military defeat or voluntary withdrawal from Indo-China, the whole of Laos and Cambodia would revert to Thailand so that it could re-establish its ''natural'' border along the Annamite chain of mountains. In return, Thailand would undertake to protect any French nationals who wished to continue to reside or work in the retroceded territories.[38]

This last concession was small comfort to Lepissier, who knew that no French government, irrespective of its political complexion, would countenance such demands. As for the Vichy regime, its Foreign Minister was Paul Baudouin, a former director of the Banque de l'Indo-Chine with large personal property interests in Cambodia. Realising full well what his attitude would be, Lepissier refused to pass on Pibul's demands, and they had to be conveyed through the Thai Minister in France. The poor man got such a rough reception that he had to be physically assisted out of Baudouin's office.[39]

Before Pibul received word from Vichy that his demands had been rejected, he held a press conference to tell the public about them; he had no other option, because during the previous few weeks, pressure had been mounting in the Assembly and the press for the return of the lost territories.[40] More important for Pibul personally was growing speculation about a plot to oust him. Some military officers were said to be dissatisfied with his lack of action over Indo-China; they had no apparent leader, but it was thought that they might turn to Sindhu to head a new government.[41] To counter any such move, Pibul stressed that he was doing his utmost to satisfy what he called Thailand's "just aspirations", but not through the use of force; he said that the country could not go to war because it lacked certain vital supplies including oil.[42] Indeed with the return of Vanich to Bangkok, it was clear that the negotiations with the Western oil companies were getting nowhere and legislation to impose petrol rationing was under discussion.

Such considerations were ignored by the irredentists, or rather the press, which was always looking for a good story to exploit especially after all the constraints to which it had been subject. Seizing on the fact that Pibul had at last acknowledged Thai demands as just, one Bangkok newspaper, which came to be regarded as the main mouthpiece of the irredentist lobby, pictured Thailand as having its territory snatched away just as a poor man might lose a beautiful wife. Now, it commented, Thailand was powerful and it was high time the French realised it.[43] As a result, many people believed, despite official denials, that Thai troops had already moved into Indo-China. Sixty members of the Assembly pledged to go to the front-line to fight, and Pibul won a massive vote of approval for the demands he had put to the French.[44]

The support was useful to Pibul in another context. He wanted to amend the constitution, a move long and vehemently opposed by active politicians from the north-east like Thong-in Buripat and Liang Chaiyakal,[45] but now they were at the forefront of the irredentist campaign, they changed their minds and expressed appreciation for Pibul's policy on Indo-China. With a lot of money also allegedly changing hands behind the scenes, the Assembly voted with the requisite two-thirds majority on September 20 to extend the ten-year transitional period provided for in the constitution before the phasing-out of its nominated members. In effect Pibul had ensured that his power would not be challenged by the democratic process for many years to come.[46]

Once he had gained his objective, Pibul adjourned the Assembly with an appeal to its members, as well as to the public, for calm and patience. He said that his government was continuing to work and hope for a negotiated settlement with the French.[47] Yet at the same time military reservists were called up, and fifty air force planes were sent to the north-east, the first time Thailand had openly admitted breaching its treaty commitments with France to maintain a demilitarised zone along the border.[48]

The immediate cause of these Thai military moves was an agreement concluded in Tokyo on September 22 allowing Japan to use three airfields in Tonkin as well as the railway from Haiphong to Yunnan. Simultaneously Japanese forces in southern China launched an attack across the border against the French garrison in Lang Son. The incident was soon resolved, but from the perspective of Bangkok it looked as if the French had been well and truly beaten and the Japanese were about to move into Indo-China in strength.[49] Then on September 27 an alliance was concluded between Germany, Italy, and Japan with the apparent intention of carving up the world between them; in other words, it seemed as if Japan had been allocated responsibility for the whole of East Asia.[50]

All these developments had a major impact on Pibul. The day after the conclusion of the Triple Alliance, he told Vanich to convey a secret message to his friend the Japanese naval attaché in Bangkok. This amounted to an offer of Thai cooperation with Japan's aims in East Asia. The naval attaché could not believe his ears, and asked for confirmation from the prime minister in person, which was provided three days later. Pibul told the naval attaché that he would allow Japanese troops transit through Thai territory and provide them with supplies if necessary. Japan could also purchase all the raw materials it needed from Thailand. There was only one condition: Pibul said that Japan would first have to guarantee to help Thailand regain its lost territories from Indo-China.[51]

Pibul's secret approach took the Japanese by surprise. They had never envisaged that he would so easily abandon the tradition of Thai neutrality. Nor had they yet formulated a policy towards Thai territorial claims on Indo-China. They had been waiting to hear what Prom Yothi and his mission had to say on the subject, but his visit now seemed irrelevant. The impression was reinforced by Pibul, who declined to grant Prom Yothi credentials to carry out any substantive negotiations during his three-week stay in Japan.[52] Even so, a Thai Deputy Defence Minister could not be completely ignored, and a programme of official calls was arranged for Prom Yothi, much to the embarrassment of the new Japanese Foreign Minister Matsuoka Yosuke.

News of Pibul's secret pledge was sent to Tokyo through restricted military channels, but Matsuoka was given some idea of what was in the wind. He now had the task of reconciling any Japanese support for Thai claims with the guarantee he had just given to respect French sovereignty over the whole of Indo-China. In this situation, Matsuoka was under pressure from a group of hot-headed military staff officers. They argued in favour of giving the Thais all the territory they wanted because in return Japan would be able to take full advantage of Pibul's secret pledge by using Thailand to mount an attack on Singapore and the Netherlands East Indies.[53]

Anyway, Pibul now appeared to take Japanese support for granted, and told the British and Americans that if Vichy did not cede the west bank enclaves soon, he would resort to force.[54] That also seemed implicit in the way the planes sent to the north-east were being deployed. According to reports in the international press, some of them penetrated up to 100 km. into Lao airspace to carry out reconnaissance and drop leaflets containing Thai propaganda.[55] On the ground, too, an anti-French campaign was being whipped up by Vichit; he toured the Mekong frontier provinces, where he had no problem in gaining support for his thesis that the Thai and Lao people were brethren. In many families it was literally true, since they spanned the Mekong and had good reason to regard it as an arbitrary border imposed by France.

Towards the end of September, an incident occurred which heightened these feelings and provided Vichit with a useful rallying cry. A Thai trader visiting Vientiane was shot dead, and overnight he became a martyr of French brutality. Even though the authorities in Indo-China tendered their apologies and proposed a joint enquiry, rallies were organised by Vichit in north-eastern Thailand to demand revenge for the murdered man.[56] Similar demands were voiced in Bangkok by a group, newly established with covert official blessing, calling itself Thai Blood.[57]

Already the government had one very useful mass organisation at its command. Under the leadership of Prayoon, the Yuvachon had grown to become a considerable force, and there were estimated to be 10,000 people present when it held its annual parade in Bangkok on October 5. Prayoon used the occasion to stress the justice of Thailand's demands for its lost territories and urge the Yuvachon to join in the struggle. He also echoed Vichit's thesis regarding the kinship between the Thai, Lao and Khmer people. His audience responded by chanting songs on this and other patriotic themes which were rapidly becoming popular throughout Thailand as well as Laos.[58] Most of these songs were composed by Vichit, who had at his disposal the machinery of the Department of Fine Arts to ensure their publication and distribution. The process was helped by Prayoon who, besides heading the Yuvachon, had been appointed deputy Minister of Education under Sindhu. As such he had virtually a free hand in dictating what went into the school curriculum. Consequently, whereas Vichit attracted the reputation of being the Goebbels of Thailand, Prayoon appeared to be emulating the head of the

Hitler Youth, although for some obscure reason he was dubbed Thailand's Goering.[59]

As irredentist agitation quickly spread through the schools and colleges of Bangkok, Pridi intervened: he was appalled by what he saw as short-sighted opportunism imbuing the attitude of Pibul and his associates towards Indo-China and the international situation as a whole. Hence he tried to stop the students of his own creation, the University of Moral and Political Sciences, from joining in demonstrations which suddenly became a feature of life in Bangkok. It seemed that everybody from schoolchildren to transport workers was on the march to demand the return of the lost territories. Pridi said that they were only increasing bitterness and making the French more intransigent in rejecting Thai demands. Such was his influence that his views were respected, at least for a couple of days; after that, restraint became impossible. The students of Pridi's university had developed a keen sense of rivalry with those at Chulalongkorn, where Pibul was rector; hence when students from Chulalongkorn University embarked on a demonstration, Pridi's disciples felt compelled to outshine them.[60]

The main destination of all these marches was the Ministry of Defence where Pibul appeared personally to greet them and express gratitude for these gestures of support for his government and its policies. Such manifestations were completely unprecedented in Thailand, and after a few days even Pibul apparently had second thoughts about what they might lead to. He ceased his public appearances, and a virtually unknown deputy army commander took over the task of saluting the marchers.[61] A government spokesman explained that Pibul still valued the marches, but he had many other matters to attend to. In any case, the spokesman added, there had been some misunderstanding of photos showing Pibul greeting the marches; he had not been giving a fascist salute in emulation of Hitler or Mussolini, but had merely raised his hand in acknowledgement. Nevertheless when Pibul next emerged to greet a public demonstration, he was pictured with his wife, and both were waving handkerchiefs.[62]

No similar caution was apparent in the Bangkok press. Ignoring the implications of the Thai military build-up along the Mekong, some newspapers noted with a sense of outrage French counter-measures such as the digging of trenches and the installation of anti-aircraft guns around townships on the Lao bank of the river. The press clamoured that Thailand should stop talking to the French and start fighting instead.[63] These demands were boosted by scare stories of an imminent invasion from southern Laos by Prince Bovoradet, portrayed as a bogey-man leading a specially recruited division of Annamites bent on over-throwing the government in Bangkok.[64] Other comments claimed that the Annamites were no good as soldiers and that the Thais were far braver.[65]

In fact, with few trained troops at their disposal the military authori-ties in Indo-China knew they could not hope to defend the long border with Thailand as well as that with China where the Japanese still threatened. Facing up to this dilemma, Decoux decided that the Thais were the main threat and ordered the majority of the troops the French could rely on to the western border. One of the main objectives of the redeployment was to reinforce the province of Battambang in western Cambodia: as one of the major rice-producing areas of Indo-China, it was considered vital to the economy of the colony, cut off as it now was from metropolitan France.

Another serious effect of Indo-China's isolation was that it no longer had a ready source of arms or reinforcements. To the anger of Decoux, the British blocked his attempts to obtain the transfer of French colonial troops from Djibouti. Likewise the Americans hesitated to agree to the departure of over 100 French military aircraft based on the island of Martinique in the Caribbean; the fear was that once these military assets were released to the French, they would be deployed not in Indo-China but rather in Europe to help the Germans.[66]

The United States was similarly concerned about Thailand disturbing the stability of South East Asia. After Pibul began to press Thai claims on Indo-China in earnest, the Americans ordered the offloading in Manila of ten fighter planes being shipped to Bangkok. They were worried the planes would be deployed against the French. The gesture was small comfort to the administration in Indo-China, but it caused great resentment in Thailand, not only among the military. The planes had already been paid for in dollars, so they were legally Thai property. Moreover, with the war in Europe ruling out any alternative sources of military equipment, moderates such as Direk thought that American sanctions would simply make Thailand more dependent on Japan.[67] What neither Direk nor most other cabinet ministers knew was how far Pibul had secretly gone in that direction already.

At that juncture, Pibul himself appears to have had doubts about his secret pledge to Japan. He quietly despatched one of his military con-fidants[68] to Singapore to sound out the situation there. Meanwhile, with a similar purpose in mind, Prayoon set off again to Europe in place of

Sindhu, who claimed that he was too busy to go. Perhaps Sindhu was also swayed by the rumours about Pibul's shaky position.

Anyway, communications with German-occupied Europe were not easy. Prayoon had to travel by a circuitous route through Iraq, and one of his tasks was to find a way of repatriating Thai students who had been caught up in the war in Europe. Above all, Pibul was concerned about his son Ananta, who had been studying in Belgium, and his daughter in Paris; both had fled before the German advance and become stranded in Portugal. By contrast, Pibul's other son Prasong was so absorbed in his naval training in Britain that he refused to return home, as his parents demanded.[69]

To add to Pibul's worries, the Japanese were pressing him for a written guarantee of the secret pledge he had only given them verbally. He attempted to get round the problem by claiming that the matter would first have to be discussed in the cabinet and hence was bound to be leaked to the British.[70] In mid-October pro-British sentiment in Bangkok was on the upswing. Apart from the impact of news about Britain's victory in its battle against the German air force, opinion in Bangkok was swayed by the publicity emanating from Thamrong's tour as he progressed from Burma to India and thence to Australia amid an aura of great honour and hospitality deliberately laid on by the British to flatter Thailand.[71]

On the other hand, the reputation of the Americans plummeted in Thai eyes following the cancellation of the aircraft delivery. The decision also dashed virtually all Pridi's hopes of raising a financial loan in the United States, a serious blow at a time of rapidly growing military expenditure. The problem dawned on Pibul as well. He tried to use economic arguments to go back on his pledge to the Japanese. As for Pridi, he armed himself with statistics about the damage the irredentist campaign was doing to the Thai economy and prepared to go into battle in the cabinet. Direk for one was ready to support him, and Pridi appeared to be making progress with other ministers when Vichit returned to Bangkok and Pibul decided to make a major broadcast on October 20.[72]

The first part of Pibul's hour-long speech contained a detailed explanation of the negotiations with France right up to Vichy's latest rejection of Thai demands on October 5. Following that, Pibul said there was no point in talking to the French any more. Thai demands were just, and the Thai people had never been so unanimous in support of their government. Military plans had already been drawn up, but

Pibul stressed that only troops would be deployed at the front line. Turning then to those he called his brethren in Laos and Cambodia, Pibul claimed that although they were all of the same race, colour, culture and religion as the Thais, they were oppressed by the French whereas the Thais had a constitution and enjoyed freedom of speech. But after a tirade of invective directed personally at Decoux, Pibul abruptly changed his tone. He said that the use of force was not always essential and in any case brought a lot of problems in its wake. Thailand had many other ways of achieving its aims since France would not rule Indo-China much longer. In conclusion, Pibul commented that the many demonstrations in support of Thai demands were useful as a warning to the French, but nobody should become disorderly because Thailand was a civilised country.[73]

To many people who heard or read this speech, it was obvious that large portions of it had been drafted by Vichit. His style was well known. Yet the speech as a whole was typical of Pibul. He had long shown a tendency to flatter his audience without committing himself irretrievably to any specific course. This accounted for the manifest contradiction between his military threats against the French and his rejection of the use of force to achieve Thailand's ends. In the circumstances, Pridi and Direk thought it a good speech which might help calm the atmosphere.[74]

On the other hand, Pibul's vituperation against the French was seen by Grant, the American Minister, as a deliberate incitement to violence. He condemned the speech as the most dangerous sort of demagogy. Anyway he was convinced that Thailand (and Pibul in particular) was dominated by a powerful military clique linked to Japan. Such views prompted thoughts in Washington of evacuating American wives and children from Thailand. Pridi was even more concerned that the United States might decide to freeze all Thailand's financial assets held in New York.[75]

Such matters did not bother the irredentists. Thai Blood immediately organised a mass rally to express support for Pibul's speech.[76] The marches too looked set to continue as stevedores, *samlor*-drivers and various other groups of workers followed the example of the students. Everybody, it seemed, was only too happy to be caught up in a wave of popular enthusiasm which was totally without precedent. Nor were the demonstrations restricted to Bangkok. Government officials travelled up-country to organise mass meetings in rural areas.[77] The extent to which the whole campaign was officially orchestrated became apparent at the end of October. Suddenly there were no more public demonstrations in Bangkok; the government evidently feared that the situation was getting out of control and decided to call a halt.[78] Anyway it had proved its point. The prospect of regaining the 'lost territories' from Indo-China had produced a real surge of national pride. Contributions flowed in to finance the anti-French campaign and by early November, nearly 70,000 men had volunteered for military service.[79]

Mixed with all this patriotism was a growing note of xenophobia. Reports in the Bangkok press alleged that French repression of the population in Indo-China included the persecution of Buddhists, with their temples being desecrated. Another recurrent claim was that Moroccan and Senegalese colonial troops assigned by the French to patrol the border provinces were raping and killing local women. Taking their cue from Pibul's speech, some newspapers also harped on the theme that French rule in Indo-China was about to end. In late October the Thai press claimed the Annamites were in rebellion, Phnom Penh had been liberated and Decoux had resigned in despair.[80] On the other hand, one of Bangkok's English-language newspapers was scathingly criticised when it published reports of demonstrations in Phnom Penh in support of the King of Cambodia and against Vichit's assertion of racial affinity between the Thai and Khmer. According to the Thai press, no such demonstrations had taken place, and *farangs* fabricating such reports were warned to take more care in future or suffer the consequences.[81]

The tone of the Bangkok press led the French to lodge an official protest. The Thais countered with another protest about the alleged infringement of their airspace by French planes. Beyond that, all other diplomatic contacts between the two countries came to a halt, and it looked as if an outbreak of hostilities was imminent.[82] Thai reinforcements were said to be moving up to Aranya Prathet, the main border crossing-point into Cambodia, where fighting had already started. But these reports were officially denied.[83]

Despite what the irredentists may have believed or hoped, Thailand was still ill-prepared to go to war.[84] Pibul's policy of using the army for his own political purposes had left the soldiers and militia in the provinces poorly trained with few arms at their disposal, a fact appreciated by the Japanese. In late October their naval attaché in Bangkok reported that the Thais would be at a distinct disadvantage in any armed confrontation with the French. He therefore recommended that urgent steps be taken to supply Thailand with various military equipment.[85]

Before anything came of the proposal, Pridi too had perforce to pay attention to the country's military needs when drawing up the annual budget. In a short and dejected speech, he said that rising military costs had forced up national expenditure by over one-third. If it could not be covered by an internal or external loan, taxes would have to go up. Pridi's warning met with little sympathy in the Assembly. Most members were in favour of increased defence expendiure, but were equally anxious to avoid the burden of paying for it. Rather, they advocated cuts elsewhere in the budget, some of them involving projects such as the construction of prestigious new office buildings by which Pibul set great store. The distribution of official medals was also decried as a waste of money.[86] In September the Council of Regents had bestowed decorations on more than 8,000 people.[87] Everybody believed that in making these awards the regents were simply acting on Pibul's behalf in trying to curry favour in as many quarters as possible, albeit apparently to little avail.

By November Pibul's position once more looked tenuous. The irredentist lobby wanted the government to declare war immediately because, it claimed, the French would otherwise collapse before the Thais had a chance to show their mettle in defeating them. This militant attitude was fanned by the Department of Fine Arts, which took over all radio broadcasts for one evening to voice public criticism of the government and its leader who were apparently afraid to use force.[88]

Privately Pibul was now hoping that Japan would come to his rescue by occupying Indo-China and allowing Thailand to reclaim its territory without having to use force.[89] The Japanese had other ideas. Having obtained more or less all they wanted from the French for the time being, they were content to let Indo-China rest while trying to come to terms with Thailand. On November 5, the inner cabinet meeting in Tokyo decided that Japan would give favourable consideration to Thai claims to the two west-bank provinces of Laos, provided that Pibul first agreed to cooperate fully in the "New Order in East Asia".[90] In other words, Thailand would have to recognise Manchukuo, participate in "cooperation conferences" and enter into various barter trade deals. As a pre-condition, the Japanese envisaged a "reform of the Thai government", meaning a purge of pro-Western elements. All these terms would have to be agreed on paper, and Pibul raised no objection when the Japanese suggested that Sindhu make a secret visit to Tokyo for the purpose. But at the last moment, just before Sindhu was due to depart, his trip was suddenly cancelled for reasons unknown to the Japanese.[91]

Prayoon meanwhile had arrived in Europe. From there he sent back encouraging reports about German and Italian support for Thai claims,[92] but it was a case of wishful thinking if not deceit. When Prayoon asked the German Foreign Minister, Ribbentrop, to bring pressure to bear on the Vichy government, he was told that Hitler wanted peace in the French colonial empire. Any Thai territorial aspirations could be satisfied later at the expense of the British, once they had been defeated and expelled from Asia.[93]

Ribbentrop's advice was of little help in coping with the strident demands of the irredentists. In one effort to placate them, Pibul announced the establishment of a new military Supreme Command with himself at its head. In addition, two special regional commands were set up in the eastern border provinces directly confronting Laos and Cambodia.[94] Yet Pibul still seemed to be hopeful of avoiding the necessity of going to war against the French. Such hopes were sustained by Prince Wan. Besides his official duties, he wrote a daily column under the thinly-disguised pen-name of Waiwan in the newspaper nominally owned by his wife.

One of Waiwan's recurrent themes was the imminent collapse of French rule in Indo-China.[95] But the nationwide rebellion predicted by the government's Propaganda Bureau did not materialise.[96] Instead a localised communist uprising, which erupted in the Mekong delta area of Cochin-China in late November, was quickly and brutally suppressed by the French. They also suspected that the Thais and, behind them, the Japanese were involved. During the uprising, communication lines within Indo-China were sabotaged and troops had to be withdrawn from the border regions to deal with the situation.[97] The Thai government's anticipation of the revolt was similarly taken into account.

Prince Wan became visibly annoyed when his articles came to be regarded as a useful barometer of Thai official thinking. He wanted to be seen as a suave diplomat.[98] Yet in mid-November when the Japanese press reported that Thailand had succumbed to Western pressure and signed secret defence pacts with Britain and the United States, he proved the point. Vehemently, both as journalist and government official, Prince Wan denied the existence of any such pacts.[99]

Similar denials were issued in Washington and London but beyond that these Japanese allegations baffled the Western powers. True they had given some thought to applying economic sanctions if Thailand attacked Indo-China, but no decision had been reached because, apart from anything else, Crosby and Grant were at loggerheads with one another in their attitude towards Pibul.[100]

Apparently unaware of these arguments, the Japanese had, it seems, been casting around for a reason to explain the cancellation of Sindhu's visit to Tokyo. One suspect was Prom Yothi. The Japanese believed he was so disillusioned by his visit to Tokyo that on his return he had set about poisoning the atmosphere both in the cabinet and the military hierarchy by encouraging pro-Western sentiment.[101] Pibul seems to have harboured similar suspicions. He appointed Prom Yothi head of the new military command confronting Cambodia, so distancing him from political intrigue in Bangkok.

In any case the Japanese were determined not to let the situation in Thailand slip any further out of their control. At another meeting of the inner cabinet held in Tokyo on November 20, the Foreign Minister Matsuoka urged that Japan should step in to prevent any more British and American meddling in the affairs of Thailand and Indo-China by offering to mediate in the dispute: he argued that it would provide an opportunity to moderate Thai demands on Indo-China while allowing Japan to gain its own ends in the region.[102]

As soon as this policy was adopted, Matsuoka asked the Germans to persuade Vichy to accept Japan's mediation offer. He added that as a gesture of solidarity with the French and a warning to the Thais, Japanese warships were being despatched to Saigon.[103] At the same time, Pibul was told that unless he accepted Japan's mediation and all its other demands, the weight of opinion in Tokyo would swing in favour of France even to the point of granting military aid to Indo-China. Pibul immediately agreed to Japan's mediation. The French took their time in considering the offer.[104]

Meanwhile, tension was rising along the border. According to the Japanese press, the French were massing troops for an invasion across the Mekong. In Hanoi Decoux claimed that the Thais were responsible for the tension. The governments in both Bangkok and Vichy continued to insist that they had no intention of going to war,[105] but on November 27 there were widespread reports in the international press as well as Japan about Thai troops launching an attack across the border into Cambodia and being repulsed.[106] By contrast the Supreme Command in Bangkok claimed the incident was started by the French.[107] The next day the Supreme Command announced more dramatically that French planes had made an unprovoked attack on Nakorn Panom, a town on the Thai bank of the Mekong, where two bombs were dropped injuring six people.[108]

Pibul immediately sprang into action. As Supreme Commander he ordered instant reprisal raids on French military installations in Laos, the call-up of all army reservists and the departure within forty-eight hours of French nationals living in north-east Thailand. A total ban was placed on any more French citizens taking up residence or even passing through Thailand. Censorship was imposed on all news reports being despatched abroad, and telegrams in code were completely forbidden. Naturally, too, Pibul broadcast to the nation and to those he called his brethren across the Mekong. With pride he proclaimed that the Thai air force had already bombed Tha Khek and Savannakhet in Laos, and warned the population there to keep well away from French military installations because there would be further raids every time the French attacked Thailand. To make sure that everybody was aware of these momentous events, Pibul asked all those with radio sets to turn them on full blast so that the whole population could hear the news.[109]

This was just what the irredentists had been waiting for. Thai Blood convoked a mass meeting to voice wholehearted support for the retaliatory raids on the French. The mood of patriotic fervour was unmistakable. When a *farang*, albeit not a Frenchman, tried to take photos of the rally, he was mobbed and almost lynched.[110] The Government Propaganda Bureau had already warned that it was difficult to distinguish the French from other *farangs*, and advised patriots to take care. Many foreign residents of Bangkok were grateful. Thai Blood was calling for a boycott of all French nationals and merchandise. Another group of self-styled patriots vowed to inflict facial knife wounds on anybody violating the boycott.[111] The virulence underlying such calls was partly attributable to Vichit, who alleged that the French had set up a secret society in Bangkok to murder all those campaigning for the return of the lost territories, with himself at the head of its death list.[112]

The brunt of the anti-French campaign was directed at the Roman Catholic Church. The bishop of the diocese of Thailand was French and although he publicly appealed to Vichy to accede to Thai demands, he was subjected to personal attacks in the Bangkok press and a boycott by his Thai parishioners; despite their small numbers, they succeeded in closing at least one church.[113] Few Thais had ever converted to Catholicism and its adherents in Bangkok were mostly Annamese. They suffered too from being suspected as fifth columnists acting on behalf of the French although irredentist propaganda claimed the Annamese were bound to side with Thailand in opposing France.[114] However, logic was not one of the strong points of the irredentist campaign.

The most virulent organ of anti-French propaganda was the government-controlled radio. Its broadcasts in Lao and Khmer as well as

Thai were couched in a style aimed at rousing a mass popular audience. The chairman of the National Broadcasting Committee was Vichit, but most radio programmes were compiled by the Government Propaganda Bureau. Its staff was expanded to include several young European-educated diplomats able to analyse foreign reports and counter them when this was deemed necessary.[115] The most popular and effective instrument of Thai radio propaganda during this period was a series of dialogues between two characters calling themselves *Nai Man* and *Nai Kong* – Mr Steady and Mr Strong. With one acting the simple peasant and the other the informed official, they explained government policy to the public. They also took great delight in trading insults with a Thai-language broadcaster on Radio Saigon, whom they dubbed Mr Kerosene because of his supposedly oily manner.[116] Similarly, the broadcasts of Mr Kerosene were used by Waiwan in his press comment as a pretext to attack French policy.[117]

Along the border itself, hostilities at first comprised mainly bombing raids. In this type of warfare, neither side was in a position to inflict much damage on the other.[118] The Thai air force was equipped mainly with light fighter planes which could only carry a couple of bombs and operate in daylight. Even the arrival of thirteen Japanese-built bombers at the end of November and another consignment a month later made little difference initially. Thai aircrew had to be retrained to use them, and the French suspected that the first raids carried out by these newly-delivered planes were piloted by Japanese.[119]

The French were far worse off. Unable to obtain planes from America or, for that matter, Japan, they had only a handful of old bombers, which because of their slowness could only be deployed safely at night.[120] Even so, they inflicted some damage on Thai military garrison towns in the north-east and had the range to bomb Bangkok, a threat often made by the French. Yet the city was ablaze with illuminations for the national holiday marking the advent of the constitution on December 10 when – in the midst of what many people, Thai and *farang* alike, considered a grave crisis – ministers abandoned their desks for three days. Perhaps they were still hoping that France would accept Japan's mediation offer. In any event there was a corresponding lull in hostilities along the border, but they soon resumed and intensified after the Thai holiday.[121]

In comparison with the fighting then taking place in the Mediterranean area, the international press tended to regard the Franco-Thai clashes as a war in miniature. The impression was reinforced by the Thai

Supreme Command announcing the defeat of a significant French incursion – comprising twenty-five men mounted on three horses, two elephants and a bicycle. Nonetheless, it was internationally recognised that there was a danger of the conflict being exploited by Japan.[122]

Certainly that was the French view. In mid-December, Decoux rejected Japan's offer to mediate because he wanted direct negotiations with the Thais.[123] The suggestion was ignored in Bangkok, where war fever was running high as the air force stepped up its raids and expanded them to include for the first time targets in Cambodia. King Sisowath Moniwong reacted angrily and urged the Cambodians to help the French.[124] Decoux was more concerned about international support. Since the Americans had declined to provide any assistance to Indo-China, that left the British. Even though relations between London and the regime in Vichy had been severed, Decoux still had many old friends among British officers based in Singapore, and decided to send his aide-de-camp there on a secret mission.[125]

In Tokyo it had been feared that something like this might happen. As soon as France rejected Japan's offer of mediation, a group of junior army staff officers condemned Matsuoka's policy as ''soft''. Instead they and their naval counterparts pressed for an immediate takeover of the whole of Indo-China and Thailand. The idea was opposed by the War Minister, General Tojo Hideki, who argued that such a move would provoke a war against Britain and the United States for which Japan was not yet prepared.[126] He was supported by Matsuoka, and for the time being the junior staff officers in Tokyo had to console themselves with the thought that the balance of power on the ground between Thailand and Indo-China was changing rapidly with the secret supply to Bangkok of four shiploads of military equipment. Much of it comprised tanks and anti-aircraft guns which were transferred to the section of the border commanded by Prom Yothi, straddling the road leading from Aranya Prathet into Cambodia. For the troops these reinforcements came as a relief, because initially they were ill-equipped to cope even with French bombing raids.[127] By the end of December, Prom Yothi even felt confident enough to order the shelling of French positions across the border in Cambodia.[128]

For Thailand, the beginning of 1941 was an important occasion. Pibul had decided to abandon the traditional Buddhist new year in April and conform with international practice in observing January 1 as the start of the year.[129] It was a controversial decision, made all the more so by Saigon Radio chiming in with allegations that Thailand was abandoning its Buddhist heritage. Yet Pibul did not advocate the adoption of the Christian calendar; 1941 would remain the year 2482 of the Buddhist era in Thailand. It simply began three months earlier than normal. Although the change was marked by special celebrations, Pibul did not participate.[130] He was pre-occupied with other matters.

In return for the military equipment being supplied by Japan, he had secretly agreed to barter tin, rice and rubber. In the longer term, Pibul also ordered all Thailand's annual tin production to be bought up for shipping to Japan, a move opposed by several ministers.[131] They pointed out that at least half the country's tin mines were owned by British and Australian companies which sold their output through the Malayan market. If the Thai government attempted to divert the tin to Japan, Britain had the means of retaliating by banning the sale to Thailand of gunny sacks from India. It was then the sole source of such sacks without which the Thai rice trade could not function. Likewise Thailand needed the foreign currency earned by the sale of its commodities to the British empire and the United States in order to purchase oil and essential manufactured goods.[132] Confronted with these economic arguments, Pibul found himself in a dilemma because of his pledge to supply the Japanese with raw materials.

Other aspects of relations with Japan also preyed on Pibul's mind. He discussed with Crosby the question of recognising the regimes in Manchukuo and Nanking without explaining precisely why it was so important; rather, he harped on the fact that he had Chinese blood in his veins.[133] His fears about the irredentist lobby also surfaced during the same conversation. He said that it was too late to check or disappoint their campaign because it would cost him his position. At the beginning of January there were once again widespread rumours of a coup being mounted by a pro-Japanese faction in the military to oust him.[134]

Neither the Thais nor the Japanese were very successful in hushing up their secret dealings. The French naturally protested to Tokyo when they discovered that Japanese planes being sent to Thailand were staging through the bases they had acquired in Tonkin.[135] The British too had an inkling of Pibul's secret pledge, and were worried lest some of the Thai tin and rubber supplied to Japan might eventually find its way to Germany. Another cause for concern in London was the prospect of Thailand falling completely under Japanese military domination, so seriously upsetting the balance of power in South East Asia at a time when Britain itself had few forces to spare to defend its own strategic interests in the region. On January 6, the British therefore proposed to the Americans that they join in offering to mediate in the dispute between France and Thailand in order to stop Japan profiting from the weakness of both sides.

Britain's move stemmed directly from the secret visit made to Singapore by Captain Jouan, the aide-de-camp to Decoux. Previously the British had doubted the will of the French in Indo-China to oppose the Japanese, but the change of heart came when Jouan requested British military and economic cooperation to strengthen Indo-China's resistance to Japan's demands. In addition Jouan and, through him, Decoux indicated that any help in mediating the dispute with Thailand would be welcome. The British immediately agreed to play such a role, but because they had no relations with Vichy, the United States had to be involved as well.[136]

While the Americans mulled over the idea, Franco-Thai hostilities on the ground escalated. In western Cambodia, the customs post at Poipet was destroyed by Thai artillery fire,[137] and from there fighting rapidly spread along most of the frontier. Martial law was imposed in all Thai border provinces, and the Supreme Command placed more restrictions on the movement of French nationals residing in Thailand.[138] As a result several French-run institutions in Bangkok quickly transferred their administration into Thai hands to avoid being closed down.[139] On January 8, tension increased further with an announcement that troops under Prom Yothi's command had advanced 30 km. along the road to Sisophon, the first town of any consequence in Cambodia en route to Battambang, which was reported to have been bombed in reprisal for French attacks on Srisaket, Ubol and Korat in the north-east.[140]

Yet neither the French nor the Thais considered these hostilities sufficient pretext to break off diplomatic relations. On the contrary, and despite having vowed never again to treat with Vichy, Pibul decided to renew contact. After several months of squabbling about the credentials of a new French Minister sent out from Vichy, he was finally accorded recognition. Direk used the occasion to convey, at Pibul's behest, a message appealing to France to cede the two provinces of Laos on the west bank of the Mekong and establish a joint commission to settle all other outstanding matters. Direk claimed that these moves would be enough to placate the irredentists and put an end to the fighting.[141] But the French remained adamant that they would only concede the redelineation of the Mekong frontier as originally agreed. The new French Minister said any other territorial adjustments would have to wait until after the end of the war in Europe. Indeed, he professed to be at a loss as to why Direk was pressing so hard for negotiations.[142] Articles by Waiwan continued to pour scorn on the whole idea.[143]

Thai policies also evoked strong American misgivings. Pibul and Direk were frequently subjected to lectures from Grant.[144] On January 13 matters reached a higher level. A young lawyer who had just been appointed to head the Thai legation in Washington was summoned to meet the US Secretary of State, Cordell Hull, to be told in no uncertain terms that Thai claims on Indo-China were a mistake because ultimately the irredentist campaign would enable Japan to swallow both Thailand and Indo-China. The new Thai Minister was not abashed. He claimed that Japan was acting altruistically in East Asia, and rebuffed any suggestion that Thailand was being opportunistic in pressing its claims against the French at that juncture. Such comments merely confirmed Cordell Hull's belief that Japan already had the Thais in its pocket.[145] Similarly, the Americans thought that Indo-China was bound to succumb soon to total Japanese control. Hence any agreement reached between Thailand and France could only be transient and subject to great Japanese pressure. The United States therefore rejected the British proposal for joint mediation.[146]

In London there was dismay. The British thought that the Americans were being short-sighted in taking Japanese domination of South East Asia for granted without making any moves to counter it.[147] Decoux, too, had not given up all hope; he continued to communicate secretly with British military officers in East Asia and sent Jouan on a second mission to Singapore.[148]

The Thai public, meanwhile, was still looking for news of a resounding victory on the battlefield. When – despite the claims of the Supreme Command – it failed to materialise, Pibul decided to issue another *Rattaniyom*. It banned all men from appearing in public bare-chested or with shirt-tails flapping. They must wear either uniform, Western-style suits or traditional Thai attire.[149] In other words the aim of the *Rattaniyom* was to ban Chinese-style pyjamas which many Thais also wore for the sake of comfort in the hot season.

Another new inconvenience to life in Bangkok was the nightly black-out. Again aliens tended to suffer most. They found themselves at the mercy of self-styled vigilante groups who interpreted the vaguely-worded black-out regulations as it suited them.[150] Increasing xenophobia was also evident in the reintroduction of a Special Courts Act to deal with alleged fifth columnists, many of them Indo-Chinese, in French employ. As a result, numerous Thais dissociated themselves from all *farangs* for fear of recriminations from the irredentists, who were becoming ever more militant and threatening.[151]

These feelings were aggravated by the lack of decisive fighting. In early January the French withdrew their forces in Cambodia some 40 km. to a hilly ridge near Sisophon which was easier to defend than the scrub jungle and paddy land closer to the border. But as soon as the foreign legionnaires and African colonial troops started to dig in, their commanders changed their minds again. It was the beginning of the dry season, and suddenly the French realised that in a protracted defensive campaign, the troops would become increasingly short of water. Consequently it was decided to switch tactics and mount a short, sharp attack into eastern Thailand. However, the troops assigned to the task were so slow in moving forward that Thai intelligence agents quickly got wind of what was afoot.[152] Hence on January 16 Prom Yothi ordered a pre-emptive strike.

Compared with battles waged elsewhere during the Second World War, it was a small encounter. Nonetheless, Thailand claimed a great victory, with forty-five *farang* soldiers captured and many more killed or wounded for the loss of only a handful of Thais. Proudly the Supreme Command also announced that no Thais had been dishonoured by being captured, and the army was now within striking distance of Sisophon. Simultaneously Thai commanders along other sectors of the border announced that their troops too were moving forward into Indo-China to pave the way for Thai administrators to assume control.[153] Not to be outdone, the navy then proclaimed a great triumph in a major battle at sea on January 17 when Thai warships, despite being out-gunned, damaged and sank the French cruiser *Lamotte-Piquet* and several of its escorts. Several days later, Saigon Radio put out a very different story about the destruction of 40 per cent of the entire Thai fleet. Only gradually over the next six months did the Thai public learn a little of what had really happened.[154]

On the evening of January 16, a French plane spotted the Thai fleet at anchor near Koh Si Chang, an island not far from the border with Indo-China. The information was flashed to the commander of the *Lamotte-Piquet*, the sole and ageing French warship in Far Eastern waters, which was already cruising off the Cambodian coast escorted by four small patrol boats. That was all the French could muster despite their belief that the much larger and recently re-equipped Thai navy was bound to stage an attack for the sake of its honour and reputation. Still, when the French naval commander received news of the whereabouts of his opponents, he decided to split his meagre forces into three with orders to slip through the channels between the off-shore islands in the early morning mists of January 17. The aim was to catch the Thai navy unawares before its ships got up steam and were able to weigh anchor. It largely succeeded. At least three Thai gunboats were sunk at their moorings and the destroyer *Thonburi* was set on fire. Even so, the Thais put up a gallant fight and managed to score several hits on the superstructure of the *Lamotte-Piquet*.

For the French it was hardly a spectacular victory although, as Decoux pointed out, it was the only naval encounter won by France during either the First or Second World Wars.[155] On the other hand, for the Thais to lose one of their two destroyers plus at least three Japanese-built gunboats was a crushing blow. Worse still, an unidentified aircraft – later suspected to be Thai – attacked the *Thonburi* when it was already on fire, causing it to be a total wreck. The loss in human life was even greater; it was several months before the Supreme Command dared admit that the commander of the *Thonburi* and most of his crew had perished with their ship,[156] and it was never explained where Sindhu had been during the battle, although he was reported to have put to sea with the fleet in late December.[157]

After so many months of pressing for military action, the irredentists did not stop to question the veracity or cost of the victories proclaimed by the Supreme Command. Rather, they exulted over the French prisoners-of-war who, to the fury of the authorities in Indo-China, were displayed in the centre of Bangkok caged like wild animals. Then as the Thai wounded from the battlefields arrived back in the city, student groups who had been collecting funds for the war quickly switched to appealing for medical equipment and relief aid.[158] Pridi too was worried that all the extra expenditure entailed by the war was rapidly depleting the treasury reserves; if it continued, he foresaw a massive budget deficit by the end of the financial year.[159] Pibul, although he did not dare to admit it publicly, was even more anxious, since he believed that Thailand did not have the resources to continue fighting for more than another two weeks, especially if the French followed up their victory at sea with counter-attacks on land.[160] Fortunately for him, the French had other ideas.

During his second visit to Singapore on behalf of Decoux, Jouan told the British that in Hanoi, if not in Vichy, it was considered unwise to push the Thais too far because this could lead to Pibul being ousted by a far more militant pro-Japanese clique. Consequently he mooted the idea of a bargain that would save face all round. It entailed France ceding the two west bank provinces of Laos, provided that the Thais agreed to adjust the Cambodian border around Aranya Prathet and further south near the coast. Jouan stressed that in putting forward these proposals, Decoux was not a free agent and would have to consult Vichy. But first he wanted to know whether Pibul was agreeable to such ideas in principle.

The British in Singapore thought that the best thing would be to sound out Thai views as quickly and discreetly as possible. Crosby agreed, and on January 17 sent a secret message to Pibul outlining the proposals put forward by Jouan in Singapore. Within twenty-four hours, the reply came back via Direk that Pibul could give no immediate answer. Instead he would welcome a secret visit to Bangkok by Jouan to explain in person what the French had in mind.[161] Pibul meanwhile had other ideas. That same night he sent Vanich to rouse the Japanese minister from his bed with the news that Decoux was in secret contact with the British and apparently trying to conclude a deal without the knowledge of Vichy.[162]

The information conveyed by Vanich about Jouan's secret mission reached Tokyo at a time when the Japanese were involved in prolonged and heated discussions about future policy towards South East Asia.[163] The debate had already been punctuated by a report from Bangkok relating Pibul's pessimism about Thailand's ability to withstand the French much longer and news of the Thai naval defeat.[164] All these developments were discussed at a special top-level civilian/military breakfast meeting on Sunday, January 19. There the military were more unanimous than ever in pressing for action leading to the assumption of complete control over Indo-China as well as the conclusion of a military pact with Thailand so that Japan could achieve its goal of ousting the British from South East Asia. Above all they argued the need to use a show of force to pre-empt British efforts to mediate in the Franco-Thai conflict.

Once more they were opposed by Matsuoka, who argued that it would be more advantageous for Japan in the longer term if it interposed diplomatically by again offering to mediate between the Thais and the French. Eventually and reluctantly, the military agreed that Matsuoka should have his way.[165] However, it was a compromise. A joint policy paper drawn up later in the day, while acknowledging that Japan's immediate aim was to preside over Franco-Thai negotiations, still spoke of applying military pressure to Indo-China and obtaining a guarantee of future cooperation from the Thai army.[166]

The next morning, Matsuoka sought an early audience with the Emperor to obtain ultimate authorisation for the policy he was advocating in the face of military opposition. He was successful; as the Emperor later indicated, he was averse to military pressure being applied to either Thailand or Indo-China.[167] Armed with this imperial mandate, Matsuoka proceeded to confront the French Ambassador in Tokyo with the information (as supplied by Vanich) of how Decoux was secretly consorting with the British to bargain away bits of Indo-China. Given these treasonable circumstances, he insisted that France must accept Japanese mediation in its dispute with Thailand.[168] Unknown to Matsuoka his threats were backed up by force. Before the military became aware of the Emperor's attitude, orders went out to move more troops into Tonkin and for several warships to station themselves threateningly off the coast of Cochin-China while another moved into the Gulf of Thailand. In this situation the French felt that they had no option but to accept Japanese mediation.[169] As for Pibul, he had made up his mind long ago, which was implicit in the way he betrayed Jouan's secret mission, an act which Crosby and the British military in Singapore branded as double-crossing once they realised what had happened.[170]

The deception continued. Whereas Thai official spokesmen denied reports from Tokyo that negotiations were about to start between Thailand and France under Japanese auspices, Waiwan simply advised his readers to watch the news from Vichy.[171] As for Pridi and Direk, they were kept in the dark for three days until Pibul saw fit to inform his cabinet that he had already accepted Japan's latest mediation offer. By that stage too, the Japanese had reputedly sent agents to Bangkok to help engineer a coup by first removing Direk and Adul from the scene. Obviously Direk's European bias was suspect in Japanese eyes, while Adul, who kept an eye on everything and everybody, simply inspired fear. Anyway the two men were forewarned and the coup attempt – if such it was – did not take place.

All the same, Direk was furious with Pibul for accepting Japan's mediation offer without consulting anybody. Prince Wan claimed that he too had been misled, but he soon went out of his way to reassure his readers and diplomats in Bangkok there was nothing to fear; Thailand, he said, was happy that Japan was presiding over the negotiations, because it was known to be fair. Prince Wan was happy as well. He had been chosen to lead the Thai delegation to Tokyo, and he clearly hoped that it would provide the opportunity to vindicate his reputation with the military, some of whom were still suspicious of his influence and ambition.[172] Before leaving for Tokyo he boasted of his intention to lead the French to "the slaughter pen" and make them sacrifice the whole of Laos and Cambodia.[173]

On the other hand, Direk was unable to conceal his distress at Japan acting as mediator, and lamented the intransigence of the French in rejecting direct talks. Some officials in Vichy felt the same when faced with the alternative of Japanese "arbitration".[174] Many French, however, tended to blame the British, and particularly Crosby whom they accused of conspiring with the Thais to wrest control of Indo-China. It was a view shared by the State Department in Washington, which had long given more credence to the French rather than the British interpretation of events. Yet, despite having refused to play any mediating role in the Franco-Thai dispute, the Americans thought Pibul's acceptance of Japan's offer was tantamount to "taking a ride on a tiger".[175]

Before negotiations could start in Tokyo, a ceasefire had to be agreed on the ground, and this gave rise to further argument. The French rejected a Japanese proposal to send a peacekeeping force to interpose between the two sides. Thai hopes of the ceasefire talks taking place at Angkor also came to nothing; instead, the Japanese flew a Thai delegation in military aircraft to their consular compound in Saigon. The Thais, believing themselves the victors in the war, complained at being confined in such quarters. The Japanese considered these protests unreasonable. They were even more incensed when the Thais and French haggled for two days over the respective position of their troops.

Finally, to stop any further prevarication, the Japanese arranged for a ceasefire agreement to be signed on January 31 aboard one of their battlecruisers; to add to the humiliation of both the French and the Thais, the warship was not on the high seas, as reported in the Tokyo press, but moored in the Saigon river close to the *Lamotte-Piquet*, which looked unscathed by battle.[176] It emerged too that the vast tracts of Indo-China which the Thai Supreme Command claimed to have conquered nowhere amounted to more than a few square kilometres. According to the agreed ceasefire lines, Thai forces had only captured about one-third of the Sayabouri area in the north and half the Bassac region in southern Laos. They had failed to follow up their victory near Sisophon, and were still 12 km. away from it. As for the rest of Cambodia, the Thais simply occupied narrow strips along the border.[177]

Nor did anybody point out what was perhaps the ultimate irony. Throughout the irredentist campaign, the Bangkok press made great play of the fact that most of the lost territories had been conceded to France under duress in 1893 when the French sent a gunboat up the Chao Phya to train its guns on Bangkok. In January 1941, as negotiations were about to start in Tokyo, Pibul had perforce to agree to the stationing of a Japanese warship in roughly the same spot. The Japanese claimed that this was necessary for communication purposes during the mediation process. In Tokyo a very different connotation was put on the development. A wave of excitement swept through military circles when it was realised that Japan's mediation in the Franco-Thai conflict had resulted in its warships being based in both Saigon and Bangkok.[178]

NOTES

1. Direk, p. 20.
2. Reports of June 13 and July 3 in F3268/3268/40 in FO371/24756.
3. Flood, p. 280.
4. BTWM, July 1, 1940; Feis, *The Road To Pearl Harbor*, p. 64; Morley (ed.), *The Fateful Choice*, p. 136.
5. Reports of July 2, *passim*, in F3690/3268/40 in FO371/24756, and Cable of July 3 in 892.00/207 in RG59.
6. BTWM, July 10, 13, 18 and 25, 1940.
7. ibid., July 10, *passim*, 1940.
8. ibid., Oct. 7, 1940.
9. Reports of July 3, *passim*, in F3268/3268/40 in FO371/24756, and Vichit, pp. 9ff.
10. Flood, p. 310n, quoting report of July 18 in GKR L3-0-0 arranging visit, and pp. 281ff on discussions.
11. BTWM, Apr. 16, 22 and 24, 1940; report of Mar. 4 in F1874/572/40; file in FO371/24754; report of May 9, 892.00/208 in RG59.
12. Flood, p. 272.
13. Jones, p. 242, and Feis, pp. 88ff.
14. Decoux, pp. 95ff, and Morley (ed.), pp. 172ff.
15. Direk, p. 21, and reports of July 21, *passim*, F2888/19/40 in FO371/24751 also demonstrate Thai suspicion of the French intention to withdraw their Minister from Bangkok even before the non-aggression pact was concluded.
16. Pibul's comments of Aug. 6, F3706/3268/40 in FO371/24756.
17. Flood, pp. 283ff.
18. ibid., p. 291, and Morley (ed.), p. 215.
19. Flood, pp. 292ff, on conversation of Aug. 17 between Pibul and Japanese Chargé d'Affaires.
20. BTWM, Aug. 5, 1940.
21. Conversation with Pibul, Aug. 6, F3706/3268/40 in FO371/24756.

22. Direk, p. 23, reporting conversations of Aug. 15. Grant was a political appointee who had contributed to Roosevelt's re-election but had no previous diplomatic experience.
23. FRUS, 1940, IV, pp. 74 and 84.
24. Direk, p. 23, and F3894/3268/40 in FO371/24756.
25. FRUS, 1940, IV, p. 91.
26. Direk, p. 23.
27. Decoux, pp. 131ff.
28. BTWM, Aug. 22, 1940, and Direk, p. 27.
29. BTWM, Aug. 22, 1940.
30. Report of Aug. 21, F4002/3268/40 in FO371/24756.
31. F3395/19/40 in FO371/24751 and BTWM, Aug. 31, Sep. 4 and 9, 1940.
32. Reports of Aug. 14, *passim*; F3706/3268/40 in FO371/24756.
33. F3771/3268/40 in ibid.
34. Flood, p. 283.
35. Morley (ed.), pp. 177ff.
36. Decoux, pp. 132ff.
37. FRUS, 1940, IV, p. 109, and Baudouin, *The Private Diaries*, p. 229.
38. Direk, p. 25, and F4185/19/40 in FO371/24751.
39. FRUS, 1940, IV, pp. 113ff; Baudouin, p. 241; French protest to Tokyo, Decoux, p. 134.
40. BTWM, Aug. 12 and 27, Sep. 5, 1940.
41. F4819/3268/40 in FO371/24756, and FRUS, 1940, IV, p. 135.
42. BTWM, Sep. 14, 1940.
43. Thai Rath comment in ibid., Sep. 23, 1940.
44. ibid., Sep. 18, 19 and 20, 1940.
45. ibid., Mar. 2, Apr. 4, May 7, June 8, July 18 and Aug. 16, 1940.
46. ibid., Sep. 20, 1940 and F4794/19/40 in FO371/24751.
47. BTWM, Sep. 23 and 26, 1940, and note delivered to French on Sep. 25 in Direk, p. 27.
48. BTWM, Sep. 26 and Oct. 2, 1940, and NYT, Oct. 5, 1940.
49. BTWM, Sep. 23, 24 and 26, 1940; Decoux, p. 114; Morley (ed.), p. 192.
50. Chariwat Santabutr, p. 195.
51. Flood, pp. 323ff, quoting diary of Commander Torigoe and other sources for interview of Sep. 28 with Vanich, and Oct. 1 with Pibul. Also Morley (ed.), p. 218. Vanich was transferred from the Fuel Oil Department to Army HQ on Sep. 27, BTWM, Sep. 30, 1940.
52. Flood, pp. 303ff. Prom Yothi visited Japan Sep. 20–Oct. 10. Lack of credentials, F4011/3368/40 in FO371/24756. BTWM, Oct. 31 and Nov. 4, 1940, on lack of publicity for visit.
53. Flood, pp. 325ff, quoting military and Gaimusho position papers on the complex factional dispute arising from Pibul's pledge.
54. F4471/3268/40 in FO371/24756, and FRUS, 1940, IV, p. 164.
55. NYT, Sep. 29, 30 and Oct. 5, 1940.
56. Vichit, pp. 72ff and Direk, p. 28.
57. BTWM, Oct. 2, 4, and 7; NYHT, Oct. 6, 1940. The head of Thai Blood was Prasert Tharisawat, an official in the Government Propaganda Bureau and younger brother to Thamrong. Siri Premchit, p. 19.

58. BTWM, Oct. 5, 1940; Decoux, p. 131; Oune Sananikone, *Kwamlang kong Karpajao*, p. 30.

59. Coast, p. 21.

60. BTWM, Oct. 7, 8 and 9, 1940, and Pridi's opposition to irredentist campaign, F3690 and F4625/3268/40 in FO371/24756.

61. This was Col. Luang Kriangsak Pichit. BTWM, Oct. 14, 1940.

62. ibid., Oct. 11 and 17, and *Daily Express*, Oct. 16, 1940.

63. Reports from Thai Rath and Siam Rath in BTWM, Oct. 10, 14 and 15, 1940.

64. Reports from Pramuan Wan, Thai Rath, Suphapburut and Thai Ekarat in BTWM, Oct. 3, 5, 7, 8 and 15, 1940. First-hand account of how French reinforced Sawannakhet in Boulle, *My Own River Kwai*, pp. 30ff.

65. Thai Rath in BTWM, Oct. 7, 1940.

66. Decoux, pp. 135ff.

67. BTWM, Oct. 11 and 14, 1940; FRUS, 1940, IV, pp. 176, 196 and 199; F4827/3268/40 in FO371/24756.

68. This was Major Mom Luang Karb Kunjara who held talks in Singapore on Oct.7. F4625/3268/40 in ibid.

69. F4669/3268/40 in ibid., and BTWM, Oct. 14 and 15, 1940.

70. Pibul's conversation with Japanese of Oct. 14 and 15 in Flood, pp. 333ff.

71. BTWM, Sep. 23 and Oct. 2, 1940, and account in Siri Premchit, pp. 268–335.

72. F4819/3268/40 in FO371/24756 and Doll's letter of Nov. 19 in 892.00/217, RG59.

73. Text in BTWM, Oct. 21, 1940, and summary in Direk, pp. 29ff.

74. F4854/3268/40 in FO371/24756.

75. F4897/3268/40 in ibid, FRUS, 1940, IV, pp. 189ff.

76. BTWM, Oct. 23, 1940.

77. ibid., Nov. 2, 1940. Some rallies in the north-east were organised by Phairote Chaiyanam, deputy Director of Government Propaganda and younger brother to Direk. ibid., Oct. 17 and 22, 1940.

78. ibid., Nov. 2, 1940.

79. ibid., Nov. 4, 1940, and Netr Khemayothin, p. 66.

80. Reports from Thai Rath, Thai Ekarat, Sri Krung and Suphapburut in BTWM, Oct. 23, 24, 26, 28 and 30, 1940.

81. ibid., Nov. 8, 11 and 18, 1940.

82. Direk, p. 31. Another reason for the hiatus was Lepissier's departure and political complexities in Vichy.

83. BTWM, Oct. 26 and 28, 1940.

84. Oune Sananikone, p. 48 recounting surprise at the poor state of Thai defences when he crossed from Laos, and Netr Khemayothin, pp. 76ff.

85. Report of Oct. 28 in Flood, p. 356.

86. BTWM, Nov. 6 and 8, 1940.

87. ibid., Oct. 4 and 23, 1940.

88. ibid., Nov. 11 and 18, 1940.

89. Conversation with Pibul, Nov. 1, F4967/3268/40 in FO371/24757.

90. Four-minister cabinet meeting, Nov. 5, in Jones, p. 235, and Flood, pp. 337ff.

91. Cancellation of Sindhu's trip noted in army general staff document, Nov. 18. Flood, pp. 339ff.

92. Conversation with Direk, Nov. 5, F5012/3268/40 in FO371/24757.

93. Prayoon's interview with Ribbentrop, Nov. 11. *Documents on German Foreign Policy* (DGFP), XI, p. 519.
94. BTWM, Nov. 14 and 16, 1940.
95. Prachachart reports in ibid., Nov. 13 and 15, 1940.
96. ibid., Nov. 14 and 20, 1940.
97. Decoux, p. 139; Gaudel *L'Indo-chine en face du Japon*, p. 105; Huynh Kim Khanh, pp. 252ff, NYHT, Dec. 4, 1940.
98. Prachachart report in BTWM, Nov. 15, 1940.
99. ibid., Nov. 20, 1940, refuting report in *Asahi Shimbun* Nov. 18, 1940.
100. NHYT and *Times*, Nov. 19, 1940, and F5196/3268/40 in FO371/24757.
101. Flood, p. 340, and Morley (ed.), p. 219.
102. Text of policy paper, ibid., p. 218; Flood, pp. 343ff; Jones, p. 235.
103. Report of Nov. 21, DGFP, XI, p. 646.
104. Flood, p. 346, and Decoux, p. 142.
105. NYT, Nov. 10 and 18, 1940.
106. NYHT, *Times* and DT, Nov. 27 and 28, 1940, including Domei report.
107. BTWM, Nov. 27, 1940.
108. ibid., Nov. 28, 1940, and Direk, p. 32.
109. BTWM, Nov. 29, 30 and Dec. 2; NYHT, Nov. 30 and Dec. 1, 1940; F5371/3268/40 in FO371/24757.
110. BTWM, Nov. 29 and 30, 1940.
111. ibid., Nov. 15, 19 and 21, 1940.
112. ibid., Nov. 25, 1940, and comments on Vichit in letter of Nov. 19, 1940, in 892.00/217 RG59.
113. BTWM, Oct. 4 and 7, and Sri Krung report, ibid., Dec. 9, 1940.
114. Thai Rath reports, ibid., Nov. 16, 21 and 28, 1940.
115. Oune Sananikone, p. 56. He was a Lao-language broadcaster and worked with Phairote Chaiyanam, Sunthorn Hongladorn (who after 1958 occupied several cabinet positions) and Dr Thanat Khoman.
116. Netr Khemayothin, p. 72, and BTWM, Nov. 13, Dec. 13, 18 and 31, 1940. Two broadcasters were Sang Pathanothai and Phra Rajatham Nitet.
117. Prachachart reports, ibid., Dec. 9, 17 and 18, 1940.
118. Gaudel, p. 95, and Boulle, p. 33.
119. FRUS, 1940, IV, p. 228; BTWM, Dec. 26, 1940; NYT, Dec. 10, 1940; Flood, pp. 357ff (quoting Japanese army staff report on the delivery of heavy bombers being a useful pretext to extend Thai airfields); Bergamini, *Japan's Imperial Conspiracy*, p. 729.
120. Gaudel, p. 35.
121. BTWM, Dec. 9; NYHT, Dec. 14, 1940; F5699/3268/40 in FO371/24757; Vichit, p. 71.
122. MG, Dec. 2; NYHT, Dec. 5, and NYT, Dec. 15, 1940.
123. ibid., Dec. 16, 1940, and Flood, p. 367. Rejection received in Tokyo, Dec. 19.
124. NYT, Dec. 17 and 19, 1940.
125. Decoux, p. 142, and F79/5/40 in FO371/28108; Jouan's visit to Singapore, Dec. 25–31, 1940.
126. Flood, p. 374, quoting military staff papers of Dec. 20 onwards, and report of military/civilian liaison conference of Dec. 26. Text in Morley (ed.), p. 223.
127. Netr Khemayothin, pp. 76ff. The first consignment of tanks was handed over to

the Thais on December 23 to mark the ratification of the Thai-Japanese friendship treaty of June 1940. Flood, p. 361.

128. BTWM, Dec. 20, 27, 28 and 30; NYT, Dec. 30, 1940; Gaudel, p. 98.
129. BTWM, Feb. 8 and Aug. 5, 1940, and Prasert Patamasukhon, p. 320.
130. Thamsook Numnonda, *Thailand and the Japanese Presence, 1941-45*, p. 23; BTWM, Jan. 4, 1941.
131. F32/32/40 in FO371/28113.
132. Direk, p. 44.
133. Conversation of Dec. 28, F79/5/40 in FO371/28108.
134. ibid;FRUS, 1941, V, p. 1; NYT, Dec. 30, 1940.
135. CSM, Jan. 6, 1941; Decoux, p. 133; F194/5/40 in FO371/28108.
136. F79/5/40 in ibid., and FRUS, 1941, V, pp. 2ff.
137. BTWM, Jan. 6 and 7, 1941, and Gaudel, p. 98.
138. Prasert Patamasukhon, p. 343; BTWM, Jan. 8; NYT, Jan. 9, 1941.
139. These included Assumption College and St Louis Hospital, both run by French Catholics. BTWM, Jan. 6, 7 and 17, 1941.
140. ibid., Jan. 8, 9 and 10, 1941.
141. The first call by the French Minister (Roger Garreau) on Direk, Jan. 8, FRUS, 1941, V, p. 7, and F142/5/40 in FO371/28108.
142. Direk, p. 34, and FRUS, 1941, V, p. 19.
143. Prachachart reports in BTWM, Jan. 3, 10, 11 and 16, 1941.
144. Direk, p. 31.
145. FRUS, 1941, V, p. 16, and Cordell Hull, *Memoirs*, p. 985.
146. FRUS, 1941, V, p. 10.
147. F142/5/40 in FO371/28108.
148. F227/5/50 in ibid. Jouan arrived in Singapore on Jan. 15, but Decoux omits to mention this second visit or his continuing exchange of messages with the British, so leading to subsequent confusion. Flood, p. 420 and n.
149. Text in Thak Chaloemtiarana (ed.), p. 252.
150. BTWM, Jan. 13, 14, 15, 17 and 18, 1941.
151. ibid., Jan. 4, 17 and 21, 1941, and report of Jan. 22 in FO371/28108.
152. Gaudel, pp. 100ff; Decoux, p. 139; Netr Khemayothin, p. 87; NYHT, Jan. 10, 1941.
153. BTWM, Jan. 20, and NYT, Jan. 21, 1941.
154. BTWM, Jan. 20, 23 and 24, and NYHT, Jan. 21, 1941.
155. Gaudel, pp. 34 and 105ff; Decoux, p. 141; Flood, p. 400.
156. BTWM, Apr. 17, and article in Nawikaset in ibid., July 12, 1941. Some survivors were rescued by a foreign cargo ship, whose captain estimated that 800 Thai sailors died. F3369/5/40 in FO371/28110.
157. BTWM, Dec. 30, 1940; Flood, p. 642; Sangworn Suwannachip, pp. 105ff, on the confusion of the battle.
158. BTWM, Jan. 22 and 24, 1941, and F328/5/40 in FO371/28108.
159. F212/212/40 in FO371/28128.
160. Pibul's comments of Jan. 17 in Flood, p. 415, and Morley (ed.), p. 227.
161. Reports of Jan. 16 and 18 in F306/5/40 in FO371/28108. Significantly Direk, who passed these messages, does not mention them.
162. The Japanese Minister's cable of Jan. 18 in Flood, p. 419.
163. ibid., p. 421.

164. Reports of Jan. 17 in ibid., p. 417. Japanese intelligence knew of the Thai naval defeat before Decoux.
165. Liaison conference of Jan. 19 in ibid., pp. 422ff.
166. Text in Morley (ed.), p. 227.
167. Flood, pp. 433, and 440ff.
168. ibid., p. 434, and Decoux, pp. 143ff.
169. Flood, p. 431; Gaudel, p. 109; FRUS, 1941, V, pp. 34ff.
170. F1208/210/40 in FO371/28120 and Allen, p. 75, quoting CinCFE.
171. Prachachart report in BTWM, Jan. 21, 1941.
172. F396/5/40 in FO371/28109. FRUS, 1941, V, pp. 41ff, and Prachachart reports in BTWM, Jan. 17 and Feb. 1, 1941.
173. FRUS, 1941, V, p. 47.
174. ibid., p. 49, and F444/5/40 in FO371/28109.
175. Decoux, p. 126; Feis, p. 151; FRUS, 1941, V, pp. 32ff.
176. ibid., p. 38; BTWM, Jan. 30, 1941; Netr Khemayothin, pp. 104ff; Flood, p. 458.
177. Ceasefire text in BTWM, Feb. 3, 1941, and F541/5/40 in FO371/28109. Compare also Gaudel, p. 109, with Vichit, p. 78.
178. BTWM, Feb. 1 and 4, 1941; F478/5/40 in FO371/28109; Flood, p. 457.

9
THE RIDE ON A TIGER

Until January 1941, the southward limit of Japanese military expansion was the Red River in Tonkin. Now, with warships in Saigon and Bangkok, Japan seemed poised both politically and militarily to take advantage of its mediation of the Franco-Thai dispute by expanding its domination over much of South East Asia and wresting control of the region's natural resources. That, at least, was the impression of the German, American and British ambassadors in Tokyo; all three reported back to their respective governments that a new Japanese southward move was imminent.[1]

In Berlin, Hitler and Ribbentrop reacted by urging Japan to forgo caution and strike immediately at Singapore in order to eliminate the British from the Far East and cripple their war effort in Europe and the Mediterranean. In Washington, Roosevelt expressed the view that a new Japanese military move southwards would take place in the second week of February, but there was nothing the United States could do to check it unless American possessions were directly attacked. In London, Churchill doubted whether the Japanese would be so precipitate. He thought that Japan was simply making military noises to conceal its diplomatic pressure on Thailand and Indo-China.[2] In the event, Churchill was right but for the wrong reason.

Unknown to the Western powers, another top-level liaison conference was held in Tokyo on January 30, when once more hot-headed army staff officers pressed for approval to take over Indo-China and force a military pact on Thailand. Again they were opposed by Matsuoka, who argued that diplomatic means must first be tried to achieve Japan's aims in South East Asia. That too remained the view of the Emperor, who indicated Japan should not seek to profit from the Franco-Thai dispute ''like a thief at a fire''.[3]

The Emperor's strictures notwithstanding, the Army General Staff had already sent two envoys to Bangkok to put pressure on Pibul to sign a military agreement. The move was stopped by the military attaché, Major Tamura Hiroshi. As an old friend of Pibul, he was aware that such tactics might prove counter-productive,[4] and his judgement was probably correct. Before Prince Wan and the rest of the Thai negotiating team left for Tokyo on February 4, again aboard Japanese military aircraft, Pibul informed Crosby that the delegation had instructions to resist Japanese pressure for military concessions.[5] Instead, once Prince Wan and those accompanying him were comfortably installed at Japanese expense in the Imperial Hotel in Tokyo (a courtesy also extended to the French), he proceeded to embarrass Matsuoka.

At the formal opening of the negotiations, which were presided over by the Japanese Foreign Minister, Prince Wan demanded the return of all the territory Thailand had lost to France since 1863. He maintained that up till then the Annamite chain of mountains had always been considered the natural border of the Thais, and they had a right to the whole of Laos and Cambodia. Even some members of the Thai delegation were astonished at the size of the demand.[6] The French were aghast at the enormity of it, and in protest they refused to have anything more to do with the Thais; the only thing they would agree to was an extension for fifteen days of the ceasefire which was due to expire on February 11.[7]

Matsuoka had been counting on a quick settlement in this, Japan's first venture into international mediation. As its chief architect, he felt his own reputation to be at stake, especially with the military still manoeuvring behind his back.[8] Anyway he was committed to leaving in early March for talks in Berlin and Moscow; hence he instructed his subordinates to persuade Prince Wan to scale down Thai demands to negotiable proportions. These efforts met with the response that Thailand had pitched its demands so high in the first place to ensure that at least the two provinces on the west bank of the Mekong would be ceded. In any event, Prince Wan boasted, Thailand would have conquered all this territory and more if only Japan had not intervened to impose a ceasefire. The Japanese were not impressed, and they recalled Pibul's fears of defeat just before the ceasefire was arranged.[9]

Prince Wan knew that he had to bargain because such high hopes had been placed on the outcome of his mission.[10] After all the excitement generated by the fighting and great victory claims, Thai public opinion was developing a momentum of its own: leaflets circulating in Bangkok demanded a resumption of war if all the lost territories were not returned,[11] and others insisted that everybody should fly flags to celebrate the country's triumph. Such uncontrolled demands worried Adul, who feared that the situation might soon get completely out of hand, and he quickly imposed a police ban on any further demonstrations or distribution of leaflets.[12]

The French were more concerned at the uncontrolled situation along the border. Despite the ceasefire, Thai troops were staging raids across the Mekong in areas where there had previously been no fighting. Yet when the French protested, they simply met with Thai counter-protests on the same score.[13] Nonetheless, in compliance with one ceasefire provision, the Thai press toned down its anti-French propaganda, though continuing to report with obvious approval the conversion to Buddhism of large numbers of Catholics living in Thailand, many of them at officially-sponsored ceremonies.[14] However, the mood of xenophobia aroused by the irredentist campaign was difficult to appease, and soon found a new target.

To ward off any more Japanese threats to the region, Britain decided to reinforce Malaya. Pibul was notified of the move in advance and assured that it was not directed against Thailand.[15] However, the Bangkok press, ignoring the broader international implications of the crisis provoked by Thai demands on Indo-China, thought otherwise.[16] Those newspapers which had previously fulminated against the French took up the war cry again. Just as they had claimed that French colonial troops in Indo-China were mutinous and disorderly, they made similar accusations against the Indian and Australian soldiers arriving in Malaya as part of Britain's efforts to strengthen its defences.[17] As a result, there were reports of British and American families being advised to leave Thailand for their own safety.[18]

Much of this tension stemmed from Tokyo, where the negotiations remained deadlocked. Prince Wan refused to budge from his initial demands, even when the Japanese argued that the terms of the settlement did not matter, since France was bound to lose the war and hence Indo-China as well in any case.[19] Matsuoka therefore tried to find some other way out of the stalemate. He did not want the talks to collapse completely because he was afraid that if the Thais failed to get what they wanted in Tokyo, they might turn to the British again for help.[20] Consequently on February 17, ten days after the abortive opening of the negotiations, he persuaded the two sides to attend a joint meeting where he proposed a compromise. Thailand was to get the two Lao west-bank provinces plus parts of north-western Cambodia in return for an indemnity of 10 million baht to be paid to the French for the assets they were losing. The deal specifically excluded the temple complexes at Angkor, which the Thais obviously coveted and which – as the Japanese knew – the French would never hand over.[21] Still, it was the money that counted.

The Thais, already disappointed at not getting Angkor, rejected any idea of paying compensation to a country they claimed to have vanquished on the battlefield. The French were equally incensed – the thought of being paid an indemnity by a country like Thailand offended their pride – but underlying their attitude was also their determination to get back any territory they were forced to cede to Thailand, once the war in Europe was over and the rule of law again prevailed in the world. Hence the governments in both Bangkok and Vichy rejected Matsuoka's proposals.[22]

To the amazement of Japanese military leaders, no ultimatum was attached to Matsuoka's proposals, and when they were rejected the Army Chief of Staff assumed that diplomacy had failed and that the military could now take action. His naval counterpart was more reticent, fearing possible Anglo-American reaction to any overt Japanese forward move in South East Asia. Matsuoka also remained opposed to the use of force;[23] his problem was time, with the ceasefire due to expire again on February 26 and indications that it might prove difficult to extend for a further period.

In Hanoi, Decoux and his war council decided that if hostilities resumed, the French this time would have to bomb Bangkok. The *Lamotte-Picquet* was also ordered to sea again, although it was now shadowed by Japanese warships.[24] Tension was rising in Bangkok as well. Pibul decided to recall the senior officers attached to the delegation in Tokyo.[25] Matsuoka too was alarmed and set to work to get the ceasefire extended for another ten days. In the case of the French it was relatively easy. Not so the Thais. Pibul was again finding public opinion difficult to control. Anyway he was disappointed by Matsuoka's failure to support Thailand's claims. He feared that the longer the negotiations dragged on, the more the Japanese would apply pressure to Thailand. In this context, Pibul was already worried because some cabinet ministers were still trying to block the delivery to Japan of all Thailand's tin and rubber production, as he had promised. Hence in the apparent hope of mollifying the Japanese, Vichit was despatched to Tokyo in great haste. At the same time, Pibul reluctantly agreed to an extension of the ceasefire until March 7.[26]

Once he had overcome this hurdle, Matsuoka tried to calm the militarists in Tokyo by drawing up another mediation plan. He stressed it was final and had to be accepted by both sides by February 28. Before the Army Chief of Staff could object, Matsuoka hastened to secure the Emperor's approval although in fact his new proposals differed little from those he had earlier put forward. France was still to cede the two west-bank provinces and north-western Cambodia. But in return Thailand, rather than paying an indemnity, had to guarantee the demilitarisation of all the retroceded territory.

Since this plan was accompanied by an ultimatum, Matsuoka had no difficulty in persuading the Thais to accept it. With a great sense of relief, Pibul cabled his agreement on February 26.[27] To get the French to do likewise, Matsuoka asked the Germans to apply pressure on Vichy and told the French directly that if they did not accept his final mediation plan, the guarantee Japan had given in August 1940 to respect the sovereignty of Indo-China would be considered null and void. Indignantly the French retorted the guarantee had already been invalidated by the territorial concessions they were being forced to make to Thailand.[28]

Yet amidst these exchanges, some French diplomats had noted that Matsuoka did not automatically sympathise with the Thais as fellow Asians and certainly did not endorse their more extravagant claims. Therefore a leading member of the French delegation thought it might be worthwhile trying to reason with Matsuoka. From the economic talks they were also holding in Tokyo, the French knew how anxious the Japanese were to buy up all the rice Indo-China could export. Since much of it came from the Cambodian province of Battambang, the French pointed out that if the province were handed over to the Thais, Japan might lose access to its rice. At once Matsuoka realised what the French were driving at and started to reconsider his mediation proposals.[29] It was too late. Japanese warships were patrolling ominously off Cap St Jacques at the entry to the Saigon river. Moves were also underway to evacuate all Japanese civilians from Indo-China as an indication of the imminent outbreak of hostilities.[30] Consequently, on February 28 the cabinet in Vichy decided that France would have to submit to Japan's ultimatum.

Still, in accepting Matsuoka's proposals, the French attached five conditions. They included the demilitarisation of all territory ceded to Thailand and the retention by France of certain sites on the west bank of the Mekong, as well as several islands in the river. Above all they demanded a guarantee that the agreement would be final and immutable. They also publicised the fact they were yielding to Japanese pressure under extreme duress and would never have surrendered to the Thais.[31]

Matsuoka's pride was hurt. He did not like being cast by France in the role of a bully, and had hoped to be able to present his military colleagues with more positive proof that diplomacy worked. He therefore reverted to the idea of leaving Battambang in French hands. The head of the

French economic delegation in Tokyo was delighted, especially since he thought the cabinet in Vichy had caved in far too quickly to Japan's ultimatum without considering any alternative solution.[32] However, any revision of the proposed terms of settlement posed other problems. First, Matsuoka had to persuade his military colleagues to agree to the change, and this was not easy. The army was poised ready to take over the whole of Indo-China and to allow the Thais to pick which bits they wanted. After considerable argument, Matsuoka managed to get the military to stay its hand at least till March 8.[33] Then he had to persuade the Thais to accept another part of Indo-China instead of Battambang. Pibul was not amenable. Having been promised Battambang, he refused to countenance any alternative proposals and certainly not, as Matsuoka advocated, a stretch of northern Laos which would give Thailand a common border with China. Prince Wan was equally adamant. In any case, he claimed that the five conditions attached to Vichy's acceptance of Matsuoka's "final" proposals invalidated the whole mediation process.[34]

The Thai press meanwhile knew nothing of the talks in Tokyo except for a few reports reprinted from Japanese newspapers. At the beginning of March, these included news that France had agreed in principle to meet Thai claims, which aroused great expectations in Bangkok; impatience was expressed there when nothing further was heard from Tokyo about an agreement being signed.[35]

The hiatus was a measure of the confusion prevailing in Tokyo. Members of the French delegation were at odds with one another over which set of Japanese proposals to accept, while the Thais insisted that they would only agree to Matsuoka's "final" proposals. The atmosphere became so tense that Matsuoka even turned to the British Ambassador for sympathy.[36] Above all, Matsuoka was concerned about his military colleagues. The Army Chief of Staff wanted to get the Emperor to approve a military take-over of Indo-China on March 8,[37] but to pre-empt such a move, Matsuoka finally managed on March 5 to persuade both the French and the Thais to subscribe to a joint communiqué announcing that they had reached agreement except for a few points of detail. Japanese elation was immediately apparent. The Stock Exchange in Tokyo registered considerable gains.[38] Even the army Chief of Staff was pleased, and drank a special cup of saké in honour of the occasion. The French had agreed to guarantee that they would refrain from any action that might be construed as hostile to Japan.[39]

Naturally, too, news of the settlement was warmly welcomed in

Bangkok. Reaction elsewhere included the comment that Thailand had now become a stepping-stone for Japan to attack Singapore. Besides the agreement in Tokyo, Japan had just been given permission to open a consulate in Songkla, not far from the Malayan border.[40] The French and British were also concerned about continuing but unpublicised Japanese arms shipments to Thailand. In addition, the Japanese warships sent to Bangkok – originally for communications purposes, so it was claimed – were making increasingly free use of the Thai naval base at Sattahip.[41] But when Crosby complained, Pibul denied that Thailand was abandoning its neutrality, claiming rather that since the Western powers were not prepared to sell arms to Thailand, he had to turn to Japan; anyway, he added, it was easy for once to get popular approval for defence expenditure. Such ingenuous remarks simply contributed to growing British disillusion with Pibul.[42]

The French, however, continued to count on Matsuoka's disillusion with the Thais, especially over the question of Battambang. Despite the joint communiqué issued on March 5, the Japanese Foreign Minister two days later sent his deputy to wake Prince Wan after midnight to argue for several hours about Thailand accepting another area of Indo-China. When the ploy failed, leaving Prince Wan not only tired but also very angry, the Japanese turned to Vanich – who, as expected, proved to be far more amenable, readily agreeing that France should retain Battambang provided that the whole Cambodian coastline were ceded to Thailand.

At that juncture the War Minister, General Tojo, intervened to protest against all the pressure being exerted on the Thais by the Foreign Ministry.[43] As a result, Matsuoka had to back down and leave his officials to draft an agreement, which was initialled by France and Thailand on March 11, pending the conclusion of a formal treaty between the two countries. Basically its terms were those originally agreed on February 28, with one significant addition. In return for Japanese supervision of the agreement, both Thailand and France bound themselves not to enter into any commitments, whether political, military or economic, which might be construed as detrimental to the interests of Japan.[44]

The implications of this clause profoundly dismayed the British and Americans, even though Matsuoka boasted that Japan had acted altruistically and not derived any benefit from its successful mediation of the Franco-Thai dispute.[45] Indeed, some military leaders in Tokyo were keenly disappointed because they saw the settlement as bringing them no closer to their objective of establishing bases throughout Indo-China and signing a military pact with Thailand.[46]

On the other hand, Prince Wan professed satisfaction with the negotiations, which he said had not been as tough as he had expected.[47] Obviously he was not prepared to admit – not to Western diplomats, at least – what he had gone through with the Japanese. Still he was heard to remark privately that the territory Thailand had acquired was devoid of all common sense, and he only hoped it was sufficient to placate the irredentists.[48] With that in mind, he made a special broadcast from Tokyo on March 11 to explain the settlement he had just agreed with the French.[49]

Prince Wan's misgivings were shared by Pibul. Apart from the province of Battambang, most of the territory Thailand had acquired from Cambodia was trackless jungle. The same was more or less true of the two west-bank provinces of Laos. These acquisitions also fell far short of irredentist demands that the Thai and Lao be reunited as brethren. Even so, Pibul did at last have something he could present as a great triumph; he proclaimed a national holiday, and ordered all official buildings to fly the Japanese flag alongside that of Thailand for three days. In similar disregard for the principles of Thai neutrality, he accepted messages of congratulation from Japan claiming that the settlement between Thailand and Indo-China would contribute to a sphere of co-prosperity in East Asia. In reply Pibul expressed the profound gratitude of the Thai people to Japan for the fulfilment of their just demands.[50] The Japanese were not deceived; they knew how disappointed Pibul was and thought he was putting on a brave show.[51] It did not end there. To mark what Pibul called this day of glory, he appealed to all Thai women to prove to the world how civilised their country was by letting their hair grow long and wearing skirts.[52]

In effect Pibul was telling Thai women to abandon tradition and adopt a more westernised appearance.[53] The proposal proved even more controversial than the *Rattaniyom* in January imposing rules on male attire. The Queen Grandmother, who had always dressed in the style of the court during the reign of her late husband, let it be known that she was complying with Pibul's dictum only with great reluctance. At the other end of the social scale, peasant women complained that it was both impractical and indecorous to plant rice or mount a water buffalo wearing a skirt. Pibul replied that they should hitch up their skirts and sit on a buffalo as if riding side-saddle.[54]

Dress reform was clearly becoming an obsession with Pibul. He seemed to be inspired by the notion that former Thai monarchs had managed to protect the country's independence by instructing their courtiers to dress properly and act in a civilised manner in the presence of foreign envoys. Now having regained some of the country's lost territories, Pibul apparently considered it even more important for the Thais to impress on the world that they were a civilised people.[55] But at least one Assembly member remarked that all the emphasis being placed on civilising the nation was more likely to make foreigners think the Thais were still very backward.[56] At home too Pibul's popularity waned markedly after he embarked on his crusade for dress reform.

Other reforms implemented by Pibul's government in the economic sphere were backfiring with even more serious consequences. Under the aegis of Vanich, the Fuel Oil Department succeeded in late 1940 in thwarting negotiations for the return of the two Western oil companies which had previously traded in Bangkok.[57] In retaliation, they barred Thailand from obtaining oil from the Netherlands East Indies, and it had to turn to other companies in the United States. Here the British warned the Americans against allowing the Thais to over-order such crucial supplies as aviation fuel which, given the reputation of Vanich, might be stockpiled for eventual use by the Japanese during operations aimed at Singapore.[58] Such representations fell on favourable ears in Washington. The United States was moving gradually towards a total embargo on the export of all strategic materials to Japan or to any other country which might be acting on its behalf. Consequently by March 1941, Thailand had to apply for licences on a whole range of imports from the United States.

Another problem was shipping. When the war in Europe curtailed the activities of Western shipping lines, Thailand was seriously affected. The state enterprise set up in 1939 to take over the shipping of all Thai imports and exports as part of the drive towards economic nationalism had only a handful of freighters at its disposal, and it could not acquire any more because of the worldwide shipping shortage. Worse still, in early 1941 the United States imposed a ban on the charter of all tankers in the western hemisphere for the transport of oil across the Pacific. The Americans also refused to grant Thailand a licence to purchase oil drums in order to transport the fuel on ordinary freighters. As a result Pibul complained that the United States was deliberately discriminating against Thailand, and made a desperate appeal to the British for help in the resumption of oil supplies from the Netherlands East Indies.[59]

Despite British suspicions of Japanese collusion with the Fuel Oil

Department, Crosby was inclined to view Pibul's request sympathetically. Even at that late stage, he thought that anything which prevented Thailand from becoming completely dependent on Japan was worth trying. The British also believed they had found a useful bargaining counter with the Thais: in return for the supply of oil, they wanted Pibul to guarantee that Thailand would not sell all its tin, rice and rubber to Japan.

First, however, the British considered it necessary to sound out American opinion. Cordell Hull's reaction was that the Thais were past praying for. They were acting in collusion with Japan and the provision of economic or, for that matter, military aid was unlikely to change the situation. On the contrary, it was more likely to benefit Japan in the longer term. These views were based on the consistently hostile assessments of Thai policy submitted by Grant in Bangkok.[60] Nor was he moved when Pibul's pleas for oil were followed by an announcement in early April that petrol rationing was being imposed in Thailand.[61]

Somewhat ironically, American disillusionment with the Thais was matched by similarly pessimistic Japanese assessments. In mid-April Tamura, the military attaché, reported back to Tokyo that most Thais appeared singularly ungrateful for Japan's mediation of the dispute with France, whereas British influence remained strong. Hence Tamura thought that Pibul would still refuse to conclude a military pact with Japan.[62] His views coincided with those of army staff officers in Tokyo. In contrast to their previous ebullience, they were now in a much more sombre mood: they had abandoned virtually all hope of making a rapid and unopposed move to give Japan the upper hand in South East Asia, since even Germany had failed to inflict a major defeat on the British.[63]

The mood was gloomy too at the Foreign Ministry in Tokyo, where progress in drawing up the formal treaty between Thailand and France was slow. The Japanese tended to blame Prince Wan,[64] who was objecting to various detailed provisions which the French wanted included in the treaty. Among their demands was guaranteed access to the site of the ancestral tombs of the kings of Luang Prabang situated in the Lao west bank province of Sayabouri, which was due to be ceded to Thailand. King Sisavangvong of Laos was so angry at losing this territory that he was threatening to abdicate.[65] If anything, the Cambodians were even more irate at losing a third of their national territory, and the death of King Sisowath Monivong in April 1941 has been attributed to his grief at this prospect.[66] As a small gesture to appease the Cambodians, the French argued at length about retaining an enclave on the west bank of the Mekong opposite Stung Treng. Other arguments arose about sovereignty over various islands in the river.

Still, the main stumbling-block was as ever financial and economic. Furious at losing Battambang, the French were determined to make Thailand pay for all the assets it was acquiring and especially a long stretch of railway line through western Cambodia.[67] Prince Wan was just as obdurate. Claiming that Thailand had won the war, he refused to countenance any idea of indemnifying the French. In any case, he maintained that Thailand was a poor country and would have to scrap the whole agreement if the French continued to insist on compensation. The Japanese were so exasperated that they pressed Pibul to give Vanich the authority to conduct the negotiations since he was far more malleable than Prince Wan. Much to the dismay of some cabinet ministers, Pibul complied with the demand.[68]

According to the Japanese press, Vanich had already paid calls on various military figureheads in Tokyo,[69] and he was also reported to have opened trade talks. Direk was worried: he knew there was little hope of Britain agreeing to supply oil from South East Asia if Vanich of all people was known to be negotiating with the Japanese.[70] Within the cabinet, too, Direk orchestrated opposition to any agreement to supply all Thailand's tin and rubber to Japan.[71] Here he had the firm support of Adul: what concerned the police chief most was apparently that in return the Japanese might step up their arms deliveries to Thailand. Besides their military purposes, these weapons could just as easily be used to mount a coup.[72]

In mid-April coup rumours were again rife in Bangkok, fuelled in part by foreign speculation. Apparently the Japanese suspected the British of manoeuvring to enhance their influence, so newspapers in Tokyo predicted an imminent Thai cabinet reshuffle. The Italian press went further and reported Pibul's assassination.[73] Official denials in Bangkok did little to boost Pibul's confidence; he always felt he was treading a precarious line amid the shifting allegiances within his cabinet. Still it was not immediately evident who might lead a coup against him. After the naval defeat in January, Sindhu had lost all credibility as a possible future strongman. Instead the name of Thamrong was being bandied around: he had long been influential among the promoters, and seemed to command respect from every clique, even though he was regarded as pro-Western.[74]

To offset all this speculation, Pibul was anxious to boost his public image by staging an impressive victory parade. Originally it was planned for mid-April, but was postponed because the treaty with France had still not been finalised.[75] Towards the end of the month, Pibul could wait no longer, and irrespective of the negotiations in Tokyo, the parade was held. Troops, who had been specially recalled from the frontier, took an hour to march past. The entire air force also participated in a fly-past. Only the navy was missing, its remaining warships and personnel being confined to the Chao Phya in mourning and disgrace. Nor was Pibul very convincing when he tried to deny that the navy had been defeated. The press had just been allowed to publish casualty figures for the war against the French. According to the Supreme Command, only 150 Thais had been killed in action and a further 500 wounded, but many believed the true figures to be far higher. British and American diplomats in Bangkok also staged a public boycott of the parade in protest against an occasion they saw as marking Thailand's acquisition of territory by force rather than the rule of law.[76]

Despite this rebuff, Pibul was still hoping that the Western powers would help with oil supplies, and decided to send a special envoy to the Netherlands East Indies.[77] He was Vilas Osathanond, a civilian promoter and member of the cabinet. More to the point, Vilas was also a leading director of various state enterprises where his business interests came into conflict with those of Vanich because they were politically opposed. Vilas was related by marriage to a leading Bangkok Chinese family closely associated with the Kuomintang; hence he had links with a wide network of Overseas Chinese businessmen throughout South East Asia.[78] Obviously Pibul was trying to exploit these links by sending Vilas to Batavia and then Singapore while Vanich was well out of the way in Tokyo.

Another of Pibul's special envoys, Prayoon, had finally just returned from his trip to Europe, albeit without the premier's children whom he was supposed to rescue.[79] Instead he had been more intent on getting the Germans to arrange for him to visit Moscow in order to establish diplomatic relations with the Soviet Union.[80] Given the continuance in force of the anti-communist act, it was a significant departure for Thai foreign policy, and Prayoon was proud of his achievement. Having travelled home via the Trans-Siberian railway and Japan, he was full of talk about new opportunities for Thai trade in selling tin and rubber to the Soviet Union.[81] Since Matsuoka too had just visited Moscow to conclude a neutrality pact, the British were afraid that this new international alignment would facilitate the export of Thai strategic commodities to Germany.[82]

In the broader context as well, it looked as if Japan, having secured peace or at least neutrality on the northern borders of its empire, could now turn all its attention southwards. Already large numbers of Japanese were being sent to Thailand on what were obviously intelligence gathering missions.[83] Yet despite his anxiety about their activities, Pibul declined to expel them. Instead he encouraged the British to send their own intelligence agents into Thailand as a counter-balance. Consequently British and Japanese officers engaged on similar missions often found themselves staying at the same guesthouses, especially in southern Thailand.[84]

One reason why Pibul was anxious not to antagonise Japan was his desire to get the negotiations in Tokyo concluded as soon as possible. Even after Vanich took over from Prince Wan, progress was slow. The French continued to insist on compensation for the assets they were relinquishing in Battambang, a demand just as adamantly rejected by the Thais. Eventually, to break the deadlock, the Japanese told Vanich bluntly that Thailand would have to pay up, but to save face this would be kept secret. Pibul was horrified. He feared that if ever word leaked out of a secret payment to France – as it was almost bound to do in gossip-prone Bangkok – he would be ousted immediately. Hence he threatened to scrap the whole agreement. The Japanese were so angry that they exerted intense pressure on the Thais as well as the French to modify their positions. In the end they both had to give way, and a treaty was concluded on May 9 that was satisfactory to neither. In return for the two Lao west-bank provinces, plus most of north-western Cambodia, Thailand had to concede the demilitarisation of all this territory as well as 6 million baht to compensate France. Pibul was utterly dismayed, and the conclusion of the treaty was not marked by any celebrations in Bangkok.[85]

In any case the Thai public, unaccustomed as it then was to economic hardship, was more preoccupied by reports of the country running out of oil. Although there were few private cars in Thailand, diesel fuel was widely used by water-borne transport including fishing boats, a lot of people cooked on kerosene burners, and most of the country's electricity was generated from oil. Consequently the British thought that they might earn some popularity by arranging an emergency delivery of oil to Bangkok.[86] They were encouraged in this view by Direk. Referring to continuing coup rumours, he claimed that Western aid would strengthen Pibul's position and help him stave off Japanese pressure.[87]

Again such arguments failed to convince Grant. The American

Minister believed all the talk about Japanese threats to Pibul's position to be simply a trick to fool the Western powers into giving aid to Thailand.[88] His reports, however, were received with increasing scepticism in Washington. There had been complaints from various quarters about his negative attitude towards the Thais, and it was decided to replace him.[89] Anyway some American officials thought a shipment of oil to Bangkok, as proposed by Britain, might do some good, especially if linked to a demand that the Western oil companies be allowed to resume business in Thailand. The British did not agree, being far more interested in linking the provision of oil to their efforts to stop all Thailand's tin and rubber going to Japan.[90]

It was too late. Although Pibul expressed his "eternal gratitude" for a British oil offer, Vanich had already arranged for emergency shipments from Japan. In return the Japanese demanded a formal guarantee that they would get all the tin and rubber they wanted from Thailand. Direk and Crosby pleaded with Pibul not to bind Thailand to Japan in this way, but without success. The Thai premier was afraid – that the Japanese would topple him from power, and that they might upset the treaty just signed with France. Moreover, given the run of German victories in Greece during May, Pibul now believed that Britain was certain to lose the war. As a result, he signed an agreement on May 20 providing for Japan to purchase 80 per cent of Thailand's annual rubber production and 50 per cent of its tin.

Even then, the Japanese were dissatisfied until Pibul indicated that they could buy up the rest of these commodities on the open market in competition with Western companies if they so wished. It sent the prices of tin and rubber rocketing in Bangkok and presented the Japanese with another problem.[91] The yen was not recognised as an internationally convertible currency, and they had few reserves of sterling or dollars to spare for commodity purchases in Thailand. That led to the despatch from Tokyo in early June of a high-ranking financial delegation to put pressure on the Thais to grant a baht credit loan.[92] Its arrival in Bangkok coincided with the return home of Vilas happily proclaiming that he had made satisfactory arrangements with the British for Thailand's future oil supplies.[93]

The Japanese reacted by launching a vicious press campaign against Vilas: he was branded as a Kuomintang agent who had gone to Singapore and Batavia to enlist the support of Thai exiles living there in ousting Pibul and placing Prince Boripat on the throne. Unfortunately for the credibility of the Japanese correspondent who filed the story, he got some of his facts wrong, including the whereabouts of Phya Song. This alerted the Thai press, which poured scorn on the anti-Vilas campaign and attributed its inspiration to Vanich, the rivalry between the two men being well-known.[94] It made Pibul more nervous than ever, and he wrote to Vilas accusing him of deliberately trying to sabotage the treaty with France which was then in the process of ratification.[95]

During the Assembly debate on the treaty, Pibul actually put in an appearance and made a lengthy speech in an attempt to ward off criticism from the irredentists. He was not entirely successful. Various members of the Assembly questioned why Thailand had not regained all its lost territories. In replying to them, it was noticeable that Pibul frequently turned to Prince Wan for advice.[96] For all his public oratory, Pibul lacked the skill of a parliamentary debater.

By that stage, too, much of the statesmanlike aura he assumed on becoming premier had been eroded. Pibul ceased giving press conferences, and his public appearances were again becoming increasingly rare. Instead personal whims seemed to play a growing part in his decisions. For instance he decreed that women should wear hats, previously used only as a shield from the sun, to prove that Thailand was civilised.[97] Now European-style hats became the fashion under the guidance of Pibul's wife Khunying La-iad, as she was officially called.[98]

Titles and ranks were another of Pibul's obsessions. After the signing of the treaty with France, all officers in the armed forces were automatically promoted one rank, including Pibul who became a lieutenant-general. Yet he was conspicuously absent during the National Day celebrations when the main event was the laying of the cornerstone of another monument, this time to mark the victory over the French. Instead the ceremony was presided over by Phya Phahol, who still enjoyed great public respect.[99] Nor did Pibul participate personally in any of the other ceremonies held to mark Thai assumption of responsibility for the territory acquired from Indo-China.

The main such ceremony took place in Battambang on July 25 with Khuang Abhaiwongse, the Director of Posts and Telegraphs, representing the Thai government; he was chosen because his father had been the last Thai governor of Battambang before the French took it over in 1907. Khuang had inherited the flag that once flew over his father's office, and he was delighted to hoist it there again. For the occasion, he was escorted to Battambang by Thai troops in apparent contravention of the treaty with France stipulating the demilitarisation of all the ceded territory. The Thais brushed aside protests on this score by claiming that the troops entered Battambang purely for ceremonial purposes.[100]

Dealing with the rest of northern Cambodia was a different problem. As Prince Wan had remarked, most of it was jungle, which Thailand lacked the resources to administer or develop. That was very evident to the Thai officer assigned to plant the flag on the country's new eastern border on the bank of the Mekong facing Stung Treng. He took a month travelling by horseback and bullock cart to reach his destination. By the time he got there, most of his transport animals had died. He too was very ill and barely capable of returning to Bangkok.[101] Such facts did not bother Pibul, and in later years he even claimed that his main reason for taking over all this territory was to push Thailand's borders further east and make Bangkok less vulnerable to Japanese attack.[102] Yet as soon as Thailand moved into western Cambodia, Japan assumed military control over the rest of Indo-China, so prompting suspicions that these operations were coordinated in advance.[103]

Japan's new southward move also followed closely on the German invasion of the Soviet Union. As such it came as a surprise to those who expected, or demanded as did Hitler, that Japan once more turn its attention northwards to help the Germans against the Russians in the spirit of the Triple Alliance between the Axis powers.[104] The idea was given some thought in Tokyo, but eventually the views of the navy prevailed. In early June, naval staff officers had drawn up a policy document based on the premise that if the New Order in East Asia was to flourish, it was essential for Japan to gain guaranteed access to South East Asia's raw materials.[105] Not only was Britain trying to block the sale of Thai tin and rubber, but the authorities in the Netherlands East Indies were also refusing to allow Japan to purchase more oil.[106] All these issues were under constant discussion in a series of top-level meetings held in Tokyo throughout June, which culminated in a decision taken on July 2 to move troops into southern Indo-China in order to establish naval and air bases there in preparation for a further southward strike.

During the imperial conference which took the decision, it was proposed that force be applied to Thailand as well to put an end to what was seen in Tokyo as British intrigue in Bangkok. This time it was the Army Chief of Staff who opposed such action, arguing that any overt military move into Thailand would certainly provoke immediate British counter-action. Although most Japanese leaders, including the Emperor, now accepted that war with Britain and the United States was probably inevitable, they still did not feel sufficiently prepared for it. Consequently the idea of using force against Thailand was shelved for the time being in the hope that the advance into southern Indo-China might in itself have a salutary effect on Pibul by scaring him into curtailing British influence and signing a military pact with Japan.[107]

For once the Americans were the first to react to Japan's new military move. All Japanese assets in the United States were immediately frozen and an almost total embargo was imposed on trade between the two countries. Britain quickly followed suit.[108] But there was little the Thais could do, and to them the threat looked far more menacing with Japanese troops now based along the entire length of their eastern border. By contrast the Americans believed that Japan would simply hand the rest of Laos and Cambodia over to Pibul.[109]

Instead the only concession the Japanese made to the Thais was to give Pibul a few hours' advance notice of their new move in Indo-China.[110] It was followed on July 25 by a series of demands. Accompanied by Vanich, the Japanese financial official who had arrived in Bangkok a month earlier called on Pibul to insist that Thailand discontinue all negotiations with Britain over oil, reaffirm its guarantee to export the major part of its tin and rubber production to Japan, join the yen currency bloc and recognise the governments in both Manchukuo and Nanking.[111] In other words, Japan was trying to enforce the terms of the secret pledge Pibul had given nine months earlier and had tried to wriggle out of ever since. That was something he refused to acknowledge. Instead, in a mood of desperation verging on panic, he convened a cabinet meeting straight away to discuss Japan's demands. Hastily he got it to agree to the recognition of Manchukuo. But the first the public knew of his reaction to the crisis over Indo-China was an announcement that he had been promoted Field-Marshal and awarded a lot more decorations.[112] As a result he now held every honour that could be bestowed in Thailand except the Chakri family order. Even then, some of his colleagues had to restrain him from using the actual Field-Marshal's baton that had previously been carried by the Chakri monarchs.[113]

In more practical vein, Pibul informed Crosby of Japan's demands almost as soon as he received them.[114] The British thought he was not telling the whole truth; they believed that Japan had also demanded military cooperation from Thailand in return for more territorial concessions in Indo-China. Direk denied it, and passed on a desperate appeal from Pibul for Western help in resisting Japan's demands. What he wanted was economic aid and particularly oil plus arms to boost Thailand's defences. Above all, he pleaded for the British and Americans to issue a firm warning to Japan to deter it from attacking Thailand.[115]

As had been the case ever since Pibul first enunciated Thailand's claims on Indo-China, the United States mistrusted him and the Thais in general. The attitude of Cordell Hull was that they had betrayed Indo-China to the Japanese, and were stringing Britain along to obtain oil and other supplies. However, the United States had no intention of being caught up in their duplicity.[116] Roosevelt was more or less of the same opinion. He said that if Japan moved troops into Thailand there would be no way of knowing whether or not they had been invited in under some clandestine military agreement; therefore, neither Western power should give any prior guarantee to defend Thai sovereignty. In any case the American president was ever mindful of the constitutional constraint requiring him to obtain congressional approval before entering into any commitments which might lead to war.[117] Even so, the State Department expanded the proposal it had just put to Japan about the neutralisation of Indo-China to include Thailand as well. The Japanese immediately countered with their own set of alternative proposals which made no reference whatsoever to Thailand.[118]

All this diplomatic activity coincided with a meeting between Churchill and Roosevelt aboard a warship off the coast of Newfoundland to sign the Atlantic Charter. In Churchill's absence from London, the British cabinet decided that the danger of Japan treating Thailand as it had treated Indo-China was so imminent that only a joint Anglo-American warning might act as a deterrent. Churchill tried to persuade Roosevelt to adopt such a course, but again Hull objected. He feared that such a warning might be used by the Japanese as a pretext to break off the bilateral talks they were holding with the United States.[119] Nonetheless, at a press conference on August 6, the American Secretary of State ventured so far as to remark that a Japanese move into Thailand would be considered a step menacing American security in the Pacific. On the same day, his British counterpart Anthony Eden warned in far stronger terms of the grave consequences that would ensue from a Japanese attack on Thailand.[120]

Although these statements were not as strong as Pibul might have hoped, both he and Direk expressed their gratitude. They also continued to plead for economic and military assistance while assuring the Western powers that Thailand would resist a Japanese invasion for as long as it could.[121] Finally Hull softened his attitude and promised that if Thailand were attacked, it would receive aid from the United States in the same way as China. In other words, once the Thais had proved in action their will to resist Japan, they could expect to receive American supplies – but not before. Here again, the British regarded the Americans as short-sighted. The view in London was that unless Thailand was reinforced in advance, it would be unable to defend itself. The British therefore embarked on interdepartmental discussions to determine whether even at that crucial stage in the war there was any military equipment that could possibly be spared for Thailand.[122]

In the meantime British forces in Malaya were moved up to the border and alerted to the possibility of a Japanese attack at any time. A British warship, the *Warspite*, was also reported to be patrolling the Gulf of Thailand,[123] although this was not true. Despite numerous pleas from Crosby for a show of British naval strength in South East Asian waters to impress the Thais and deter the Japanese, no capital ships were available for the purpose until at least the end of 1941 because of the priority given in London to the war in the Mediterranean and the Battle of the Atlantic.[124]

Such considerations were ignored by the Japanese press, which seized on the British military moves in Malaya and the alleged presence of the *Warspite* in the Gulf of Thailand to claim that it was the British who were threatening the Thais and creating an atmosphere of crisis in East Asia. Equally, the Japanese branded the warnings issued by Hull and Eden as "unwarrantable".[125] Pibul was so worried that he made an impassioned broadcast to proclaim that Thailand would defend itself and never yield an inch to any external aggression, no matter whether it came from Britain, Japan or anywhere else. He even called on members of the public holding stocks of poison gas to place them at the disposal of the army![126]

In private Pibul's mood was very different. He was desperately trying to devise ways of rejecting as many of Japan's demands as he dared. In his eyes, the decision to recognise Manchukuo was simply a sop to appease Japan, since it was not a matter of great principle as far as Thailand was concerned; on the other hand, he was determined not to recognise the government of Wang Ching-wei in Nanking, and thought he could maintain that line on the grounds that Thailand had never had any diplomatic relations with China. The demands for tin and rubber were more difficult to cope with: here Pibul came up with the idea of scrapping all his previous commitments on commodities, whether with Britain or Japan, and placing all supplies on the open market where any country was welcome to buy provided it could pay the price. The unspoken intention was to place the Japanese at a disadvantage because of their lack of convertible currency. They realised it and countered by applying even more pressure in the financial sphere.[127]

At first Pridi was successful in warding off Japanese demands for baht credit loans. He argued that there was no precedent and no need for such arrangements since Japan could easily obtain dollars or sterling. The situation changed when the Americans and British imposed their freeze on Japanese assets. Pridi thought it prudent to modify his stance and agreed to a consortium of Thai banks extending a 10 million baht credit to Japan but only on condition that the equivalent in gold be deposited in Bangkok and not in Tokyo as the Japanese proposed. He had no intention of being tricked into transferring part of Thailand's national reserves to Japan so forcing it to join the yen currency bloc being created as part of the ''New Order'' in East Asia.

In mid-August the Japanese tried again. Claiming that the 10 million baht credit was already exhausted, they demanded a further 25 millions. Pridi refused, especially since the Japanese wanted to impose far stiffer conditions than before. That involved him in a furious quarrel with the head of the Japanese financial delegation, who went straight off to Pibul to denounce Pridi as cantankerous and an obstruction to good relations between the two countries. Initially the Thai premier was inclined to back his Finance Minister, but on August 20 the Japanese, with the help of Vanich, brought further pressure to bear on Pibul, who forced Pridi to compromise. Another baht loan was agreed, although again only on condition that the counterpart in gold was deposited in Bangkok.[128]

In his efforts to resist Japanese pressure, Pridi knew that he now had the support of public opinion. With the Japanese advance into Indo-China, any lingering traces of euphoria generated by the settlement in Tokyo were dissipated. Even Vichit moderated the tone of his speeches. Everyone was scared by reports of Japanese troops being stationed along the east bank of the Mekong.[129] Pibul was utterly dismayed, especially when he recalled how during the negotiations in Tokyo the Japanese had rejected Thai proposals for a demilitarised zone on the French side of the border. Now it seemed clear that Japan had simply been paving the way for its own troops to move in and threaten Thailand.[130]

Other aspects of his past policies were also causing Pibul problems. Japan insisted that he suspend Thailand's newly established diplomatic relations with the Soviet Union.[131] Meanwhile, through Prayoon the Germans warned him not to trust Japan.[132] To cope with these conflicting cross-currents Pibul decided on August 21 to appoint Prayoon and

Vichit deputy Ministers of Foreign Affairs on a par with Direk. Immediately Crosby warned that in promoting such well-known pro-Axis sympathisers Pibul risked forfeiting any aid from Britain and the United States. The threat had its effect. Pibul decided to appoint Direk Minister of Foreign Affairs in place of himself, and several days later he got rid of his other ministerial responsibilities. Prom Yothi became Minister of Defence and another military promoter took over the interior portfolio.[133]

This cabinet reshuffle was not arranged in the usual way through a caucus of the promoters. The first Direk knew of his new appointment was when Pibul's aide-de-camp[134] mentioned it casually a couple of hours before a broadcast announcement.[135] Simultaneously, in another surprise move, Adul was named deputy premier, a position which had not previously existed; in the past, when Pibul was temporarily absent from Bangkok, Pridi had automatically taken over. Now that he had obviously antagonised the Japanese, Pibul possibly thought it wiser to nominate an alternative.

Still, having rearranged the government to function without him, the Field-Marshal had himself appointed Commander-in-Chief of all three armed forces. As a result, some people thought he was preparing to assume royal powers; he was known to admire Napoleon, with whose early career his own bore some resemblance.[136] There was also the precedent of the first Chakri monarch who started his rise to power by campaigning to reunite and expand the kingdom after it had fallen apart under the previous dynasty. Others, including Pridi, believed that Pibul was modelling himself more on Mussolini, and that by divesting himself of ministerial responsibilities, he was merely creating scapegoats to take the blame if any major misfortune should befall Thailand.[137]

Anyway, all these changes left Pibul free to turn once more to the issue of Thai civilisation. After an interval of nine months, another *Rattaniyom* emerged on September 8, which instructed the Thais to organise their lives by dividing the day into three: between six and eight hours had to be allocated to sleep, the daylight hours to work with only an hour off for lunch, and the rest of the time to physical exercise, gardening, cultural pursuits and listening to the radio. The *Rattaniyom* also decreed that Thais should eat no more than four meals a day.[138] At the same time orders were issued reinforcing previous strictures against disorderly behaviour such as pushing on to buses. The dress rules too were reiterated and elaborated. Women were advised to wear not just skirts and hats but also gloves with matching handbags and shoes. Men entering government offices were required to wear a hat and doff it in a bow rather than a *wai* – the customary Thai greeting with palms pressed together.[139]

In attempting to popularise these measures, Pibul resorted again to the radio dialogues of *Nai Man* and *Nai Kong*. This time, their task was more difficult than during the irredentist campaign. In one broadcast explaining the dress and conduct rules, they admitted that some people thought the Prime Minister had become insane in concentrating on such trivialities when the world was in crisis and Thailand possibly on the brink of war. Others questioned how the poor could find the money to buy hats and shoes at a time of constantly rising prices.[140] Racial discrimination was involved too. Beside the ban on Chinese pyjama-style trousers, Indian women wearing saris were barred from public buildings and buses. Others who suffered were Thai Muslims, and in their case religion impinged as well. The anti-Catholic movement during the irredentist campaign developed into a ban on all non-Buddhists working in government or military service, and many were forced to convert.[141] Pibul caused further resentment by issuing decrees banning aliens, often at short notice, from living in areas considered to be strategically important, such as the vicinity of Thai military garrisons. As a result, numerous Chinese and Indian traders had to abandon their businesses and homes at great financial loss. Yet despite the influence of such Nazi sympathisers as Prayoon and Vichit with Pibul, he never attempted to emulate Hitler's more extreme measures against the Jews.[142]

Far from being a ruthless dictator, Pibul in some respects was very timorous. After Japan moved into southern Indo-China, he was afraid to announce the mobilisation of the armed forces to meet the new threat to Thailand's borders for fear of provoking a Japanese reaction. Instead, secret orders went out by letter instructing the army to prepare for the possibility of war.[143] *Nai Man* and *Nai Kong* were also stopped from warning the public about the potential Japanese threat. Rather, Pibul asked the British to carry out the task through a radio station broadcasting in Thai from Penang.[144] The furthest Pibul himself dared venture was to get the Assembly to pass legislation making it mandatory for every citizen to oppose anybody violating Thai sovereignty. It was to be done by pursuing a scorched earth policy and denying all food and property to the enemy. So drastic was the wording of the law that it opened up visions of the whole of Thailand being reduced to a wilderness in the face of an enemy attack.[145]

The public was far less reticent than Pibul in identifying the potential source of aggression. Japanese claiming to be businessmen, doctors or even tourists were turning up everywhere including remote villages which the Thai military barely knew existed.[146] The influx of Japanese spies was particularly blatant in Bangkok, where some local people became distinctly hostile. Following several brawls and stabbing incidents, the Japanese ambassador warned his compatriots to comport themselves more carefully in Thailand.[147]

The hostility was extended to Japan's friends within the Thai administration. Obviously the most prominent was Vanich, who had been promoted to a senior position in the Foreign Ministry at the same time as Prayoon and Vichit. That led to the circulation of a clandestine leaflet accusing Vanich of embezzling government funds and acting as a fifth-columnist for Japan. Similar suspicions had long been harboured by Adul and the secret police, who backed up public calls for an official committee to investigate Vanich. It comprised Thamrong, Pridi and Direk. Like the police they found it hard to charge Vanich with being a fifth-columnist because he was acting so openly on behalf of the Japanese. Indeed, he made frequent visits to the Japanese embassy to report how the investigation was proceeding.[148]

Pibul was so obviously worried that Crosby sought to help him out by suggesting that the best way to deal with Vanich would be to send him off as ambassador to Tokyo. The Thai legation there had just been upgraded to an embassy because the Japanese had insisted on raising the status of their diplomatic relations with Thailand. Since the United States and Britain declined to follow suit, Japan now took pride of place in the diplomatic sphere, and Pibul said that Vanich was far too junior to be appointed to Thailand's first and only ambassadorship. In any case, he told Crosby, the Japanese might construe it as banishment.[149] The press in Tokyo had weighed into the controversy by claiming that Vanich was being victimised by Prom Yothi.[150]

Following their long-held belief that Prom Yothi was pro-Western, the Japanese now had extra cause for concern because of his appointment as Minister of Defence. On the other hand, his role in leading the army in the war against the French had made him a national hero in the eyes of the Thai public. Prom Yothi gambled on this popularity in protesting against the Japanese allegations by tendering his resignation from the Defence Ministry. Finally Pibul decided to try and appease everybody by declining to accept Prom Yothi's resignation and retaining the services of Vanich both at the Foreign Ministry and the Department of Commerce.[151]

Japanese pressure on Pibul was being deliberately intensified.[152] On September 6, another imperial conference held in Tokyo had formally decided to complete preparations for a war against Britain, the United States and the Netherlands East Indies by the end of October. In these plans it was assumed that Thailand would side with Japan.[153]

Irrespective of how much Pibul was actually told of the decisions taken in Tokyo, he certainly knew that the threat of war was growing. In mid-October he made a desperate plea to the British and Americans for military equipment and particularly aircraft to boost Thailand's defences, but even in making the request, he had to be careful: the Japanese had noted the number of times he saw Crosby, and complained. Hence Pibul resorted more than ever to the services of Direk as a messenger. In particular he used this channel to enquire what Britain would do if Japan invaded Thailand. Pibul also wanted to know what steps the Thais could take to coordinate their military planning with the British in Malaya.[154]

Ever since the strengthening of the naval base at Singapore, the British had obviously been thinking about the defence of Malaya, but there were still divided opinions among military planners as to where the Japanese might strike first. The picture changed when Japan started building bases in southern Indo-China only a few hundred miles across the Gulf of Thailand from the Malayan peninsula.[155] There was now a distinct possibility of Japanese troops landing along the Thai coast south of the Kra isthmus, which prompted the British military in Singapore to draft a plan, code-named Operation Matador, providing for forces based in northern Malaya to cross the border and take up positions around Songkla and its adjacent beaches twenty-four hours before the Japanese landed there.[156] Still the planners were mindful of Thai neutrality. The launching of Operation Matador was made conditional on the Japanese first violating Thai sovereignty elsewhere. This was inherently unlikely if Japan's aim was to use Thailand to invade Malaya, but the British were reluctant to get round this fatal flaw in their planning by seeking prior approval from Pibul to move troops into Songkla and its environs.[157]

Even without American penetration of Japanese cypher traffic, the British knew from previous experience that their dealings with Pibul were almost invariably leaked to Tokyo. Another factor giving rise to mistrust in Singapore was the continuing deployment of Thai troops in the south along the border with Malaya: in British eyes, they should have been moved to confront the Japanese in Indo-China where the real threat to Thailand lay.[158] Consequently, many British and Americans thought Pibul insincere in requesting Western aid, and that he had already entered into some sort of military alliance with Japan.

One of the few *farangs* who continued to have some faith in Pibul was Crosby, and it was largely due to his efforts that Thai pleas for military aid received further consideration in both London and Washington. There was little the British could offer. They themselves were now very dependent on US military equipment. Even though the Americans were still reluctant to become directly involved in the war, they were also providing arms to China and the Soviet Union and claimed that they too had none to spare for Thailand. All they would concede was that if the British felt strong enough to defend themselves against the Japanese threat in the Far East, there would be no objection to the supply to Thailand of various items of American military equipment such as aircraft already delivered to Singapore.[159]

The idea did not appeal. The military in Singapore were not prepared to hand over any of the planes they were counting on for the defence of Malaya. Their overall view was that if Japan invaded Thailand, any military equipment supplied to it would soon be captured. Even so, as a gesture of goodwill, the British offered to provide the Thai army with howitzers and shells to the value of £250,000 and this was welcomed by a military delegation Pibul had sent to Singapore.[160] His own reaction was just the opposite; he dismissed the British offer as so insignificant as to constitute an insult to Thailand. His attitude did not endear him to officials in London, where every gun and shell was considered precious in the life-and-death struggle Britain was still waging against Germany.[161]

Anyway, in early November neither the British nor the Americans thought an attack on Thailand was imminent, but their assessments were based on several serious miscalculations. British officers in Singapore believed that the Japanese were unlikely to plan landings in southern Thailand during December or January because the terrain there would be too waterlogged to push on into Malaya. As for the airfields which the Japanese were constructing in southern Indo-China, the Americans thought they would not be ready for use at least till the end of February, by which time the rainy season would make flying impossible. Here the British quickly pointed out that the dry season in mainland as distinct from peninsular South East Asia usually lasts until May. Even so, American analysts thought that Japan's next objective would be a push through southern Yunnan to cut the Burma Road and the flow of Western supplies to Chiang Kai-shek.[162]

Another factor affecting American attitudes was the talks they were holding with the Japanese in Washington, which continued despite the decision taken in Tokyo at the beginning of September to prepare for war against the Western powers. The situation was re-assessed at a further imperial conference held on November 5, when it was agreed that unless a satisfactory settlement was reached in the Washington talks within the next three weeks, Japan would declare war in early December. In that event, a document approved by the Emperor provided for close military relations to be established with Thailand just before the outbreak of hostilities.[163] The Japanese were worried that if they moved any earlier to cement relations with Pibul, it might give the game away and provoke an immediate British reaction.[164]

Nonetheless, the Japanese were intent on exploiting such leverage as they already had over the Thais. For instance, under the Franco-Thai treaty they had gained the right to preside over a joint commission whose task was to resolve any financial, administrative, political or border problems arising from the territorial transfer. The commission was based in Saigon until early November, when the Japanese suddenly demanded that it move to Bangkok. The Thais were not so easily deceived. In contrast to the acrimony preceding the conclusion of the treaty, the commission had few problems to contend with and certainly none which justified a further Japanese demand to base aircraft in Thailand to help the commission by conducting aerial surveillance of the border with Indo-China. Hence the cabinet rejected both these demands. Not so Pibul: through one of his protégés who was a member of the joint commission in Saigon,[165] he agreed to its transfer to Bangkok, and its Japanese members immediately set off to travel there by land from Saigon. At the border they were all subjected to intensive customs checks, and protested vehemently to Pibul, who reacted by venting his anger on Pridi as the minister ultimately responsible for the customs department.[166]

Such outbursts by Pibul against his colleagues were becoming ever more frequent. He was clearly in a state of nervous apprehension born of fear. With the Japanese manifestly building up their military strength in Indo-China, he still did not dare to take overt steps to strengthen Thailand's eastern border defences. Instead, referring to rising tension in all directions, the Field-Marshal reconstituted the Supreme Command with himself at its head.[167] He also secretly instructed the army Chief of Staff[168] to draw up plans to counter a Japanese invasion as well as a British attack.[169]

Another of Pibul's ideas was to move the government, so that Bangkok could be spared damage by being declared an open city. Others thought that the real intention was to base the government up-country where it was easier to resist the Japanese. While acknowledging that it would be more natural for the Thais to move north in these circumstances, the British still hoped that the government would consider going south to facilitate military liaison with Malaya. In any event, nothing was said to Pibul about the idea lest it prejudice the secrecy of Operation Matador.[170]

Despite similar Japanese concern about maintaining secrecy, the purpose of some of their moves was blatantly obvious. Japanese resident in Thailand were trying to amass as much small coinage as they could, and pressure was again exerted on Pridi to authorise another baht loan, this time to be paid in cash rather than commercial credits. Direk too suspected an ulterior motive when for once Japanese diplomats tried to court his friendship. He was convinced that Thailand would be Japan's next target.[171]

The Western powers now tended to agree. Their problem was to determine whether Japan's next forward move would be limited to Thailand alone. Neither Britain nor, even less, the United States was prepared to risk war with Japan simply for the sake of defending Thailand.[172] As a result, Pibul and Direk received no positive response throughout November to their numerous pleas for some sort of undertaking or public statement from the Western powers about taking action in the event of a Japanese attack on Thailand.[173]

Towards the end of November, perceptions of the imminence and scope of the next move by the Japanese changed rapidly. They were observed to be moving supplies and manpower southwards through the East China Sea to the island of Hainan, where a large quantity of Japanese shipping was gathering. To monitor further developments, the Western powers agreed to coordinate aerial reconnaissance over the sea-lanes around the southern tip of Indo-China.[174] The next major development occurred in Washington where the Japanese-American talks became deadlocked on November 27. The US Navy was immediately issued with a war warning specifying the targets of probable Japanese attack as the Philippines, Thailand and British North Borneo.[175]

At the same time the British Commander, Far East, asked London for permission to launch Operation Matador without having to obtain prior cabinet authorisation.[176] Churchill was reluctant. Pre-occupied with the war in Europe, the last thing he wanted was hostilities in the Far East.

But he had to take into account the attitude of the British dominions such as Australia which believed that the whole empire would be at risk if Thailand fell to the Japanese.[177] Equally crucial for Churchill was the American attitude. On November 29, the British ambassador in Washington was told to ask Hull what the United States would do if Japan invaded Thailand. There was no direct reply.[178]

The next day American intelligence intercepted and deciphered a cable to Tokyo from the Japanese ambassador in Bangkok about a plan to entice the British into invading southern Thailand, so providing Japan with a pretext to rush in troops to its defence.[179] Obviously it made the authorisation of Operation Matador even more difficult, but in Washington the intercepted Japanese message, coupled with other intelligence reports, prompted Hull to recall Roosevelt from his weekend retreat.[180] As soon as the President arrived back in Washington, he gave the British an undertaking that if they moved into southern Thailand, American support would be forthcoming. Only first before making any public commitment, Roosevelt decided to make a direct personal appeal to the Emperor of Japan for peace.[181]

Meanwhile on the basis of Roosevelt's pledge, Churchill's cabinet gave the British Commander, Far East, the go-ahead to launch Operation Matador on his own initiative as soon as the situation warranted.[182] For the first time, too, Crosby was sent details of the plan and asked to make discreet soundings about likely Thai reaction. In reply he and Direk sent back a joint appeal "for God's sake" not to permit British troops to occupy an inch of Thai soil unless or until Japan struck the first blow. They insisted that at all costs Thai neutrality must be respected.[183]

In associating Direk with his appeal, Crosby was acting beyond the bounds of normal diplomatic practice, but clearly he felt the situation merited it, especially since he regarded Pibul as having the mind of a child with little grasp of strategic realities.[184] Had Crosby known what was happening behind the scenes, his disillusion would have been even greater. At several cabinet meetings from November 18 onwards, Pibul developed his ideas on how Thailand should react to what he foresaw as the inevitable war between Japan and Britain. He did not seem to envisage the Americans being involved, and predicted that the British would soon be overwhelmed. In any case, he claimed, Britain would never come to the defence of Thailand. Therefore the Thais should side with Japan from the first in order to save their country from becoming a battlefield.[185]

The idea of minimising the damage suffered by Thailand was also the

main topic of Pibul's frequent conversations with Tamura, which led
the military attaché to believe that his old friend was about to give Japan
all it wanted. In Tokyo General Tojo, the War Minister, who had just
taken over the premiership as well, was still not convinced. On December 1 at the final imperial conference before the outbreak of war,
he continued to express doubts about where Pibul's real allegiance lay.[186]
Hence there were no last-minute changes in Japan's plans relating to
Thailand. They entailed waiting until a couple of hours before Japan
declared war on the Western powers; then, and only then, Pibul was to
be asked for transit rights and facilities for Japanese troops moving into
Thailand as a prelude to a full-scale military alliance.[187] Instructions to
this effect were despatched on December 2 to Tsubokami Teiji, the
newly-arrived Japanese ambassador in Bangkok. What he was not told
was the timing of the call he had to make on Pibul. That crucial piece of
information was to follow later.

The embargo contained in these instructions presented Tsubokami
with a difficult decision later that evening when Pibul asked to see him
to beg that Thailand be spared the suffering of war. The moment seemed
opportune to propose the conclusion of a military pact which would
mean that Pibul need no longer fear a Japanese invasion. In the event,
Tsubokami chose to ignore the embargo and take his chance.[188] Pibul,
however, made no direct response – possibly he did not feel brave
enough to face up to the decision confronting him – but he pleaded once
more with Tamura "for the sake of Thailand's honour" that no
Japanese troops move into Bangkok or the heartlands of the Chao Phya
basin. In return for such a favour, Pibul promised to close his eyes to a
Japanese move into the area south of the Kra isthmus. That still did not
amount to the pledge of full cooperation he had given at the height of
the irredentist crisis, but even so Tamura expressed gratitude and,
promising to do what he could, quickly flew off to put the proposition
to the Japanese high command based in Saigon.[189]

Meanwhile Pibul, knowing that he had to justify his secret diplomacy
with the Japanese to his colleagues, tried a new tack. At a cabinet
meeting on December 3, he argued that if the Thais fought the Japanese,
they would not simply be beaten; the Japanese would also get rid of the
government which had plunged Thailand into war and replace it with a
compliant regime composed of opponents of the promoters such as Phya
Thephatsadin.[190] Bangkok, on the other hand, was once more rife with
rumour about an imminent coup by pro-Japanese elements within the
military in preparation for an invasion expected at any moment.[191]

All the main Japanese military and naval commanders received a message on December 2 which simply said "Climb Mount Niitaka 1208". Its recipients knew that it meant they had to attack their designated targets soon after midnight Tokyo time on December 8.[192] The fleet which the Western powers had noticed assembling off Hainan immediately started embarking troops, before setting sail on December 4.[193] Two days later it was seen rounding the southernmost tip of Indo-China. The observation was made by an Australian reconnaissance plane operating out of Kota Bahru on the east coast of Malaya at the farthest extent of its range. Hence it had little time before returning to base, to determine where the Japanese fleet was heading. There seemed to be several possibilities including an anchorage off Cambodia, the mouth of the Chao Phya, southern Thailand or even Malaya.

Still despite several further sightings of Japanese warships in the Gulf of Thailand on December 7, senior British officers hesitated to order the launching of Operation Matador. Among other things, they were mindful of Crosby's warning about the need to respect Thai sovereignty which had apparently not yet been violated by the Japanese. For the British on the ground in northern Malaya, the situation was particularly frustrating. Thai troops on the other side of the border were observed digging in and strengthening their positions, while the forces assigned to launch Operation Matador were ordered on to the alert in atrocious weather pending a further decision when the situation became clearer.[194]

This was precisely the dilemma with which the Japanese hoped to confront the British. After rounding southern Indo-China, the Japanese fleet was under instructions to set a course apparently heading in the direction of the mouth of the Chao Phya and Bangkok until 0900 hours local time on December 7. Only then were the ships involved to disperse and head for their designated landings in Thailand and Malaya. These orders involved a gamble.[195] The Japanese were hoping for bad weather in the Gulf of Thailand to prevent aerial reconnaissance of their movements. On the other hand, the early onset of the north-east monsoon would make their planned landings on the east coast of southern Thailand and Malaya extremely difficult.[196] They were lucky. Because of poor visibility throughout December 7, British aircraft were unable to determine the size and destination of the Japanese fleet without being shot down; and late that evening, when a report was received in Singapore that Japanese warships had been sighted off Songkla, it was decided that no further action could be taken till next morning, when it was hoped the weather would clear up.[197]

In London there was a greater sense of urgency. Churchill decided that he must send a personal message to warn and reassure Pibul. It was despatched from London early in the afternoon of December 7,[198] which, because of the time difference, was already well into the evening in Bangkok. However, Crosby had already received word direct from Singapore of the Japanese fleet movement, and decided to warn Direk. Since the two men knew each other well, he called uninvited at Direk's house that Sunday evening. Reacting as a Foreign Minister, Direk insisted that his fellow-countrymen would resist a Japanese invasion. The Assembly had just passed a bill for the call-up of all able-bodied men, and according to the press more than one million had already volunteered for military service.[199] Even so, Direk said that Thailand felt like a five-year-old child in the warpath of an elephant.[200]

That same evening Direk had invited Adul to dinner, and on his arrival told him of Crosby's warning. It came as little surprise, because through his own secret intelligence channels the police chief had already heard from Saigon about the movement of the Japanese fleet. What was more puzzling was Pibul's sudden departure from Bangkok, leaving Adul as acting premier. While he and Direk were discussing these developments, the telephone rang with a call for Adul. He refused to answer because nobody was supposed to know where he was and he feared a trap, especially with the Japanese about to invade Thailand. Eventually a compromise was reached: Adul agreed to meet his caller at secret police headquarters, and hurried off without eating. All he told Direk was that the situation was critical.

Later that evening Direk's phone rang again with a call for him. He was summoned urgently to Suan Kularb, which served both as Pibul's residence and Government House. On arrival there Direk noticed the Japanese ambassador and some members of his staff waiting in a downstairs reception room, and to avoid them took the back stairs to the upper offices. There he found Adul, who explained that Tsubokami had demanded an urgent interview with Pibul and on finding him absent had asked to see his deputy. Adul was reluctant to meet the ambassador; he had always kept aloof from the diplomatic corps, and in any case he considered it more appropriate for an ambassador to be received by the Foreign Minister. Direk agreed and went downstairs to meet the Japanese who were accompanied by Vanich.[201]

Tsubokami had received instructions from Tokyo only that morning concerning an approach he had to make before midnight to Pibul and nobody else. But on the previous day Pibul had notified the Japanese that he was leaving Bangkok, and had not said when he would be back. Somehow he had to be contacted and persuaded to return before the deadline expired. The Japanese could not very well go chasing around the country looking for him. Nor was there anybody readily available to help them: Sindhu, as usual every weekend, was away with the navy somewhere in the Gulf of Thailand, and even Vanich proved difficult to locate. Tamura, who had just returned more or less empty-handed from his flying visit to Saigon, spent all Sunday morning searching Bangkok in vain. Finally Vanich was discovered in mid-afternoon at the Assembly, which was meeting in emergency session to decide whether or not to adjourn as usual every year for the holiday surrounding Constitution Day. In their frantic concern to contact Pibul, the Japanese had forgotten such niceties. Anyway Vanich, once he was found, enlisted the help of his friend, the Minister of Economic Affairs,[202] who phoned Adul at Direk's house. Meanwhile, twenty members of the staff of the Japanese embassy, plus a senior military officer specially detached from the military headquarters in Saigon, as well as Vanich, gathered in the early evening, and then proceeded in an impressive convoy of cars to Suan Kularb for what turned out to be an interview with Direk.[203]

Tsubokami immediately launched into a prepared statement. Japan, he said, had been subjected to intolerable pressure by the Western powers and had decided to rise up in self-defence and declare war on its oppressors. The ultimate goal was to implement a policy of Asia for the Asians. In the spirit of this doctrine, Tsubokami formally requested permission for Japanese troops to pass through Thailand in order to attack the British in Burma and Malaya. He asked for a reply by 2 a.m. In other words, it was an ultimatum which left the Thais barely three hours to make up their minds.

Direk's instinctive reaction was to refer to Thailand's traditional policy of neutrality and then to the law binding all Thais to resist any foreign troops setting foot on their national territory. The only person who could countermand the legislation was the Supreme Commander, Pibul, and until he returned to Bangkok, Direk said, no response could be given to the Japanese demand. Here one of the military officers present interjected that a delay would lead to unnecessary bloodshed, since Japanese troops were about to enter Thailand in strength. Detailed maps were then produced showing where Japanese operations were planned. Direk was shocked, having never envisaged that Japan had such elaborate and extensive plans. Tsubokami claimed that Japanese action was justified because the British had already violated Thai sovereignty by crossing the border from Malaya. All Direk could say in response was that he would have to go and consult Adul and any other cabinet ministers who could be summoned to an emergency meeting. Eventually the Japanese agreed, although to impress on the Thais the urgency of the situation Tsubokami insisted that he and his colleagues would remain at Suan Kularb until they received an answer.[204]

It was then nearing midnight, and some ministers had already gathered at Suan Kularb. The main absentee was still Pibul. He was thought to be inspecting Thai defences somewhere near Aranya Prathet, and Adul sent several telegrams to the military garrison there as well as a plane to pick him up. The hope was that Pibul would return to Bangkok before the Japanese ultimatum expired. In the mean time, Adul ordered the police on to full alert and told a Defence Ministry official to issue similar orders to the army since Prom Yothi too could not immediately be found. As time was so precious, Adul then asked Direk to explain what had transpired at his meeting with the Japanese. Those present agreed that no decision could be made on Japan's ultimatum until Pibul returned. Meanwhile all they could do was to ask the Japanese to postpone the entry of their troops to Thailand. The request was conveyed by Direk now backed up by Pridi and Prince Wan. In response Tsubokami claimed that all communication with the troops entering Thailand had to go through Saigon, so it was no longer possible to delay their action. Instead he reiterated his demand for transit rights and insisted that he would continue to wait at Suan Kularb until the matter was resolved.

In a desperate attempt to pre-empt the ultimatum, Adul and Direk rushed off to the Post Office to try to reach Pibul by telephone. Simultaneously, another minister set off by car in the direction of Aranya Prathet in the hope of speeding the premier's return.[205] None of these moves was successful. By 2 a.m., when the ultimatum expired, it was apparent that Pibul would not get back before dawn. Once Tsubokami realised this, he and his party agreed to depart for the time being. The overall plan for the Japanese declaration of war and the launching of their attacks in Asia and the Pacific had been carefully synchronised. At 1.20 a.m. Bangkok time on December 8, 1941, Japanese aircraft operating on the other side of the international dateline dropped their first bombs on Pearl Harbor.[206]

NOTES

1. NYT, Jan. 29, 1941; DGFP, XI, p. 1231; FRUS, 1941, V, p. 62; Woodward, *History of British Foreign Policy in the Second World War*, II, p. 120.
2. DGFP, XII, pp. 144ff; Woodward, II, p. 121; Churchill, III, pp. 156ff; Jones, p. 250.
3. Flood, pp. 462ff; Morley (ed.), p. 231; Feis, p. 95; Nobutake Ike, *Japan's Decisions for War*, p. 26.
4. Flood, p. 470, quoting Tamura papers.
5. F690/246/40 in FO 371/28131.
6. Flood, pp. 476ff, and Netr Khemayothin, pp. 131ff.
7. FRUS, 1941, V, p. 87, and F931/5/40 in FO 371/28109.
8. Matsuoka proudly offered to mediate between Britain and Germany. Jones, p. 248.
9. Deputy Foreign Minister Matsumiya Jun held numerous meetings with Prince Wan from Feb. 9 onwards, Flood, pp. 479ff.
10. FRUS, 1941, V, p. 43.
11. BTWM, Jan. 30 and 31; NYT, Jan. 31, 1941.
12. BTWM, Feb. 3 and 7, 1941, and F1204/246/40 in FO 371/28131.
13. NYT, Feb. 4 and 8, 1941; FRUS, 1941, V, p. 86; and Flood, p. 482.
14. BTWM, Feb. 6, 10 and 13, 1941.
15. F2696/246/40 in FO 371/28131, and Allen, p. 53.
16. *Chicago Daily News*, Feb. 7, 1941.
17. Thai Rath and Sri Krung reports in BTWM, Feb. 14, 20, 22, 24 and 25, 1941.
18. ibid., Feb. 20 and DT, Feb. 25, 1941; FRUS, 1941, V, p. 404.
19. Flood, p. 483.
20. DGFP, XII, p. 115.
21. Flood, pp. 485ff; Gaudel, p. 115; FRUS, 1941, V, p. 87.
22. ibid., pp. 89 and 91; DGFP, XII, p. 200; Flood, pp. 492ff.
23. Army staff papers and records of liaison conferences of Feb. 20 and 23 in Flood, pp. 487ff, and Morley (ed.), p. 238.
24. NYT, Feb. 24 and 25, 1941; FRUS, 1941, V, p. 89; and F1240/210/40 in FO 371/28120.
25. BTWM, Feb. 25, 1941.
26. Flood, pp. 497ff; FRUS, 1941, V, p. 91; F1327/5/40 in FO 371/28110; Vichit, p. 57; BTWM, Feb. 26, 1941.
27. Flood, pp. 511ff.
28. DGFP, XII, pp. 115 and 179.
29. Flood, pp. 515ff, and F1685/5/40 in FO 371/28110.
30. *Chicago Daily News*, Feb. 28; NYT, Mar. 1, 1941; Vichit, p. 86.
31. Flood, p. 517, and NYHT, Mar. 6, 1941.
32. Flood, p. 522, and F1685/5/40 in FO 371/28110.
33. Record of March 1 liaison conference in Morley (ed.), p. 233, and Flood, p. 519.
34. ibid., p. 523; FRUS, 1941, V, p. 102; F1724/5/40 in FO 371/28110; *Times* and NYT, Mar. 7, 1941.
35. BTWM, Feb. 28, Mar. 1, 5 and 6, 1941.
36. F1572/5/40 in FO 371/28110.

37. Flood, pp. 529ff.
38. NYT, Mar. 8, 1941.
39. March 6 liaison conference record in Flood, pp. 531ff.
40. BTWM, Mar. 5 and 6, 1941.
41. FRUS, 1941, V, p. 92; F2121/210/40 in FO 371/28121; NYHT, Mar. 3, 1941.
42. F1451/438/40 in FO 371/28135.
43. Flood, pp. 541ff, and NYHT, Mar. 12, 1941.
44. ibid., Mar. 13, 1941, and Flood, p. 553.
45. F1951/210/40 in FO 371/28120.
46. Flood, p. 564.
47. NYHT, Mar. 14, 1941.
48. F1964/210/40 in FO 371/28120, and FRUS, 1941, V, pp. 109 and 113.
49. Text in BTWM, Mar. 13, 1941.
50. ibid., Mar. 12, 1941, and F1944/210/40 in FO 371/28120.
51. Flood, p. 570.
52. BTWM, Mar. 14 and 15, 1941.
53. M. Smith, pp. 78–80, for description of traditional attire.
54. BTWM, Apr. 2, 1941.
55. Charnvit Kasetsiri, loc. cit., p. 42.
56. BTWM, Sep. 23, 1940.
57. F5604/572/40 in FO 371/24754.
58. FRUS, 1941, V, p. 82.
59. ibid., pp. 120ff; Feis, pp. 157ff; Martin, "Thai-American Relations in World War II", *Journal of Asian Studies*, 4 (1963), pp. 455ff; F2462/1281/40 in FO 371/28140.
60. F2846/1281/40 in ibid., and FRUS, 1941, V, pp. 120ff.
61. BTWM, Apr. 8 and 14, 1941.
62. Report to Generals Tojo and Sugiyama of Apr. 16 in Flood, p. 568.
63. Military policy paper of Apr. 17 in ibid., pp. 595ff.
64. ibid., p. 576.
65. Decoux, p. 292.
66. Norodom Sihanouk, *Souvenirs doux et amers*, p. 51.
67. Gaudel, p. 115.
68. F3408/5/40 in FO 371/28111 and Flood, pp. 577ff.
69. BTWM, Mar. 14, 1941, and F2225/210/40 in FO 371/28121.
70. BTWM, Apr. 17, 1941; F3171/32/40 in FO 371/28113; FRUS, 1941, V, p. 149.
71. Direk, p. 44.
72. F4019/210/40 in FO 371/28122.
73. BTWM, Apr. 17 and May 1, and NYHT, Apr. 26, 1941.
74. Flood, p. 607, and F3568/246/40 in FO 371/28132.
75. F3032/5/40 in FO 371/28111.
76. F3311/5/40 in ibid., BTWM, Apr. 24, 25, 28 and 29, 1941, and Sangworn Suwannachip, pp. 107ff.
77. BTWM, Apr. 29, 1941.
78. Vilas was married to a daughter of Seow Hood Seng (Hsiao Fo Cheng), who was Minister for Overseas Chinese Affairs in several Kuomintang cabinets. Landon (1941), p. 291.

79. BTWM, Apr. 25, 1941, and F2961/210/40 in FO 371/28121.
80. Diplomatic relations between Thailand and the Soviet Union were established in February 1941. Prayoon, pp. 427ff; FO 371/28139; DGFP, XI, pp. 517ff. The Soviet Union believed Thailand to be virtually a Japanese colony. McClane, p. 341.
81. BTWM, Mar. 14, May 17 and 19, 1941.
82. F4132/1281/40 in FO 371/28141.
83. *Chicago Daily News*, Mar. 27, and *Straits Times* report in BTWM, Apr. 24, 1941; F4019/210/40 in FO 371/28122.
84. F3852/246/40 in FO 371/28132; Allen, p. 94; Cruikshank, *SOE in the Far East*, p. 70.
85. Flood, pp. 579ff, and F3408/5/40 in FO 371/28111.
86. F3854/1281/40 in FO 371/28140 and Direk, pp. 49ff.
87. F3965/210/40 in FO 371/28121.
88. FRUS, 1941, V, p. 146.
89. F5009/246/40 in FO 371/28133, and *Chicago Daily News*, Mar. 13, 1941. Howard Grant left Bangkok in August 1941. Direk, p. 54.
90. FRUS, 1941, V, p. 152, and F4161/1281/40 in FO 371/28141.
91. F4164/1281/40 and file in ibid.
92. BTWM, June 10, 1941.
93. ibid., June 2, 7 and 12, 1941.
94. ibid., June 12, 16 and 17, and NYT, June 4, 1941.
95. F5447/210/40 in FO 371/28122.
96. BTWM, June 10, 1941, and Prasert Patamasukhon, p. 345.
97. BTWM, June 17 and 21, 1941, and Gilchrist, *Bangkok Top Secret*, p. 12.
98. BTWM, Oct. 20, 1939, when Pridi's wife was similarly honoured.
99. ibid., June 19 and 21, 1941.
100. F7559/5/40 in FO 371/28112.
101. Netr Khemayothin, pp. 159ff.
102. Ananta Pibulsongkram, II, p. 167.
103. FRUS, 1941, V, p. 236, and NYT, Aug. 6, 1941.
104. ibid., Aug. 3, 1941; Feis, p. 214; Woodward, II, p. 136; Morley (ed.), p. 99.
105. Text in Ike, p. 51, and Flood, pp. 611ff.
106. The British were aware that their discussions with the Thais on commodities had been leaked to Tokyo. F6777/246/40 in FO 371/28134.
107. Records of liaison conferences and imperial conference of July 2 in Ike, pp. 53ff, and Morley (ed.), pp. 92ff.
108. Feis, pp. 227ff, and Woodward, II, p. 140.
109. FRUS, 1941, V, p. 219; NYT and NYHT, Aug. 2, 1941.
110. FRUS, 1941, V, p. 231, and F6695/210/40 in FO 371/28123.
111. F6798/1281/40 in FO 371/28143; FRUS, 1941, V, p. 233; Flood, pp. 615ff.
112. F7037/3906/40 in FO 371/28157, and Ananta Pibulsongkram, II, p. 192. In testimony to a war crimes tribunal on Oct. 19, 1945, Prince Aditya claimed that Prayoon brought pressure to bear on him to promote Pibul to Field-Marshal, while Adul testified that the regent had strong misgivings.
113. Thawee Bunyaket in Ray, p. 74, and NYT, July 30, 1941.
114. F6759/438/40 in FO 371/28135, and FRUS, 1941, V, p. 248.
115. ibid., p. 236, and F7085/210/40 in FO 371/28123.

116. FRUS, 1941, V, p. 242.
117. Woodward, II, p. 142, and F7171/210/40 in FO 371/28123.
118. Cordell Hull, p. 1014, and Ike, pp. 118ff.
119. Jones, p. 281, and Woodward, II, p. 144.
120. FRUS, 1941, V, p. 264; F7583/210/40 in FO 371/28124; *Times* and NYT, Aug. 7, 1941.
121. FRUS, 1941, V, p. 266, and F7622/210/40 in FO 371/28124.
122. FRUS, 1941, V, pp. 268ff, and FO 371/28158-28161.
123. NYT and *Chicago Daily News*, Aug. 4, 1941.
124. Churchill, III, pp. 523 and 768ff.
125. NYT, Aug. 7 and 8, 1941, and F7361/246/40 in FO 371/28134.
126. NYT, Aug. 8, and DT, Aug. 12, 1941.
127. F7316/210/40 in FO 371/28123.
128. F7551/210/40 and file in ibid.; Direk, p. 45, and FRUS, 1941, V, p. 283.
129. *Times*, Aug. 8; NYT, Aug. 10 and 23, 1941; F7858/210/40 in FO 371/28124.
130. F9437/210/40 in FO 371/28125.
131. FRUS, 1941, V, p. 234.
132. F6821/766/40 in FO 371/28137 and Prayoon, pp. 427ff.
133. This was Luang Chawaengsak Songkram. F8285/3906/40 in FO 371/28157 and FRUS, 1941, V, p. 284.
134. This was Major Pao Sriyanond.
135. Direk, p. 55.
136. Thawee Bunyaket in Ray, p. 75.
137. F8771/3906/40 in FO 371/28157.
138. Text in Thak Chaloemtiarana (ed.), pp. 253ff.
139. ibid., p. 257.
140. ibid., pp. 267ff.
141. BTWM, May 6, 1941, and F14074/3906/40 in FO 371/28153.
142. Skinner, p. 270.
143. Pibul in Thak Chaloemtiarana (ed.), p. 353, and F8295/7221/40 in FO 371/28158.
144. Despatch of Aug. 23 in F9437/210/40 in FO 371/28125.
145. Text in Thak Chaloemtiarana (ed.), pp. 448ff.
146. Netr Khemayothin, p. 221.
147. NYT, Sep. 23 and Oct. 9, 1941; F9697/210/40 and file in FO 371/28125; Flood, p. 636; Fujiwara Iwaiki, *F Kikan*, p. 25.
148. ibid., pp. 646ff, and Adul in Suphote Dantrakul, p. 72.
149. F10641/210/40 in FO 371/28125, and Direk, p. 37.
150. *Tokyo Nichi Nichi*, Oct. 7, 1941, as quoted in F3288/396/40 in FO 371/31856.
151. Flood, p. 648.
152. Statement by General Tojo at Nov. 5 imperial conference, in Ike, p. 235.
153. Record of imperial conference in ibid., pp. 133ff.
154. F10827/210/40 in FO 371/28125; Direk, p. 56; FRUS, 1941, V, p. 320.
155. Allen, pp. 45ff.
156. ibid., pp. 92ff, and Kirby, *History of the War with Japan*, I, p. 76.
157. F10967/210/40 in FO 371/28126.
158. F4626/1281/40 in FO 371/28141.
159. F11157/9789/40 and file in FO 371/28161, and FRUS, 1941, V, pp. 325ff.

160. Allen, pp. 87ff. The Thai delegation comprised Luang Suranarong and an air force officer, Thawee Chullasap. The British were wary of showing them too much of Malaya's defences for fear that information would be leaked to the Japanese. Such suspicions proved justified in December 1941 when Pibul attached Thawee Chullasap to Japanese staff headquarters during the campaign to capture Malaya. Thawee Chullasap, *Chart Yoo Nua Sing Dai*, pp. 29ff.
161. F12666/9789/40 in FO 371/28162, and Direk, p. 57.
162. FRUS, 1941, V, p. 340; Feis, p. 299, and NYT, Oct. 31, 1941.
163. Ike, p. 209.
164. ibid., p. 235, and Flood, p. 659, quoting conclusions of Nov. 12 liaison conference.
165. This was Major Chai Pratipasen. Ananta Pibulsongkram, II, p. 209.
166. F12028/5/40 and file in FO 371/28112 and F12159/210/40 in FO 371/28126.
167. ibid., and Prasert Patamasukhon, p. 375.
168. This was Lt.-Gen. Chira Vichitsongkram.
169. Thawee Bunyaket in Ray, p. 76, and Flood, p. 655.
170. FRUS, 1941, V, p. 342, and F12453/9789/40 and file in FO 371/28162.
171. FRUS, 1941, V, pp. 356ff; F13176/210/40 in FO 371/28126; Direk, p. 57.
172. Woodward, II, p. 154; British decision that the Japanese attack on Thailand was not a *casus belli* in F261/210/40 in FO 371/28120; American decision in Feis, p. 302.
173. FO 371/28162, and FRUS, 1941, V, pp. 342ff.
174. Kirby, I, p. 173.
175. Wohlstetter, *Pearl Harbour Warning and Decision*, p. 45.
176. F12981/9789/40 in FO 371/28162, and Allen, p. 95.
177. ibid., p. 96, and Churchill, III, p. 534.
178. Woodward, II, pp. 168ff.
179. Wohlstetter, pp. 48ff.
180. ibid., p. 270.
181. Woodward, II, pp. 170ff, and Allen, pp. 97ff.
182. ibid., and Kirby, I, p. 175.
183. F13116/3906/40 in FO 371/28157 and F13332/9789/40 in FO 371/28163.
184. F13164/3906/40 in ibid.
185. Flood, pp. 680ff, and Thamsook Numnonda, *Foon Adit*, p. 172, quoting Thai cabinet records.
186. Record of imperial conference on Dec. 1 in Ike, p. 281.
187. Plans outlined at Nov. 12 liaison conference (ibid., p. 242) and approved at Nov. 22 liaison conference, ibid. p. 253, and Flood, pp. 665ff.
188. ibid., p. 682.
189. ibid., p. 685, quoting Tamura papers.
190. Tamsook Numnonda (1979), p. 174, and Ananta Pibulsongkram, II, p. 267, quoting Dec. 3 cabinet record.
191. NYT, Nov. 20, and *Times*, Dec. 5, 1941, and F12688/210/40 in FO 371/28126.
192. Allen, p. 101.
193. Tsuji Masanobu, *Singapore: the Japanese Version* p. 72ff.
194. Allen, pp. 104ff, and Kirby, I, pp. 180ff.
195. ibid., p. 179.
196. Tsuji, pp. 76ff.

197. Allen, pp. 109ff.
198. Woodward, II, p. 175, and F13329/9789/40 in FO 371/28163.
199. NYT, Dec. 4 and DT, Dec. 6, 1941.
200. Direk, p. 61.
201. ibid., p. 62, and Adul in Suphote Dantrakul, pp. 75ff.
202. This was Phra Boribandh Yutthakit.
203. Flood, pp. 693ff, and Fujiwara, p. 57.
204. Flood, p. 700; Direk, p. 62; Ananta Pibulsongkram, IV, pp. 408ff, quoting record of cabinet meeting.
205. This was Phra Muni Vechayan Rangsit.
206. Direk, p. 63; Thawee Bunyaket in ibid., p. 110; Adul in Suphote Dantrakul, pp. 77ff; Flood, p. 701.

Part IV
WAR AND PEACE,
1941-1945

10
THE COCK AND THE RISING SUN

Why Pibul was out of Bangkok on the night the Japanese invaded Thailand has never been satisfactorily explained. Many people jumped to the conclusion that he had been forewarned and was panic-stricken at the fate about to befall the country. Others have suggested that he wanted to make scapegoats of his colleagues by leaving them to take the crucial decision on how to respond to Japan's invasion.[1] This theory was later partly confirmed by Pibul in his complaint that Adul and Prom Yothi should have taken action against the Japanese in his absence.[2] After the war, Pibul also claimed that while he had no foreknowledge of the timing of the invasion, reports of the Japanese build-up in southern Indo-China prompted him to go and inspect Thailand's eastern border defences. Then, having got as far as Aranya Prathet, he was persuaded to go on to Battambang, which he had never previously visited.[3] Yet when leaving Bangkok on December 6, Pibul sent word to Tamura that he had received reports of a Thai official being beaten up by the Japanese on the border near Angkor, an incident he was determined to investigate personally.[4] Nonetheless, despite Pibul's ambivalence about where he went and why, he was apparently on his way back to Bangkok before Japanese troops started to move into Thailand.

Japanese operations in South East Asia came under the overall command of Count Terauchi, based at Southern Military Headquarters in Saigon. Under him, General Yamashita commanded the 25th Army responsible for operations south of the Kra Isthmus aimed at Malaya and Singapore. The rest of Thailand was left to the 15th Army, most of whose divisions were still in China in early December because the Japanese counted on meeting little Thai resistance. Instead several ceremonial units of the Imperial Guard, which had far less combat experience than most Japanese troops, were temporarily assigned to take control of Bangkok and the heartlands of central Thailand. They simply drove across the border from Indo-China with a couple of battalions being landed as an advance party at the mouth of the Chao Phya.[5] The Japanese were right in thinking they would meet little opposition. One or two Thai fighter planes which attempted to challenge their advance from Indo-China were soon shot down.[6] Otherwise Thailand seemed so peaceful that a Japanese battalion commander volunteered to drive on ahead alone to ascertain the situation in Bangkok. Unexpectedly, near Don Muang airfield he encountered an angry crowd of Thai civilians who dragged him from his car and killed him on the spot.[7]

He seems to have been the only Japanese casualty in the capture of Bangkok, which the advance party that had landed at the mouth of the river more or less completed by the evening of December 8. Indeed, it all happened so quickly that Thai staff officers proceeding to work as normal that Monday morning were amazed to see Japanese troops already taking over parts of the city.[8] The Chief of Staff had accompanied Pibul to the border and in his absence little had been done to alert his subordinates or the Bangkok garrisons to the invasion. In these circumstances, the efforts of the police ordered by Adul to block the road into the capital from the coast came to nothing. The navy too was taken by surprise. In attempting to make his way back from Sattahip to attend the cabinet meeting, Sindhu was temporarily detained by the Japanese.[9]

Elsewhere the picture was somewhat different. When the Japanese fleet dispersed in the Gulf of Thailand on December 7, several troop transports with a light naval escort headed towards Prachuap Kirikhan, Chumpon and Nakorn Srithamarat to land detachments of the 15th Army. Their task was to seize control of rail and road links between central and southern Thailand as well as stage a lightning strike across the peninsula at British forces in the southernmost tip of Burma. During their landings they met with considerable resistance from local Thai garrisons backed up by police and Yuvachon.[10] Without waiting for orders from Bangkok, they all acted on the law making it mandatory to oppose any foreign forces setting foot on Thai soil. Much further south too, at Pattani near the border with Malaya, the Thai army put up stiff resistance against units of Yamashita's 25th Army, which had to fight their way ashore.[11]

There were other problems at Songkla where Yamashita and his staff were due to land. They were preceded ashore by 1,000 Japanese troops dressed in Thai military uniforms. Their orders were to procure some local transport plus the cooperation of Thai forces so that they could all proceed rapidly down the only motorable road in the area to the Malayan

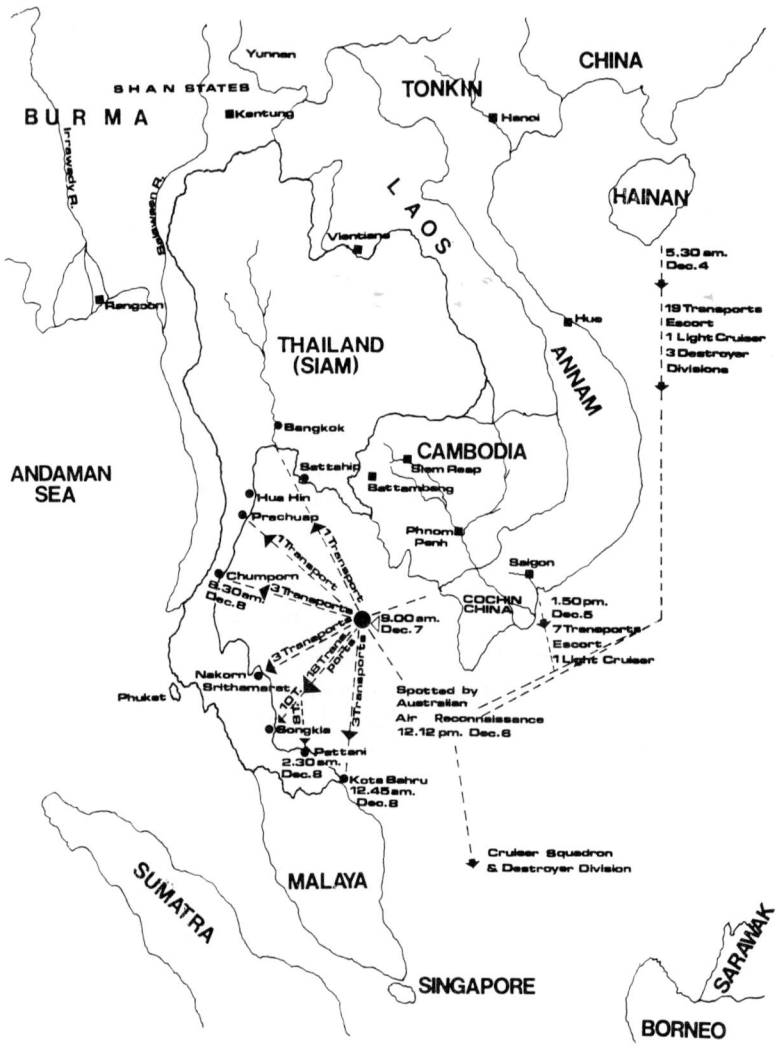

South East Asia, showing Japanese Fleet movements, December
4–8, 1941

border under the pretence they were fleeing the Japanese. Then having fooled the British and been allowed to cross into Malaya, their objective was to seize vital bridges to stop them from being blown up.[12]

The plan did not succeed. The troops involved in this special operation expected to find a Japanese army colonel, who had been working incognito at their consulate in Songkla, waiting to meet them on the beach with their transport already lined up. He was nowhere in sight; in an excess of zeal, he had destroyed his codes too early and was unable to make sense of the message conveying the invasion date. Thus the officer commanding the landing party had to commandeer a *samlor* to get to the Japanese consulate where he was greeted in astonishment by an official who had had several drinks too many. It led to considerable commotion and more delay. The Thai police, too, became suspicious when a group of Japanese soldiers tried to hire transport and bribe their cooperation with a large sum of money brought ashore specially for the purpose. Fighting broke out, units of the Thai army joined in, and it was about twelve hours before the Japanese gained control of the situation in Songkla.[13]

Reports of the fighting in southern Thailand began to reach the cabinet in the early hours of December 8. Its members kept an all-night vigil and at one stage were joined by the regents and Phya Phahol. None of them felt there was any more they could do until Pibul arrived back. There were even suspicions that he might be deliberately delaying his return because he had ignored the plane sent to pick him up and travelled by car. In the mean time, the cabinet had to put up once more with the Japanese ambassador and his delegation, who re-appeared at Suan Kularb at 5 a.m. The deadlock was only broken two hours later when Pibul finally arrived.

Immediately he was informed by Adul of the night's developments, including initial reports picked up from foreign radio stations about Japan's attacks on Malaya, the Philippines, Hong Kong and Pearl Harbor. Before Pibul could comment, Pridi warned that the world would judge the Thais by their reaction to the situation, but Pibul as ever was more concerned about the damage being done to Thailand. He asked everybody present in turn, whether a ceasefire should be declared. The replies were mixed. In the end it was Adul who proved decisive: he said it was pointless to continue fighting if the Japanese were only passing through Thailand. They were too strong for the Thais to oppose, and they had in fact threatened to bomb Bangkok unless white sheets were laid out on the race course at the Royal Turf Club as a sign of Thai non-resistance. Naturally such threats made Pibul all the more anxious, and at 7.30 a.m. he proposed, and the cabinet agreed, that a ceasefire should be declared straight away.[14]

Once the decision was taken, Pibul hurried downstairs to tell the Japanese waiting below. For them, however, a ceasefire was not enough. The previous evening Tsubokami had deliberately refrained from mentioning anything beyond the transit of troops, because his instructions were to talk only to Pibul. Now he outlined a series of proposals concerning Thailand's future relationship with Japan. They entailed the conclusion of either an offensive or defensive pact which could, if Pibul wished, be extended to enable Thailand to join the Triple Alliance between the Axis powers. Moreover, Tsubokami added, once Pibul agreed to any or all of these proposals, Japan would ensure the return to Thailand of more of its lost territories. But he warned that Thailand would not benefit if it merely agreed to grant Japan transit rights and the facilities needed for attacks on Burma and Malaya.

Pibul's first reaction was to complain of the presence of Japanese troops in Bangkok and central Thailand in complete disregard of all his previous pleas, but Tamura replied that Japan had no intention of dishonouring Thailand. It was simply a matter of operational necessity in order to defeat the British. Pibul did not bother to argue any more, but simply asked for copies of the proposed alliances so that he could go and consult the cabinet. Tamura then became impatient at what he saw as a delaying tactic. He told Pibul to make up his mind there and then, because once the decision had been taken everybody would follow his lead. The peremptory tone of Tamura's remarks dismayed Vanich, the only other Thai in the room. He burst into tears and begged the Japanese not to coerce Pibul. That only made matters worse. One of the more hot-headed Japanese officers present became abusive, threw a copy of the proposed alliances on the floor and stamped on it. More alarmed than ever, Vanich sobbed that this was no way to treat a prime minister and would ruin future cooperation between Thailand and Japan. Eventually the Japanese calmed down and after about an hour agreed that Pibul should go and consult the cabinet.[15]

When Pibul returned upstairs, he does not appear to have given his colleagues much account of his stormy encounter with the Japanese. Instead he asked Vanich to explain Japan's various proposals. They were complex and, somewhat ironically, were set out in English. Hence there were prolonged discussions about what precisely was involved. For Vichit the debate was largely irrelevant; he was in favour of concluding all the proposed alliances, including that with the Axis powers, so that Thailand could derive the greatest possible benefit from the new international situation. Pibul was inclined to agree and several other ministers, having no definite views of their own, were ready to go along with him.

Here Pridi, Adul and Direk intervened to pose in one form or another the question of what would happen if Thailand simply agreed to the transit of Japanese troops. Thus they focussed attention on the issue of Thai sovereignty and the future of the armed forces; in other words, whether they would be disarmed. To find out, Vanich and other envoys including Prince Wan, who was present as always, went downstairs to ask the Japanese. After several such sorties, it transpired that the Japanese were prepared to conclude an agreement which merely provided for the transit of their troops through Thailand coupled with guarantees of respect for Thai sovereignty in future.

At once, the mood changed. There was no more talk of alliances. Instead Pibul told Direk to go and conclude an agreement with the Japanese for the peaceful and swift transit of their troops through Thailand in return for a guarantee that it would be final and that no more demands would be made. It was signed by Direk and Tsubokami at noon on December 8. A few minutes later the cabinet decided to adjourn on the understanding that it would convene again soon to review the overall situation.[16]

Although this was one of the longest cabinet meetings in Thai history, some of its members had little time for rest. Vichit was instructed by Pibul to draft a public statement about the ceasefire. It was issued to the press and broadcast that afternoon. Simultaneously Direk hurried off to tell foreign diplomats in Bangkok what had happened. He was on the verge of tears when he explained to Crosby and the American Minister how powerless the cabinet had felt in the face of Japan's ultimatum. As for the agreement which had been reached with the Japanese, Direk stressed that it only entailed transit rights, so Thailand would continue to maintain normal relations with the Western powers. He also promised that British and American subjects, as well as their property, would enjoy full protection.[17] These assurances were received with gratitude. Furthermore the American and British ministers expressed sympathy for Thailand's predicament, but, as he later came to realise, Crosby played a significant role in shaping the Thai attitude towards the ceasefire.[18]

During the night on which the Pacific War started, he received from

London the message Churchill had addressed to Pibul. It read: ''There is a possibility of an imminent Japanese attack on your country. If you are attacked, defend yourself. The preservation of the full independence and sovereignty of Thailand is a British interest and we shall regard an attack on you as an attack on ourselves.'' Though clearly overtaken by events, Crosby conveyed the message as it stood, in a secret letter despatched to Pibul at 8 a.m. on December 8. When Pibul read it is not clear. Crosby also did not explain that Churchill had sent the message before the Japanese invasion.[19] Pibul might have deduced this from the text, but if he did he omitted to reveal the fact. Instead, in propaganda to convince the public and the armed forces of the need for the ceasefire, Churchill's words ''Defend yourself'' were quoted out of context as evidence that Britain had refused to come to Thailand's aid.[20] In reality, Pibul phoned Crosby on the afternoon of December 8 to say that there would be no Thai objection or resistance to British troops crossing the border from Malaya.[21]

As part of Japan's propaganda campaign, Domei, the main news agency in Tokyo, reported that Japanese troops had entered Thailand to repel prior British aggression. The story was carried by several Bangkok newspapers,[22] but it was not true: Operation Matador was not launched till 3 p.m. on December 8, which was far too late to achieve any of its objectives, let alone pre-empt the Japanese landings at Songkla and Pattani. In addition, despite what Pibul had said, British or rather Indian troops encountered Thai roadblocks and sniper fire as soon as they crossed the border. Hence they only advanced about 3 miles along the road to Pattani before nightfall.

Meanwhile the Japanese had already put ashore at Songkla 12,000 troops, five tanks and 400 trucks, which soon began to deploy southwards. Equally, they made immediate use of the airfield at Songkla as a base for their fighter-bombers to raid British positions in northern Malaya in support of their hard-fought landings at Kota Bahru on the east coast. In retaliation, British planes struck back at Songkla airfield on December 9, and met with heavy Japanese anti-aircraft fire.[23]

That same day, in Bangkok, the Assembly met in emergency secret session to debate the ceasefire. As on previous occasions when he was unsure of his reception, Pibul stayed away and delegated Thamrong to deploy his ''golden tongue'' to explain the situation and fend off awkward questions, of which there were many. Most of them demanded assurances on the maintenance of Thai sovereignty, political, military and financial. Thamrong frequently had to plead reasons of security for not answering in detail. At the end of the day, however, the Assembly accepted his promise that Thailand would remain faithful to its policy of neutrality throughout the war. After that hurdle had been crossed, Pibul plucked up courage to make a broadcast explaining – contrary to everything he had previously said about pursuing a scorched earth policy against any invading force – that the ceasefire had been ordered to save further unnecessary bloodshed.[24] To some who heard the broadcast, it seemed as if Pibul's voice was trembling as he spoke.[25]

Only at Prachuap Kirikhan was the ceasefire seriously ignored. The garrison there continued fighting for forty-eight hours until envoys were sent from Bangkok to interpose.[26] Elsewhere, the Thai response appears to have been mostly one of shocked surprise at the speed of the Japanese action. The deployment of their forces had been well planned in advance. Using agents secretly implanted at strategic points throughout Thailand, they quickly took control of the entire rail and road network to facilitate the movement of units of the 15th Army towards Burma. Its commanding general flew into Bangkok on December 9, and was soon ensconced in private conversation with Pibul about future cooperation. The Field-Marshal promised that there would be no problems provided that Thailand received military and economic support in return. Even so, he said that public opinion would have to be watched because many people were still subject to British and Kuomintang influence.[27]

The Japanese needed no such reminder. One of their first objectives in Bangkok was to seize the Chinese Chamber of Commerce for use as their main military headquarters. The move was approved by a joint Thai-Japanese military commission, which Pibul agreed to set up with Prayoon as one of its principal members. It also authorised the Japanese cavalry to take over the stables at the Royal Bangkok Sports Club, which had previously been used mostly by *farangs*. As for the Japanese infantry, it set up camp in Lumpini Park, and from there, before some cabinet ministers realised what was happening, they fanned out to place guards on the nearby American and British legations by the evening of December 9 while interning certain Western nationals in Bangkok and expropriating their property.[28]

Crosby immediately protested to Direk that the Japanese had no right to act in such a way since Thailand remained a sovereign state. Direk agreed, but was powerless to stop the Japanese. He had already told Pibul that he had no wish to stay on as foreign minister because he felt he could no longer usefully serve Thailand in that capacity. In his stead, Vichit quickly assumed charge at the Foreign Ministry and readily cooperated with the Japanese in restricting the activities of *farang* diplomats and expatriates.[29]

One of the most telling blows to British prestige in the Far East was the Japanese sinking of the battleships *Repulse* and *Prince of Wales* within sixty hours of the outbreak of war. The impact on Pibul was tremendous. Previously, in his efforts to stiffen the Thai will to resist Japan, Crosby had pointed to the arrival of these two warships in Singapore as evidence of British determination to oppose the Japanese.[30] Soon after their sinking, Pibul called in the Japanese ambassador to say he was about to proclaim martial law, and Tsubokami responded by producing a copy of an offensive and defensive alliance between Thailand and Japan. This time Pibul did not hesitate.[31]

At a cabinet meeting the next morning, when some ministers complained of the way the Japanese were abusing Thai sovereignty and the agreement signed two days earlier, the premier cut them short. He walked out at 11 a.m., saying he had an appointment with Tsubokami, returning half an hour later with the news he had just signed a military alliance with Japan. All that his colleagues could say at such a precipitate abandonment of Thai neutrality was that care would have to be taken in informing the public. Again Pibul turned to Vichit. The upshot was another typical example of their joint rhetoric which the Field-Marshal broadcast on December 12.[32]

He claimed that Thailand was being buffeted by remorseless storms, and that despite being a nation of great warriors it had to learn to adapt and make sacrifices. Part of the process was to recognise who its true friends were. Britain, he said, could no longer be counted as such because it had long deprived Thailand of some of its territory. Pibul did not elaborate, since the Japanese had specifically asked him not to reveal any details of their alliance for the time being. Instead he requested his compatriots to treat the Japanese in their midst with courtesy and kindness.[33] His appeal was echoed by a Japanese professor long resident in Bangkok. Apologising for any lack of good behaviour or cleanliness on the part of the troops, he called for the understanding and cooperation of the Thai people as fellow-Buddhists.[34]

Among those most dismayed by the way the Japanese were behaving were the friends of Pridi. Soon after the ceasefire, some of them made their way discreetly to his house to discuss whether there was any action that could be taken. One idea that came from several up-country Assembly members was to use their constituencies as a base for an anti-Japanese resistance movement. Another suggestion put forward by a maverick military promoter was for several pro-Western cabinet ministers, plus part of the army, to make their way to Burma to continue the fight against the Japanese from there.[35] That, however, was soon ruled out by the speed and strength of the Japanese invasion, although a few individuals, mostly *farangs*, did manage to make their way to Burma and thence to India.[36] Yet there remained one glimmer of hope for Pridi and his friends: they heard a statement by the Thai Minister in Washington, broadcast from San Francisco, denouncing Pibul and his government for failing to resist the Japanese and calling on all Thais to rise up and reassert the sovereignty and independence of their country.[37]

In fact Pibul's government was by no means unanimous in its reaction to the new situation. At one cabinet meeting, a fist-fight broke out between Sindhu and Vilas who, as a leading director of the Thai national shipping line, was apparently held responsible for the sequestration of all its freighters which happened to be in British-controlled waters at the outbreak of war. Anyway, Vilas soon resigned from the cabinet – fortunately for the Japanese, who were about to insist that he be ousted because of his well-known Kuomintang sympathies.[38] They also wanted to pave the way for his arch-rival Vanich to join the cabinet. The prospect worried Adul, who feared that henceforth all Thai cabinet business would automatically be leaked to the Japanese.[39] Indeed Vanich continued to serve them faithfully by conveying their requirements for the provisioning of Japanese troops in Thailand, including the printing of more money.

Already, through regular banking channels, the Japanese were pressing for increased baht loans in cash to purchase what they wanted in Thailand. But unlike previous such transactions, they insisted that the counterpart in gold would now be earmarked for Thailand and held in Tokyo till the end of the war.[40] Pridi was furious and told the cabinet that Japan's financial demands would cause inflation and the eventual devaluation of the baht. As a way out, he suggested that the Japanese should be asked to print their own military scrip which could easily be withdrawn at the end of the war. That in turn angered Pibul, who claimed that it would imply a partial loss of Thai sovereignty. Pridi instantly retorted that, judging by the number of Japanese swarming all over the country, it had been lost already.[41]

The Japanese were not surprised by Pridi's attitude. His name was also on their list of people to be removed from the cabinet, because obviously if he remained Minister of Finance he would try to block their plans for closer economic cooperation with Thailand within the framework of the New Order in East Asia. Yet it was no easy matter for Pibul to dispense with Pridi, given his reputation and his popularity. The problem was resolved by the Japanese: they proposed, and Pibul agreed, that Pridi should be relieved of his cabinet post by elevating him to an empty seat on the Council of Regents. In other words, he was "kicked upstairs".[42] However, certain royalists took a different view; they had not forgotten how Pridi had penned the Manifesto of the Khana Ratsadorn attacking the Chakri family and subsequently been branded as a communist. Now, after all Pibul had done to undermine the standing of the royal family, some of its members were even more perturbed by Pridi's nomination as regent at a time when the young King, though safe in Switzerland, seemed unlikely to return to his kingdom for a long time to come.[43]

Another problem for Pibul was what to do with Direk. Adul suggested that he would be suitable for the new post of Thai ambassador to Japan, and Pibul agreed, in the belief that a period in Tokyo might wean Direk away from his pro-Western views. Adul had a very different idea in mind. Knowing Direk as a friend whom he could trust, he wanted him in Tokyo where he could report back on the true situation in Japan. The difficulty was to get Direk to accept the post; he claimed that to do so would besmirch his family honour because his friends, both Thai and *farang*, would consider him a traitor. Adul countered that on the contrary, since Direk was known to be pro-Western, everybody including the Japanese would respect his position. It was to no avail. Even in the face of one of Pibul's tantrums, Direk remained adamant in rejecting the ambassadorship and turned to Pridi for support. The new regent had ideas similar to those of Adul: he suggested that in Tokyo, Direk might somehow be able to pass a message to the Western powers advising them that there were many influential people in Thailand opposed to Pibul's alliance with Japan. But, Pridi added, Direk should insist on choosing his own staff to accompany him to Tokyo so that he would be surrounded there by trustworthy people. Under these conditions, Direk finally agreed to take up the post and, armed with a secret code to communicate direct with Adul, he left for Japan in early 1942.[44]

Underlying Direk's reluctance to go to Tokyo was the rapidly developing relationship between Thailand and Japan. On December 14, Pibul signed a secret agreement with the Japanese committing Thai troops to fight in Burma.[45] On December 21 matters were taken a step further by the conclusion of a formal treaty of alliance between the two countries. To emphasise its solemn and binding nature, the treaty was signed by Pibul and Tsubokami in front of the Emerald Buddha, considered the most sacred object in the whole of Thailand.

No treaty with a foreign power had ever before been concluded in such a manner and Pibul left it to Vichit to secure the Assembly's approval. It was obtained by means of three documents distributed to each representative. First there was the text of the treaty and then a copy of an exchange of letters between Pibul and his Japanese counterpart General Tojo. Most significant of all, the third was a secret Japanese guarantee to return to Thailand the territory it had ''lost'' to Burma and Malaya. Vichit warned the Assembly that its existence must not be publicly revealed until its terms could be fulfilled. However, it was sufficient to silence most of those voices which might have been raised against the alliance with Japan and the consequent abandonment of Thai neutrality. Nor was any serious opposition expressed when Vichit indicated that Thailand might declare war on the Western powers.[46] In private Pibul had already committed himself to such a move, provided he was given time to prepare public opinion.[47] He also had to pluck up courage to face personal repercussions because two of his children were in the United States and another was in Britain.[48]

In Washington and London little was known about what was happening in Bangkok since communications were cut soon after the Japanese occupied the city. The main remaining source of information was what could be gleaned from monitoring radio broadcasts plus reports from the few people who managed to escape to Burma. The latter suggested that most Thais were opposed to the Japanese, and as a result the initial reaction of Britain and the United States was cautious. They simply declared Thailand an enemy-occupied country for the purposes of trade, and as a precautionary measure froze all its financial assets in London and New York. Otherwise both the Western powers tended to regard Thailand as the innocent victim of Japanese aggression.[49]

Towards the end of December, this attitude became difficult to sustain especially in London. Reports of Thai troops invading Burma transformed into anger the dismay already felt about Japan's use of Thailand for attacking neighbouring British colonies. For instance, Japanese bombers based at Don Muang launched a series of air raids on Rangoon. In retaliation, the British struck back at communications links and other facilities enjoyed by the Japanese in Thailand. On January 24, after a particularly heavy raid on Rangoon, they included targets in the Bangkok area. The British claimed to have damaged the port and an electricity generating plant used by the Japanese.[50]

However a couple of stray bombs fell near the Assembly building. Although it was not damaged, Pibul seized on the incident as a pretext to declare war on the Western powers straight away. His haste was compounded by what he regarded as an auspicious date: January 25 was celebrated as the anniversary of one of his heroes, King Naresuen, who vanquished the Burmese during the seventeenth century. There was only one snag. Before the declaration of war could be promulgated, it had to be signed by all three regents, and on January 25 Pridi happened to be away visiting his home-town of Ayuthya. Unable to wait for his return, Pibul prevailed on the senior regent Prince Aditya to write in Pridi's name on the declaration of war. News of its promulgation was then broadcast by Vichit, who later claimed that it had been ''the most memorable day of my life''.[51]

Any scruples Pibul may have had about the fraudulent way the declaration of war was signed were soon forgotten in his anxiety to justify the abandonment of Thai neutrality. He was not so much worried about his cabinet colleagues, who accepted the argument that to save the armed forces being disbanded, Thailand had to side with Japan against the Western powers. The problem was how to convince the public. Pibul asked Vichit to search through history for anything justifying Thai hostility towards its new enemies. One of the more far-fetched ideas he came up with related to the United States. Vichit alleged that in 1893, when the Thais were embroiled in a dispute with the French over Laos, the Americans had shown a hostile attitude by failing to intervene with an offer of mediation.[52]

Despite or because of such claims, the declaration of war was soon subject to criticism in leaflets circulated clandestinely in Bangkok. They were signed, like the earlier pamphlets criticising Vanich, by a group calling itself ''Thai Issara''. In neither case was it apparent who was directly responsible.[53] Obviously one of the most suspect elements in Bangkok was the Chinese community and particularly those members of it who were associated with the Kuomintang. After the Japanese invasion, some of them fled and others were arrested.[54] At the same time, the sole remaining Chinese newspaper published in Thailand was taken over and run by the Japanese. The same fate befell Bangkok's two English-language newspapers.[55] There remained, however, one medium of mass communication neither the Japanese nor Pibul could control.

Many Thais continued to listen to British and American radio broadcasts, which after January 25 denounced Pibul as a quisling.

To counter Western propaganda, Pibul relied even more on the radio dialogues of *Nai Man* and *Nai Kong*, to which he himself was an avid listener. If he happened to miss one of their broadcasts, he often insisted that it be repeated or the script sent to him.[56] During the opening months of 1942, *Nai Man* and *Nai Kong* took great glee in talking about how the British had lost Hong Kong, Borneo, Malaya and Singapore in quick succession, and claimed that nobody could have faith in Britain any more. From there, at the apparent instigation of Vichit, they went on to broadcast slanderous attacks on the British royal family. Ironically too, turning full circle from their previous anti-French diatribes, *Nai Man* and *Nai Kong* accused the British of treachery in burning Joan of Arc at the stake and sending Napoleon into exile on the island of St Helena.[57] It was all music to Pibul's ears. His main concern, he confided to an army staff officer, was to ensure that Thailand was on the side of whomever won the war. According to that criterion, he had apparently made the right choice.[58]

At last too, after all the strains to which he had been subjected, Pibul felt that he could enjoy the fruits of power. Publicly he was referred to as "The Leader" – *Poo Nam* – the Thai equivalent of *Der Führer* or *Il Duce*. Bangkok newspapers carried bannerheads with such slogans as "Our Nation's Security Depends on Believing in Our Leader", "The Nation will survive if we believe in Pibulsongkram" or, more simply, "Hail Pibulsongkram". Those not complying with the practice soon found their supply of newsprint cut off. Another aspect of Pibul's growing personality cult was an order for his picture to be displayed in every home.[59]

Pibul himself contributed to the propaganda campaign with articles written under various patriotic-sounding pseudonyms. His main theme was the need for all Thais to contribute to building their country into a great nation worthy of membership of Greater East Asia.[60] Unfortunately the term *Mahamitr*, used to describe Japan as a great friend, could easily be transformed by a slip of the tongue to mean "friend of a dog". Another derogatory name used by some Thais in talking of the Japanese was "disreputable dwarfs". Beyond that, however, there was little incidence of Thai-Japanese friction in the early months of 1942.[61]

What weighed on most Thais far more heavily were renewed attempts by Pibul to reform their dress and manners according to his concept of what befitted a great nation. The wearing of hats was now strictly enforced under the slogan "Hats Lead a Nation to Power", and guidelines were issued on the materials, colours and patterns from which they should be made. Women were encouraged to wear skirts, gloves and shoes, stockings being optional.[62] They were advised to dress in sombre colours: grey, blue or khaki for outdoor work, dark blue for housework. As for fashionable women, *Nai Man* and *Nai Kong* suggested that white or pastel shades were more suitable than gaudy floral outfits, especially when travelling abroad. Their radio broadcasts also told Thais to use knives, forks and spoons, because only savages ate with their hands.[63]

After the war Pibul claimed that all these reforms had had an ulterior motive which he could not explain at the time. The drive for women to wear Western dress was intended to deter them from adopting the kimono. Likewise, the use of Western-style cutlery was a counter to chopsticks. Pibul alleged that he had similar aims in launching other campaigns to enforce adult literacy and reform Thai spelling. He was deliberately trying to keep the Thai people busy learning and relearning their own language so they would have no time for Japanese lessons which were part of the overall drive to impose *Nippon-go* as a lingua franca throughout the Co-Prosperity Sphere.[64]

Different impressions prevailed in 1942. Many Thais thought that Pibul was trying to simplify their language because the Japanese had complained about its complexity. This created a lot of resentment, as too did Pibul's attempts to impose rules on how Thai children were named: he decreed that girls should be named after fruit or flowers and boys after martial attributes. He said that his aim was to correct the Thai failure to make any distinction between male and female names. This diktat especially infuriated the Queen Grandmother, whose personal name was one of those designated for men. She let it be known that her father King Mongkut was well aware of her sex when he conferred a name on her and she had no intention of changing it.[65]

Yet despite Pibul's increasingly idiosyncratic rule, it looked to the public as if he continued to enjoy the support of his colleagues. True, Pridi and Direk had left the cabinet, but they still occupied official positions rather than retiring from the political arena completely. Nor were there any significant changes when Pibul reshuffled his cabinet in March 1942. Thamrong, Prom Yothi and Khuang, all of whom had been considered pro-Western, continued in office. Even more significant was the emergence from retirement of Phya Phahol. Apart from his early contact with Japan, he was not identified in the public mind with either militarism or pan-Asian policies.[66] But at Pibul's behest he agreed to head a goodwill mission to Tokyo to place a ritual seal of approval on the alliance with Japan. It seemed to symbolise the general feeling that Pibul had adopted the only reasonable course open to Thailand.[67] But the mission included Vanich who as soon as he entered the cabinet was appointed Deputy Minister of Finance.[68]

Thanks to Pridi's careful husbanding, Thailand's finances were in a healthy state at the outbreak of war. As he foresaw, however, the situation changed rapidly as soon as the Japanese arrived. Government revenue slumped catastrophically because it was derived mainly from tariffs on foreign trade, which soon ground to a halt. The Japanese simply bought up everything they needed on the spot without paying any duty. Apart from that, a supplementary budget, virtually doubling defence expenditure, was adopted in January once Pridi was ousted from the Ministry of Finance and replaced by the far more malleable Minister who had previously been in charge of economic affairs under the influence of Vanich. The Japanese were delighted with these changes, and quickly invited Vanich to Tokyo to work out the details of Thailand's role within the Co-Prosperity Sphere.[69]

Before Phya Phahol arrived at the head of the goodwill mission, Vanich had already concluded an agreement to establish parity between the baht and the yen. In effect it amounted to a devaluation of about one-third, because the rate of exchange had previously been 155 baht to 100 yen. The Japanese explained the change by claiming that the yen had appreciated in value.[70] Later, after participating in the hospitality lavished on Phya Phahol's mission, Vanich stayed on in Tokyo to negotiate various other deals. The net result was that Thailand had to hand over its raw material production to Japan in return for manufactured goods and other essential imports as and when they could be supplied. For example, the first consignment of oil to reach Thailand after the outbreak of the Pacific War was delivered in September 1942.[71] Several months earlier, Pibul declared in his National Day speech that the country was on the verge of bankruptcy.[72]

Thailand's impecunious state was mainly due to the demands made by the Japanese. They needed the equivalent of 13 million yen a month to cover their local military costs. They also required roads to be built through the difficult terrain of north-west Thailand to speed their advance into Burma.[73] That led to an official recruitment drive for what were called construction units. *Nai Man* and *Nai Kong* were at pains to stress that these units were not some sort of forced labour. Although they engaged in road building and irrigation work, they were basically an extended form of military service designed to promote a sense of discipline, so it was claimed. To set an example, some high-ranking officials and even ministers, dressed in the uniform blue caps and short trousers of the construction units, were reported to have volunteered to work on some of their projects.[74]

As for the regular armed forces, Pibul was worried about their morale now they had been outfaced by the Japanese, and had no obvious role in defending the country. Hence he conceived the idea of creating a new Northern Army to take control of Burma east of the Salween and attack Kuomintang forces in southern Yunnan. Since Thailand had already been promised parts of Burma that were regarded as "lost territory", the Japanese did not object in principle, but they were not prepared to allow Thai claims to the Karen State, and insisted that Pibul limit his territorial aspirations to the Shan States. The Japanese also realised, as apparently the Thais did not, that a military campaign in north-eastern Burma was no easy matter.

The Northern Army was formed under the command of Luang Seri Roengrit, one of the more venal military promoters and best known in Bangkok for his prominent patronage of the Turf Club. He had, however, staked another reputation during the campaign against the French, when as Director of State Railways he had organised the transport of military equipment to the Cambodian border. The logistical problems he had to cope with in the Shan States were very different. The Thai railway system only reached as far as Chiengmai, and from there the troops had to make their way with their supplies along rough mountain tracks. Many of the soldiers assigned to the campaign came from the north-east and had not been resupplied with weapons since the war against the French. Nor were they equipped to cope with the climate in the northern mountains. Above all, they had little idea who they were supposed to be fighting.[75]

After Japan's declaration of war in December 1941, Chiang Kai-shek cabled to Roosevelt and Churchill offering his full cooperation. In particular, he suggested that Chinese troops should move into northern Burma to help the British protect the vital supply route whereby American military equipment delivered to Rangoon was transported overland up the Burma Road to China. The offer was accepted, and units of the 93rd Division of the Chinese Army based in Yunnan moved south down the Salween valley. There they contributed little to the defence of Burma, and soon retreated out of the way of the Japanese to settle in the Shan States and live off the land.[76] Their peace was shattered when Thai planes bombed Kengtung on May 3 as a prelude to the arrival of the Northern Army several weeks later. It enabled Pibul to vindicate the reputation of the armed forces by announcing proudly that the capital of the eastern Shan States had been liberated from the enemy, although which enemy remained unspecified. What is more, the territory was renamed the "Original Thai United State".[77]

The victory in the Shan States came just in time to salvage the National Day celebrations. Otherwise, given Thailand's increasingly dismal economic situation, they might have been a very gloomy affair, although it was the tenth anniversary of the end of the absolute monarchy.[78] Then another national holiday was proclaimed to mark Pibul's birthday on July 14, and Vichit wrote a special play for the occasion. Meanwhile, all cinemas were instructed to display Pibul's picture at the end of every performance as if it were the King's portrait, and the audience were expected to rise and bow. Another aspect of Pibul's growing personality cult was becoming apparent in official décor. According to the eastern zodiacal system, he had been born in the year of the cock, and this symbol began to replace the wheel (representing the Chakri dynasty). Similarly Pibul's auspicious birth-colour, green, was used in official decorations. More ominous still in the eyes of some promoters was an idea mooted by Pibul to institute a new system of titles to replace that inherited from the absolute monarchy.

There were in fact a few promoters who still cherished the original ideals of the Khana Ratsadorn. In late 1941, for example, they succeeded in having all official titles abolished. For people like Pridi, who had been known throughout his official life as Luang Pradit Manudharm, it made little difference. They simply reverted to their original names. Not so Pibul: reluctant to lose his identity by going back to plain Plaek Kittasangka, he coined the name P. Pibulsongkram,[79] and in that type of formulation he was followed by, among others, Vichit, Adul and Thamrong. Even so, Pibul was not happy with the change and, given his addiction to honours, proposed the introduction of new semi-regal titles.

For once he was over-ruled. Those promoters who had advocated the abolition of the earlier system of titles pointed out forcefully that they had put an end to the absolute monarchy in order to do away with privilege, and certainly not to create a new ruling dynasty. The regents too expressed distinct misgivings because, no matter what Pibul might think, they still represented the monarch. Hence, on his birthday he honoured his wife: Khunying La-iad was appointed a lieutenant colonel and royal aide-de-camp, the first time a woman had ever been commissioned in the Thai armed forces. Later a women's army corps was set up, and Khunying La-iad further expanded her influence by establishing a national women's organisation of which she was, of course, president.[80]

Pibul also continued to flatter the Japanese. In an interview published in Singapore, he said he was so busy studying the secret of Japanese invincibility that he had given up his favourite pastime of tennis and restricted his horse-riding. These remarks were made while welcoming to Bangkok a high-ranking Japanese mission reciprocating the visit made to Tokyo by Phya Phahol. Pibul naturally played the effusive host to the delegation, which was likewise headed by a former premier.[81]

Still it seemed to be Vichit who was doing most to forward Japanese policies. Proclaiming himself a firm believer in the doctrine of Asia for the Asians, he presided over the opening of a conference held in Bangkok to set up the Indian National Independence League and Army inspired by Subas Chandra Bose and sponsored by Japan.[82] At the Foreign Ministry Vichit also pursued the idea, originally proposed by the Japanese, that Thailand should join the Triple Alliance between the Axis powers. He was not being altruistic; he wanted Thailand to have the right to participate in any conference convened by the Axis powers to carve up the spoils of war. Vichit therefore instructed the Thai ambassador in Tokyo to raise the matter officially. Direk was dismayed, yet he duly submitted the proposal to the Japanese and was all the more relieved that they found it unwelcome.[83] What worried them was the Germans who were taking advantage of the Triple Alliance to buy up a lot of tin, rubber and tungsten in Thailand for shipping back to Europe. These and similar German purchases in Indo-China and the East Indies clearly did not conform to the concept of Asia for the Asians or the Greater East Asian Co-Prosperity Sphere.[84]

Even within this sphere Japan was experiencing problems. Despite continuing pressure, Pibul had still not recognised the government in Nanking. The idea was resurrected when Thai and Chinese troops clashed in the Shan States. Since Pibul was reluctant to declare war openly on Chiang Kai-shek's regime because of possible repercussions among the Chinese community in Bangkok, the Japanese suggested that Thailand should demonstrate its hostility by recognising Wang Ching-wei as China's head of state. Again the idea was readily taken up by Vichit, but when the regime in Nanking responded with a request to set up an embassy in Bangkok, the old problem of Thai relations with

China resurfaced. Irrespective of who governed China, there was an innate Thai belief that if ever a Chinese diplomatic presence were established in Bangkok, it would become an alternative focus of loyalty for anybody with ancestral links to the Middle Kingdom. Here the Japanese sympathised and stopped the government in Nanking from pressing to set up an embassy in Bangkok.[85] Japan was above all anxious not to stir up trouble among the 3 million-strong Chinese community in Thailand. No matter whether they were supporters of Wang Ching-wei or of Chiang Kai-shek, they were still prepared to trade with the Japanese, especially if there was a profit to be made.

On the other hand, the Chinese were also united in opposing Pibul's policies. Early in 1942 he resumed his nationalist campaign with a decree reserving twenty-seven occupations and professions exclusively for Thai citizens. These ranged from the legal profession to the makers of umbrellas and sellers of charcoal. Some of them, such as barbering and the making of Buddha images, have remained prohibited to aliens on and off ever since.[86] The problem for Pibul was to persuade Thais to take over these jobs. He was particularly anxious that they should take up noodle-vending, and coined the slogan ''Noodle is your lunch''.[87]

Another of Pibul's concerns was to minimise political opposition to his rule. In June 1942 various communist suspects were rounded up and imprisoned.[88] Likewise, several leading journalists were detained after the passing of a new Press Act,[89] which empowered Pibul and Prom Yothi (who had become Minister of the Interior) to prevent the publication of any material considered detrimental to the national interest. In other words, newspapers were instructed to print only good news emanating from Axis sources, while sarcastic comments about the internal situation were banned. One of the most prominent victims of this edict was Prince Prem Purachatra who, in a column penned jointly with his wife, had been making barbed comments about Pibul's cultural innovations. They were censored, but soon resumed writing under a different pen-name.[90]

Other members of the royal family found alternative ways of expressing their views on Pibul's policies. Like most of the population, they resented above all the hat edict. One princely scholar pointedly put hats on his four Great Dane dogs to take them for their daily walk, while going bare-headed himself. The Queen Grandmother, too, was irate; when asked to contribute a photo of herself wearing a hat to promote Pibul's campaign, she allegedly retorted she would sooner have her head cut off.[91]

Pibul also found it difficult to contend with the Thais abroad. Besides, their radio broadcasts facilitated by the Western Allies, it was hard to explain why most of them refused to be repatriated under an agreement between the Japanese and their opponents for the exchange of enemy aliens. In July 1942, all American, British and other Western diplomats interned in the Far East, including Bangkok, as well as some civilians, were taken by ship to Mozambique. There they were exchanged for Japanese and Thais from the United States and Britain. Among them were Pibul's son Ananta and his daughter Chirawat from the United States as well as his other son Prasong and the Thai Minister, who had been interned in London. Otherwise most Thai diplomats and students in both America and Britain refused to be repatriated. In welcoming his children home, Pibul was particularly scathing about the Thai Minister in Washington, whom he condemned as a rebel for failing to return. Pibul alleged that such people were trying to set up a resistance movement abroad and had attempted, albeit unsuccessfully, to recruit the King in Switzerland to their cause. They were unpatriotic Thais who must be stripped of their nationality.[92] Even so, the Field-Marshal received no reply to a message he sent appealing to the King to return home to learn Japanese.[93]

One of the few members of the royal family who continued, as ever, to cooperate with Pibul was Prince Wan. He was appointed head of a National Cultural Council, which issued a whole series of edicts, many of them related to the finer points of etiquette, such as when to bow and when to kneel at royal and state ceremonies. Other instructions concerned the use of visiting cards and whether one or two should be sent and on which occasions. For the lower classes, the guidelines issued by the National Cultural Council were equally specific. The people were forbidden to wash in public, sit or sleep on footpaths, or climb on the railings of bridges. At home Thais were told to sit on chairs rather than squat in traditional fashion; nor were they to carry children on the hip. Such practices were said to be unhygenic. In the same spirit, a Ministry of Public Health was set up for the first time in Thailand.[94] It soon received a spate of instructions from Pibul.

Unfortunately, in October 1942 Bangkok and the Chao Phya basin were hit by the worst floods since 1917. They caused widespread damage and epidemics. The situation became so bad that Pibul had to explain on the radio that floods were a natural phenomenon arising from meteorological causes rather than an omen from on high.[95] Japan reacted with an offer of aid. However, even before the floods, economic problems had been causing unrest in Bangkok.[96] According to the Bank of Thailand's statistics, the cost of living in the city doubled between 1938 and the end of 1942; simultaneously standards of living fell. Soon after the Japanese occupation, soap and basic medicines disappeared from the shops; sugar, matches, cooking oil, kerosene and other petroleum-based products were all rationed. Bangkok's buses were even reduced to running on charcoal burners, although to the annoyance of the public Japanese military vehicles still sped through the city.[97] Basically it was a lack of shipping which caused so many shortages in Thailand, dependent as it was on imports for most manufactured goods. At the same time, its traditional exports such as rice and teak piled up at the ports or up-country. The concept of Thailand as a major source of raw materials for the whole of Greater East Asia thus became a mockery.

Yet, to the dismay of some of its members, the ideals of the Co-Prosperity Sphere were still being pursued in Tokyo. A new Greater East Asia Ministry was created in September 1942 to oversee all the countries where Japan held sway. Among those who viewed the development with concern was Direk: despite his status as ambassador of an independent country, he found himself being treated by the Greater East Asian Ministry on a par with representatives of the former Western colonies in South East Asia.[98]

In Japanese eyes, Thailand's most important role was as a hub of communications since its road and rail systems interlinked with those of Indo-China and Malaya. To protect this vital network, Japan kept an army of never less than 50,000 men in Thailand throughout the war. Another of its tasks was to supply the army in Burma. In early 1942, the Thais helped to construct a road from Tak to Mae Sot to facilitate the Japanese attack on Moulmein and the capture of Rangoon. After that, Japanese communications problems became more acute as they expanded their campaign in Burma before being able to secure the shipping lanes through the Andaman Sea from Allied attack. Hence, in June it was decided in Tokyo to have a railway built connecting Thailand and Burma. For months the Thais haggled over costs, and only in November was it announced that agreement had been reached on the construction of a railway across the Three Pagodas Pass so linking Bangkok eventually with Rangoon. It entailed cutting through some of the most inhospitable mountainous jungle in the world. For that reason, Western engineers had long since rejected such a project as unrealisable. Significantly, in resurrecting the idea, Japan gave no public indication of the labour force to be used in building the railway.[99]

Despite such efforts at concealment, Japan's shipping and transport problems were very obvious to the Western Allies who, in late 1942, resumed bombing facilities used by the Japanese in Thailand including certain targets in Bangkok.[100] Coming on top of the floods, these raids dealt another blow to public morale, as was implicitly acknowledged by Pibul in his New Year address at the beginning of 1943. Yet he claimed that Thailand had never before been so prosperous, and determined to fight side by side with its great friend Japan to achieve total victory. As for the 600 Thai soldiers killed during the war, Pibul promised that their names would be inscribed on the monument originally constructed to mark the victory over the French in 1941. What he did not say was why a lot of soldiers were still dying.[101]

Although the onset of the rainy season in mid-1942 brought a halt to the fighting in the Shan States, it only increased the hardships the troops there had to suffer. They were woefully lacking in food and medical supplies. Hence deaths from malaria and jungle fevers far exceeded those in battle.[102] The problem finally came to Pibul's attention in January 1943, and he ordered ten tons of quinine to be sent to the Northern Army. When he actually went north later that month, his demands became even more exaggerated. Orders came flooding back to Bangkok for uniforms, staff officers, sugar, money, doctors and a hundred ox-carts of bananas to be sent to the troops in the Shan States.[103] In the same peremptory vein, Pibul ordered the construction within four months of hundreds of kilometres of roads to link up the towns and villages of the Shan States with Thailand.[104] But when some of the sick troops were sent down to Bangkok for medical care, they noticed with resentment that nobody in the capital seemed to know or care about all the hardships they had suffered.[105] Meanwhile Pibul created panic in the six northern provinces of Thailand by suddenly banning all aliens from residing there. Apparently he was worried that they might be spies since his tour had been punctuated by Allied bombing raids. Nevertheless the Northern Army continued to announce new victories.[106]

Such news was met with increasing scepticism. The Japanese had already reported the liberation of the Shan States as well as the rest of Burma.[107] Pibul's credibility was further strained by broadcasts from Allied sources. As a result both he and the Japanese sought to ban the use of short-wave radios in Thailand, though to little avail. In January 1943, news from the West made compulsive listening. The defeat of the Germans and Italians in North Africa as well as the Soviet victory at Stalingrad provided the first signs that the tide of war might be changing in favour of the Allies. As the possible implications for Thailand were being assessed, Bangkok Radio announced the resignation of Pibul from the premiership.[108]

According to one account, Pibul's resignation was prompted by an argument he had with his wife.[109] The reasons he himself gave in a letter to the regents on February 13 announcing his intention to resign were poor health and frequent headaches, but this seemed so implausible that the senior regent Prince Aditya was reluctant to take the letter seriously and called in Thawee Bunyaket, the cabinet secretary, to enquire what truly underlay the premier's action. Thawee was aware of various clashes of personality in the cabinet, mainly centring around Prayoon, who was generally considered to be inefficient as well as personally vindictive. More to the point, perhaps, Pibul had been angry about a caretaker premier being appointed while he was on tour up north. Even so, Thawee could think of no compelling reason why Pibul should decide to resign. Still baffled, Prince Aditya asked Thawee and the official secretary to the throne to call on Pibul to determine whether he was acting on a mere whim. In the event Pibul agreed to see only the royal secretary, who was a military promoter and member of his personal clique.[110] During their meeting the premier once more affirmed his intention of resigning and Prince Aditya was informed accordingly.

By that stage the senior regent had been joined by Pridi, Adul and Khuang, all of whom read Pibul's letter and were equally unsure what to make of it. In another effort to find out, Prince Aditya tried to reach the Field Marshal by telephone, but without success. Adul then offered to go and talk to Pibul. After several hours, he returned to tell Prince Aditya that the premier had reaffirmed his wish to resign, and that the only explanation he would offer was poor health. Next morning Thawee, who felt responsible for the cabinet and feared recriminations if anything went wrong, took the advice of Pridi and wrote to Pibul requesting his confirmation that he still wished to resign. An affirmative reply came back in writing. After that Prince Aditya felt confident enough to call in the Speaker of the Assembly to start off the constitutional process for selecting a new premier. At the same time, Thawee drafted a statement announcing Pibul's resignation, which was broadcast on the evening of February 14.

Within a couple of hours, Pibul's military secretary[111] arrived at the radio station and insisted at gunpoint that the announcement be retracted. The head of the Government Propaganda Bureau, who happened to be Direk's younger brother,[112] refused pending further instructions from Thawee. Later that evening, Prayoon phoned both Prince Aditya and Adul, claiming that he was being besieged by Japanese generals demanding to know what was going on and adopting threatening attitudes. Adul was furious at receiving such a call; throughout the war, he had made a point of avoiding all direct contact with senior Japanese officers based in Thailand – which his close friends regarded as a remarkable act of defiance and ingenuity, especially in view of Adul's position.[113] And he was not about to break his record now. Angrily he demanded a confrontation with Prayoon in the presence of Pibul. There Adul berated his colleague for embroiling the Japanese in Thai internal politics and seeking to exploit their presence. Prince Aditya, however, was more intimidated by Prayoon's call. Together with his wife, he fled his home that night, to seek refuge with Pridi.

On becoming regent, Pridi had moved to Ta Chang, a residence pleasantly situated on the banks of the Chao Phya, not far from the royal palace compound. It also turned out to be politically convenient, because Pridi was quickly able to call up aid from friends he had long been cultivating in the navy. Prince Aditya too had naval connections, and both felt reassured when a gunboat appeared in the river off Ta Chang to counter the armoured vehicles emerging ominously elsewhere in the city.[114] The army then turned its attention to intimidating the staff at the radio station, and next morning a statement was broadcast retracting Pibul's resignation.[115]

After that, the premier ordered everybody involved in the events of the past twenty-four hours to attend a meeting at Suan Kularb. Some people, such as the radio announcer who broadcast the news of Pibul's resignation, complied, whereas others, including the regents and the Speaker of the Assembly, refused to attend on the constitutional grounds that the prime minister had no right to command the presence of representatives of the Assembly, let alone the monarchy. Thawee too did not put in an appearance; he was beginning to fear for his life and asked Khuang to report back on what happened at the meeting. It was probably just as well. Pibul lashed out at everybody who had had any part in announcing his resignation, and particularly Thawee whom he accused of instigating the whole incident. Afterwards he phoned Thawee to ask why he had not been present. The reply was frank. Thawee said he had no wish to be killed by Pibul's henchmen. Immediately Pibul changed his tone and promised that all the tanks would be withdrawn to barracks. As soon as that happened later the same day, Thawee agreed to meet the premier.

It was a stormy encounter. Pibul demanded to know why his letter of resignation had been taken at face value. In reply Thawee enumerated all the attempts to cross-check the premier's true intentions. Anyway, he added, given the changing trends in the war, he thought that Pibul might have decided to resign in order to spare Thailand and its government from suffering for their collaboration with the defeated Axis powers. The suggestion infuriated Pibul. He told Thawee he thought too much, and accused him of entering into a conspiracy with the regents to install a new premier. As for the letter of resignation, it had simply been intended as a test of loyalty, especially in the case of Prince Aditya.[116] For Thawee that was the last straw. He turned on Pibul and accused him of lacking all moral scruples, even to the point of pillorying the radio announcer who had simply been doing his duty. Somebody would have to accept responsibility for such unpardonable conduct, and if Pibul was not prepared to do so, Thawee felt it only right to tender his own resignation.

Soon afterwards Khuang, who was similarly disillusioned with Pibul's machinations, likewise resigned from the cabinet. As for Adul, who had been present throughout the confrontation between Pibul and Thawee, he thought of doing the same. He had experienced growing misgivings about Pibul's conduct ever since December 1941 but had also been asked by several senior princes to help protect the monarchy and the nation from Pibul. In these circumstances, Adul decided to remain in the cabinet where he could observe at close quarters what Pibul got up to next.[117]

None of these arguments was revealed to the public. Yet even the Thais abroad and the Allied powers, cut off as they were from all inside information concerning events in Bangkok, deduced from the conflicting broadcasts about Pibul's resignation there was some sort of crisis within the ruling élite.[118] Furthermore, Chinese officers based near the border with the Shan States received what they believed to be a significant offer from a Thai commander there to defect to the Allies with all his troops.[119] All these developments prompted Chiang Kai-shek to declare in a broadcast on February 23 that China was ready to help those Thais who wished to liberate their country from Japan. Two weeks later, Roosevelt made a similar statement on behalf of the United States. The British did not follow suit.[120] Even so the Chinese and American statements were enough to give Pridi and his friends new heart.

Since becoming regent, Pridi had ostensibly been busy carrying out the duties that went with that position; these included looking after the safety and wellbeing of the royal family and principally the Queen Grandmother. Being of an advanced age, she was naturally very perturbed by the bombing, and eventually sought refuge at Bang Pa-in, a country retreat her husband had built near Ayuthya. In helping to make the Queen Grandmother comfortable, Pridi managed to overcome some of the royal family's suspicions about his basic loyalty.[121] His frequent trips up-country on royal business also served as useful cover for attempts to outwit the Japanese.

During 1942, Pridi sent several missions overland to China to contact the Allies, but they disappeared without trace.[122] Nor did he receive any direct response to secret messages sent through the British and American internees repatriated in July 1942.[123] Pridi was even more disappointed when the Thais returning home in this exchange brought no indication from those remaining abroad about their plans.[124] Thus fourteen months passed without Pridi and those of his friends opposed to the Japanese receiving any word from the other side except what they could hear on the radio. After Pibul's abortive resignation, they decided to try again to set up a direct channel of contact. With the help of two leading princes who were worried by Pibul's dynastic ambitions, Pridi sent another envoy to China in late February.[125]

The crisis surrounding his abortive resignation made a deep impression on Pibul as well. He had to put up with a lot of questioning from the Japanese about what underlay his move. He tried to convince them that it was simply a misunderstanding between himself and the regents. As for the reported offer of a Thai general to defect to the Chinese, Pibul dismissed it as pure propaganda on Chiang Kai-shek's part. More difficult to contend with was a wave of gold speculation which hit Bangkok in early March. This seemed to have various causes. The unrest created in the north by the sudden ban on alien residents spread to the capital as thousands of displaced families, many of them Chinese with widespread business interests, flooded in. On top of that, Pibul's own actions had an unsettling effect on the political climate.[126]

Realising that he could no longer even count on the loyalty of some of his close associates, the Field-Marshal banned the discussion of politics in official quarters. He also decreed that no individual could be given personal protection except on the express orders of the Supreme Command. Clearly he wanted to prevent a repetition of the move made by the navy to protect the regents, as Adul for one appreciated: he reminded the police they had a duty to protect everybody irrespective of politics.[127] Pibul countered by drafting another decree authorising the

Supreme Command to take control of the cabinet and all government departments in a state of emergency. Again Adul expressed misgivings. Only the regents were bold enough to support him. They returned the decree to Pibul unsigned, together with a memorandum explaining that it violated the constitution.

Pibul was so incensed by this act of defiance, in which Prince Aditya had clearly been influenced by Pridi, that he ordered both regents on March 30 to report in person to the Supreme Command.[128] Prince Aditya complied, but Pridi did not, protesting once more that the premier had no constitutional right to issue orders to the monarch's representatives. Next day Pibul calmed down and released Prince Aditya, perhaps as the result of some feminine intervention. Significantly he instructed that Mom Kobkaeow, the wife of the senior regent, be invested immediately as a lieutenant-colonel in the Cavalry. He then got the Assembly to grant emergency powers to the Supreme Command, albeit in a form that was a modification of his original proposals.[129]

Far more controversial for most Thais was Pibul's order banning the chewing of betel-nut, about which even his mother is said to have protested. Still, provincial governors were instructed to destroy all betel trees unless some industrial use could be found for them.[130] The idea was again to prove that the Thais were civilised. Now Pibul had another obsession: he wanted to increase the population to match his claim that Thailand was a great power. All babies born on January 1, 1943, were designated "Greater Asia Children", with a right to free education throughout their lives. Group weddings were introduced to encourage the habit of marriage by cutting down the cost. On the other hand, a punitive tax was imposed on bachelors. It was followed up by an official campaign to encourage husbands to respect their wives. Women were no longer to be treated, according to the traditional saying, like the hind-legs of an elephant. In other words they were not to be beaten or treated as slaves. Pibul decreed that men should allow their wives to rule the household and kiss them on the cheek before leaving for work.[131]

No matter what motivated Pibul to issue such idiosyncratic decrees – and many of the élite believed it to be his wife – he was also under pressure to grant equal status to Japanese culture, as befitted two nations cooperating in the development of Greater East Asia. The foremost proponent of this argument was Vichit, who urged the conclusion of a cultural agreement with Japan: it would prove, he claimed, that one of the world's major nations was prepared to acknowledge Thai culture as worthy of recognition.[132] Yet the agreement he negotiated in late 1942 was slow to be gazetted in Thailand, and its conclusion was not fêted in Bangkok as it was in Tokyo. Instead a Japanese official was said to have gone to Bangkok to "enforce" the treaty.[133] What the Japanese planned was the construction in Lumpini Park of a replica of one of the temples at Nara to be used as a cultural centre for teaching *Nippon-go* and the arts of flower arrangement and drama.[134]

Coincidentally a new university was set up in Bangkok for the study of Thai arts. Silpakorn University began by offering free five-year courses in music, drama, painting and sculpture.[135] Its inception clearly owed a great deal to Vichit, whose wife was one of the University's lecturers. She was a prominent dancer and choreographer, and as such was commissioned by Pibul to set up a Western-style *corps de ballet* for the air force. It came to nothing as did another of Pibul's ideas: to create an orchestra comprising 100 instrumentalists capable of playing Western music to outdo a similar Japanese ninety-man orchestra. On the other hand, Vichit applied very strict criteria when it came to Thai music and dancing. Several traditional instruments were banned because they were judged to be un-Thai. So too were puppet shows and *Likay*, a popular form of comedy show performed in many villages. In contrast the *ramwong*, a dance originating in the north-east, was popularised throughout the country, including Bangkok, where officials were ordered to spend every Wednesday afternoon practising its sinuous movements instead of carrying out their normal duties.[136]

Many of these reforms aroused resentment, especially at a time of constantly rising prices when official salaries remained frozen at pre-war levels. Pibul seemed to have lost all touch with reality, as had his immediate entourage. The public identified its members as Vichit, Vanich, Prayoon and Prince Wan.[137] Another important, although less well-known figure was Pibul's military secretary, Chai Pratipasen, who significantly was the youngest general in the army. His main function was to act as chief Thai representative on the committee liaising with the Japanese.

Chai had established his reputation as a liaison officer when he was a member of the mixed commission set up in Saigon after the conclusion of the Franco-Thai Treaty in 1941.[138] At that time he was regarded as one of a coterie of French-educated officers who were protégés of Prom Yothi. By 1943, however, Prom Yothi's star had waned and he was no longer considered as a possible heir to Pibul. Here the Japanese may have played a role, since they had never trusted Prom Yothi. His resentment was obvious in the alternatively sycophantic and truculent attitudes he adopted towards Pibul. Such behaviour further tarnished Prom Yothi's reputation among both the promoters and the public.[139]

By contrast there was little that either the Japanese or Pibul could do to dent Pridi's popularity, and he continued to build up his network of friends and useful contacts, including Thawee. Soon after he resigned from the cabinet, he was asked by Pridi to help set up a government-in-exile to cooperate with the Allied powers. What Pridi had in mind was to ensure that the annual reselection of the Assembly speaker in June resulted in Thawee being chosen for the position with Khuang as his deputy. After that Thawee, the constitutionally elected leader of the Assembly, together with Pridi as regent and another friend who was a cabinet minister,[140] would find some way of escaping from Thailand to set up a government abroad which could legally claim to represent all three branches of the Thai body politic. Both Thawee and Khuang agreed to play their designated roles in the scheme and, with Pridi deploying his influence behind the scenes in the Assembly, they were elected as planned on June 26.[141]

These manoeuvres did not escape Pibul's attention. In congratulating Thawee on his election as speaker, the prime minister hinted at problems with the Japanese; he claimed that they regarded Thawee as pro-Western and might intervene to impose military rule on Thailand. Hence Pibul suggested that Thawee should relinquish his new position for the sake of the country's independence. Thawee would have none of it: he told Pibul bluntly to inform the Japanese that the speaker of the Thai Assembly was elected by due constitutional process, and nobody had the right to intervene.

Pibul then tried a different tack. Since Thawee was one of the original promoters from the French nucleus, Prayoon was sent as an old friend to plead with him to comply with Pibul's wish and resign. In addition, Prayoon suggested that Thawee would find the mortgage on his house paid off. Thawee replied angrily that he would never accept a bribe from anyone, and told Prayoon to leave and never cross his threshold again. Among the promoters, such an argument was unusual, but Thawee no longer had much faith in their secret oath forbidding mutual recriminations. Friends in the cabinet had warned him that Pibul was considering his arrest.

Thawee immediately made plans to leave Bangkok the next morning on the southern express for Hua Hin. At least, that was the story his wife told Prayoon when he called again looking for Thawee. The news of his departure was welcome to Pibul, since there would no longer be any need to arrest him – a move opposed by many friends of the two men. Instead Pibul addressed a letter to the Assembly claiming that its speaker was apparently afraid of assuming the position since he had left for Hua Hin.

That was what Thawee thought might happen. Hence he had arranged, with the help of Khuang, to leave the southern express at a station not far from Bangkok and make his way back to the capital by car with a few phone calls en route to check what was taking place in the Assembly. He also wrote a lengthy memorandum setting out his position in detail just in case anything untoward befell him. As it turned out, he reached the Assembly in time to attend a secret session specially convened to hear Pibul's message. It was conveyed by his military secretary, Chai, who was visibly surprised to see Thawee arrive and ostentatiously seat himself between two naval promoters. The implicit challenge was so clear that Chai quickly requested the temporary adjournment of the Assembly; he said Pibul wished to attend but had been delayed. This was simply a pretext to gain time.

Pibul, as usual, had no intention of putting in an appearance on such a delicate occasion, and yet again delegated Thamrong to speak on his behalf. Using the frequent Thai excuse that there had been a misunderstanding, Thamrong tried to explain how the prime minister had come to interpret the speaker's departure for Hua Hin as resignation. Here Thawee intervened: basing himself on his memorandum, he outlined to the Assembly the course of events since his election as speaker. For once it was too much for Thamrong: he said that he had simply conveyed Pibul's message as instructed and then bowed out. At that one of Pibul's close military associates took the floor to claim that Japan was bound to impose military rule if Thawee became speaker. The argument had a major impact on the Assembly, even though it had earlier failed to impress Thawee himself. His appointment as speaker was quickly rescinded, and one of Pibul's friends was selected in his stead. Likewise Khuang was replaced as deputy speaker.

Even then Pibul was not content. Just as he had previously done with the regents, he ordered Thawee to report to the Supreme Command for military duty. Having no special status to fall back on, Thawee felt he had to comply or face a court-martial. A few days later he was released, and Pibul tendered his apologies for the whole incident, saying that he had simply lost his temper. He even invited Thawee to return to the cabinet. The proposal was firmly declined.[142]

Although Pibul's fears of a Japanese military takeover were obviously exaggerated for his own political purposes, his relationship with them was becoming very ambivalent. After his trip north in January, he sought to extend the regulations controlling aliens to include Japanese residents. Likewise, he expressed concern at their activities in other areas.[143] He also made one excuse after another for declining to visit Tokyo or sending his children there to be educated.[144]

On the other hand Japan had not fulfilled its pledge incorporated in the December 1941 military alliance to restore to Thailand the territory "lost" to Burma and Malaya. Even when the Japanese Minister for Greater East Asia visited Bangkok in April 1943, there was no reference to the subject in a joint communiqué he issued with his hosts. The fact was that the promise had begun to embarrass the Japanese, especially now that they were on the point of granting independence to Burma. Anyway Pibul was still demanding the Karen as well as the Shan States.

The matter was finally resolved at a meeting of the Imperial Council held in Tokyo at the end of May 1943 when, despite considerable opposition, General Tojo managed to secure agreement for Thailand to be given the eastern Shan States as well as the four northern states of Malaya. He wanted the issue settled because he was just about to embark on a tour of South East Asia and the Pacific during which, amongst other things, he hoped to placate Pibul.[145]

For obvious security reasons, the Japanese went to great lengths to ensure that Tojo's itinerary remained secret. Direk, for instance, was told that the Japanese prime minister would be meeting his Thai counterpart in Singapore. Instead, to flatter Thailand and Pibul, Tojo made a special visit to Bangkok. Yet, when he arrived at Don Muang on July 3, he was snubbed: Pibul had arranged for his Foreign Minister, Vichit, to greet the Japanese premier. Still, as soon as it was realised the main purpose of Tojo's visit was to announce the transfer of the "lost territories", Prayoon organised a massed rally of the Yuvachon in celebration. In Tokyo, however, the press characterised the news as "sensational" and attributed it to "Thailand's long-cherished aspirations for new territory". By contrast when Vichit informed the Assembly in Bangkok on July 23 that the legal formalities involved in transferring the lost territories were underway and Japan had demanded nothing in return, Pibul was given a massive vote of confidence.[146]

This was opportune, since Pibul was not feeling at all confident. The Allied landings in Italy had given him reason to fear that the tide of war was turning fast, and he did not want to give the impression he had aligned Thailand with Japan simply in order to gain new territory. Anyway he would have preferred more of Laos and Cambodia, particularly since France looked unlikely to emerge victorious from the war and thus in a position to demand the return of its territory.[147]

Pibul's anxiety was also manifest in other directions. On July 18, he suddenly ordered a road and railway to be built up a remote and virtually uninhabited valley north-east of Lopburi. A month later he designated Petchaboon, a township at the head of the valley, as the site of a new city destined to be the capital of Thailand.[148] The move seemed prompted by the fear that just as the Allies had landed troops in southern Italy to threaten the capital, Rome, they might do likewise near Bangkok.

Developments in Italy created other uncomfortable precedents. During a conversation with Prince Aditya, Pridi remarked what a pity it was that Thailand had no figurehead to depose its dictator as Marshal Badoglio had just done with Mussolini in Italy. Immediately the senior regent went and reported Pridi's comment to Pibul, who construed it as treason and convened a special meeting of the promoters to carry out an interrogation. Despite his status as regent, Pridi submitted to the process but managed to brush aside his remarks as simply intended as a joke.[149] Pibul was still not completely reassured. He was worried by the way Pridi had engineered the election of Thawee and Khuang to the speakership. Hence the premier ordered the dismissal from office of the Assembly's secretary, a close friend of Pridi, plus several naval promoters.[150] Direk then used a genuine, albeit temporary illness as a pretext to resign from his post as ambassador in Tokyo.

To keep a close watch on Direk's activities when he returned to Bangkok, Pibul unexpectedly appointed him Foreign Minister again, a move arranged in a very hasty and arbitrary way. Direk first learnt of his new appointment on October 20 when listening to the news on the radio. Once more he felt that Pibul was coercing him and refused to accept the position until, as before, Adul was sent to coax him. However, this time Direk had little to do on taking over the Foreign Ministry except cope with the Japanese.[151] It was not easy, as Pibul also realised.

In an obvious attempt to allay Japanese suspicions that Thailand might be wavering in its allegiance, Pibul soon appointed Vichit as ambassador in Tokyo to replace Direk. The move led the Japanese to believe that Vichit was being banished and not simply because he remained an uncritical advocate of cooperation with Tokyo. Within the cabinet Vichit had also acquired a reputation for being personally vindictive. Still he was reluctant to go to Tokyo, where he knew that Pibul would count on him to smooth over any awkward points in Thai relations with Japan.[152]

The first test of Vichit's ability to keep the Japanese happy came in November when Pibul declined to attend a conference, convened in Tokyo, of the heads of government of the Greater East Asia Co-Prosperity Sphere. Even though he had professed friendship for Japan long before Ba Maw of Burma and Laurel in the Philippines, let alone Subas Chandra Bose, the head of the Indian Independence League, Pibul had no wish to be classed with them as Japanese puppets. Possibly, too, he was worried that he might be ousted from power if he was absent from Bangkok.[153] Instead Thailand was represented at the Greater East Asia Conference by Prince Wan. It was in any case just as well for Pibul's nerves. On its way to Tokyo the plane carrying Ba Maw crashed, although he escaped with his life. Simultaneously Prince Wan's flight was delayed by mysterious engine trouble. Both incidents occurred at Saigon, which the Japanese thought might be no coincidence.[154]

Yet once the conference in Tokyo ended with ringing declarations about the need for ever greater solidarity among the peoples of East Asia in their efforts to oppose any attempt by the Western powers to reassert their influence in the region, Pibul duly subscribed to its aims. In a broadcast addressed personally to Chiang Kai-shek, the Thai Prime Minister called on him to join all the other countries of East Asia in fighting against the Americans and British. Thus, outwardly at least, Thailand remained firmly aligned with Japan in pursuing the doctrine of Asia for the Asians at the end of 1943.[155]

NOTES

1. Thawee Bunyaket in Ray, p. 77.
2. Ananta Pibulsongkram, IV, p. 176.
3. Pibul in Thak Chaloemtiarana (ed.), p. 354.
4. Flood, p. 692, and Fujiwara, pp. 55ff, on Japanese dismay at the incident which involved Thanat Khoman.
5. Allen, pp. 116ff, and *Operations of 15th Army*, Japanese Monograph AL5192.
6. ibid.; Flood, pp. 668ff; Netr Khemayothin, p. 231.
7. Tsuji, pp. 104ff, and Prayoon, p. 477.
8. Netr Khemayothin, p. 231.
9. Flood, p. 702; Adul in Suphote Dantrakul, pp. 78ff; and Sangworn Suwanna-chip, pp. 111ff.
10. AL5192, pp. 8ff.
11. Tsuji, p. 92.
12. ibid., pp. 65ff.
13. ibid., pp. 83ff.
14. Direk, p. 63; Thawee Bunyaket in ibid., pp. 111ff; Adul in Suphote Dantrakul, p. 86. The incident with the sheets is related in several accounts in Phra Phinit Chonkadi, *Nitan Tamruat* (unpaginated), although Fujiwara, p. 59, claims that the sheets were quickly removed by Thai police.
15. Thawee Bunyaket in Direk, p. 113, and a cabinet record in Ananta Pibulsong-kram, IV, p. 442, suggest that Direk accompanied Pibul contrary to accounts of Direk, Pibul and Japanese records: Direk, p. 64, Pibul in Thak Chaloemtiarana (ed.), p. 356, and Flood, pp. 706ff. Pibul is also wrong in claiming that he was threatened by Japanese generals since nobody present was of that rank.
16. Direk, p. 64; Thawee Bunyaket in ibid., p. 114; cabinet record in Ananta Pibul-songkram, IV, pp. 440ff, despite various contradictions.
17. Direk, p. 64; FRUS, 1941, V, p. 378; F13492/210/40 in FO 371/28126.
18. F7656/1083/40 in FO 371/31860.
19. F13329/9789/40 in FO 371/28163 and Ananta Pibulsongkram, IV, p. 398.
20. Netr Khemayothin, p. 241, and text of broadcast in Thak Chaloemtiarana (ed.), p. 307, but Coast, p. 18, is wrong in stating that the message came from Singapore.
21. F13417/210/40 in FO 371/28126.
22. F13522/13522/40 in FO 371/28164.
23. Kirby, p. 185, and Tsuji, pp. 87ff.
24. Thamsook Numnonda (1977), pp. 2ff, and Prasert Patamasukhon, p. 379.
25. Crosby, p. 135.
26. Sriphanon Singthong, p. 292.
27. Conversation between Pibul and General Iida on Dec. 9 in Flood, pp. 716ff.
28. Prayoon, pp. 477ff; FRUS, 1942, I, p. 917; Office of Strategic Studies (OSS), *The Japanese Domination of Thailand*, p. 8.
29. Crosby, pp. 131ff, and Direk, p. 65.
30. Thawee Bunyaket in Ray, p. 79.
31. Flood, p. 720.
32. Direk's account in Nicol Smith, *Into Siam: Underground Kingdom*, p. 265, and

Ananta Pibulsongkram, IV, pp. 526ff.

33. Thamsook Numnonda (1977), p. 4.
34. OSS, p. 35.
35. Pridi in Thak Chaloemtiarana (ed.), p. 377, and Nai Chantana (pseud.), *XO Group*, pp. 25ff.
36. Gilchrist, pp. 208ff.
37. Text of broadcast in F2213/1341/40 in FO 371/31862.
38. 892.00/233 in RG59; Flood, p. 725; Adul in Suphote Dantrakul, p. 90.
39. ibid., p. 92.
40. Correspondence on Thailand's financial dealings with Japan in 892.515/3-2348 in RG59.
41. Thawee Bunyaket in Ray, p. 79 and Prasert Patamasukhon, p. 380.
42. Adul in Suphote Dantrakul, p. 91; Pridi in Pramote Pungsunthorn, p. 55; Gilchrist, p. 15. Japanese concern about Pridi led to a flying visit to Bangkok in Jan. 1942 by Phra Sarasat Pholkand, former Minister of Economics and head of the Thai-Japanese propaganda unit in Tokyo. They argued as Pridi testified in Phra Sarasat's trial as a war criminal in Feb. 1946. Thak Chaloemtiarana (ed.), pp. 379ff. Also WO 208/1923 (54a).
43. Momchaoying Aphasrapa Tevakul in Pramote Pungsunthorn, pp. 26ff.
44. Direk, p. 73; Adul in Suphote Dantrakul, pp. 94ff; Konthi Suphamongkol *Karnvithesobai kong Thai*, p. 99.
45. Ananta Pibulsongkram, IV, p. 260, and Thamsook Numnonda (1977), p. 5.
46. ibid., pp. 6ff. Text of treaty in Thak Chaloemtiarana (ed.), pp. 450ff. According to Bangkok rumour, the real statue was hidden beforehand, so the treaty was not binding.
47. Flood, p. 719.
48. Having fled the German invasion of Belgium and France, Ananta and Chirawat Pibulsongkram eventually flew from Portugal to Washington, where in Dec. 1941 Congress was considering a bill for Ananta to enter West Point. Martin, loc. cit., p. 461n. Pibul's concern about his children in note of Dec. 20, 1941, in 892.01/16 RG59.
49. FO 371/28164; FRUS, 1941, V, pp. 392ff; FRUS, 1942, I, p. 913.
50. NYT, Jan. 9, 11, 14 and 21, and *Times*, Jan. 26, 1942. Kirby, II, pp. 25ff.
51. Thamsook Numnonda (1977), pp. 7ff; Prasert Patamasukhon, pp. 383ff; Thawee Bunyaket in Direk, p. 116. In testimony to The War Crimes Tribunal on Oct. 19, 1945, Prince Aditya said that Pibul sent a declaration of war to the regents three days earlier, so prompting Pridi to absent himself.
52. Thamsook Numnonda (1977), pp. 7ff, and *Democracy*, Jan. 3, 1946.
53. Thamsook Numnonda (1977), p. 17, and Batson, *The Fall of the Pibul Government, 1944* (JSS 1974), p. 97n, and NYT, Jan. 29, 1942.
54. Skinner, p. 272. Adul testified after the war that he ordered the arrest of some Chinese known as anti-Japanese to protect them from detention and interrogation by the Kempei while helping others to escape to China. Adul in Suphote Dantrakul, pp. 101ff.
55. The *Bangkok Times* closed down in 1942, but the *Bangkok Chronicle* continued publication throughout the war under Japanese Foreign Ministry supervision. *Magic*, Aug. 9, 1942.

56. Thamsook Numnonda (1977), p. 30.
57. Text of broadcasts in Thak Chaloemtiarana (ed.), pp. 286ff and F7656/1083/40 in FO 371/31860. Ananta Pibulsongkram, III, p. 562, claims that attacks on George VI were simply in reaction to Western criticism of Pibul.
58. Netr Khemayothin, II, p. 3.
59. Adul in Suphote Dantrakul, pp. 109ff, and Thamsook Numnonda (1977), p. 29.
60. ibid.; Thawee Bunyaket in Ray, p. 87; and Ananta Pibulsongkram, III, pp. 62ff.
61. Thamsook Numnonda (1977), p. 51.
62. ibid., pp. 31ff.
63. Broadcast of June 5, 1942, in Thak Chaloemtiarana (ed.), pp. 308ff.
64. Pibul's statement of Sep. 1945 in ibid., pp. 363ff.
65. Thamsook Numnonda (1977), p. 34; article in *Bangkok Post*, Aug. 7, 1977; Coast, p. 22.
66. Crosby, pp. 105ff.
67. Coast, p. 21.
68. The mission included Thamrong. *Syonan Times*, Apr. 24 and 28, 1942.
69. British Financial Adviser's report on repatriation, F7086/2317/40 in FO 371/31864; Ingram, p. 162; Adul in Suphote Dantrakul, p. 173.
70. *Syonan Times*, Apr. 23 and 24, 1942.
71. ibid., Sep. 2, 1942.
72. Thamsook Numnonda (1977), pp. 83ff; Batson (JSS 1974), p. 95 and report of Aug. 22, 1942, in 892.00/233 RG59.
73. AL5192, p. 14 and *Magic*, July 23, 1943, summarising Japan's financial demands on Thailand.
74. Broadcast of May 9, 1942, in Thak Chaloemtiarana (ed.), p. 301, and Prasert Patamasukhon, p. 402.
75. *Magic*, May 8 and 12, 1942, reporting Pibul's concern. Varying accounts of the campaign in biographies of Field-Marshal Phin Chunhawan in Sriphanon Singtong, pp. 99ff; Field-Marshal Sarit Thanarat in Thak Chaloemtiarana (ed.), p. 693; Oune Sananikone, pp. 83ff.
76. Kirby, II, pp. 16ff.
77. *Magic*, May 30, and *Syonan Times*, May 29, Jun 3 and 17, 1942.
78. Conflicting accounts of austerity and joy in ibid., June 23 and 27, 1942.
79. This accounts for irreverent references to "Field-Marshal Pee".
80. BP (articles by Thamsook Numnonda), July 31 and Aug. 7, 1977; Adul in Suphote Dantrakul, pp. 106ff; and Prince Aditya's testimony of Oct. 19, 1945, claiming Pibul had monarchical ambitions.
81. *Syonan Times*, June 23, July 1, 16, 21 and 24, 1942. The mission was headed by Koki Hirota, subsequently hanged as a war criminal. One of Hirota's tasks in Bangkok was possibly to secure Pridi's cooperation. They had met in Tokyo in 1936. Given Japan's own imperial tradition, Hirota may also have warned Pibul against pursuing his dynastic ambitions WO 208/1923 (54a).
82. *Syonan Times*, June 16, 1942.
83. Direk, pp. 76ff, and Konthi Suphamongkol, p. 104.
84. *Magic*, May 29 and July 9, 1942, which helped the Allies intercept and sink German shipping. Lewin *The Other Ultra*, p. 206.
85. Direk, p. 78 and complex negotiations between Bangkok, Tokyo and Nanking in *Magic*, May 13 and 25, June 22 and Oct. 6, 1942.

86. Skinner, p. 276.

87. BP (article by Thamsook Numnonda), July 31, 1977.

88. Coast, p. 22, and MG, June 10, 1942.

89. They included Kularp Saipradit, editor of *Suphap Burut*; Kumut Chandruang, editor of *Thailand Illustrated* and Suri Thongvanit, proprietor of *Siang Thai*.

90. Thamsook Numnonda (1977), p. 18, and Batson (JSS 1974), p. 112n. Also banned was a book apparently referring to Pibul's minor wife which angered Khunying La-iad. Adul in Suphote Dantrakul, p. 111. Pibul's attitude towards the press in Ananta Pibulsongkram, III, p. 77.

91. Thamsook Numnonda (1977), p. 33.

92. Batson (JSS 1974), p. 97.

93. NYT and NYHT, May 22, 1942, and 892.001/456 in RG59.

94. BP (article by Thamsook Numnonda), Aug. 7, 1977, and Coast, p. 26.

95. Thamsook Numnonda (1977), p. 51, and *Magic*, Oct. 4 and 13, 1942.

96. ibid., Oct. 17, 1942 and *Syonan Times*, Nov. 11, 1942. Aid also came from the Chinese community whose charitable organisations continued to operate clandestinely. Skinner, p. 278.

97. Thamsook Numnonda (1977), p. 88, and *Magic*, Aug. 19, Sep. 4, 28 and 29, Oct. 5 and 19, reporting demonstrations in Bangkok during August and subsequent attempts to get supplies of oil and consumer goods to Thailand.

98. Direk, pp. 84ff.

99. AL5199, p. 8; AL435, pp. 4ff; Bergamini, pp. 966ff.

100. NYT, Nov. 29, 1942.

101. *Syonan Shimbun*, Jan. 4, 1943, and Ananta Pibulsongkram, III, p. 280.

102. Report by the Japanese consul in Chiengmai in *Magic*, Jan. 26, 1943, and Oune Sananikone, pp. 93ff.

103. Pibul's orders in Ananta Pibulsongkram, III, pp. 281ff.

104. ibid., pp. 487ff.

105. Thawee Bunyaket in Ray, p. 92.

106. Chiengmai reports in *Magic*, Feb. 3, 1943.

107. *Chicago Daily News*, Jan. 22, 1943.

108. *Magic*, Dec. 18, 1942, and Jan. 28, 1943, and Coast, p. 23.

109. Thawee Bunyaket in Ray, p. 92.

110. This was Khun Nirandonchai.

111. This was Maj.-Gen. Chai Pratipasen.

112. This was Phairote Chaiyanam.

113. F3490/738/40 in FO 371/46562.

114. Gunboat commanded by Lt. Vacharachai Chaisitthivet, who later became Pridi's personal bodyguard. Sangworn Suwannachip, p. 118.

115. Statement broadcast by Deputy Director of Government Propaganda, Phra Rajatham Nithet, one of the *Nai Man* and *Nai Kong* team.

116. Disappearance of letter from Regents' office and suspicion that Khun Nirandonchai removed it on Pibul's instructions, WO 208/1923 (54a).

117. Testimonies by Thawee Bunyaket and Prince Aditya in Oct. 1945; Adul in Suphote Dantrakul, pp. 60ff; Khuang, loc. cit., p. 73 (he misplaces the incident); Sangworn Suwannachip, pp. 117ff.

118. NYT, Feb. 15, 1943, also referring to broadcasts by Pibul seeking to explain his personal wealth.

119. ibid., Mar. 3, 1943. Details of the incident in cremation volume of Gen. Harn Songkram, Commander of the Third Division in the Shan States. He was told by Gen. Chira Vichitsongkram, then Commander Northern Army, to repatriate some Chinese prisoners to Yunnan with a message that Thailand was the unwilling ally of Japan and wished to cooperate with the United Nations. It is unclear whether Pibul authorised the contact or if it affected his decision to resign.

120. FRUS, China, 1943, pp. 13 and 36; FO 371/35983.

121. Momchaoying Aphasrapa Tevakul in Pramote Pungsunthorn, pp. 30ff.

122. Nai Chantana, p. 50.

123. Gilchrist, p. 19, and secret meeting between Pridi and local manager of Hong Kong Shanghai Bank before repatriation in F7578/396/40 in FO 371/31856.

124. Nai Chantana, p. 58.

125. They were Prince Damrong and Prince Dhani Nivat who gave the envoy, Chamkad Balankura, letters of introduction to the French historian, Georges Coëdes in Hanoi. WO 208/1923 (54a).

126. Pibul's interview with Tsubokami and newly-arrived Japanese garrison commander on Mar. 2 in *Magic*, Mar. 11, 1943.

127. Adul in Suphote Dantrakul, p. 115.

128. ibid., pp. 143ff; Prince Aditya's testimony of Oct. 19, 1945, and Pridi in Pramote Pungsunthorn, pp. 61ff. The third regent, Chao Phya Phityenthornyothin, died in Sep. 1942 and was not replaced.

129. Pibul's orders of Mar. 30 and 31 in Ananta Pibulsongkram, III, pp. 88ff.

130. ibid., p. 220, and Thamsook Numnonda (1977), p. 33.

131. BP (article by Thamsook Numnonda), Aug. 7, 1977, and Prasert Patamasukhon, p. 427.

132. Charnvit Kasetsiri, loc. cit., p. 58; Direk, p. 83; *Magic*, Nov. 16, 1942.

133. Text in Thak Chaloemtiarana (ed.), pp. 452ff, and *Syonan Shimbun*, Apr. 15, 1943.

134. OSS, p. 39.

135. Ananta Pibulsongkram, III, p. 239, and Thamsook Numnonda (1977), p. 37.

136. ibid., p. 38; Coast, p. 25; Ananta Pibulsongkram, III, p. 267.

137. Coast, p. 23, and Thamsook Numnonda (1977), p. 45.

138. See above, p. 204, fifth paragraph.

139. Flood, p. 275, and Adul in Suphote Dantrakul, pp. 124 and 174.

140. This was Mom Luang Kri Dechatiwong, Minister of Communications.

141. Thawee Bunyaket in Direk, p. 117.

142. Thawee Bunyaket in Ray, pp. 96ff. Khuang also refers to the incident, but confuses it with Pibul's resignation. He too was ordered to report to Supreme Command.

143. Ananta Pibulsongkram, III, pp. 85, 94, 96, 159, 342 and 546.

144. Coast, p. 24, and *Magic*, July 9, 1943, listing all Pibul's excuses.

145. ibid., and Jones, pp. 349ff.

146. Direk, pp. 91ff; *Times* and NYT, July 6; and *Syonan Shimbun*, July 24, 1943.

147. *Magic*, Oct. 14, 1943, as compared with Thamsook Numnonda (1977), p. 48.

148. Pibul's orders of July 17 and 18 and Aug. 11 in Ananta Pibulsongkram, III, pp. 417ff.

149. Pridi in Pramote Pungsunthorn, pp. 62ff; Adul in Suphote Dantrakul, p. 160; Prince Aditya's testimony of Oct. 1945.

150. Pibul's orders of June 30, July 7 and 8, reprimanding and dismissing Thongpleow Chollapum, Secretary to the Assembly, and naval promoters Pan Navavichit and Sangworn Suwannachip in Ananta Pibulsongkram, III, pp. 98ff and Prasert Patamasukhon, p. 420.

151. Direk, pp. 84ff.

152. *Magic*, Oct. 14, 1943.

153. ibid. and Batson (JSS, 1974), p. 95.

154. Allen, *The End of the War in Asia*, p. 44.

155. Konthi Suphamongkol, p. 113.

11

THE OTHER SIDE

During the Japanese occupation of Thailand, radio became the main way of bridging the gap with the rest of the world in ʰoth directions. Just as many Thais listened to foreign broadcasts, so the Western Allies monitored Bangkok Radio to try to find out what was happening in Thailand. In reading between the lines of propaganda and wartime censorship, the British and Americans were helped by some of the Thais who were resident abroad at the outbreak of war and decided to remain there. Most prominent among them was the Thai Minister in Washington, Mom Rajawong Seni Pramoj.

As his title indicates, Seni was a junior member of the royal family.[1] He was a great-grandson of the second Chakri monarch but the Pramoj family remained influential; Seni's father was Director-General of Police for fifteen years till his retirement in 1929, and he sent his sons abroad to be educated. Consequently Seni spent most of his youth at a typical English public school, an experience he does not appear to have enjoyed.[2] He went on to take a degree at Oxford and qualify as a barrister. Thus, on his return to Siam in 1929, he was entitled to a district judgeship in Bangkok as well as an official position in the Ministry of Justice. Yet, unlike his contemporaries in the Ministry, Seni played no part in ending the absolute monarchy. He has claimed that his career suffered as a result, and he was assigned to the arduous work of codifying Siamese law to provide the legal basis for Pridi to renegotiate the treaties with the foreign powers in 1937. Seni's qualifications also enabled him to lecture at the University of Moral and Political Sciences. There, he has alleged, he became so popular that Pridi got jealous and engineered his unexpected transfer to Washington as Thai Minister in April 1940.[3]

The Americans took a different view. They regarded Seni as Pibul's appointee since he was in charge of foreign affairs at the time. Moreover, Seni defended Thai claims against Indo-China so assiduously that Cordell Hull thought Seni was – like Pibul – a creature of the Japanese.[4] Seni also seemed unduly friendly towards the other Axis powers.[5] Perhaps it was simply inexperience. Aged only thirty-five, he was the youngest head of mission in Washington.

Anyway, given Seni's record, Hull was surprised to receive a call from him on December 8, 1941, when everyone in Washington was preoccupied with Japan's attack on Pearl Harbor. Seni wanted to inform the United States officially of the Thai legation's desire to cooperate with the Americans in opposing Japan. As for the ceasefire proclaimed in Bangkok, Seni told Hull that it was the work of pro-Japanese elements acting against the will of the Thai people.[6] Seni was all the more incensed because the first two cables he received from Bangkok after the Japanese invasion were instructions from Pibul to hand over large sums in dollars to his two children in the United States.[7] Only a couple of days later, he was officially notified of the ceasefire and Pibul's subsequent decision to conclude a military alliance with Japan.

Before receiving news of this development, Seni gave a press conference on December 11 to repudiate Pibul's collaboration with the Japanese. Nor did he not hesitate to communicate his views to the Foreign Ministry in Bangkok.[8] Subsequently he claimed that he decided to dissociate himself from Pibul's policies in the belief that the Americans would eventually win the war. In other words, Seni, just like Pibul, wanted to be on the winning side, although he thought it would take the United States several years to build up its armed strength and that initially America might be over-run by the Japanese.[9] Still, such fears were not apparent in broadcasts made by Seni which were transmitted around the world by a radio station in San Francisco. His aim was to denounce Pibul's pro-Japanese stance and call on all Thais to unite in fighting for the restoration of their country's independence.[10]

Seni's attitude led to an exchange of telegrams between Washington and London about the possibility of setting up a Free Thai movement modelled on those representing several German-occupied countries in Europe. At the beginning, the British were more optimistic than the Americans about the Thai will to resist the Japanese; yet both Western powers agreed that much would depend on the personality of Thai resistance leaders.

This caution was overtaken at the end of December 1941, when the Americans decided in principle to recognise a Free Thai movement headed by Seni, although his status obviously differed from those Europeans who had set up resistance forces under governments-in-exile. Even so, early in 1942, when twenty-six countries pledged in the name of the United Nations to cooperate in defeating the Axis powers, Seni made a similar declaration on behalf of all Thais. For the time being, it was kept secret because the Americans were concerned for the safety of their diplomats in Bangkok.[11] Contrary to normal international diplomatic procedure, they were confined to their legation and denied communication with Washington long before Thailand declared war on the United States.[12]

In later years, Seni made much of the claim that he declined to deliver Thailand's declaration of war to the Americans and kept the document firmly locked in his desk-drawer.[13] Strictly speaking, it is not true. When he finally received notification from Bangkok of the state of war between the two countries – a message delayed because of the severance of communications between Washington and Bangkok – Seni conveyed the text to the State Department with the comment that it was simply intended for the record because he himself was ignoring it.[14] That too was the reaction of Roosevelt who recommended Congress to treat Thailand's declaration of war with contempt by ignoring it just like those of Hungary, Bulgaria and Romania. Only if Thai forces engaged in military operations against the United States or its Allies was Thailand to be regarded as an enemy. Rather it was classed as an enemy-occupied state, which entailed freezing Thai financial assets in the United States, whereas Thai citizens residing there were not considered enemy aliens.[15]

Even so, Pibul's declaration of war led to the severance of diplomatic relations between Thailand and the United States which caused problems about Seni's status in Washington. Following standard international procedure, the Foreign Ministry in Bangkok asked Switzerland to take care of all Thai interests in the United States for the duration of the war, and the Americans thought that Seni should comply by handing his legation over to the Swiss.[16] Seni demurred. He had no intention of forfeiting his home or his diplomatic standing in Washington. On the contrary, he was determined to stay where he was and use his position to promote the cause of a Free Thai movement in the United States.[17] His decision was reinforced by the support of the Thai military attaché in Washington, Mom Luang Colonel Karb Kunchara.

A more junior member of the royal family than Seni, Karb was one of Pibul's more urbane military protégés who was sent to Washington in October 1941 with express instructions to do everything possible to improve Thai-American relations.[18] Another of Karb's tasks was apparently to keep an eye on Pibul's children. Anyway, in carrying out his duties Karb soon established contacts with the American military which came in useful after the outbreak of war in the Pacific. Karb quickly suggested that he and some of the Thai students currently in the United States could help the Allies fight the Japanese in South East Asia.

At first the Americans were unsure how far they could trust Karb, given that he had previously worked closely with Pibul. These doubts were brushed aside by Seni, who personally vouched for Karb's reliability and dedication to the Free Thai cause. Hence, in June 1942 thirteen Thai students specially selected by Karb began a three-month course of intensive military training, although they were not enlisted in the US Army. Instead, they came under the Office of Strategic Services (OSS), set up by General William Donovan, with the blessing of Roosevelt, specifically to carry out clandestine warfare behind enemy lines. As such, OSS was already working with several resistance groups in German-occupied Europe. When it assumed responsibility for the Thai students, most of whom were post-graduates, they were adjudged to be one of the most intelligent groups with whom OSS was working.

To distinguish them from the collaborationists back home, Karb personally invested them as officers in the Free or Seri Thai army, which Seni agreed should be financed out of Thai assets frozen in the United States.[19] Further, to ensure that there was no misunderstanding about Seri Thai aims, Seni placed on record a statement disclaiming any intention of forming a political party or becoming involved in controversy over the succession to the throne. Instead, he stressed that the purpose of the Seri Thai was to liberate their country from Japan.[20] After that, another eighteen Thai students in the United States were trained by the OSS and some of them, together with the first batch of trainees, embarked in March 1943 on a voyage to India and eventual infiltration into Thailand.

At the same time, a group of thirty-six Thai students from Britain was likewise on its way to India. To get there they had to cope with far more problems than their compatriots in the United States. In the first place, unlike Seni, the Thai Minister in London did not denounce Pibul's alliance with Japan. Nor was there any question of Britain ignoring Thailand's declaration of war. It was in flagrant breach of the non-aggression pact between the two countries, and to make matters worse there were reports of Thai troops moving into Burma. Hence Britain reacted by declaring war on Siam – as it was again referred to in London.[21]

Under these circumstances all Thai citizens in Britain became in theory enemy aliens subject to internment. In practice, only the staff at the Thai legation in London had their movements restricted until those who so opted were repatriated, together with a mere handful of students who chose to follow them.[22] Despite the dangers and difficulties of life in wartime Britain, most of the Thai community decided against returning home. They then had to contend with the freeze imposed on all Thai financial assets held in London. It hit those students who had Thai government scholarships particularly hard.

One reason why most of these students refused to be repatriated was their awareness of Seni's move to establish the Seri Thai in the United States. They wanted to do something similar in Britain, but their problem was how to obtain official British agreement. For obvious reasons they could not seek the help of their legation in London, and the only other Thais in Britain with influence in official circles seemed to be members of the royal family. The students were reluctant to involve princes in their plans. As part of the post-1932 generation, they had been educated to believe that the aim of the royal family was to restore the absolute monarchy. One possible exception in Britain was Prince Chula Chakrabongse, who had visited Bangkok several times since 1932, and was apparently not totally opposed to constitutional rule. By 1942, however, Prince Chula had married an Englishwoman and settled in Cornwall, where he joined the local Home Guard. His cousin, the racing driver Prince Bira, followed a similar course, and neither of them was prepared to play any further role relating to their homeland. That left the close relatives of ex-King Prajadhipok as the only other potentially influential figureheads amongst the Thai community in Britain.[23]

The former monarch died in May 1941 at the home he had acquired just outside London.[24] He was survived by his wife, Queen Rambhai Bharni; she was comforted in her dowagerhood by her brother, Prince Subha Svasti or Tan Chin as he was familiarly known. Their father, the controversial Prince Svasti, died in 1935 in Penang. Yet the family reputation lived on. Because of his involvement in the Bovoradet rebellion, Tan Chin was regarded as a royalist diehard who was likely to be arrested if he returned to Bangkok.[25] Consequently he lived in England where he had been educated, and like many other Chakri princes obtained a commission in the British army. He reminded Churchill of the fact in August 1941 when amid the growing atmosphere of tension surrounding Thailand, Tan Chin asked to return to active military service. The request was referred to the Foreign Office, which pointed out Tan Chin's political handicaps in any duties relating to Thailand. Hence he was employed by the War Office in a back-room job up-dating maps of South East Asia.[26] Even so, at the outbreak of the Pacific War, Tan Chin was already in uniform with military contacts which could be useful to the students; however, they wanted nothing to do with him.

Instead they sent a telegram to Seni in Washington asking for help in setting up a Seri Thai group in Britain.[27]

After official consultations between Washington and London, it was agreed that Mani Sanasen, a Thai diplomat formerly with the League of Nations and now in the United States, should travel to Britain as Seni's representative to contact the students and ascertain their views. The task was completed in July 1942 when Mani reported to the Foreign Office that most Thai students in Britain wished to cooperate with the Allies and liberate their country from the Japanese, provided that they were not used to serve the interests of any particular political faction and above all not the princes. The stipulation was appreciated by British diplomats who had experience of Thailand, and were aware of continuing manoeuvring among various branches of the Chakri family over the succession to the throne. But the students' desire to help the Allies raised other problems as well.[28]

In comparison with the Free French or Free Poles, the Thais were few in number with little apparent military potential and no government abroad to represent them. Technically, as enemy aliens, the only military avenue open to them was to join the Pioneer Corps which enlisted people of various nationality and race mainly for manual work. The idea did not appeal to the Thai students. They regarded the Pioneer Corps as a very dubious body lacking in status, where they feared they might be treated simply as "coolie labour".[29] Eventually they agreed to join on condition that they be kept together as a group and deployed on duties relating to their homeland. These terms were agreed in August when more than thirty Siamese students were enlisted in the British army to spend the next few months on a rigorous course of basic military training. Again, like their counterparts in the United States, the Thais joining the Pioneer Corps earned the compliments of their officers. Hence at the start of 1943 they were on their way to India for further training in preparation for the tasks on which they were to be deployed.[30]

In early 1943 the Americans and much less the British had barely recovered from the shock of Japan's onslaught, so their planning of major counter-offensives was still in the initial stages. Clearly the Americans were determined to liberate the Philippines as soon as possible, just as the British wanted to avenge their defeat in Malaya and Singapore. These objectives left the question of who was to defeat the Japanese in Thailand and Indo-China rather indeterminate, and for the time being the Allies allocated responsibility for the two countries to China's theatre of operations. The decision was taken more out of a desire to boost Chiang Kai-shek's prestige as one of the Allies rather than any belief that the Chinese could effectively challenge the Japanese presence in South East Asia.[31]

Chiang Kai-shek took his new responsibilities seriously. Noting that Pibul had not declared war on China, his first thought in early 1942 was to issue a statement expressing sympathy for Thailand as the innocent victim of Japanese aggression.[32] The idea was quickly abandoned when the clashes in the Shan States were followed by Pibul's recognition of the Wang Ching-wei regime in Nanking; the move was strongly condemned by the press in Chungking, which claimed that Pibul had forfeited Thailand's right to independence.[33]

Some six months later, Chiang Kai-shek had second thoughts. The offer to defect made in February 1943 by a Thai general in the Shan States led the Chinese to believe that it might after all be worthwhile issuing a public statement to encourage other Thais to oppose the Japanese. As a result, Chiang Kai-shek broadcast a personal message to the Thai people. Referring to their traditional friendship with the Chinese including the 3 million residing in Thailand itself, the Generalissimo said that China wanted to help the Thais liberate their country from the Japanese. He was careful to stress that China had no designs on Thai sovereignty.

A similar statement, including a pledge to respect Thailand's independence, was issued by Roosevelt a few days later. After that the Foreign Office in London thought that Britain should follow suit, and a draft statement was submitted to the war cabinet. There it fell foul of what virtually amounted to a veto by Churchill. Still smarting from the loss of Malaya and Singapore, he ruled that before making any public commitment on the future of Siam, consideration must first be given to imposing some sort of protectorate over the Kra Isthmus region to prevent history from repeating itself.[34]

The absence of a British statement on future policy towards Siam did not immediately affect the students in the Pioneer Corps. Once they reached India, they were assigned to various specialised training courses under the aegis of Force 136, a clandestine paramilitary organisation officered by British businessmen, civil servants and diplomats with previous experience of the Far East. Force 136 was in fact the South East Asian branch of Special Operations Executive (SOE) which, like its American counterpart OSS, undertook such operations as dropping agents behind enemy lines, collecting intelligence and carrying out sabotage, if possible with the cooperation of local resistance movements.[35] But in the case of Thailand, neither Force 136 nor OSS was sure at the beginning of 1943 whether an underground resistance movement existed.[36] After the messages which Pridi managed to smuggle out with the repatriated Allied internees, nothing further was heard about the situation inside Thailand until Chamkad Balankura suddenly appeared in southern China in March 1943.[37]

Chamkad was the envoy whom Pridi had authorised to travel to China following Pibul's abortive resignation.[38] Chamkad was motivated by a desire to free Thailand not merely from the Japanese but also from Pibul. As a student at Oxford and head of the Thai Student Association in Britain in 1938, Chamkad had written an article critical of the lack of democracy in Siam,[39] which caused such a stir in Bangkok that Pibul angrily barred him on his return home from entering government service. Instead he worked privately and was able to slip out of the country virtually unnoticed with travel documents stating that he was visiting Japan on business.

Chamkad left Bangkok at the end of February accompanied by a Sino-Thai acting as companion and interpreter. Travelling by public transport, they soon reached Hanoi. From there, with the help of some French contacts, they were taken by boat and bus to Mong Cai on the border of Tonkin and crossed into a part of China not occupied by the Japanese.[40] There Chamkad's youthful enthusiasm took over. Ignoring the fact that all telegraphic traffic in wartime is monitored by many interested parties, he fired off a series of telegrams addressed to Seni in Washington, the British and American embassies in Chungking, and Chiang Kai-shek personally.[41] From all of them he requested help in arranging a high-level conference. Immediately Chinese suspicions were aroused and Chamkad was detained. Somehow he managed nevertheless to make his way to the British consulate at Kweilin where he introduced himself as the secretary of the Seri Thai and its executive committee, the XO Group.

Naturally the first reaction of the Chinese and British to Chamkad's sudden appearance was to check whether or not he was a Japanese agent. His identity was soon established. His tutor at Oxford remembered him well, and Crosby stated that he knew Chamkad's family. Additional confirmation of the family's standing came from Seni in Washington.[42] But the XO Group was a different matter. According to Chamkad, the name was a secret password given by Pridi to Western internees repatriated in 1942.[43] If so, the information did not reach Crosby, who denied all knowledge of the XO Group. Nor did anybody in Washington appear to know of it. Yet, since Chamkad's personal identity had been vouched for, the Chinese made arrangements for him to be flown to Chungking where he was accorded an interview with the Deputy Foreign Minister.[44]

To all his official contacts, Chamkad had various proposals to make. He wanted a seaplane or submarine sent to Hua Hin before mid-May because the two regents and several cabinet ministers were there on holiday. Chamkad claimed they were all Seri Thai who wished to leave the country to set up a government-in-exile in India. When questioned further about who precisely was involved, Chamkad was vague; instead he was more intent on going to London to meet Crosby and other British officials who had previously worked in Thailand, as well as Seni and various friends from Washington. Such a meeting would discuss a series of political proposals which, Chamkad said, came from Pridi: they were based on the premise that Thailand's declaration of war against the Western powers was invalid because Pridi's signature on it was a forgery. Proceding from that, Chamkad demanded the unfreezing of Thai funds in London to finance a government-in-exile and a Seri Thai army based in Yunnan. He envisaged that it would march south, liberate Chiengmai, cut off the Japanese army in Burma and eventually free the whole of Thailand and Indo-China from the Japanese.[45]

As Chamkad piled these proposals one on top of another, he began to appear to the British and Chinese, as something of a megalomaniac especially since they were still not sure whether he represented Pridi or anyone else apart from himself. Anyway he seemed to have no conception of the bitter struggle still being waged to contain the Japanese, let alone defeat them. Even the despatch of a seaplane to an uncertain rendez-vous in the Gulf of Thailand hundreds of miles behind enemy lines involved risks the British were not prepared to take. They also thought the "exfiltration" of Pridi and members of the cabinet might prompt Japan to stage a complete take-over of Thailand which would create even more difficulties for the Allies. The British mentioned some of these misgivings to the Chinese. Instead of keeping quiet about them, the Chinese passed them on to Chamkad in a form which made it look as if Britain was fundamentally hostile towards him.[46]

The Americans too had little interest in the proposals Chamkad had put forward. General Stilwell, commander of the China-Burma-India theatre of operations as well as Chief of Staff to Chiang Kai-shek's forces, considered operations to liberate Thailand to be low on his list of priorities. His main preoccupation was the reopening of the Burma Road to overcome the problem of transporting all US military aid to China by air over "the Hump" from India. The limitations imposed by these hazardous flights meant that American military equipment could not be supplied to large sections of the Chinese army, let alone a Thai army as proposed by Chamkad. In any case Chinese troops based in southern Yunnan along the border with the Shan States and Indo-China did not receive American aid. They were regarded by most generals in Chungking as the levies of local warlords whose value was doubtful. Partly for these reasons, Stilwell also told the Chinese to discourage the Thai army in the Shan States from defecting, as its commander offered to do in February 1943. The American general had no wish to provoke the Japanese into counter-action in an area where he had little control.[47]

For obvious security reasons, such tactical considerations were not explained to Chamkad and he became increasingly depressed at the apparent lack of interest in his proposals on the part of any of the Allied powers. Moreover he was accommodated in Chungking in what was officially termed a guest house but where in reality all his movements were subject to strict surveillance by the Chinese authorities. Once the British and Americans realised this, they concluded that Chamkad had been taken over by one or other of the Chinese intelligence agencies to manipulate him for its own purposes.[48]

Having been allocated Thailand as part of his theatre of operations, Chiang Kai-shek was determined to make the most of the opportunity. In other words, if a Thai government were set up in exile, the Chinese wanted it based in Chungking and not in India where it would come under British influence. That in particular was the view of General Tai Li, the head of the Kuomintang's top intelligence agency. He had a personal grudge against the British and refused to cooperate with SOE. The feeling was becoming mutual. A group of Sino-Thais recruited by the British for infiltration into Thailand turned out to be agents of Tai Li sent to infiltrate Force 136.[49] On the other hand, Tai Li was much more ready to cooperate with the Americans. He had cultivated the friendship of Captain Milton Miles, a senior US Navy officer based in Chungking. On the strength of their close relationship, Miles was appointed head of OSS operations in China. An agreement was then concluded between OSS and Tai Li whereby Chinese manpower and facilities were to be used in clandestine operations against the Japanese with the Americans supplying the arms, equipment and finance.

Under these arrangements, OSS planned to use Chinese territory to infiltrate into Thailand the students recruited in the United States with the aim of gathering intelligence and building up an underground resistance network.[50] Tai Li had other ideas. He already had plenty of intelligence agents in Thailand. The Kuomintang had long since established its own clandestine network in Thailand with the means to communicate secretly with Chungking.[51] Now Tai Li wanted to reap the benefit by sending in an army of 10,000 troops equipped and financed by the Americans. To gain the support of OSS for his plan, he agreed to the Seri Thai students from the United States accompanying his army into Thailand.[52]

As official liaison officer between OSS and the Seri Thai, Karb flew into Chungking in June to make advance preparations for the students who were undergoing jungle warfare training in India. Clearly, in carrying out his task, it would have been useful for Karb to meet Chamkad and learn at first hand about the situation in Thailand. Permission for such a meeting was refused.[53] Suddenly, despite his earlier testimonials to Karb's reliability, Seni reversed his position. He now claimed that Karb could not be trusted because he had expropriated vast sums of money to equip the Seri Thai and pay their travelling expenses. In any case, Seni alleged that Karb was notorious, having been sent to Washington in the first place as Pibul's spy. He would not therefore be trusted by anybody emerging from Thailand as an envoy of the resistance movement.

Given all that had gone before, Seni's accusations were attributed to jealousy since Karb was regarded by many Americans as a far better and more charismatic leader of the Seri Thai.[54] One person who was particularly impressed with Karb was Miles. He took the Seri Thai officer under his wing and introduced him to Tai Li, who realised that it might be useful in many ways if Karb assumed the leadership of the army to be sent into Thailand.[55]

Meanwhile Chamkad continued to demand an interview with Chiang Kai-shek to outline what he said were Pridi's plans. Eventually, once the Chinese had obtained confirmation from Bangkok that he was a genuine envoy and not a Japanese agent, Chamkad's request was granted. Yet when he actually met Chiang Kai-shek at the end of July, Chamkad's main concern was apparently to get permission to travel to Washington to talk to Seni. The Generalissimo's reply was cautious. He said it was for the Americans and Seni to decide whether such a visit was welcome,[56] but officials in Washington saw it more as a matter to be sorted out between the Thais and Chinese. However Seni's messages to the Chinese about Chamkad evoked little response.[57]

To add to this complex situation, Tan Chin arrived in Chungking in July. Despite continuing discussions in London about whether he should be involved in Free Siamese activities, SOE sent him to China to meet Chamkad.[58] His arrival was not welcome to the Americans. They, or at least Miles, thought that the British wanted Tan Chin to become leader of the entire Seri Thai movement and on the strength of that take over the throne as well. In harbouring such suspicions, Miles was perhaps unaware that one of Tan Chin's younger brothers was among the Seri Thai students trained by OSS. Some of them flew into Chungking in August when Miles found them to be ''as much fun and as unpredictable as a litter of tiger cubs''. Anyway both they and Karb were barred from meeting Tan Chin.[59] Here the British were quietly relieved. They too had come to the conclusion Karb was unreliable.[60]

On the other hand the British now believed that some sort of resistance movement existed in Siam and was worth encouraging in the longer term. That was why they wanted Tan Chin to meet Chamkad. Finally, in early August, the Chinese allowed the interview, which convinced Tan Chin and the British ambassador to China that Chamkad really was Pridi's envoy.[61] Moreover, in London some merit was seen in Chamkad's proposal for a Thai government-in-exile to be set up, provided it was in India rather than anywhere else. Underlying this thought was an agreement just reached between Churchill and Roosevelt to establish in India a joint Anglo-American military command to direct operations aimed at the defeat of the Japanese in South East Asia.

The Chinese were not involved in the discussions about this new operational command, and apparently saw it as a threat to their own ambitions in South East Asia, especially where Thailand was concerned. Suddenly Chamkad disappeared from the ''guest house'' where he was staying in Chungking having been spirited away, so it transpired, by Tai Li who tried to bribe him to form the nucleus of a Thai government in exile based in China.[62] The attempt was overtaken by the arrival in China of another Thai mission sent from Bangkok.

Having heard nothing from Chamkad, Pridi was getting worried. His anxiety increased in June 1943 when Pibul foiled his plan to get Thawee elected speaker of the Assembly. The incident prompted Pridi to send another mission to China to try to contact the Allies. This time, perhaps fearing that Chamkad had failed because of his lack of official status, Pridi decided to send somebody better known. His choice fell on

Sanguan Tularaks, a promoter and one of his close associates in 1932, in drafting the constitution and propagating the idea of democracy.[63] Subsequently, Sanguan acquired considerable notoriety as the director of a penal colony for political prisoners, but in 1943 his main function was managing the state tobacco monopoly, in other words the Bangkok factory of a major Western cigarette company which had been expropriated by Thailand.

Occupying such a conspicuous position, Sanguan could hardly slip out of the country unnoticed. Hence he obtained official approval to travel to Japan to purchase materials necessary for the production of cigarettes. He also arranged to take his wife and children with him because he was worried that they might not be safe once Pibul realised that he had escaped to China. In addition Sanguan sought to add prestige to his mission by asking Seni's younger brother Kukrit to accompany him.[64] The request was declined and instead a Foreign Ministry official, Deng Gunatilaka, agreed to accompany Sanguan and his family.[65] They set off on July 14 to travel through Indo-China to Hanoi and thence to Mong Cai as Chamkad had done before. On arrival in China, they were accorded a very different reception.

The Chinese immediately arranged for Sanguan and his party to travel to Chungking, where he had a meeting with Chiang Kai-shek straight away. Then, just like Karb and Chamkad, Sanguan and Deng found themselves taken into the protection of Tai Li, much to the dismay of some Americans in Chungking. They suspected Tai Li of trying to gain control through devious means with the help of Miles of the entire Thai underground resistance network, including that trained by OSS.[66] In Washington Seni was even more alarmed. He reminded the State Department of his warnings about Karb's reliability. He tried unsuccessfully to persuade OSS to recall Karb from Chungking, and when he discovered that Karb and Sanguan after initial suspicions got on well together, he alleged that they were conspiring with Chinese encouragement to set up a Seri Thai government in Chungking.

Such anxieties prompted the US Embassy in Chungking to take a new interest in trying to get Chamkad out of China, and if possible Sanguan and Deng as well.[67] These efforts gave Chamkad reason to hope, at last, after so many months of frustration in Chungking, that he might finally achieve his objective of meeting Seni. It was not to be. Throughout his stay in China, Chamkad suffered from poor health and in September he was admitted to hospital.[68] The British, alert as ever to Tai Li's machinations, suspected the worst and managed through a ruse to get Chamkad transferred from a Chinese hospital to one run by Canadian missionaries. There a doctor diagnosed that Chamkad had cancer of the liver. Even so, many people were surprised when he died on October 7. More ominously, Sanguan refused to authorise a post-mortem and both he and Tai Li were present to oversee Chamkad's cremation a few days later.[69] In these circumstances the British were not alone in suspecting that Chamkad had fallen victim to Tai Li.[70]

For obvious reasons, all these developments in Chungking were unknown to the public in Bangkok. Still, as soon as Pibul realised that Sanguan had defected to China, he drew attention to the fact. Sanguan was officially declared a rebel and stripped of his Thai citizenship and property.[71] At a time when he was worried about developments in Italy, Pibul clearly hoped that his move against Sanguan would deter anybody else whose loyalty was wavering. Another cause for concern in August 1943 was the decision by Roosevelt and Churchill – the leaders of the two countries on which Pibul had declared war – to set up a joint command to defeat Japan and its collaborators in South East Asia.

The new South East Asia Command was envisaged by the Western Allies on a par with the joint commands already established in Europe and the South West Pacific under Generals Eisenhower and Macarthur respectively. Their counterpart in South East Asia was a British officer, vice-Admiral Lord Louis Mountbatten. Despite Roosevelt's approval, his appointment aroused mixed feelings among many Americans who were convinced anti-imperialists: in their eyes Mountbatten, a great-grandson of Queen Victoria with close relatives in most of Europe's royal families, looked likely to have as his main objective the restoration of the British empire in the Far East. Consequently SEAC, the initials which designated his command, were quickly read by some Americans as "Save England's Asian Colonies".[72] Fears were expressed too that, with Mountbatten in command of this theatre, Britain would seek to expand its empire to encompass Thailand.

At times such suspicions stemmed from simple misunderstandings. For instance, an American diplomat based in Delhi discovered by chance that the British were secretly training a group of Thais in India, and construed this as evidence of a deeply laid British plot to manipulate Thailand's post-war future with the help of these "hand-picked" infiltrators. In fact they were the students from Britain who had volunteered to help liberate their homeland in the same way as the Seri Thai who were being trained by OSS.[73]

Yet underlying American misgivings was Churchill's failure to

follow Chiang Kai-shek and Roosevelt in issuing a public statement
about policy towards Thailand. To compensate for the omission, some
British diplomats pointed to the Atlantic Charter where Churchill and
Roosevelt had jointly pledged that during their efforts to defeat the Axis
neither of their countries would seek territorial aggrandisement or
changes in national sovereignty, contrary to the wishes of the people
involved.[74]

Such reassurances did not convince Seni, for one. He never forgot that
at a conference of the Institute of Pacific Relations towards the end of
1943, he had heard a British delegate advocate the need for Pibul's collaboration with the Japanese to be taken into account when Thailand's
post-war future came to be considered. Seni immediately took this to be
an expression of official British policy rather than an issue put forward
for discussion at an academic conference.[75]

Similar problems arose from a lecture given in London by Crosby in
1943. By then he had retired from official life and was speaking in a
personal capacity when he proposed some sort of international mandate
be established to guide Siam's political and economic development in the
first few years after the war. Again the statement was seized upon as
evidence of British designs on Thailand's independence. What neither
Seni nor the Americans who harboured such fears knew was that in
submitting his views to the Foreign Office, Crosby had suggested that
the United States rather than Britain would best be able to help Siam
progress towards democracy and prosperity. The idea was however
strongly challenged with the argument that because the Americans were
so closely allied to Chiang Kai-shek, any influence they might have over
Siam would be exercised to the advantage of the Chinese and the
detriment of the Thais. Indeed, far from having any ambitions to expand
their Asian empire, one of Britain's underlying concerns throughout the
war was to stop China seeking to exploit its status as an Allied power to
establish a dominating influence over South East Asia.[76]

China's attitude was a matter of even more immediate concern to
Mountbatten. Soon after assuming his command, he flew to Chungking where one of the issues he wanted to discuss with Chiang Kai-shek
was the authorisation of operations in Thailand and Indo-China. Their
talks were not very successful. China's leader had no wish to share
responsibility for any of the territory allocated to his theatre of operations; all he would concede was that, as the war progressed, there might
be some overlap between SEAC and the Chinese theatre.[77] On that basis,
Mountbatten concluded what he regarded as a "gentleman's agree-

ment'' with Chiang Kai-shek. In Mountbatten's eyes, it allowed for his command to authorise clandestine operations in Thailand as long as the Chinese were informed of what was going on. As a result Force 136 and OSS now received the go-ahead to mount operations to infiltrate Thailand with forces based in India.[78]

First off the mark was Force 136, which had a team of three Free Siamese trained and ready. They were headed by Puey Ungpakorn, who had given up a fellowship at the London School of Economics to join his compatriots in the Pioneer Corps and was regarded as their *de facto* leader.[79] Now, too, realising that invidious comparisons might be drawn between the status of these students and those recruited by OSS as Seri Thai officers, the British army awarded commissions to the twenty-two Siamese who completed a course of training with Force 136 in India. In addition, two of them who were to accompany Captain Puey were also trained as radio operators.

As planned by Force 136, the aim of their mission was to make a clandestine landing from a submarine off the west coast of the Kra Isthmus, establish direct radio contact with India and eventually, if possible, link up with local resistance forces under the leadership of Pridi. The groundwork was laid when Tan Chin visited Chungking: he gave Chamkad a microdot message to be conveyed somehow to Pridi through Chinese channels with the help of some gold and precious stones to speed it on its way. The gist of the message was a request that signals be made from a specified beach during one week in December, so indicating to the submarine a safe reception awaited Puey and his colleagues; Force 136 had no wish to risk their lives in a ''blind'' landing. However, the message conveyed through Chamkad did not reach Pridi until July the next year, so there were no signals when the submarine arrived off-shore. Since its commander had orders not to land the Free Siamese in such circumstances, Puey and his colleagues spent an uncomfortable three weeks cramped aboard the submarine before being returned to India.[80]

By comparison OSS was making even less progress. After Chamkad's death, Sanguan and Deng were extracted from Chungking by the Americans as quickly as possible lest they too should fall victim to Tai Li.[81] He and Miles were now talking of creating an army out of the many Sino-Thais who had fled to southern China to escape the Japanese.[82] As for the Seri Thai recruited by OSS in the United States, they were getting nowhere. Seni was continuing to make accusations against Karb and demand his recall from China. This simply added to the problems

created by Miles and Tai Li, which prompted the head of OSS to visit
Chungking in December 1943 to try to sort the situation out.

Before General Donovan left Washington, Seni asked to see him, but
the interview was not a success. Donovan had little sympathy for Seni's
complaints against Karb. Like most of his staff, the head of OSS still
had a high opinion of Karb and his ability to lead the Seri Thai on a
dangerous mission. All he would concede to Seni was that Seri Thai
operations would be restricted to military objectives and not become
involved in politics.[83]

Once he got to Chungking, Donovan was far more concerned with
the organisational problems of OSS in China. Straight away he dismissed Miles from his position as chief local representative, and bluntly
told Tai Li that the Americans had no time for his devious and obstruc-
tionist tactics.[84] This forthright attitude was of little help to the Seri
Thai students, who now found themselves stranded in Kunming where
Tai Li's agents obstructed their attempts to obtain the transport and
guides they needed to continue their mission southwards.[85]

Tai Li still had reason to hope that he might achieve his aims in
Thailand through other channels. One idea promoted by Sanguan on his
arrival in Washington was the creation of a Sino-Thai army in southern
China. He claimed that he already had the permission of a Chinese
general to set up such an army, and all that was needed was the provision
of US arms and radio equipment.[86] In justification of his efforts, Sanguan
stated that he was President of the Committee for Siamese National
Liberation, a different organisation from that represented by Chamkad,
although they both had the same objectives and owed allegiance to Pridi
as head of anti-Japanese resistance in Thailand. Furthermore, Sanguan
asked for help in enabling Pridi and other leaders of the resistance to
escape from Thailand to set up a government-in-exile. Before that he
wanted guarantees that such a government would be internationally
recognised and frozen Thai funds released to finance it.

Sanguan's demands were forwarded to the Americans by Seni, who
initially had considerable misgivings about them. He remembered his
declaration a year earlier disclaiming any political intentions for the Seri
Thai, which was difficult to reconcile with the proposal to set up a
government-in-exile. At the urging of Sanguan, however, Seni soon
changed his mind and started to press the Americans to favour the idea.

Reactions in Washington were mixed. All the dissension between
Seni and Karb did not seem to augur well for the Thais in exile getting
together. The Americans also thought that Britain would be opposed to

recognising a government-in-exile. Then there was the Chinese attitude
to be taken into account, as well as their attempts to dominate any Thai
government set up abroad. As for the proposed army, it is not clear
whether the State Department knew how deeply Tai Li was involved in
the project. Anyway, the idea was vetoed by the War Department. Just
like Stilwell earlier, it pointed to the difficulty of transporting supplies
to the Chinese army and hence the impossibility of undertaking to equip
a Sino-Thai army as proposed by Sanguan.[87]

Little about Sanguan's proposals and American reaction to them was
revealed to the British, who were worried because, on his way through
India to the United States, he had told British officials that Pridi was
desperate and afraid for his life. Naturally the British wanted to know if
the Americans were planning to exfiltrate him since it would affect the
thinking of Force 136.

Anyway, the overall view in London remained that it would do more
harm than good to bring out Pridi, because Japan was likely to react
with violence. For the same reason, doubts were expressed about the
wisdom of setting up a Thai government-in-exile. There was also the
question of what sort of recognition could be accorded to the Free
Siamese cause abroad. With only a handful of them in the United States
and even fewer in Britain, some British officials thought it would be
pretentious for the Free Siamese to claim equal status with, for instance,
the Free French. Furthermore, as the Treasury pointed out, even de
Gaulle had not been given unlimited access to France's funds frozen in
Britain. Thus there was no question of allowing the Free Siamese to do
what they wanted with frozen Thai assets. Such hardline attitudes
worried some Foreign Office officials, who recalled the Thai tendency to
use one power to apply pressure on another and feared that the Americans acting at Siamese instigation might soon urge Britain to change its
views on all these issues.

From the perspective of SEAC, the problem looked somewhat different. For the sake of future joint operations, Mountbatten's political
adviser insisted that it was essential for Britain to bring its policy into
line with that of the United States by issuing a public statement on Siam.
This view was appreciated in the Foreign Office, if not throughout
Whitehall. For instance, it was pointed out that no statement had been
issued on Poland's post-war status or boundaries, despite British support
for the Free Poles. In any case, some ministers failed to see the need to
express any attitude about what seemed in the global context to be an
insignificant South East Asian country which had chosen to ally itself

with Japan. Here wartime secrecy played a part: knowledge about the missions sent out by Pridi was restricted to a very few people.

Even so, the Foreign Office managed in early 1944 to win cabinet approval for a statement expressing support for the concept of Thai independence. But it also incorporated the idea that Siam would have to atone for Pibul's quisling behaviour by "working its passage home" – in other words, contributing to the anti-Japanese struggle – before it could be considered as one of the Allies. As a matter of routine wartime cooperation, this statement was shown to the Americans before being issued. They were appalled, and protested that Britain's harshness towards the Thais was bound to be counter-productive. At this point, Eden lost patience; he characterised the American attitude as "tiresome" and refused to go through the lengthy process of obtaining cabinet approval for a revised statement. As a result, Britain remained officially silent on its policy towards Siam.[88]

None of this had much immediate effect on Force 136 which, after the failure of its submarine mission, was reassessing its plans. Of far greater consequence was the departure of Sanguan and Deng from Chungking. Force 136 had hoped to use them to try to smuggle another message to Pridi, but now there was no option but to send a mission into Siam by parachute without any prior arrangements for its safe reception.

Originally this method of infiltration had been considered too dangerous. Distance and weather made flights from India to Siam and back a hazardous operation for the planes SEAC had at its disposal. Besides the terrain into which the parachutists would be dropped was a very different proposition from that in Europe where such methods of infiltration were often used. In Thailand, too, Pibul had warned the population to be vigilant and report any parachute landings to the authorities. Such warnings were thought likely to be heeded, since Thais are superstitious about any signs from the sky. It was therefore with considerable misgivings that Force 136 sent Puey and his colleagues off on another course, this time in parachute training.[89]

The delay involved was another annoying factor. Mountbatten was anxious to get men operating on the ground in Thailand to sabotage Japanese lines of communication. He knew, through the interception of their secret telegraphic traffic, how heavily the Japanese depended on Thailand for transport facilities;[90] furthermore the construction of the Thailand-Burma railway across the Three Pagodas Pass was speeded up, at the cost of thousands of lives, so that it could be opened to traffic in October 1943.[91] Japan wanted to use the railway to reinforce Burma in preparation for a new westward thrust into India, two years after it had first declared war on the Western powers.

NOTES

1. *Mom Rajawong* is usually shortened to M.R., leading Seni's younger brother M.R. Kukrit to quip that the initials stand for "minor royalty". Only members of the Thai royal family with the rank of *Mom Chao* (royal grandson) and upwards are normally referred to as "prince".
2. Seni in Ray, p. 186.
3. ibid., pp. 147ff, and Kruger, pp. 82ff.
4. See above, p. 000 fourth paragraph.
5. F4881/246/40 in FO 371/28133.
6. FRUS, 1941, V, pp. 376ff.
7. Thai aide-memoire of Dec 20, 1941, in 892.01/16 RG59.
8. Memo of Dec. 12, 1941, in 892.01/12 and 24 RG59, and FRUS, 1941, V, pp. 382 and 389.
9. Seni in Ray, p. 152.
10. Thamsook Numnonda (1977), p. 63, and NYT, Dec. 25, 1941.
11. FRUS, 1941, V, p. 387, and Martin, loc. cit., pp. 640ff.
12. FRUS, 1942, I, pp. 921ff, protesting through Swiss channels at the treatment of American diplomats in Bangkok who fared worse than their colleagues in Tokyo.
13. Seni in Ray, p. 151, and R.H. Smith, *OSS*, p. 294.
14. Note of Feb. 11, 1942, in 892.01/2-1142 RG59.
15. FRUS, 1942, I, pp. 913ff.
16. 892.01/1-3042 RG59.
17. Seni in Ray, p. 152.
18. Ananta Pibulsongkram, II, p. 78.
19. ABC 000.24 Thai (8.20-42) RG165, memo of Nov. 13, 1943, in 792.93/57 RG59 and Nicol Smith, pp. 17ff.
20. 892.01/12-842 RG59.
21. Correspondence in FO 371/28164 and FO 371/31856.
22. FO 371/31859 and *Daily Express*, Mar. 14, 1942.
23. Puey Ungpakorn in Direk, p. 125; Chula Chakrabongse, *The Twain Have Met*, pp. 237ff; F13945/13522/40 in FO 371/28164.
24. *Times* and NYT, May 31, 1941.
25. Queen Rambhai in Thak Chaloemtiarana (ed.), p. 27.
26. FO 371/28159 and letter from Tan Chin to Seni. F5006/1341/40 in FO 371/31862.
27. Puey Ungpakorn in Direk, pp. 125ff. Telegram sent by Snoh Tanbunyuen, a broadcaster with BBC Thai Service throughout the war and long afterwards.
28. FO 371/31862.
29. Seni Pramoj, *Chumnum Wannakhadi tang Karnmuang*, p. 3, alleging fundamental British hostility towards the Seri Thai.
30. Puey Ungpakorn in Direk, pp. 126ff, contradicting the assertion by Gilchrist,

p. 29, on Major Arun (code-name for Tan Chin) helping the students' enlistment.
31. Thorne, p. 217.
32. Correspondence in FO 371/31866 and FRUS, 1942, China, pp. 32ff.
33. Ta Kung Bao, July 27, 1942, in 892.01/19 RG59.
34. FRUS, China, 1943, pp. 13ff, FO 371/31867. For the complex course of British wartime policy towards Siam, see Tarling, *Absolution Before Atonement* (JSS 1978).
35. Gilchrist, pp. 24ff.
36. Unlike Malaya, SOE left no "stay behind" agents in Siam. In 1941 all SOE operations in Thailand were blocked by Crosby. Cruikshank, p. 32.
37. Gilchrist, p. 20 and R.H. Smith, pp. 297ff.
38. Decision taken on Feb. 17, 1943, according to Chamkad's statement to British Military Attaché (Col. Ryde) in Kweilin on Mar. 12, 1943. WO 208/1723, Nai Chantana, pp. 67ff. Further details in Phaisal Trakuli (Liu Hui-sheng), *Virabutr Niranam*, the Sino-Thai who accompanied Chamkad.
39. See above, p. 000, n 30.
40. Chamkad did not hack his way through jungle as was frequently claimed, for example by Thawee Bunyaket in Direk, p. 117.
41. Chungking cable, Apr. 14, 1943, in 792.93/29 RG59.
42. F2015/169/40 in FO 371/35977 and WO 208/1923 (26a) and F2214/1010/40 in FO 371/35982.
43. Nai Chantana, p. 59 and reports of British repatriates in FO 371/31855.
44. F2190/69/40 in FO 371/35977 and Nai Chantana, pp. 89ff.
45. WO 208/1723.
46. F2299/69/40 and file in FO 371/35977; Chungking cable, Apr. 29, 1943, in 792.93/32 RG59; Nai Chantana, pp. 104ff; Gilchrist, p. 23.
47. Chungking cable, Apr. 29, 1943, in 792.93/31 RG59.
48. Chungking cable, July 9, 1943, in 792.93/37 RG59.
49. Gilchrist, p. 33, and Cruikshank, pp. 13ff.
50. R.H. Smith, pp. 247ff.
51. Skinner, pp. 276ff, and Milton Miles, *A Different Kind of War*, p. 180, as compared with Nicol Smith, pp. 142ff, showing how little Chinese intelligence on Thailand reached OSS field officers.
52. Miles, p. 166.
53. Nicol Smith, p. 67 and Nai Chantana, pp. 114ff.
54. Memo of Nov. 13, 1943, in 792.93/57 RG59.
55. 892.00/9–3044 RG59.
56. Chungking cable, Aug. 1, 1943 in 792.93/38 RG59 and Nai Chantana, pp. 117ff.
57. 792.93/31, 34 and 39 RG59.
58. F5313/169/40 in FO 371/35978.
59. Miles, pp. 164ff, claiming that Mountbatten told him of British plans for the Thai throne.
60. F3647/169/40 in FO 371/35977.
61. F4478/169/40 in ibid.
62. 792.93/42 and 892.00/11-2443 RG59.
63. See above, p. 19.
64. Nai Chantana, p. 155. According to Chamkad, the Japanese wanted to get Kukrit to Tokyo as a hostage against Seni's actions in Washington. WO 208/1923 (54a).
65. Deng was the brother of Khuang's wife, Khunying Lekha. Their father was a

prominent lawyer, Phya Attakorn Prasit, born in Ceylon as William Alfred Gunatilleke, which became Gunadilok in Thai, but Deng used other versions which led OSS and SOE to question whether he was really Thai.

66. Nai Chantana, pp. 155ff, and Chungking cable, Sep. 8, 1943, in 792.93/42 RG59.
67. 792.93/45 and file RG59.
68. Nai Chantana, pp. 148ff.
69. Cruikshank, p. 105.
70. Netr Khemayothin, II, p. 385; R.H. Smith, p. 300; 792.93/47 RG59.
71. Prasert Patamasukhon, p. 435 and Gilchrist, p. 21.
72. R.H. Smith, pp. 286ff, and Thorne, pp. 336ff.
73. 892.01/32 and 39 RG59.
74. WO 193/606 and F3617/2873/40 in FO 371/31866.
75. Seni, p. 2, and Seni in Ray, p. 156.
76. Thorne, p. 347; FO 371/35979; Darling, p. 40.
77. WO 203/5627 and FRUS, China, 1943, p. 840.
78. Mountbatten, *Report of the Allied Supreme Commander, South East Asia*, pp. 3ff, and Thorne, p. 301.
79. Like all Free Siamese, Puey's identity was protected by a code-name. His was "Khem", meaning "determined", which Puey resurrected in 1972 when he again found himself abroad and opposed to government in Bangkok.
80. Puey in Direk, p. 131; Gilchrist, pp. 44ff; Nai Chantana, pp. 142ff; Cruikshank, pp. 105ff. Two other Free Siamese attached to ISLD (wartime cover for Far East operations of SIS) were landed on the west coast of the Kra Isthmus in November 1943. They were not carrying radios and their mission was to spend six weeks gathering information on Japanese troop deployments in southern Thailand before being taken out again by submarine. They were successful but the submarine due to pick them up was delayed by Japanese action and failed to make the pre-arranged rendez-vous on time. They then managed to hide till late 1944, when subsequent developments enabled them to make contact with local Seri Thai and ultimately the British again. Adul in Suphote Dantrakul, p. 228, and unpublished memoir by Chundaeng Rintakul.
81. 792.93/47 RG59.
82. OPD 353/Case 494 RG165.
83. 792.93/50 RG59.
84. R.H. Smith, p. 258, and Miles, pp. 177ff, although his account of subsequent developments in Thailand contains several obvious inaccuracies.
85. Nicol Smith, pp. 96ff.
86. Lt.-Gen. Chiang Kai-men, Director of Chinese Military Intelligence and sub-ordinate of Tai Li.
87. 892.01/47 and 892.01/12-3143 RG95; FRUS, 1943, III, pp. 1119ff; ibid., 1944, V, p. 1311.
88. Correspondence in FO 371/35978 and 41844, and FRUS, 1944, V, pp. 1351ff.
89. Gilchrist, pp. 42ff.
90. Zieger, *Mountbatten*, p. 268, and *Magic*, Oct. 12, Dec. 2 and 5, 1943.
91. AL5199.

12

THE ECLIPSE

On the second anniversary of the Japanese move into Thailand, there was certainly nothing to celebrate in Bangkok. The economy was continuing to deteriorate. Inflation was spiralling. The scarcity of consumer goods in the markets was increasing. Hoarding and speculation were rampant, so much so that in December 1943 all trading in gold was officially suspended throughout the country. On top of all that, the Allies intensified their bombing raids.

With the opening of the Thailand-Burma railway, large quantities of supplies destined for the Japanese campaign in Burma were offloaded in Bangkok for onward transport by rail. Hence godowns and communications facilities in and around the Thai capital became a vital target for the Allies. These raids, being heavier and more frequent than anything the Thais had previously experienced, caused widespread panic, although the Allies had no intention of conducting a blitz against the civilian population, as happened in European cities.[1]

Pibul thought otherwise. Through Swiss diplomatic channels, he protested to the Americans about homes, temples and schools destroyed in indiscriminate bombing contravening the Geneva Conventions on methods of warfare.[2] And as if to create permanent monuments to such acts, he at first forbade the repair of damaged buildings and had the areas surrounding them barricaded off. The population of Bangkok also had to contend with an inadequate air raid warning system and the complete lack of shelters.

Pibul's solution to these deficiencies was to issue a frantic series of orders for roads to be built out of Bangkok into the countryside to facilitate a total evacuation.[3] He proclaimed that there was no longer any reason for anybody to reside in Bangkok because it had ceased to be the capital. Ministries, government departments, military units, factories and businesses were all instructed to move within the space of a couple of weeks to Petchaboon, the new capital in the north.[4] But obviously these hastily-ordered moves, together with Pibul's schemes to build roads, railways and cities where none had previously existed, imposed a tremendous strain on Thailand's resources. Labour had to be specially conscripted, and to finance the projects the Field-Marshal decreed the expropriation of royal assets by the Supreme Command.[5]

At the same time the Thai economy was burdened by growing Japanese demands for loans to finance their military activities. In January 1944 the amount involved was doubled to 45 million baht a month. Although this entailed printing more money and so further fuelling inflation, the Japanese continued to count on the compliance of Vanich at the Finance Ministry. They were therefore completely taken aback when he was dismissed from office on February 1 and promptly arrested. What is more, Pibul rejected all Japanese pleas for his release. Vanich had been detained on charges of speculation and was held responsible for the crisis six weeks earlier when all trading in gold had to be suspended.[6] But the Japanese suspected that politics might also be involved. After the bombing began in earnest, they noticed that the Thais ceased broadcasting any criticism of the Western Allies in the apparent hope of ending the raids. The Japanese believed that Pibul subscribed to the adage ''No anger falls from gods we have not offended.''[7]

Once the war was over, Pibul tried to explain all his manoeuvring as part of a deeply-laid plan to outwit the Japanese. For example, he claimed to have chosen to site the new capital at Petchaboon because it was so inaccessible that the Japanese would never have been able to capture it. Another advantage was Petchaboon's location in the north of the country where most of the Thai army was also based. Pibul alleged that his intention was to position both the government and the armed forces where they could easily link up with the Allies moving south from Yunnan. What these arguments overlooked was the ease with which the Japanese could have surrounded and starved out Petchaboon once the government and military had abandoned Bangkok and the central plains. Nonetheless, with hindsight Pibul's claims did have some plausibility.[8]

In southern Yunnan various developments were taking place. One was the construction of an airfield at Szemao for the 14th US Air Force, often called the Flying Tigers. They were responsible for many of the raids on Bangkok, and during their operations one Flying Tiger pilot crash-landed in Thailand. By chance the news came to the ears of Nicol Smith, the OSS officer in charge of the Seri Thai students stranded in Kunming. A bargain was quickly concluded. On January 15, 1944 the Seri Thai in Kunming were flown to Szemao in return for a promise to rescue the Flying Tiger pilot as soon as they managed to get to Thailand.[9]

From Szemao it was only a seven-day pony trek to China's southern border, and then what local guides said was at most a three-week journey through northern Indo-China into Thailand. At last, after all their frustrations, it seemed to the Seri Thai students that they were finally within sight of their goal. Their hopes were reinforced by several Sino-Thais who had managed to escape from Bangkok to Szemao without any apparent problems. Hence five Seri Thai left Szemao on February 29 cheerfully expecting to be back home before long. Six weeks later they were still in China. Their guides through Indo-China turned out to be agents of Tai Li.

Since the rainy season was fast approaching, this new delay really infuriated Nicol Smith, but luckily, together with Karb, he had meanwhile explored other potential infiltration routes including a sector of China's southern border with Burma controlled by the 93rd Division of the Chinese army. Its local commander was very hospitable and readily agreed to allow a Chinese Christian missionary with widespread local knowledge to guide a Seri Thai group through the Shan States – in other words, through territory controlled by the Thai army.

Karb's enthusiasm grew further when he discovered that an informal ceasefire had been observed along the border between southern Yunnan and the Shan States since early 1943 with the arrangement being cemented from time to time by gifts of Thai whisky, cigarettes and guns presented to officers of the 93rd Division by their Thai counterparts. On perusing a list of Thai officers participating in these exchanges, Karb saw the name of one of his former students at the military academy in Bangkok. With the permission of Nicol Smith, Karb penned a letter to him plus another to be forwarded to Pibul if possible. The commander of the 93rd Division agreed to hand over Karb's missive to the Thais at their next meeting.[10]

How much Pibul previously knew about all the comings and goings between Thai and Chinese officers in southern Yunnan is not clear, but in January 1944, when his nerves were strained by the bombing, he instructed officers of the Northern Army to contact the Chinese. Then, on receipt of Karb's letter, he designated an army staff officer to go and participate in the next meeting with the 93rd Division. The eventual aim was to get Karb to secure Chiang Kai-shek's agreement for the despatch of Prayoon and Adul disguised as Chinese soldiers on a secret mission to Chungking. The idea raised a few eyebrows at army headquarters, since Pibul could have thought of nobody more unsuitable to disguise as Chinese. Prayoon was distinctly Caucasian in appearance, whereas Adul was tall and swarthy like his Indian forebears. As it turned out, the problem did not arise. Karb was not present at the meeting

which the Thai army staff officer held on April 2 with representatives of
the 93rd Division; hence, he could report back to Pibul no more than a
few Chinese courtesies and perhaps the possibility of getting in touch
with Chiang Kai-shek sometime in the future.[11]

The Chinese had reason for caution. Chiang Kai-shek had not
forgotten Pibul's broadcast after the Greater East Asia Conference in
Tokyo, appealing to the Kuomintang to change its mind and oppose the
Western powers.[12] The Japanese had just made similar suggestions
through clandestine channels. In early 1944 they also embarked on a new
campaign, known by the code-name *Ichi-Go*, aimed at south-west
China. Likewise the Chinese were worried about Thai support for Subas
Chandra Bose whose forces had just launched an offensive backed by the
Japanese to capture Imphal and move into eastern India.

Anyway Pibul's interest in contacting the Chinese was soon overtaken by other preoccupations. The campaign to urge people to leave
Bangkok was extremely unpopular: there were suspicions that the Field-
Marshal was deliberately abandoning the capital founded by the Chakri
dynasty to promote his own royal ambitions.[13] Furthermore officials
were reluctant to move to Petchaboon because of the lack of facilities
there. Electricity and water supplies, shops and telephones were all non-
existent, as Pibul himself realised. Even the road to get there was not
being built as fast as he hoped. The valley up which Petchaboon was
situated was so insalubrious and inhospitable that thousands of conscript
labourers were dying of malaria, inadequate medical care and lack of
food. Still Pibul did not desist; he ordered the removal of all royal and
national treasures to Petchaboon and the building of a grandiose temple
there for the Emerald Buddha. Almost as magnificent was the new
government house planned for himself.[14] To set the seal on all these
developments, the premier intended to visit Petchaboon on April 23
with the Supreme Patriarch of the Buddhist Sangha for the ceremonial
laying of the cornerstone of the new capital. But when news of these
plans was broadcast, it evoked comment from a Thai-language radio
station based in India, which led Pibul to fear that the ceremony would
be disrupted by an Allied bombing raid.[15]

The British, however, had other plans. Once Puey and his colleagues
in India had completed parachute training, he was selected to head a
group of three to be dropped into Siam during the full-moon period in
March on an operation code-named ''Appreciation''. Since they were
going in ''blind'', Force 136 tried to choose a landing zone as far away
as possible from known Japanese encampments. It also needed to be

remote from cultivated land and villages but with thick cover nearby where the parachutists could hide themselves and their equipment. The area selected was a valley in Nakorn Sawan province to the north of the central plains. Although the drop seemed to take place without any hitch, no radio reports were heard from Puey and his colleagues about their safe landing.

On the April full moon, Force 136 tried again. A second Appreciation mission comprising three more Free Siamese was dropped at another site some 40 miles from the first. Once more radio monitors in Calcutta failed to pick up any signals from the mission. In May Force 136, now desperate, changed tactics. A group of Sino-Thai agents was landed by flying-boat off the west coast of the Kra Isthmus with instructions to contact the local Chinese community, organise sabotage along the rail link between Bangkok and Malaya much used by the Japanese, and report back to Calcutta by radio. This mission turned out to be an even greater failure. The noise of the flying-boat alerted local villagers, who reported its arrival to the police. A fight ensued during which several Force 136 agents were killed and the rest captured. Worse still for the morale of Force 136, Bangkok Radio reported the capture and inter-rogation by the Japanese of the first two parachute missions sent into Thailand.

Instead of being dropped in a remote valley, Puey and his colleagues had come down through an air navigational error in a populated area of Chainat province. One of their supply parachutes even landed in the middle of a village which soon drew attention to their presence. Hence they abandoned all their equipment except the radio transmitter and made off for a nearby forest where they managed to hide for two days while trying in vain to contact Calcutta. They also had to forage for food and water, which was particularly difficult for Puey who had injured his ankle on landing. In the absence of his companions, he was tracked down by villagers and handed over to the local police, who took him to the provincial jail. Regarded more as a curiosity than as a danger-ous enemy agent, he was on the whole kindly treated before being transported down-river to be imprisoned by the Thai secret police in Bangkok. There he met up with his two companions; ironically, they had been arrested in the first place not as infiltrators but because, in violation of Pibul's edict, they were found eating in a public place without wearing hats! Later they were joined in prison in Bangkok by members of the second Appreciation mission, who had also been dropped in the wrong place, as well as the survivors of the Sino-Thai party landed in the Kra Isthmus.[16]

To their surprise, the Force 136 infiltrators were well looked after by the secret police. In return they were required to write a report on the situation in Europe and the rest of the world from the Allied point of view. They also had to sign a personal confession of loyalty to Pibul, which was virtually dictated to them by Adul, who wanted to lull Pibul's suspicions that the parachutists were rebels who had come to overthrow his regime rather than the Japanese. After that, Adul managed to keep the Free Siamese under the protection of his own men, although he could not block all Japanese access to them. Consequently Adul helped Puey concoct stories to outwit Japanese interrogation.[17]

However, all this Thai manoeuvring did not fool the Japanese. They knew of Pibul's contacts with the Chinese in Yunnan.[18] They questioned him too about the parachutists.[19] Furthermore, they suspected that he was deliberately spending long periods in Petchaboon to avoid them. His frequent absence from Bangkok also led to the collapse of public morale in the capital; indeed, after the January bombing raids, the government seemed to disintegrate as most ministers and officials fled either to Petchaboon or the countryside around Bangkok. Nor did Pibul have much impact when he promulgated a code of moral and martial values bearing a close resemblance to *Bushido*, the Japanese code of valour.[20]

Politically conscious Thais were far more interested in indications that the Americans were advancing by leaps and bounds through the islands of the Pacific towards Japan. In early June too came the news of the Allied capture of Rome, followed two days later by the D-Day landings in Normandy. Although Japanese reverses were always reported in the Bangkok press as great victories with thousands of American dead and wounded, the censors interfered little with news of German defeats in Europe. Anyway, despite the official ban, most people with short-wave radios listened to Allied broadcasts which, apart from providing news, also indulged in psychological warfare. For example, the BBC broadcasting in Thai warned that everybody continuing to support Pibul, especially Assembly members, would be tried as war criminals after the Allied victory.[21]

Bangkok radio reacted by claiming that the Thai people, despite wartime inconveniences, were not anxious for a change of leader.[22] The Japanese knew better. They had been aware at least for the past four months that many Thais from Pridi downwards wanted to oust Pibul from power, but were fearful of the army's reaction. This made the Japanese uncomfortable; they were worried lest Pibul's unpopularity should reflect on their own position. Hence they began to make their own soundings in royalist circles about setting up an alternative government. These moves were soon noticed by Adul, whose vigilance had earned him the nickname "the Fierce-Eyed General".[23]

Adul had particular reason to be vigilant with the Japanese. In May, Vanich died in prison shortly before he was due to stand trial. According to one rumour, the Japanese had somehow managed to dispose of him for fear of embarrassing evidence coming to light in court. Others thought that Adul, seeing which way the tide of war was turning, had sought to prove his loyalty to the Allied cause by getting rid of Vanich.[24]

Such suspicions bothered Pridi, who had never really trusted Adul because their attitudes were so different. For instance, Adul was aware of, but unsympathetic towards, Pridi's anti-Japanese activities since he believed that some people within the Seri Thai were trying to use the movement to restore the absolute monarchy. Still, with Direk's return to Bangkok, Adul and Pridi had a friend in common who tried to bring them together for the sake of liberating Thailand from the Japanese. This led Adul to produce a suicide note proving that Vanich had not been murdered; he also informed Pridi of Japanese moves to promote a coup. In return the regent asked for a relaxation of police vigilance on Assembly members opposed to Pibul.[25] Towards the end of June, when a new session of the Assembly was convened, Pridi's request bore fruit. Pibul's friends in the Assembly were no longer strong enough to block the selection as speaker of a British-educated official[26] with Khuang as his deputy.

Even more significant was an Assembly debate which took place on July 20, two days after General Tojo was forced to resign from the Japanese premiership. It also happened to coincide with a serious but unsuccessful attempt to assassinate Hitler.

Pibul had asked the Assembly to endorse a decree promulgated several months earlier on the construction of Petchaboon, which everybody knew had long been under way. Thus the move to legalise it at this late stage was criticised on constitutional grounds. Some Assembly members also questioned the wisdom of embarking on such an expensive project at a time of war and financial stringency. As ever, the most vocal criticism came from Thong-in and other north-eastern representatives, who claimed that the labour force at Petchaboon had been conscripted

Pridi Banomyong

mainly from their constituencies and that at least 10 per cent of the 100,000 workers involved had already died of malaria and other diseases. Hence the bill was defeated by a margin of twelve votes.[27]

After the war, Pibul claimed that the outcome of the vote had been due to his inability at the time to explain Petchaboon's real purpose as an impregnable fortress safe from the Japanese. He also said that the Assembly deliberately sabotaged the bill.[28] Yet two days after its defeat, Prayoon introduced another somewhat similar measure, this time to approve an emergency decree establishing a Buddhist sanctuary near Saraburi.[29] Later Pibul alleged that this too was part of his plan to foil the Japanese since they intended to move into the strategic area around Saraburi. In addition, he said that the sanctuary would have provided a safe haven for civilians when hostilities broke out.

On July 22 in the Assembly, Prayoon said that the sanctuary was intended as a world Buddhist centre in much the same way as Rome and Mecca served as places of pilgrimage for Catholics and Muslims, a contention hard to challenge. Instead the government was again criticised for issuing decrees and trying to obtain legislative approval afterwards. In reply, Prayoon pointed out that the decree on Saraburi was auspiciously promulgated on a Buddhist holy day despite previous official strictures against superstition and the traditional custom of regarding certain dates and omens as auspicious. The representative for Saraburi also protested that the sanctuary would involve expropriating a lot of land in his constituency. Others questioned how monks at Saraburi would support themselves when even some *wats* in Bangkok had to purchase food because most people were now too poor to donate in the traditional manner. Hence this second bill was defeated by 43 votes to 41, the low figures being attributable in part to the absence on duty up-country of many of the Assembly's military members. Undoubtedly, too, there was considerable political manoeuvring behind the scenes, even though Pibul had not indicated beforehand whether he regarded these two votes as an issue of confidence in his government.[30]

Irrespective of Pibul's intentions, it was immediately presumed that he would resign the premiership. For example, Prince Prem, using the allegorical style he had adopted to beat the censors, commented in his regular newspaper column that a partial eclipse of the sun had been observed in Bangkok and that it was worth watching for further unusual phenomena.[31] Everybody knew what he was hinting at. A Japanese diplomat, who had just called on Direk to explain General Tojo's resignation, requested another interview to enquire about Pibul's position: in view of what had just happened in Tokyo, Direk pointed out that Thai internal developments could be just as complex and would only suffer from foreign intervention.[32]

As it was, Pibul did tender his resignation in the apparent belief that he was indispensable and would quickly be asked to resume office. Among those sharing the view was Prince Aditya; he remembered all too well what had happened over Pibul's letter of resignation in 1943 and was reluctant to accept it this time. But the climate of opinion had changed. Prince Aditya was soon subject to so much criticism that he joined Pridi on July 26 in announcing that the regents had accepted the prime minister's resignation and asked the Assembly to nominate his successor.

Almost automatically everybody, including the Japanese, thought of Phya Phahol who, however, declined the position. Publicly the reasons he gave were poor health plus a vow never again to enter politics. Later it became known that Phya Phahol had received what he construed as a threatening visit from Pibul's military secretary, Chai.[33]

Such behind-the-scenes pressure made the choice of a new premier even more delicate, especially since there was no other obvious candidate. At first Pridi thought of Thawee Bunyaket, who had performed effectively as cabinet secretary and, besides, was popular with the Assembly, as his aborted election to the speakership had proved. In addition Pridi knew that he could count on Thawee to work with the Seri Thai. But there was one snag: by nature Thawee was a very forthright character who did not mince words, and this might be a handicap in a premier who had of necessity to deal with the Japanese. Hence Pridi turned his attention to Khuang, who had proved equally popular with the Assembly and had the reputation of being able to talk his way out of any situation. These considerations led Pridi to recommend his friends in the Assembly to choose Khuang as prime minister.[34]

Accounts vary about what happened in the next secret session of the Assembly, and no official record appears to have been kept. The nomination of Sindhu, Adul and even Pibul is said to have been discussed before Khuang emerged as the clear choice of most members.[35] He himself did not take part in the debate, claiming to be unwell. He was raised from his sickbed by a summons to Ta Chang, where Pridi told him that he must accept the premiership for the good of the country, especially since nobody else had the courage to succeed Pibul.

By contrast Prince Aditya warned Khuang against taking over because it might provoke a military coup leading in turn to Japanese intervention and the end of Thailand's independence. When Khuang brushed these cautions aside, Prince Aditya pointed out that he was not a military man, nor did he command the respect of all the promoters. Consequently, before endorsing his appointment as premier, the senior regent wanted to know whether he would be able to form a cabinet and who its members would be. Still undaunted, Khuang replied that he fully intended to become prime minister because it was the wish of the Assembly, but he could not start forming a cabinet until his appointment was officially approved by the regents.

At that point, Prince Aditya decided to consult Pibul, whom he located on the golf course at Chitralada Palace. They were joined there by Adul, who as usual was keeping a close eye on developments, which was probably just as well. Pibul reacted to Khuang's nomination by commenting that the Assembly must be mad because it had chosen a madman as premier. Anyway, Pibul claimed that the appointment was bound to provoke strong opposition within the army and possibly even a coup. In this context he mentioned certain key units based in Bangkok and the Shan States which were particularly loyal to him. Inevitably, too, the bogey of Japanese intervention was again raised. These threats worked, as Pibul no doubt intended. Prince Aditya refused to endorse Khuang's appointment as premier.[36]

The Japanese were indeed, as Pibul suggested, observing the crisis in the Thai leadership very closely. Two of their military attachés called on Pridi at Ta Chang to enquire what was happening about Khuang, since they had never had any contact with him. In reply the regent suggested that they should refrain from worrying too much about Thai politics and judge Khuang by his performance in office. The problem remained how to implement the process.

Adul thought Prince Aditya's refusal to endorse Khuang's appointment was a constitutional matter to be sorted out between the Assembly and the regents. Direk and Thamrong agreed. Pibul, meanwhile, convened a meeting in the apparent hope of resolving the crisis in a way leading to his resumption of the premiership. He was soon disillusioned. Some promoters told him bluntly that he no longer had the right to try to chair a cabinet meeting, let alone dictate its decisions. It was then made clear to Prince Aditya that he had to make the next move. He was still reluctant, feeling that he had become involved in an internal power struggle among the promoters. Besides, he was fearful of possible retribution from the army. Hence, rather than authorising Khuang's appointment, Prince Aditya tendered his own resignation. It was promptly accepted by the Assembly, which voted at the same time to approve Pridi as sole regent. As a result, on August 1, 1944, Pridi issued a royal proclamation appointing Khuang as prime minister. Immediately afterwards Pibul and his personal entourage left Bangkok for the military base at Lopburi.[37]

The next day, in his first speech to the Assembly as premier, Khuang pledged that he would uphold the constitution, the monarchy and the six principles of the Khana Ratsadorn. He also promised to tackle the nation's economic problems and develop relations with friendly countries, especially Japan.[38] These comments were part of a bargain he had concluded with Pridi. In return, the regent promised to support Khuang as premier provided that he humoured the Japanese and turned a blind eye to the activities of the resistance movement. The two men also agreed that the interests of the Seri Thai would be principally represented within the cabinet by Thawee Bunyaket: he was reappointed as its secretary, and took over the education portfolio to undo the damage caused by Prayoon and organise students in underground work against the Japanese.[39] On the other hand, Direk declined to continue as Foreign Minister, claiming that he could serve the country better in other ways.[40] Instead the portfolio went to an *ancien régime* official who had earlier spent several years in Tokyo as Thai minister.[41] Various other well-known officials also re-emerged to take over seats in the cabinet, although it continued to be dominated by promoters.

In ousting Pibul's army clique, Khuang replaced it with civilian promoters as well as some from the navy. Sindhu agreed to undertake the difficult task of following Pibul as Defence Minister while Supha, his major rival among the naval promoters, took over the Interior Ministry. Finally, to set a seal of authority on his new cabinet, Khuang approached Phya Phahol. The elder statesman eventually agreed to become a minister without portfolio on condition that his name appeared at the bottom of the cabinet list. Even then, Khuang could not rule out a potential military coup and appealed to Adul for help.[42]

The police chief felt that he had a constitutional duty to protect Khuang's government, and paid a call on the general commanding the Bangkok military region whom Pibul had referred to as one of his most loyal supporters.[43] Bluntly Adul asked whether a coup was in the offing, and was told in reply that the army intended to arrest Khuang's entire cabinet including Phya Phahol. To register his profound disapproval. Adul left it to his deputy, the head of the secret police,[44] to express the anger which the detention of Phya Phahol in particular would cause not just among the promoters but also throughout the country. Adul and his close colleagues then went out of their way to warn numerous military figureheads that any coup attempt would be firmly opposed by the police and the navy. Still, the rumours of plotting persisted; even at that critical juncture in the war, some army officers were apparently more concerned about their personal interests than the fate of the country.[45]

In the midst of this tension, Pridi and his friends received an unexpected boost to their morale. At long last, all their efforts to establish direct communication between Thailand and the Western powers bore fruit, largely due to Puey. Soon after his imprisonment in Bangkok, he secured the friendship of a police officer who, like himself, was a graduate of the University of Moral and Political Sciences. Through this contact a clandestine meeting was arranged between Puey and Pridi at the home of the University's Secretary-General.[46] It was even kept secret from Adul: despite, or perhaps because of, his sinister reputation, he did not command the complete loyalty of all his subordinates. The loophole was exploited by Pridi to spirit Puey and his colleagues in and out of prison and provide them with access to their radios in the hope of getting in touch with Force 136, but it was to no avail. Having learnt from Bangkok Radio of the arrest and interrogation of the Free Siamese parachutists, Force 136 had given up monitoring the wavelengths on which they were supposed to report back. In desperation, Puey then compiled an encyphered message to be carried overland and delivered if possible to the British consulate in Kunming.[47]

In developing his Seri Thai network, Pridi used all the resources he could muster, including his family as well as his political friends. A younger brother, Louis Banomyong, was a Chinese-educated banker who occupied an important position in the Thai financial world as *comprador* for the Bank of Asia. Usefully for the Seri Thai, the bank had branches in various towns throughout the country as well as a network of regional contacts. Arthakit, another of Pridi's brothers, happened to be in charge of the Thai legation in Berne when war broke out. Given Switzerland's role in maintaining residual contacts between Thailand and the Western powers after Pibul declared war, Arthakit was supposed to remain diplomatically neutral. His delicate position seems to have been respected till 1944, when need drove Pridi to reactivate a secret family code to ask Arthakit to inform Force 136 that the men they had parachuted into Thailand were safe and anxious to establish radio contact. At first the British were suspicious of the secrecy of Arthakit's communications with his brother.[48] But then Puey's message to the same effect was somehow delivered to the British consulate in Kunming. The news aroused such excitement at Force 136 headquarters in Calcutta that the officer responsible for parachuting Puey and his colleagues into Thailand fainted when the first direct radio contact with Bangkok was made on August 22.[49]

Irrespective of whether Khuang was informed of the radio link with the Allies, some of his cabinet colleagues took new heart from it. Thawee in particular stressed that something had to be done to wrest control of the armed forces from Pibul, who as Supreme Commander was continuing to issue orders from Lopburi. For instance, he demanded the speeding up of construction work at Petchaboon and on the road leading to it because the project was vital to national security. Likewise, Pibul summarily ordered the imposition of military rule over the provinces of Lopburi, Saraburi and Petchaboon. The Supreme Commander also appointed Prom Yothi as his deputy, and compensated other friends dropped from the cabinet with prestigious military positions. Hence it began to look as if Thailand had two separate and rival administrations, since the new prime minister was also very active.

First Khuang moved to abrogate some of Pibul's more arbitrary dictates. Compulsory dancing practice for officials was abolished, and provincial governors were told to forget the hat edict. Controls on what the Bangkok press could publish were also relaxed, much to the dismay of Pibul, who promptly came under attack and reacted by ordering the head of government propaganda to report to the Supreme Command at Lopburi. Then referring to his powers under martial law, he demanded that all broadcasts be subject to military censorship. However, his views were no longer heard on the radio. The two broadcasters who had personified *Nai Man* and *Nai Kong* left with him for Lopburi. Pibul further sought to expand his personal empire by attempting to transfer the departments responsible for roads and railways to the jurisdiction of the Supreme Command.[50]

All these blatant efforts to undermine the authority of the new government worried Adul, who responded to Khuang's appeals for help by advising him to visit Lopburi to sort matters out personally with Pibul. Before taking such a step, the prime minister decided to determine where he stood internationally by calling in the Japanese and German envoys in Bangkok for consultation. The move was useful for Khuang's self-confidence. The Japanese assured him that there would be no outside intervention in any showdown between the government and forces loyal to Pibul. Still, Khuang remained anxious about his personal safety in going to Lopburi or, as he later put it, 'to visit the tiger in his cave'. He asked Adul to obtain a guarantee that he would not be arrested by Pibul's henchmen. The police chief did more than that, persuading two senior generals[51] to accompany the prime minister to Lopburi. For good measure, the head of the secret police offered to join the party as Khuang's personal bodyguard. Another problem was how to make the journey. Pibul had taken the entire fleet of governmental cars with him to Lopburi, and Khuang had to beg transport, tyres and petrol to get there. Despite the loss of face involved in arriving at Lopburi in a motley collection of cars, the new prime minister was greeted in friendly fashion by his predecessor. What is more, Pibul agreed to sign a statement saying that he regarded Khuang as a younger brother and had no intention of opposing his government. Once Khuang had returned safely to Bangkok, the statement was given the widest possible publicity. Nonetheless, it failed to dampen rumours that the army was still unhappy and intended to taking action to oust Khuang.[52]

The most important factor which appears to have deterred Pibul from taking this course was his fear of Adul, who continued to threaten action against anybody violating the constitution. When word of Adul's threats reached Pibul, he wrote to enquire whether he was likely to be arrested. Adul replied affirming that anybody who launched a coup would definitely be detained. Pibul then started to bargain; he hinted that he might quit the Supreme Command voluntarily on condition that he was appointed senior regent, a position which he suggested would be appropriate for a former prime minister. To many people, it looked more as if Pibul was angling for a post where he could continue to pursue his dynastic ambitions as well as outmanoeuvre Pridi. Instead, all the cabinet were prepared to concede to Pibul if he resigned from the Supreme Command was his appointment as Superior Advisor to the armed forces. In other words, it was a sinecure with a grandiloquent title, a ploy frequently used by Pibul himself in trying to dispense with rivals like Phya Song and Pridi.[53]

To Thawee such tactics seemed irrelevant. He argued that Pibul could easily be stripped of his powers by virtue of the constitution, which stipulated that the monarch was Supreme Commander of all three armed forces. Hence Thawee offered to draft a public statement explaining the constitutional issues involved. The proposal worried Khuang, until

Thawee also volunteered to accept sole responsibility if anything went wrong. In return he requested from the premier full discretion over the timing of the move.

After all his confrontations with Pibul, Thawee realised that words alone would not budge the Supreme Commander. A show of force was also needed. Thawee knew he could count on the support of the police under Adul's leadership. The navy too was bound to oppose the army in any showdown involving Pibul; the question was whether the army as a whole supported him. First Thawee set out to gain the sympathy of Luang Sinad Yotharaks, a general who was one of the few non-promoters to survive Pibul's purge of senior military officers. More to the point, Sinad had command of troops in Bangkok. Once his cooperation was secured, Thawee turned to Prom Yothi for help. However the new deputy Supreme Commander maintained that Pibul was still very popular within the army and it would be suicidal to make any move against him. Hence Thawee resorted to Phya Phahol: he was asked to become commander-in-chief of the armed forces, a titularly different position from that occupied by Pibul. Phya Phahol would not have much to do beyond acting as a figurehead. Sinad had agreed to serve as his deputy and carry out all the actual work involved.[54]

Even then, Thawee felt that one last effort should be made to persuade Pibul to retire with dignity, and accordingly on August 23 Khuang reluctantly made a second trip to Lopburi, albeit not without his secret police bodyguard. This time their reception was far less cordial. Pibul's determination to hang on to office had been strengthened by the arrival in Lopburi of the influential military governor of the Shan States.[55]

As soon as Khuang returned to Bangkok empty-handed, Thawee decided that no time was to be lost: the same evening, before the army could mount a coup, Thawee asked a private printing press, well protected by armed police, to prepare for distribution the next morning a million copies of a statement he had drafted. It declared Pibul's position as Supreme Commander unconstitutional and the appointment of Phya Phahol as Commander in Chief of the Armed Forces with Sinad as his deputy. To save face for Pibul, the statement added that he had been promoted to the newly-created position of Superior Adviser to the armed forces.

Immediately the printing of the statement was under way, Thawee disappeared from his home to spend the night with Supha under naval protection. As for Phya Phahol, who was genuinely unwell, an ambulance picked him up and whisked him away to the comparative safety of the naval headquarters in Thonburi, where he was joined by Khuang. Meanwhile, Pridi and Adul set to work to lull the suspicions of Pibul's friends. In this they were successful. Early next morning, when the army was deemed to have lost the advantage in mounting a coup, copies of the statement drafted by Thawee were widely distributed throughout Bangkok. Simultaneously orders went out in the name of Phya Phahol instructing military officers to obey only orders from him. Nonetheless Phya Phahol is said to have grumbled that never before had a Commander-in-Chief had to assume office in such clandestine circumstances while the prime minister accompanying him had to sleep on a table.[56]

Once the order announcing Pibul's demotion was broadcast, neither the new Commander-in-Chief nor the premier had much time for rest. Khuang issued a supplementary statement claiming that the military changes were for the good of the nation, and that there was no basis for rumours alleging that Pibul was dissatisfied.[57] Phya Phahol and Sinad meanwhile convoked a meeting of senior military officers, ostensibly to explain the changes but in reality to keep generals and colonels occupied well away from the troops under their command. The manoeuvre seems to have foiled a move by Pibul ordering various military garrisons to rally against the government. Yet what appears to have deterred Pibul's supporters most of all was the argument, widely disseminated by Adul, that a coup might provoke Japan to intervene and disarm the Thai military.[58]

When it became apparent to Pibul that he had lost out, he wrote to Khuang saying he was leaving Lopburi to retire to the countryside. In the same letter he said that he would have resigned voluntarily, had it not been for pressure from his entourage.[59] After the war Pibul's wife claimed he had stepped down because of his belief in democracy and the sacred nature of the constitution. Anyway she added that by 1944 Pibul thought the Allies would win the war and that it would be better for Thailand if he were no longer premier.[60] Another subsequent claim made by Pibul and his wife was that his ousting from power constituted the first major split among the promoters. Clearly what they were referring to was not so much the rivalry with Pridi but rather the rift between Pibul and Adul.[61]

NOTES

1. Mountbatten, p. 94, and *Magic*, Dec. 30, 1943, Jan. 19, 20 and 25, 1944.
2. FRUS, 1944, IV, pp. 1321ff.
3. Ananta Pibulsongkram, III, pp. 358ff.
4. ibid., p. 182, and Prasert Patamasukhon, p. 430.
5. Ananta Pibulsongkram, III, pp. 75 and 468.
6. Direk, p. 96; Batson (JSS 1974), p. 98; *Magic*, Jan. 16 and June 4, 1944.
7. ibid Feb 26, 1944.
8. Pibul in Thak Chaloemtiarama (ed.), p. 369.
9. Nicol Smith, p. 115.
10. ibid., pp. 127ff; R.H. Smith, p. 301; Netr Khemayothin, II, p. 19; Cremation volume of General Harn Songkram, Commander. Third Division, based in Kengtung.
11. ibid., Netr Khemayothin, II, pp. 21ff; Adul in Suphote Dantrakul, p. 197.
12. Konthi Suphamongkol, pp. 343ff, recounting Chiang Kai-shek's recollections in 1946.
13. La-iad Pibulsongkram in Ray, p. 204, and *Magic*, Apr. 28, 1944.
14. Ananta Pibulsongkram, III, pp. 445ff and 520ff; NYT, Apr. 13, 1944; Coast, p. 26; Batson (JSS 1974), pp. 98ff.
15. Ananta Pibulsongkram, III, p. 464.
16. Puey in Direk, pp. 132ff; Gilchrist, pp. 45ff; Cruikshank, p. 114.
17. Puey and Adul in Suphote Dantrakul, pp. 43 and 202ff, but Ananta Pibulsongkram, III, p. 617, has the wrong date.
18. AL5199, p. 21, and Sangworn Suwannachip, p. 123.
19. Ananta Pibulsongkram, III, pp. 12 and 136, and *Magic*, June 25 and 30, 1944.
20. ibid., May 20, 1944, and Thamsook Numnonda (1977), p. 37.
21. Thawee Bunyaket in Ray, p. 83, and Pridi in Pramote Pungsunthorn, p. 66.
22. Batson (JSS 1974), pp. 97ff.
23. Pridi in Pramote Pungsunthorn, p. 66.
24. XL 22759 in RG226, and *Magic*, June 4, 1944.
25. Adul in Suphote Dantrakul, p. 236, and Pridi in Thak Chaloemtiarama (ed.), pp. 383ff.
26. This was Phya Manavarat Sevi, then known as Vichien na Songkla.
27. Batson (JSS 1974), pp. 100ff.
28. La-iad Pibulsongkram in Ray, pp. 203ff.
29. Decree promulgated June 5, 1944, in Prasert Patamasukhon, p. 431.
30. Batson (JSS 1974), p. 101.
31. ibid., p. 113n.
32. Direk, p. 98.
33. Pridi in Pramote Pungsunthorn, pp. 67ff; Adul in Suphote Dantrakul, pp. 119ff; Khuang, loc. cit., p. 75.
34. Pridi in Pramote Pungsunthorn, p. 68; Thawee Bunyaket in Ray, p. 101; *Magic* of Apr. 12, 1944, showing that Pridi's plans for the premiership dated back at least as far as Feb. 1944.
35. Batson (JSS 1974), pp. 109ff, and Adul in Suphote Dantrakul, p. 121.
36. ibid., p. 122; Prince Aditya's testimony to the War Crimes Tribunal, Oct. 19, 1945; Khuang, loc. cit., p. 76.

37. Adul in Suphote Dantrakul, pp. 124ff; Pridi in Pramote Pungsunthorn, p. 69; Prince Aditya's testimony. In 1946 Pridi testified that he also asked Phra Sarasat in Tokyo to help persuade Japan to accept Khuang as premier. Pridi in Thak Chaloemtiarama (ed.), p. 388.

38. Text in Prasert Patamasukhon, p. 439, and Domei News Agency, Aug. 3, 1944. Summary of reports monitored from Domei and Bangkok Radio in F6998/296/40 in FO 371/46522.

39. Pridi in Pramote Pungsunthorn, p. 68 and Thawee Bunyaket in Ray, p. 101.

40. Direk, p. 98.

41. This was Phya Srisena.

42. Batson (JSS 1974), p. 111; Adul in Suphote Dantrakul, p. 134; Khuang, loc. cit., p. 77.

43. This was Maj.-Gen. Plot Porapaks.

44. This was Khun Srisakorn (Chalaw Srisakorn), a promoter who always opposed Pibul's self-aggrandisement.

45. Adul in Suphote Dantrakul, pp. 135ff; Netr Khemayothin, II, p. 40; and *Magic*, Aug. 9, 1944.

46. This was Vichit Lulitanond.

47. Puey's tribute to Adul in Suphote Dantrakul, p. 45; Puey in Direk, pp. 139ff; Gilchrist, pp. 55ff.

48. F3836/23/40 in FO 371/41845 and Nai Chantana, pp. 238ff, on the Banomyong family code originally devised in 1933 for secret messages when Pridi was banished.

49. Gilchrist, pp. 60ff, and Cruikshank, p. 107.

50. Pibul's orders from Lopburi in Ananta Pibulsongkram, III, pp. 597ff.

51. These were Gen. Kriangsak Pichit, just appointed army commander by Pibul, and Gen. Chai Pratipasen, his military secretary.

52. Thawee Bunyaket in Ray, p. 81; Batson (JSS 1974), p. 111; Adul in Suphote Dantrakul, pp. 128ff; Khuang, loc. cit., p. 77.

53. Adul in Suphote Dantrakul, pp. 139ff.

54. Thawee in Ray, p. 81, and Adul in Suphote Dantrakul, p. 175.

55. ibid., p. 149; Khuang, loc. cit., p. 78; Prayoon, p. 522; Pin Chunhawan, military governor of Shan States, in Thak Chaloemtiarama (ed.), p. 568.

56. Thawee in Ray, pp. 82ff; Adul in Suphote Dantrakul, p. 152; Batson (JSS 1974), pp. 111ff; Khuang, loc. cit., p. 78. Text in Prasert Patamasukhon, pp. 441ff.

57. Bangkok Radio, Aug. 25, 1944.

58. Thawee Bunyaket in Ray, p. 83; Adul in Suphote Dantrakul, pp. 153ff; Pin Chunhawan in Thak Chaloemtiarama (ed.), p. 569.

59. Batson (JSS 1974), p. 112.

60. La-iad Pibulsongkram in Ray, p. 205.

61. La-iad Pibulsongkram's tribute to Adul in Suphote Dantrakul, p. 39.

13
THE YEAR OF DISSIMULATION

The Japanese were happy to see Pibul go. They had found him increasingly uncooperative and ineffective. In Tokyo the main news agency bluntly stated that Pibul had become unpopular because of his dictatorial rule. The report also claimed that Khuang's government was far more pro-Japanese than its predecessor.[1]

The Americans, on the other hand, viewed the fall of Pibul and Khuang's advent to power as a distinct advantage to the Allied cause.[2] Such enthusiasm alarmed Sanguan, Pridi's envoy in Washington, who pointed out that Khuang's government still had to live with the Japanese presence, and any overt American support would create difficulties for it. Instead Sanguan, backed up by Seni, suggested that the Allies should stop bombing Bangkok as a gesture of gratitude for the change of regime.[3] The Americans did not respond because the raids were intended to destroy installations used by the Japanese rather than strike at Thailand for its own sake. In any event, the British would not have agreed to halt the bombing; they remained doubtful of the will or ability of any Thai government to oppose the Japanese. When this view was challenged in Washington, Eden replied that the Siamese needed "a spur rather than a sugar plum" to assist the Allies.[4]

These doubts were not shared by SOE, which was now receiving numerous messages from Pridi. Via his brother in Switzerland, he asked for another Seri Thai group to be parachuted in, this time to a pre-arranged landing zone where their arrival could be kept secret from the Japanese.[5] Then, through the new direct radio link set up by Puey between Bangkok and Calcutta, one of Pridi's first messages expressed fears that either Prince Aditya or Pibul had betrayed Seri Thai activities to the Japanese, so setting back all the efforts to build up an underground resistance network. Another of Pridi's concerns was about the fate of the envoys he had sent to China. In particular he asked that Deng Gunatilaka, if he were still alive, be parachuted back into Thailand with a radio operator to set up an alternative channel of communication with the Allies. This was easier said than done.[6]

After their discussions in Washington with Seni and various American officials interested in Thailand, Sanguan and Deng had little to do and were transferred to Kandy in Ceylon, where SEAC had established its headquarters and where, too, OSS had decided to set up an office to oversee its operations in East Asia.[7] Somewhat ironically in the light of American suspicions of British intentions in South East Asia, Mountbatten – unlike his counterpart Macarthur, the Supreme Commander in the Pacific – did not object to OSS operating in his theatre. However, attempts were made to minimise friction and competition between OSS and Force 136 by creating a special department in Kandy to coordinate their operations.[8] Yet they still tended to vie with one another and go their own separate ways: hence, when the British won the unofficial race to set up direct links with Bangkok, the Americans were very envious.[9]

By comparison, OSS had made far less progress; it had heard nothing from all the Seri Thai infiltrated through Yunnan except for one short, sad message received in July. Two of the Seri Thai students guided through northern Indo-China by Tai Li's agents were killed on crossing the Mekong into Thailand. The motive of their assailants was apparently robbery; they had been carrying gold to meet all eventualities on their journey. Still, Bangkok Radio reported that an enemy patrol trying to infiltrate Thailand had been repulsed: this alerted the Japanese, who increased their patrols along Thailand's northern borders, which had hitherto been left mainly to the Thai army to guard.[10] All these developments naturally dismayed OSS. Hence, it responded favourably to a British proposal to parachute Deng into Thailand, but unfortunately he injured a leg in training and the idea had to be abandoned.[11]

As it turned out, Force 136 had to contend with many other problems in meeting Pridi's request for another parachute mission. After a disastrous experience in Europe when the Germans captured several Allied agents parachuted into the Netherlands and manipulated them into sending back false information, SOE had qualms about the reliability of Puey's radio messages, especially since he was known to have been interrogated by the Japanese. Another worrying factor was the role of Adul: echoes of his sinister reputation lingered on. Hence Force 136 was instructed by SOE in London to carry out an elaborate security check to determine whether Puey really was in contact with Pridi and not simply sending messages dictated by the Japanese or Adul.[12]

Once this was successfully achieved, other snags arose. To gain Pridi's confidence and ensure his full cooperation, Mountbatten wanted to send him a personal message. Here the Foreign Office in London raised objections. True, Mountbatten was an Allied Supreme Commander on a par with Eisenhower and Macarthur, but he was still British and, given the state of war between Britain and Siam, his idea of communicating directly with someone who was in effect head of an enemy state was considered highly irregular. Eden in particular was a stickler on the point. With no personal experience of South East Asia and little interest in it, the British Foreign Secretary referred to the Siamese regent as "a collaborationist and creature of the Japs".[13]

Eden's attitude accounted in part for Britain's continuing failure to issue a statement on policy towards Siam. Despite numerous high-level representatives from Washington,[14] British officials still felt constrained by Churchill's dictum of 1942 about imposing a security guarantee on the Kra Isthmus area to prevent history from repeating itself, although the idea now looked outdated. Analysts in the Foreign Office pointed out that once Japan was defeated, there was no other regional power capable of taking advantage of the Kra Isthmus. But another problem had arisen with the transfer to Thailand of parts of Burma and Malaya. The Colonial Office insisted that the territory had to be returned before any friendly gesture was made to Siam. There were also misgivings in the Foreign Office about Mountbatten sending a message direct to Pridi because it might be construed as a sign that Britain favoured one political faction in Siam as against another.[15]

While all these issues were being discussed in London, Mountbatten cut through the bureaucratic tangle by signing a message addressed to no-one in particular, requesting Siam's full cooperation with the Allies.[16] Before London could object, the message was carried into Siam by another Force 136 mission. In an operation code-named "Brillig", three Free Siamese were dropped in early September near Hua Hin at a landing zone previously arranged with Pridi.[17] In fact it was so well illuminated by fires lit on the ground that the pilot of the aircraft dropping the Free Siamese was afraid that they would be burnt on landing.

These fears were misplaced. Pridi's men soon had the Brillig mission on a boat bound for a secret hiding-place in Bangkok. From there, within a couple of days of landing, the Free Siamese established an independent, direct radio link with Calcutta without their presence being known either to the Japanese or to Adul. After that, Force 136 had little doubt about Pridi's ability as a resistance leader or his loyalty to the Allied cause. The feeling was mutual. Putting his trust in Force 136, Pridi proposed a visit to Kandy by a Thai delegation led by Direk to annul the state of war with Britain and discuss future military cooperation.[18]

The thought of holding political discussions with the Siamese, especially with an ex-Foreign Minister who had recently served as ambassador in Tokyo, again raised the hackles of British officialdom. There was little understanding of a country which wanted to talk peace terms with Britain while still ostensibly collaborating with Japan. Hence, Force 136 officers were instructed to tell Pridi that political discussions were out of the question at that stage in the war. Noticeably upset, Pridi cancelled the idea of sending anyone to Kandy; Force 136 replied sharply that there was no room for personal pique in the middle of a war, and operational considerations must take priority over politics.

Instead of pursuing the argument, Pridi showed how politically adept he could be. Through the radio link operated by Puey, to which Adul had access, the regent stressed the high level of organisation already achieved by the Seri Thai and invited a British officer to come and see for himself. Then, through the new radio link set up by the Brillig mission, Pridi told Force 136 that its tough talk had been useful in persuading those who had qualms about Seri Thai political intentions that they must cooperate for the sake of defeating Japan. Pridi indicated that he was thinking in particular of Adul; above all, the police chief was worried because the Free Siamese group in Britain included Queen Rambhai and Tan Chin. Adul regarded them as political enemies whose main aim was to restore the absolute monarchy rather than oppose the Japanese. He also had doubts about Seni since he too was a junior member of the royal family. In these circumstances, Pridi told Force 136 that its message had been valuable in demonstrating to Adul and other doubters that the defeat of Japan took precedence over all Thai political considerations.[19] Still, they could never be completely ignored.

After Pibul was eased out of the Supreme Command, a series of orders was issued in the name of Phya Phahol reorganising the army, navy and Defence Ministry hierarchies. As a result, members of Pibul's personal entourage, the military governor of the Shan States and Prayoon were all dismissed from office.[20] The purge was master-minded by Sinad despite the risk of alienating many other military officers.[21]

At the same time, Pridi and Khuang set out to court support for the new administration from other quarters. Given the widespread dismay over the way Pibul had treated the royal family, the King's birthday on September 21 was quickly reinstated as a national holiday. Among the first officials to react was Prince Wan: demonstrating his accustomed ability to adjust to the prevailing political climate, he broadcast a speech extolling the virtues of a constitutional monarchy. More significant still was the proclamation of a royal amnesty for political prisoners.[22]

This move was fraught with problems. Not only Pibul but Adul too was held responsible for having arrested the political prisoners in the first place. Once again Thawee showed his courage in arguing the case for their release and drafting the necessary legislation. But he was careful to exclude from the amnesty those who had been detained for supporting the Allied cause. Thawee was afraid they might simply be re-arrested by the Japanese and suffer an even worse fate.[23] Nevertheless, on the King's birthday in 1944, more than sixty people were released from prison, including Prince Sitthiporn who had been detained since the Bovoradet rebellion in 1933, part of the time on Terutao island. Likewise, Phya Thephatsadin and Prince Rangsit benefitted from the amnesty. And in another gesture to heal old wounds, Pridi as regent presided over a special royal ceremony to re-invest Prince Rangsit with all the ranks and titles of which he had been stripped in 1939.[24]

These developments made OSS feel all the more frustrated. The Seri Thai infiltrators from Yunnan, if they were still alive, had orders to concentrate on building up a clandestine military network up-country without becoming involved in politics or attempting to approach Bangkok. These instructions stemmed from Seni's suspicion of Karb and Donovan's undertaking to restrict the activities of any Seri Thai associated with him. Obviously these limitations became very irksome once Pibul was ousted from power and Force 136 established direct radio links with Bangkok. Hence OSS decided not to send any more Seri Thai to Szemao where they might come into contact with Karb and the Chinese. Instead they were placed at the disposal of the OSS office in Kandy from where it was hoped to open up a channel for political liaison with Pridi.[25]

To achieve their objective, the Americans swallowed their pride and asked the British to pass a message to Pridi about arranging a dropping zone for a group of Seri Thai parachutists. The area suggested by OSS was near Chiengmai. Without having to consult Bangkok, Force 136 knew that the idea was impracticable because the internal resistance movement had no organisation in the north capable of arranging to receive a parachute drop. But when the information was conveyed to OSS, an over-zealous British officer made it look as if Pridi had rejected the whole idea of an American parachute mission.[26] Consequently, much to its annoyance when it later discovered it had been misinformed, OSS decided to embark on a "blind" drop, and in September two Seri Thai were parachuted by the Americans into the central plains. As they landed their radio was smashed, both were injured, and one of them was immediately arrested by the police.[27]

Up-country Adul had built up a loyal personal network known as the field police. They were ordered to increase their vigilance after it was discovered that the two Seri Thai killed in July on arrival from Yunnan had been carrying a personal letter addressed to Adul from a prominent Sino-Thai whom he had helped to escape to China at the start of the war. Adul feared that if any more attempts were made to smuggle in such messages, his position could be jeopardised.[28]

As it turned out, the vigilance of the field police proved helpful for the other Seri Thai infiltrators from Yunnan. Once they crossed into Thailand, they were all intercepted by their compatriots rather than the Japanese and sent straight to Bangkok. Particularly grateful was the group of four Seri Thai, who had set off to cross the Shan States under the guidance of a Chinese missionary. They spent eighty-seven days trekking through monsoon-swept jungles with frequent detours to avoid Japanese patrols; they only survived by eating roots and berries while trying to fend off tropical diseases. Finally, they were picked up by the field police, escorted to Bangkok and, like their predecessors from Force 136, accommodated at secret police headquarters. They were not, however, given access to their radios; Adul was apparently wary of their previous association with Karb and Tai Li. Only when the Seri Thai parachuted in by OSS from India arrived was direct radio contact allowed between the agents infiltrated by the Americans and the outside world. In Szemao, the receipt of their first message on October 5 caused great joy and relief.[29]

OSS then received another surprise. After all the time and effort expended in attempting to infiltrate Thailand, Nicol Smith was amazed when one of his Seri Thai protégés, a few weeks after reaching Bangkok, reappeared in Yunnan with various prominent Thais including a member of the Assembly.[30] They had been guided out of Thailand through northern Laos by Chinese agents following long-established opium trails about which OSS knew little. What is more, Tai Li had deliberately concealed other contacts with Thailand from the Americans.

The Seri Thai who returned to Yunnan so quickly was Karoon Kengradomying, one of four children sent to study in the United States by their father Luang Kad Songkram, a maverick military promoter and cabinet minister. Having opposed the Japanese from the start of the war, Kad resigned from the cabinet in July 1943 and quietly disappeared to China with his wife and personal entourage. On arrival in Chungking, he was taken in charge by Tai Li, who tried to persuade him to set up a government-in-exile. He refused and eventually in August 1944 his

presence in China became known to the Americans.[31] Then, three
months later, his son Karoon arrived back in Yunnan with Thawil
Udol, the Assembly representative for Roi Et.[32] Immediately, before any
Americans could talk to him, Thawil was whisked off by plane to
Chungking thanks to a high-ranking Kuomintang official based in Kun-
ming who had organised his escape from Thailand.[33]

Still, in September when he left Bangkok, Thawil informed Pridi who
seized on the opportunity to send a personal appeal to Chiang Kai-shek
for news of all the other envoys he had despatched to China in the hope
that they could act in setting up a provisional government abroad. Naturally the Chinese were delighted to receive Pridi's message, and quickly
created a special committee to discuss matters with Thawil.[34] However,
these deliberations had already been overtaken by other messages sent by
Pridi through the direct radio channels to the British and Americans.

To extend his options for dealing with the great powers even further,
the Thai regent instructed his brother Arthakit to move from Berne to
Stockholm where he might be able to contact the Soviet Union. In
Sweden Arthakit continued, as in Berne, to receive coded messages to
pass to the other Allied powers. One was a plea for Churchill to issue a
statement on policy towards Thailand similar to those already put out by
Chiang Kai-shek and Roosevelt. Pridi said that it would help him unite
all Thais in opposing the Japanese.[35] Arthakit was likewise asked to
suggest to the American embassy in Stockholm that Seni travel to
Sweden to discuss setting up a government-in-exile. Like the British
earlier, the Americans were suspicious of Arthakit and the security of his
links with his brother. More than that, Seni believed that Pridi's use of
the Swedish channel was a trap designed to betray all the Seri Thai
abroad. The allegation turned out to be groundless, as the Americans
soon discovered by cross-checking with Bangkok.[36]

Seni's suspicions of Karb were another matter. OSS finally agreed to
recall him from China, only to find more accusations lodged against him
by Seni. The result was a major split among the Seri Thai recruited in the
United States, much to the dismay of OSS.[37] Seni also quarrelled with
Tan Chin and continued to voice suspicions of British intentions
towards Thailand. His fears were fuelled in part by Mani Sanasen who,
in travelling between Washington, London and later Kandy as Seni's
personal envoy, spread some very wild rumours about Western policy
regarding Thailand. They had little effect on the British, who considered Mani a troublemaker. Nonetheless, some Americans believed
him.[38]

Pridi still knew little of all the dissension among the Seri Thai abroad. He was concentrating on building up his internal network as well as keeping a close watch on the rapidly changing position of the Japanese. Towards the end of 1944, the Allied campaign in Burma was at last making significant progress, while in the Pacific theatre troops under Macarthur's command, who for so long had seemed bogged down in the remote jungles of New Guinea, suddenly made a successful landing in the Philippines. The Japanese reacted quickly. Realising that the Americans might soon be able to cut the shipping of supplies from the home islands to South East Asia, orders went out from Tokyo to all Japanese commanders in the region to redeploy their forces and develop self-reliance. The result in Thailand was the formation of a new army under the command of General Nakamura Akito.[39] He had been garrison commander in Bangkok since January 1943 and had gained considerable experience of the local scene, as was very evident as he set out to tackle his new responsibilities. First he confronted Khuang with the information the Japanese had accumulated about Allied infiltration, and demanded that the parachutists be executed immediately. When the Thai premier tried to dodge the issue, Nakamura threatened a military take-over if any more pro-Western plotting was discovered. He also demanded more loans from Thailand to finance his expanding army. All that Khuang could do in the circumstances was agree to pay up, despite the already abysmal state of the Thai economy.

Some Japanese diplomats at least appreciated that Khuang, unlike his predecessor, was making efforts to cope with Thailand's economic problems.[40] He ordered the cessation of work on the Petchaboon project and the investigation by an official committee of all other public expenditure.[41] As Finance Minister in his own cabinet, he also tried to stamp out racketeering that resulted from the Japanese presence, as well as the longer-term tendency of many promoters to pack the boards of state enterprises. The trouble was that such moves prompted Pibul's supporters to find ways of circumventing them.

Nevertheless, Khuang continued to dismantle the legacy he had inherited from Pibul. The unpopular bachelor tax was abrogated, as were the spelling reforms. Khuang also decided to abolish the decree banning the use of official ranks, although he himself chose not to resume his former title.[42] Far more significant for many people was his promise of greater freedom of speech. Some Assembly members immediately pressed for the right to form political parties. But again Pibul's supporters sought to take advantage by making similar demands.

It was on such occasions, when dealing with awkward issues, that Khuang earned the reputation of being a comedian. He quipped that, rather than thinking of the future, ambitious politicians would do better to concentrate on dodging bombs.[43] The remark was very apposite: with the end of the rainy season, the Allies were once again intensifying their raids on Bangkok. Unwittingly they enabled the government to embark on other reforms. The Ministry of Education under Thawee was anxious to purge the school curriculum of the extreme nationalism with which it had been imbued during the Pibul era. Using the bombing as a pretext, all educational establishments in Bangkok were ordered to close from the end of December. All the same, the government wanted more people to evacuate to the comparative safety of the countryside.[44]

As the Seri Thai leadership now knew from its direct contacts with the Western Allies, the purpose of the bombing was to destroy installations used by the Japanese. But in Bangkok, the tendency to put up makeshift homes wherever possible often resulted in civilians becoming casualties of bombs intended for military targets nearby. Even so, thanks to the intelligence provided by Pridi's network about facilities used by the Japanese, Allied raids became more accurate and effective. For instance, on November 27 the railway marshalling yards at Bangsue were destroyed, the Bangkok cement works was put out of action, and hits were scored on several wharves in the port. Five nights later the main target was the Rama VI bridge carrying rail traffic across the Chao Phya en route to Burma and Malaya.[45]

Many of these raids were carried out by Allied planes based in India. Given the distance involved and the lack of emergency landing strips anywhere in South East Asia, one major concern of the pilots was the weather and the complex pattern of monsoons in the region. Uncertainty about flying conditions was also the main reason why Force 136 did not take up Pridi's invitation to send a British officer to Bangkok. For such a mission to be effective, the person concerned would have to make a brief visit and the only way of extracting him from Thailand was by means of a Catalina flying-boat. Allied pilots believed that from November onwards the north-east monsoon would make the Gulf of Thailand too rough for landings.[46]

Anyway, Force 136 was still worried about the security of its contacts with the internal resistance network because they were concentrated in Bangkok where Japanese surveillance was most intense. For that reason the British had long been considering setting up a clandestine base in a remote area of north-eastern Thailand. The idea materialised in late

1944, when another group of Free Siamese recruited in Britain was dropped at a site in Khonkaen province previously agreed with Pridi and Adul. All the arrangements for the landing zone and reception party were made through the field police in a way which led Force 136 to realise that Adul wanted to vet and control everybody sent into Thailand.[47] Force 136 was therefore happy when, unknown to Adul, one of Pridi's friends in the Assembly, representing Sakol Nakorn in the northeast, offered to set up a secret resistance base in his constituency. In return he wanted a radio transmitter and weapons for his local supporters, some of whom were already under para-military training.[48] Once Force 136 agreed to the plan, the Seri Thai leadership in Bangkok further arranged for a group of Lao refugees, who had fled to Thailand in 1940 during the irredentist campaign, to go to Sakol Nakorn. From there it was hoped that their leader Oune Sananikone could contact his compatriots across the Mekong in Laos and so expand anti-Japanese resistance.[49]

At the same time, to placate Adul and ensure his continuing cooperation, Force 136 arranged to exfiltrate a group of police officers for paramilitary training in India. Somewhat ironically they were picked up by seaplane off the coast of Terutao Island, the former penal colony; situated in the Andaman Sea, it was more sheltered from the north-east monsoon than the Gulf of Thailand. Even so, the operation was still risky and nearly went wrong.[50]

All this activity by Force 136 simply strengthened American suspicions of British aims in Thailand. In yet another high-level Anglo-American exchange of correspondence about Britain's policy, Eden for the first time told the Americans of Churchill's concern to obtain a security guarantee covering the Kra Isthmus area.[51] The information was seized on in Washington as substantiation for a rumour purveyed by Mani Sanasen. He alleged that Britain had already chosen as its future governor of Thailand a businessman representing an Anglo-Indian company which wanted the rights to exploit all the natural resources of the Kra Isthmus.[52] The idea was pure fantasy, and the British would have told the Americans so had the matter been raised, but as matters turned out, it was not. Roosevelt had a brief to challenge Churchill on the question of Thailand when they met at the Yalta conference in February 1945. In the event other arguments over Europe's post-war future took priority.[53]

Even so, on the ground OSS was more determined than ever to outflank Force 136 activities. The Americans were already starting to extract Seri Thai groups for paramilitary training in India. The problem was they were dependent on the same flying-boats as Force 136.[54] But as the pilots flying these missions – who were mainly British and Australian – built up their experience, they realised that there were gaps in the monsoon when it was possible to land in the Gulf of Thailand. OSS immediately seized the opportunity to send two officers to Bangkok. The plan was for one of these Americans to return to Kandy after a week with a first-hand account of the situation in Thailand, while the other remained in Bangkok to liaise directly with Pridi. The Seri Thai quickly agreed to the idea, and on January 25 the two OSS officers were landed by a British Catalina near Hua Hin and swiftly taken off by a Thai customs boat direct to a secret hide-out in Bangkok.[55]

Pridi was delighted that OSS had sufficient confidence to entrust him with the safety of its officers in the heart of Japanese-occupied Bangkok. To register his gratitude he presented a gold cigarette-case to Roosevelt and a set of embossed cuff-links to General Donovan.[56] The gifts were despatched on their way with the OSS officer returning to Kandy. He also took with him a comprehensive military plan drawn up by the Seri Thai leadership. It envisaged the landing of two US Army divisions, one near Hua Hin and the other on the opposite side of the Gulf at Sattahip to carry out a pincer movement with the help of local forces to capture Bangkok and eventually liberate the whole of Thailand, as well as Indo-China, from the Japanese. But before the Thais could undertake their part in the plan, Pridi requested that they be supplied with large quantities of arms.[57]

Through OSS, Pridi also arranged to send another envoy to Washington. This was Konthi Suphamongkol, a young diplomat who had previously worked under Direk at the Thai embassy in Tokyo and could provide the Americans with up-to-date information on the Japanese capital just before it was subjected to a major bombing campaign.[58] However, Konthi's main task in Washington was to liaise with Seni in pressing for international recognition of the Seri Thai in the shape of either a government-in-exile or a liberation committee. To legalise any such move, Konthi had credentials signed by Pridi as regent, authorising Sanguan to act on his behalf in coordinating Seri Thai activities abroad.

The ever-increasing flow of envoys and messages emerging from Pridi was becoming confusing, especially to Seni. He did not know what to do; in principle he remained opposed to the idea of a government-in-exile, and told the Americans that he would only agree to it if directly ordered by Pridi or if Japan staged a complete military takeover.[59] The

Americans too had still not made up their minds. After all the arguments between Seni and Karb, they wondered whether the Seri Thai abroad were capable of any united action.[60]

Another factor worrying the Americans was continuing Chinese efforts to dominate the Seri Thai movement. In fact, OSS had become so disillusioned with Tai Li's machinations that it decided to close down the base in Szemao and transfer responsibility for all its operations directed at Thailand to Kandy, where they would come under the aegis of SEAC.[61] Even so, Donovan refused to countenance any joint operations with Force 136 in Thailand.[62]

Of course the Thai public knew nothing of all these developments, its main concern, particularly in Bangkok, being the bombing. Because one of the electricity power plants was put out of action, the pumping of water was curtailed and supplies were cut off completely during the hours of darkness. In order to inconvenience the Japanese, no effort was made to repair the damage and restore supplies. The Thai public also had to cope with a growing shortage of cloth and other essential imported goods. Again the Allies were indirectly responsible since, to stop Japanese military supplies reaching the port of Bangkok, they dropped mines in the approaches to the Chao Phya river. As a result the Japanese gave priority to their own shipping needs, leaving Thai imports to be transported overland from Saigon and Singapore whenever possible.

Matters became so bad in January 1945 that Khuang – in complete contrast to the Pibul era – told everyone from ministers downwards to wear only shirts, trousers and shoes. He set an example by appearing informally clad in the Assembly and elsewhere. Less easy for him to deal with was a sudden increase in rice prices during February, prompting a crisis of confidence in the government. Khuang reacted by giving a pep-talk to all senior officials on the need for the whole nation to pull together and cooperate in a difficult situation.[63]

Khuang's strictures also served Pridi's purposes. He was worried that Pibul and his henchmen were still conspiring in secret to exploit the loyalty of some military units. The air force had not yet been brought under the control of officers whom the Seri Thai could trust and the situation in the navy was extremely complex.[64] While some officers continued to maintain the close links they had long had with Japan, somewhat paradoxically Admiral Sangworn Suwannachip, who was regarded as a leader of the pro-Japanese faction in the navy, decided to cooperate with the Seri Thai. His attitude was much appreciated by Pridi because the admiral had under his command a special security unit which protected the personal safety of the Seri Thai leadership.[65] As for the army, it had now been sufficiently purged of Pibul's supporters for Sinad to feel confident enough to issue secret orders about thwarting any Japanese attempt to stage a military takeover. But to carry out these orders, the Thai army wanted more weapons.[66]

When Pridi received no immediate reply to the military plans and pleas for arms he had sent to Washington via OSS, he resurrected the idea of sending a mission to Kandy. Again the British were wary. With envoys already in Washington and Chungking, Pridi now appeared in a good position to start bargaining. Anyway, the mission Pridi proposed sending to SEAC still included Direk, which made it apparent that the Seri Thai continued to hope for political as well as military matters to be discussed. That was impossible as far as the British were concerned. The debate in London about future policy towards Siam was still tied up in inter-departmental red tape. Yet some officials appreciated that Pridi might easily take offence if Britain kept on refusing to receive a mission that included Direk. Worse still, it could cause a setback to the operational cooperation SEAC needed with the Seri Thai, especially to interdict traffic on the Siam-Burma railway and rescue the Allied prisoners-of-war working there.[67]

Since 1943 the Western powers had been aware that, in contravention of all international conventions on the treatment of prisoners-of-war, Japan was using them as slave labour on the railway being constructed between Siam and Burma. Most of those working on the Thai side of the border were British, Australians and Dutch captured in 1942 during the collapse of Malaya and the Netherlands East Indies. In addition, the Japanese conscripted Chinese and Indian labourers from the territories they conquered as well as some in Thailand. When reports of the appalling conditions under which all these men were forced to work began to filter out, the Western powers protested vigorously to Japan. Similar protests to Thailand were also considered, but initially there was little public criticism in the West. British officials decided to limit publicity about prisoners-of-war working on the railway to avoid causing undue distress to the families of those involved.[68]

The position changed in late 1944 when the Americans sank a Japanese cargo ship in the South China Sea. Its holds were found to have been crammed with prisoners-of-war who, after the completion of the railway, were being shipped to Japan for further forced labour. When the few who were rescued told their stories, news of the brutality suffered by prisoners-of-war in Thailand could no longer be hushed up.[69] In Britain, public opinion thought that Siam must be at least partly responsible for the inhumane conditions along what became known as the "Death Railway". After all, Siam had declared war on Britain in apparent collaboration with Japan. Such views were also widely held in Whitehall, where wartime secrecy restricted knowledge about the Seri Thai and their sympathetic attitude towards the plight of the prisoners-of-war. But those officials who were aware of the true situation saw it as a good reason for strengthening military cooperation with the Seri Thai. Hence SEAC was given the go-ahead to welcome a mission from Pridi provided that its political role was strictly circumscribed.[70]

Unlike the envoys sent by Pridi to China and the United States, those going to SEAC were to return to Thailand after only a few days. For the people involved, the risks were very apparent; if ever the Japanese found out that they had been to Kandy, there would certainly be serious repercussions, especially for Direk. Even after relinquishing the Foreign Affairs portfolio for the second time in 1944, he had maintained friendly relations with General Nakamura.[71] It may have been shrewd policy on Direk's part, but Nakamura too was adept at dissimulation. With the Thais he cultivated a benevolent image; for instance, when several Thai monks were caught helping workers along the Death Railway, they were not physically punished because Nakamura knew that this would violate local custom. Instead he ordered them to pay a fine and then donated the money to charity.

Yet before coming to Thailand, Nakamura had been an officer in the *Kempei*, the notorious Japanese military police. This meant little to most Thais. Compared with other parts of the Co-prosperity Sphere, the *Kempei* kept a low profile in Thailand. However, the Japanese were aware that Sanguan, Deng, Thawil Udol and various other Thais had escaped to China. The activities of Adul and the police under him were also beginning to look increasingly suspicious in Nakamura's eyes, and in late 1944 he told the *Kempei* to step up surveillance of the entire Thai leadership.[72]

Japanese fears of being double-crossed were matched by those of the Allies. The Americans had just got wind of possible collusion between certain high-ranking Kuomintang officials and Japan; hence they insisted that nothing further should be revealed to the Chinese leadership about clandestine Western contacts with the Seri Thai. The ban applied especially to Direk's proposed visit to Kandy. As a result, Mountbatten reluctantly broke the "gentleman's agreement" he had concluded with Chiang Kai-shek about informing each other of their respective links with Thailand, although it had of course long been ignored by the Chinese.[73]

In SEAC's view, the main interest in extracting a mission from Siam lay in its military value. Besides Direk, Pridi had indicated that he was sending out the Army Chief of Staff-designate[74] with a great deal of military intelligence and a brief to discuss future operational cooperation with the Allies. The third member of the mission was Thanat Khoman, a young diplomat who till recently had worked at the Thai embassy in Tokyo and could therefore provide the Allies with first-hand information about the situation in Japan. These three Thais were picked up by flying-boat from the Andaman Sea near Terutao Island on February 25 and flown to Trincomalee in Ceylon. There they were greeted by Andrew Gilchrist, a Force 136 officer who knew Direk well, having worked as a diplomat in Bangkok up till the Japanese invasion.

Overjoyed at re-encountering an old friend, Direk launched straight into explaining that his main aim was to persuade Britain to disregard Pibul's declaration of war and put out a statement of friendly intent towards Thailand. Gilchrist cut him short. He told Direk that while he himself appreciated the Thai position, all that Churchill and the British public knew about Siam was that it had declared war and seized large tracts of Burma and Malaya. In these circumstances Gilchrist advised Direk that rather than seek friendly statements from Britain, he would do better to keep quiet about politics and concentrate on military cooperation in defeating the Japanese so that after the war Siam could claim to have made amends for Pibul's erroneous policies. In other words, Gilchrist was stating what by then had become standard British policy towards Siam.

Direk was clearly taken aback by such toughness. His previous experience of British diplomats had led him to expect a more sympathetic attitude; he had apparently forgotten Gilchrist himself had been subject to some pretty rough treatment under Thai internment for seven months at the beginning of the war. Even so, Direk heeded the advice of an old friend. During the first two days of consultations with officers at SEAC, the Thai mission concentrated on military matters. The Army Chief of Staff elaborated on the intelligence he had brought out about Japanese troop dispositions in Thailand, and offered to place the Thai armed forces under the command of SEAC provided that weapons could be provided. He then produced a long list of Thai military requirements ranging from tyres and car-batteries to bren-guns and tanks.

After that, Direk was accorded an interview – not with Mount-batten, as he had hoped, but with Esler Dening who had been seconded from the Foreign Office as political adviser to SEAC. Dening again pointed out, as Gilchrist had done, that Britain still officially considered Siam an enemy country, and it was up to the Thais to prove in deeds rather than words that they were now prepared to work with the Allies. A statement to this effect was also handed to Direk to take back to Pridi. The atmosphere then thawed a little. Before returning home, the mission was entertained at a party in Kandy arranged by various officers from SEAC and Force 136. Perhaps as a result of this hospitality, Direk reported back to Pridi in fairly optimistic terms despite the harshness of the British stance. In any case, the two sides now had a better appre-ciation of each others' position although the Thais failed to understand why the British were cautious about their request for arms. As Mount-batten later put it, ''It was sufficiently unusual to be offered command of an enemy army in war, but to be asked to equip it as well seemed a shade over the odds.''[75]

Somewhat different criteria prevailed in the case of Indo-China, where the administration headed by Admiral Decoux continued, at least on the surface, to collaborate with Japan despite the end of the Vichy regime and the establishment of a Free French government in Paris. Given such an anomalous situation, the Japanese naturally realised that many French in Indo-China were anxious to cooperate with the Allies. Secret contacts had in fact long been set up, and Force 136 was starting to drop weapons to the French when the Japanese struck. On the night of March 9 the colonial administration in Indo-China was ousted and French forces were disarmed in a *coup de force* paving the way for a com-plete Japanese military takeover.

Several hours before Decoux was due to be arrested, the Japanese in Bangkok gave Khuang and Sindhu, as Defence Minister, advance warn-ing and requested their cooperation. What Japan wanted was for the Thais to seal the border to prevent any French escaping from Indo-China and to detain all French citizens already resident in Thailand. Since Khuang always tried to appear as cooperative as possible, he readily agreed to the first demand, but he claimed that internment of the French was a different matter because Thailand was a sovereign state and the cabinet would have to give its approval. That provided Nakamura with a pretext to keep Khuang and Sindhu talking until well after the planned time for launching the coup in Indo-China. The Japanese were right in suspecting that the Thais would pass the information on to the Allies as soon as possible.[76] Pridi not only used the direct radio links with OSS and Force 136 to inform them of all that the Thais knew about the situation in Indo-China, but he also warned that something similar might happen in Thailand. In a show of strength, the Japanese had moved tanks into the streets of Bangkok.[77]

Up till then Pridi had thought that Japan would refrain from intervening directly in Thailand. During his visit to Kandy, Direk told SEAC that the Seri Thai leadership believed the Japanese would never dare to curtail or tamper with the independence of the only South East Asian country which had managed to escape colonial domination.[78] But in January 1945 Nakamura made several preparatory moves for disarming the Thai military and police. The question of staging a complete takeover was further discussed at southern headquarters in Saigon, where Count Terauchi remained responsible for implementing Japanese military policy throughout South East Asia. Yet among his staff officers the prevailing attitude seemed to be that it would be a cowardly and dirty trick to stage a takeover of a weak country like Thailand.[79]

Another factor which apparently militated in Thailand's favour was the lack of anybody who could be depended upon to set up a client regime in Bangkok as was happening in Indo-China. Following the abrupt termination of French rule, the Japanese planned to install local politicians whose friendship they had been cultivating at the head of ostensibly independent governments. The Seri Thai were aware of the manoeuvre. The prime ministers-designate of both Vietnam and Cambodia passed through Bangkok on their way home to take up the positions Japan had arranged for them. Then it began to look as if the Japanese had something similar in mind for Thailand when it was reported that Phra Sarasat, the former Minister of Economic Affairs, was returning home in March.

Throughout the war Phra Sarasat had broadcast propaganda on Japan's behalf, and on his way back to Thailand he was accompanied by various potentially influential young Thais, like the son of Prince Wan who had been studying in Tokyo. The official reason given for their departure from Japan was that they were being evacuated for their own safety. The Americans had just launched a series of devastating firebomb raids against Japanese cities.[80] But there was alarmed speculation in Bangkok about Phra Sarasat and the students returning with express orders to form the nucleus of a pro-Japanese government, a move which would have been very unpopular. Because of his broadcasts from Tokyo and outpourings on the Thai economy, Phra Sarasat had forfeited all respect, and the feeling was that he was bound to be assassinated if ever he tried to take over the premiership.[81]

Still, coinciding with his return, Khuang was invited to visit Tokyo, which simply added to Pridi's suspicions that the Japanese were attempting to engineer a change of government in Bangkok. In fact almost the opposite was true. Japan wanted to cement its relations with Khuang and with Thailand as a whole by using his visit to Tokyo as the occasion for convening a second conference of all the heads of government in the Greater East Asia Co-Prosperity Sphere. As it turned out, these plans did not materialise for a variety of reasons. Yet Pridi continued to think that a Japanese coup in Bangkok was imminent and sent desperate pleas to the Americans for aid.[82]

According to Sinad's plan for opposing a Japanese takeover, the Thai army envisaged holding out in Bangkok without any outside assistance for a month, but much longer if the Allies supplied anti-tank guns. The assessment was based on the assumption that the Seri Thai leadership would know of an impending coup at least three days in advance since Sinad and Adul had a lot of spies watching every Japanese move. Adul also had plans to assassinate all the main Japanese officers in Bangkok while Pridi, Direk, Thawee and the other Seri Thai civilian leaders escaped up-country or to the coast to set up a "liberation government" proclaiming allegiance to the Allies.[83]

All these ideas flooding out of Bangkok somewhat perplexed the Americans. They were still considering Pridi's earlier proposals to set up a government-in-exile or otherwise a Seri Thai liberation committee abroad. The situation was further confused by a spate of messages from Chungking where Chiang Kai-shek, spurred on by Thawil's presence, kept coming up with different ideas for meetings and committees to discuss Thailand's future. These proposals seemed to be overtaken by a message sent to Seni through OSS channels, stating that Pridi intended to deal direct with the Allies in settling Thailand's problems. But, again, that seemed to conflict with what Direk had told the British in Kandy about Pridi's intentions.[84]

Such problems did not bother General Donovan. He had no doubt what the Seri Thai wanted. OSS still had its own officer in Bangkok liaising with Pridi (or "Ruth", the code-name used to protect his identity). It was through this OSS channel that Seri Thai fears of a Japanese takeover were transmitted. Donovan used these messages to reinforce a submission he had already made to the Joint Chiefs of Staff in Washington for sympathetic consideration of Pridi's original ideas for two US army divisions to be landed at Hua Hin and Sattahip.

The Chiefs of Staff were not enthusiastic. Allied plans gave priority to Pacific Command under Macarthur, who had instructions to strike north towards Japan as soon as possible. Any US landings in Thailand would involve diverting troops from Macarthur's campaign. Like it or not, the Americans knew that any forces entering Thailand had to come from SEAC. But Mountbatten planned, after defeating the Japanese in Burma, to capture Malaya and the Straits of Malacca instead of sending his troops on another foot-slogging campaign through more mountains and jungles into Thailand. The idea was endorsed by the US Chiefs of Staff, and all that they would concede to Donovan was that if arms stockpiled by OSS in Calcutta were not needed by the Chinese, they could be sent to Thailand. Even then, OSS was told that it must supply weapons only to the Seri Thai guerillas. American generals were totally opposed to equipping the Thai armed forces, which had served for so long simply as a prop for a military dictatorship and its pro-Japanese policies.[85]

In effect, Allied reluctance to aid the armed forces encouraged the expansion of the Seri Thai. Numerous Bangkok students were sent secretly to the area surrounding the naval base at Sattahip, which Admiral Sangworn considered as his private fiefdom. There guerilla training was provided by some of the Seri Thai originally recruited in the United States, until OSS sent in more specialised instructors and light arms. In the north-east Tiang Sirikhan, the representative for Sakol Nakorn, claimed after receiving a radio transmitter and small arms from Force 136 to have 5,000 men under training. They also constructed an airstrip where, later, supplies from OSS were landed. Other north-eastern Assembly members such as Thong-in from Ubol and Chamlong Daoruang from Mahasarakham followed suit.[86] Elsewhere, Force 136 provided assistance to a Seri Thai group in the northern province of Tak through which, it was thought, Japanese troops in Burma might try to retreat. Further south, other Seri Thai groups based near the Siam-Burma railway and at Hua Hin eventually received aid from OSS.[87]

During the early months of 1945, it was difficult to ferry aid to the Seri Thai. British and American air force units had more than enough to do in coping with the major campaign unfolding in Burma, and from their bases in India it was a long and perilous flight, sometimes lasting up to twenty hours, to drop supplies and agents into Thailand. Some sort of "cover" also had to be provided to prevent Japanese detection of the supply drops; this usually took the form of bombing raids or the scattering of propaganda material from the air. During his visit to Kandy, however, Direk said it was a waste of effort to drop propaganda leaflets as everyone was already anti-Japanese. Instead, Force 136 had the idea of dropping books of matches, and these proved very popular because matches had long been in short supply throughout Thailand.[88]

One of Pridi's main concerns in developing the resistance movement was financial. He asked OSS to arrange somehow for the transfer to Bangkok of $500,000 from Thai assets frozen in the United States. Eventually the sum was scaled down to $50,000 worth of gold, which was delivered to the Seri Thai leadership by two OSS officers sent to Bangkok in April to join John Wester, the liaison officer who had been there since January.[89] They were all accommodated in a secret hideout at one of the royal palaces, where the Seri Thai sought to make the Americans as comfortable as possible. Even so, the OSS officers had to put up with some of the inconveniences suffered by the rest of Bangkok's population – for by then conditions of life in the city had deteriorated further. The nadir was reached on April 14 when an Allied raid destroyed the one power-station still operating. The result was panic: all central electricity supplies ceased and with them the pumping of water. Worse still, there was an outbreak of cholera and typhoid.[90]

Wester too fell ill, although he was more acclimatised than most Americans to Thailand's tropical weather, having previously spent sixteen years as a businessman in Bangkok. At first he was thought to have malaria, but he responded adversely to the usual drugs. In a fit of delirium, he tried to betray his presence to the Japanese, and the OSS hideout had to be quickly moved. The incident also led the Seri Thai leadership to believe that because Wester had remained cooped up in hiding for three months, his illness was more psychological than physical. Hence he was introduced to some congenial feminine company. Many of the ladies of Bangkok were already working for the Seri Thai by seducing Japanese for the purposes of intelligence gathering and robbery; however, their charms failed to alleviate Wester's condition, and arrangements were made for him to leave Thailand bound eventually for a hospital in Calcutta.[91]

Even on his way out of Bangkok on a launch of the Thai Customs service, which was also cooperating with the resistance, Wester almost betrayed his presence to the Japanese. It could have been fatal to OSS operations in Thailand. Also aboard the launch was an American pilot from the Flying Tigers who had been smuggled out of a Japanese prison camp by the Seri Thai at the specific request of OSS. Another member of the launch party was one of the few Thai air force officers involved in resistance work, on his way to India to liaise with his American counterparts in SEAC.[92]

As the campaign in Burma was progressing well, SEAC was pressing ahead with planning the next stage in its operations. Mountbatten wanted to carry out amphibious landings on the west coast of Malaya aimed at capturing Singapore as soon as possible. As a prelude he planned to seize Phuket island off Thailand's west coast for use as a forward air base and naval anchorage without bothering to occupy the rest of the Kra Isthmus region. However, moves clearly had to be made first to stop the Japanese from bringing in reinforcements to oppose the capture of Phuket.

To help carry out "Operation Roger", as it was code-named, Force 136 was asked to provide local intelligence and on-the-spot assistance to commando teams to be sent into the Kra Isthmus area. Yet although Seri Thai agents trained in India were used for the purpose, Force 136 was strictly warned not to allow any hint of the forthcoming operation, due to take place in May, to reach Pridi. The British were worried news of the operation might be leaked inadvertently or otherwise to the Japanese. In addition, SEAC did not want the Seri Thai to use the capture of Phuket as a cue for staging a nationwide uprising.[93] Intelligence estimates suggested that the Japanese would easily crush the Thais unless they received outside help, and Mountbatten wished to avoid diverting resources from the Burma campaign or the planned invasion of Malaya to help the Thais. Instead, despite his reservations about equipping the Thai armed forces, he pressed London to agree to the provision of some weaponry for their use in the event of an emergency during Operation Roger.[94]

In these circumstances, the British regretted all the more their failure to take up Pridi's invitation in November for Force 136 to send a liaison officer to Bangkok – a feeling aggravated by the way OSS had now stolen a march. The rivalry between the two organisations acted as a spur, and Force 136 decided to send a mission to Bangkok headed by Brigadier Victor Jacques, an officer who had seen active service in both the World Wars. More to the point he had worked in the interim in Bangkok as a lawyer, and spoke fluent Thai.[95] Thus he seemed a good choice for serving as liaison officer with the Seri Thai, except that in 1935 he had acted as defence counsel for Phya Thephatsadin and was identified with the royalist cause.[96]

Worse still from that point of view, the British defence heirarchy decided that Jacques should be accompanied to Bangkok by Tan Chin. Force 136 was appalled at the idea because it could cause numerous political repercussions. Hence a personal message was sent to Pridi enquiring whether he would welcome a mission that included Tan Chin. He replied in the affirmative, but Force 136 thought that he was simply being diplomatic and privately asked Puey for his opinion. Tan Chin too had qualms about going to Bangkok and enquired in yet another message whether the amnesty proclaimed the previous September applied to political exiles like himself who would have been arrested if they had returned during the Pibul era.[97] Once more, both Puey and Pridi replied reassuringly and to prove the point a decree was issued in early May specifically extending the amnesty to Thai political exiles living abroad.[98] Ostensibly the first to benefit were the dead. The ashes of Phya Song, who had died in Indo-China in 1944, were repatriated with honour. Likewise, Prince Boripat's exile in Java since 1932 ended when his remains were brought back to rest in Bangkok in preparation for a royal cremation ceremony.[99]

Meanwhile, Jacques and Tan Chin slipped clandestinely into Bangkok at the end of April. To impress them and avoid Japanese surveillance one evening of their brief sojourn in Thailand was arranged as a launch party cruising up and down the Chao Phya. Those present included Pridi, Direk, Thawee, Adul, Supha and Sinad: in other words, all the main Seri Thai leaders except Admiral Sangworn, who as usual was away at Sattahip. During the cruise Pridi explained to Jacques how the Seri Thai operated with the tacit connivance of Khuang, who was kept deliberately in ignorance of resistance activities so that he could parry any Japanese protests in good faith.

For his part, Jacques outlined the objectives of Force 136, and claimed that it was not competing with OSS or hostile towards Siam.[100] In this context there was one particular incident which needed sorting out. Pridi had expressed fears to the Americans about the aims of a Force 136 group parachuted into the Shan states. OSS seized on the issue to claim that the British were trying to sneak into Thailand via the back door without official permission from either Washington or Bangkok. Jacques told Pridi that this was not true; all the British wanted to do was cut off every route by which the Japanese could retreat from Burma. Jacques also suggested to Sinad that the Thai army should withdraw from the Shan States to avoid clashes with the advancing Allied forces.[101]

In any case, Pridi had already told the British that Thailand intended to return the Shan States as well as the four northern Malay states as soon as possible.[102]

Sinad was more interested in pressing for arms, especially now that it looked as if the war in Europe was drawing to a close and the Allies could divert all their military resources to East Asia. Furthermore, Sinad wanted all British military aid to go to the Thai armed forces. As a professional and hitherto apolitical general, he made it clear that the army deeply resented having its needs neglected while Allied arms were supplied to Seri Thai guerillas of whom, according to Pridi, there were now about 100,000 under training.

Here Jacques discerned the makings of future conflict. Likewise he realised that the Thai military, schooled as it was in the doctrine of conventional warfare carried out by career officers, could not comprehend why it was denied direct contact with its British and American counterparts in SEAC, and had to deal with such apparently unorthodox bodies as Force 136 and OSS which were staffed by amateur soldiers.[103] However, Jacques had been warned in both London and Kandy not to discuss politics or commit Britain to anything during his visit to Bangkok.[104] The whole question of British policy towards Siam and the possibility of granting military aid to it had now become the responsibility of a special committee set up by the cabinet in London to consider Far Eastern affairs.[105]

Nonetheless, in reporting back to Kandy, Jacques agreed to take with him a Thai army officer designated by Sinad to carry out military liaison with SEAC. Somewhat ironically, the officer chosen was Colonel Netr Khemayothin, whom Pibul had sent a year earlier to liaise with the Chinese in Yunnan. Netr left on the same flying-boat as Jacques and Tan Chin. Also accompanying them was Puey; after all his exploits, including a year spent in a Bangkok prison, Force 136 thought that he deserved a holiday. But Pridi asked Puey when he got to London to act as a Seri Thai envoy in trying to persuade the British to adopt a more flexible attitude towards Thailand.[106]

Meanwhile Jacques soon returned to Bangkok as permanent liaison officer with the Seri Thai. This time he was accompanied by another Force 136 officer who had previously worked as a banker in Bangkok. Although Tan Chin had apparently received a friendly welcome from Pridi and Adul on their first encounter, the British decided it would be wiser to assign him to help train a Seri Thai guerilla group in Tak province.[107] Anyway, Jacques caused problems enough: to prove that he was a soldier not a spy, he insisted on wearing British military uniform throughout his stay in Bangkok. Hence he had to be kept well concealed. The hideout selected for him by the Seri Thai leadership was part of the University of Moral and Political Sciences next to the site where several hundred Western civilians caught in Thailand in December 1941 were still being detained in Thai custody. For Jacques the location was particularly poignant; many of the internees were personal friends whose voices he recognised. Yet he did not dare to reveal his presence even to them. Apart from the security risk, it might have raised their hopes of escape, which was impossible given the numbers involved.[108]

After their experience in getting the Flying Tiger pilot out together with Wester, the Americans too were becoming more cautious. The OSS mission was eventually rehoused at Suan Kularb, previously used by Pibul as government house. The Thais told the Japanese that the former palace was now occupied by the secret police – this served as a cover story for the large volume of radio traffic emanating from the building. The precaution was necessary because the Japanese had started using mobile equipment in Bangkok to detect clandestine radio transmissions. Another security measure at Suan Kularb was Pridi's selection of a deaf-and-dumb servant to look after the OSS mission. Even so, knowledge of the presence in Bangkok of American and British officers, some of whom were well-known local figures, soon began to percolate through the city's élite. The Thai tendency to gossip proved far stronger than the need for wartime security.[109]

In any case, after the fall of Berlin and the end of the war in Europe, most Thais believed that the Japanese would soon be defeated, an impression reinforced by the Allied capture of Rangoon in early May. With war-weariness running high in Bangkok, there were widespread hopes that Japan would now sue for peace. Yet, despite their awareness of these feelings, the Japanese had other plans. In March, at a meeting held in Bangkok, they had drawn up a strategy to continue the struggle against the Western powers in South East Asia even if Japan itself were invaded and occupied.[110] In this spirit their forces in Thailand were instructed to strengthen their positions and stand ready to fight to the death. Reinforcements were already arriving.

In January 1945, a division based in Sumatra, plus troops from Indo-China, was ordered to move to northern Thailand to protect Japanese lines of communication with Burma. But their redeployment took place more slowly than planned.[111] Thanks to a Thai officer on the special military coordinating committee set up with the Japanese, news of their moves was passed daily through Pridi to SEAC. As a result Allied bombing was playing havoc with road and rail links in Thailand, a tactical necessity not always appreciated by the local population or armed forces.[112] Furthermore, the Japanese had virtually no fighter planes left in Thailand to oppose Allied bombers.[113]

Despite such problems, Nakamura soldiered on trying to strengthen the defence of Thailand. However, his moves were ignored by Colonel Tsuji Masanobu, an influential Japanese staff officer wounded in the fighting in Burma. On arrival in Bangkok, Tsuji, whose reputation for brutality had made him notorious among both his fellow-officers and the Allies, criticised the way his compatriots were continuing to live comfortably in apparent oblivion of the hardships of war and the approaching crisis. Hence he ordered the closure of Bangkok's geisha houses and banned local dancing-girls from all Japanese military premises. But his efforts to get new defensive positions constructed made a fortune for several Thai black-marketeers supplying building materials to the Japanese.[114]

In the longer term, these measures made little difference. Following the capture of Rangoon earlier than planned, Mountbatten decided to scrap Operation Roger for the seizure of Phuket and accelerate the invasion of Malaya. That meant SEAC would have no troops available to move into Siam at least till December, when it was envisaged that airborne landings could be made in the plains around Bangkok. Force 136 was very disappointed because much effort had gone into preparing for Operation Roger – and, looking ahead, the decision to by-pass Siam might deprive the Seri Thai of the opportunity to show its mettle in cooperating with the Allies.[115] Still, Pridi could not complain since he had been kept in the dark about SEAC planning. Instead, he was informed in May that OSS intended to supply small arms to the Seri Thai, although the message was coupled with a warning to refrain from taking any precipitate action against the Japanese until the Allies indicated that they were ready to provide back-up support. While Pridi replied to OSS expressing gratitude for the promise of arms, he said that restraint might prove impossible because Japan was again threatening a military take-over of Thailand. The Americans were now more sceptical and thought that Pridi was simply stepping up pressure to obtain more weaponry following the end of the war in Europe.[116] Rather the Japanese increased their pressure on Khuang's government in mid-May by demanding an immediate loan of 100 million baht.[117]

As a former Finance Minister, Pridi was well aware that Thailand's total annual budget had never amounted to more than 100 million baht till 1939. Since then inflation had taken its toll, but even so Japan's demand was enormous and Pridi decided to make the most of it. In similarly worded messages designated "very important", the regent informed the US Secretary of State and Mountbatten that the Thai government intended to reject the Japanese loan demand and resign to make way for a new administration which would promptly declare all Pibul's alliances with Japan invalid while calling for a national uprising. Before taking such action, Pridi wanted an assurance of Allied support for the Thai people who were prepared to sacrifice everything to regain their independence.

In his message to Washington, the Regent further requested an American statement according recognition to Thailand as a member of the United Nations Organisation, which was at that moment convening in San Francisco to draw up a charter. No Thai representatives had been invited to attend because only those countries which had fought actively against the Axis were considered eligible for UN membership. That too had a bearing on Pridi's message. As a dedicated internationalist, he wanted to establish Thailand's right to join the new world body by fighting the Japanese before they were defeated.

However, Pridi's messages were seen in another light in Washington, London and Kandy where it was considered suicidal for the Thais to attempt an uprising against the Japanese. Besides, it would disrupt Allied plans since they would feel morally obliged to come to Thailand's aid with troops and arms needed elsewhere. Indeed, while the Thais might think that the defeat of Germany would result in the redeployment of Allied resources to South East Asia, virtually the opposite was true. Germany had to be occupied and its armed forces disbanded. In Britain there were demands for demobilisation of the forces after more than five weary years of war. As for the Americans, they were concentrating all their efforts for a final onslaught on Japan itself. For once, therefore, the Western Allies were unanimous. Both the US Secretary of State and Mountbatten replied to Pridi expressing sympathy for Thailand's desire to cooperate with the Allies but advising him not to take any action against the Japanese. On the contrary, Pridi was asked to do everything possible to avoid a premature uprising and to continue stringing the Japanese along. Mountbatten also advised the Seri Thai to refrain from acts of sabotage since they might provoke Japanese retribution.[118]

Disappointed as Pridi was by these replies, he did heed them. Instead of rejecting the Japanese loan demand, Khuang bargained and managed to get it reduced by half. Pridi promised too that he would try to restrain his forces, although it might prove difficult.[119] By then the Japanese were so unpopular that some Thais simply took action against them on their own initiative. For instance, in March a Seri Thai unit based near Tak attacked a Japanese detachment killing fourteen men, an incident which infuriated Nakamura.[120] Likewise, meat deliberately poisoned by Thai traders caused the decimation of a Japanese battalion near Nakorn Nayok.[121]

This small town north-east of Bangkok, with easy access to Cambodia, was where the Japanese, using prisoner-of-war labour, planned to build a redoubt for a last stand in the event of an Allied invasion or a local uprising. Both these possibilities weighed heavily on Nakamura. In early June he ordered all Japanese troops in and around Bangkok to fortify their barracks, stockpile provisions and ammunition, and build defensive positions around strategic targets. For example, at Don Muang casemates were built near the runway and an additional artillery battery was installed. When all these reinforcements were completed, various Thai officers were invited to inspect them. The Japanese thought they were impressed and intimidated. The opposite was true: the Thais took note of the Japanese fortifications to plan how best to attack them.[122]

The growing possibility of open conflict in Thailand acted as a spur to OSS. For Donovan it was also a matter of prestige. Now the war in Europe was over, he had to justify the continuing existence of his organisation and Thailand was one of the few places where his men were allowed to participate in the struggle against Japan. Hence, as soon as OSS was authorised to supply weapons to the Seri Thai, Donovan drew up elaborate plans to drop arms and training teams to provide instruction in their use.[123] The problem was still lack of transport. By June OSS had only been able to parachute five tons of supplies and one training team into Thailand. By comparison Force 136 had thirteen clandestine transmitters operating in various parts of the country but had supplied few weapons.[124]

At that juncture a US Air Force general came to the rescue of OSS. The planes under his command had completed their mission in Burma and were about to be transferred to China. While the move was underway, the general offered OSS the use of two squadrons for a month to drop supplies into Thailand. The idea appealed so much to Donovan's American pride that he feared Mountbatten would veto it.[125] On the contrary, it was agreed at a special SEAC meeting: the Americans would deliver 200 tons of supplies plus three OSS guerilla training teams at a rate of 8–10 tons a night as long as adequate diversionary cover could be provided.

The biggest problem seemed to be on the ground. Doubts were expressed about whether the Seri Thai could organise reception for all the supplies to be dropped in and manage to conceal them before the Japanese realised what was happening. Therefore it was proposed that Pridi should personally give clearance for each sortie in advance. Naturally he was delighted at the prospect of such a massive influx of supplies and asked only that the drops be made at night to avoid Japanese detection. At first his request seemed impossible to meet because of the difficulties involved in timing long and hazardous flights from India. Then the problem was suddenly resolved when the airfield at Rangoon was put back into service much more quickly than expected.[126]

Yet the Thais needed medical supplies more than weapons. With the breakdown of public utilities in Bangkok, the incidence of smallpox and cholera was reaching epidemic proportions.[127] Hence to boost Thai morale and discountenance the Japanese, a daring project was conceived to drop fifty parachute-loads of medicine in broad daylight on June 18 into the heart of Bangkok at Sanam Luang, the large open space in front of the royal palace compound, usually known to *farangs* as the Phramane Ground. The cover was a military parade arranged by the Seri Thai leadership at Sanam Luang, with police waiting hidden around the area to take possession of the parachutes and their precious loads before the Japanese, who were mostly garrisoned on the other side of the city, could arrive on the scene.

As it turned out, everything went according to plan until the plane making the drop circled to make sure that the parachutes had landed on target. Suddenly it was fired upon by the Thai navy moored in the river nearby. Since the loyalty of some naval officers was still suspect, they had not been given advance warning of the operation. The crew of the Allied plane, reacting automatically, returned fire and in the heat of the moment sprayed the nearby university area where Jacques and the *farang* internees received a nasty shock but fortunately escaped injury.

Meanwhile the Japanese, arriving late on the scene, managed to capture one parachute and its load. They found each batch of medicine contained a warning about poison being added if it fell into Japanese hands. Nakamura was furious and demanded an urgent interview with the Thai premier. Aware of what was coming, Khuang feigned a bad headache. The general responded by sending him some of the medicine supplied by the Americans, complete with the poison warning![128]

That, at least, was the story told to the Americans. In reality, the Japanese appreciated that Khuang had a difficult role to play: he was still trying to be cooperative despite growing public disillusion with his administration and political infighting between the pro-Pridi and pro-Pibul factions, especially over the issue of Japan's financial demands and their effect on the Thai economy. In June, for the first time ever, the matter was openly raised in the Assembly.[129] But again Khuang used his wit to cope with an awkward situation. In reply to calls for an end to the privations caused by the war, he compared Thailand's position to a house in the midst of a forest fire where nothing can be done until the blaze is put out. Pridi, too, in his speech as Regent opening the new Assembly session on June 24, warned of the war reaching a climax in which Thailand might become a battlefield. If that happened, the Regent stated all Thais had a duty to rise up and re-establish the independence of their country. When the Allies saw reports of this speech, they thought Pridi was being too outspoken and asked him to be more cautious, particularly since the massive airlift of American supplies had started on June 20.[130]

During the first week of nightly drops, everything seemed to go smoothly and the Americans managed to parachute in 74 tons of supplies to sites designated by Pridi in various provinces. However, some of the weapons were subsequently smuggled into Bangkok to be hidden at the University of Moral and Political Sciences and the homes of the Seri Thai leadership for use if the Japanese attempted to seize control of the city.[131] With that in mind, Pridi warned his colleagues to be more vigilant than ever, reminding them in particular that before staging their coup in Indo-China the Japanese had organised various parties for the French. Hence the Seri Thai leaders were wary of accepting Japanese hospitality and always briefed their deputies on what to do in an emergency.

These precautions were timely. On the evening of June 28, the Japanese held several parties, to one of which Pridi was invited. He decided to attend, accompanied by a large bodyguard. The dinner passed off without incident, although the Japanese were well aware that the Allies were parachuting in large quantities of arms. Hence they expected a Thai uprising at any moment and on June 30 the Japanese ambassador officially warned Prince Wan that stern counter-measures would be taken. Immediately news of this interview was flashed to Kandy with a request from Pridi for the Americans to stop their supply drops without suspending all aerial activity, because that would simply add to Japanese suspicions. His wishes were complied with, even though SEAC did not initially understand why there was so much panic in Bangkok. Then Jacques reported that Khuang had received yet another Japanese loan demand, this time for the massive sum of 1,000 million baht. Again he was involved in bargaining.[132]

With the Japanese determined to maintain their influence in South East Asia despite the outcome of the war, they were open to all sorts of deals. Khuang, too, had interests, which might be jeopardised by an Allied victory. Through his family connexions with Battambang, he had benefited greatly from Thailand's acquisition of the province and its fertile ricelands. He showed his concern by arranging for elections to be held in Battambang and the other provinces acquired from Indo-China so that they could be represented in the Assembly in Bangkok on a par with the rest of Thailand, a constitutional nicety which Pibul had ignored. At the same time, the Japanese decided to evacuate their women and children resident in Bangkok to Battambang where they could count on the protection of Khuang's family network.[133] Further, to shore up Khuang's internal position, the Greater East Asia Ministry in Tokyo agreed for the first time since December 1941 to transfer to Bangkok some of the gold earmarked to cover Japanese borrowings from Thailand.[134]

Even so, Khuang could not afford to be too jubilant. Like Pridi and the rest of the Seri Thai leadership, he noticed that he was increasingly subject to surveillance by the *Kempei* and protested to the Japanese ambassador, threatening to resign if he was no longer trusted.[135] In view of the agreement Khuang had just concluded to lend Japan a further 700 million baht, his resignation was the last thing the ambassador wanted. As a result the Japanese visibly reduced their pressure and Pridi felt confident enough on July 7 to send a message to Kandy indicating that arms drops could be resumed to a few selected zones provided that adequate forewarning was given.[136]

Four days later one of the continuing bombing raids hit Bangkok with force. The target was the main railway station, but some bombs fell in the densely-populated surrounding district where more than 100 people were killed, partly because the houses there were wooden and fires quickly spread. Immediately the OSS team in Bangkok protested about the raid and pointed out that Allied bombers were supposed to attack only strategic targets. This led to an official SEAC enquiry on the conduct of the raid, although the Americans in Bangkok later admitted that their alarm had initially been prompted by being on the receiving end of bombing to which no counter-measures were taken.[137] The Japanese were worried too. Colonel Tsuji set off to find Khuang whose home was close to the railway station. There he was amazed to find the Thai premier, informally clad with sparks flying around him, calmly contributing to the relief operations with no ostensible concern for his own safety or status.[138] Nakamura was more concerned with what was going on up-country. In mid-July he referred openly to guerrillas active near Sakol Nakorn as the personal army of Tiang Sirikhan, which was not far from the mark.

Pridi had warned Force 136 and OSS that they could not expect any officers they sent to the Sakol Nakorn area to control operations because all the Seri Thai there owed their primary allegiance to Tiang. His well-known autonomy was even regarded as a bonus by Pridi. He told SEAC that if the Japanese protested about the base area at Sakol Nakorn or attacked it, the Seri Thai leadership would treat it as an isolated case for which it bore no responsibility. Nonetheless Pridi warned Tiang to take care, especially after Nakamura remarked that the Lord Buddha would keep him informed of what was going on, even if the Thai authorities did not.[139]

This comment was construed as a reference to Japanese aerial surveillance aimed at detecting clandestine airstrips being constructed up-country. When the Japanese protested about them, Pridi pointed to pre-war legislation requiring all provincial governors to establish local landing sites for use in case of emergency. But Khuang dismissed the idea with the claim that fields up-country were simply being cleared to plant peppers. In reality these remote airstrips were being used ever more frequently by the Allies to land weapons and personnel now the situation in Burma shortened supply flights and facilitated the use of smaller planes.[140]

Among the people arriving on such flights were some of the Thais sent to India for guerrilla training. Their safe return was a relief to the Seri Thai leadership. Although Adul and Supha, for instance, were aware that their sons had gone to India, other families were worried at the unexplained disappearance of their children. In these circumstances, those returning from India, including Colonel Netr who had gone there for liaison purposes, found it difficult to conceal where they had been and it was becoming an open secret in Bangkok that many Thais were visiting Kandy.[141]

This aroused concern within Force 136 and OSS about the security of their own officers sent into Thailand. Secrecy was so strictly observed

among them that British and Americans working up-country often had no knowledge of each other's presence and were surprised when they happened to meet. Sometimes, too, it simply heightened rivalry between Force 136 and OSS.[142] The Americans were still suspicious of Britain's ultimate intentions in Thailand, whereas they viewed their own role in a much more benign light. One story recounted by many Americans with great glee was about an OSS officer parachuted into a remote up-country district who delighted his reception committee by stating in rudimentary Thai: "American officers hate Japs, love Thai people. Otherwise no good. All the time drink whisky, shoot crap, fornicate and masturbate."[143]

Previously most *farangs* with whom the Thais had come into contact sought to project a very different image. Indeed the easy going American attitude was not always completely welcome. Preoccupied as he was by the day-to-day course of the war, Pridi still found time to express concern about the longer-term effects of the Americans on those Thais trained by them: for instance, he had to remind some of the original Seri Thai students recruited in the United States and subsequently employed on liaison work in Bangkok that it was still the Thai custom to show deference to one's elders and not slap them on the back American-style. Likewise he wondered how all the Thais trained in clandestine warfare would adjust to the post-war world.[144]

Pridi expressed these views to Nicol Smith, the OSS officer who had been mainly responsible for Seri Thai infiltration from Szemao. He made a brief visit to Bangkok in July, partly to impress on the Seri Thai leadership the need to abstain from precipitate action against the Japanese. Instead he was treated to a display of how many risks the Thais were prepared to take. On being landed in an Allied Dakota at Pukio airstrip near Pibul's abandoned Petchaboon project, Nicol Smith was picked up by a Thai air force plane: it was piloted by Thawee Chullasap, who had spent a brief spell as Seri Thai liaison officer with the Americans at SEAC. Thawee revelled in his clandestine activities and flew the OSS mission straight off to Don Muang where there was still a large Japanese military presence. When Nicol Smith expressed apprehension, Thawee brushed it aside by claiming that the Japanese would never dream that a Westerner might dare to breach their security so flagrantly.[145]

Even so, Nicol Smith only narrowly escaped Japanese detection at Don Muang and had a similar experience on an excursion by car to Sattahip to meet Admiral Sangworn. On both occasions the Seri Thai said that if ever the Japanese caught them with a *farang*, they had a ready alibi: they would simply explain that the Westerner was an infiltrator who had just been captured and was en route to detention in Thai custody. Nicol Smith was not completely reassured. He knew that in theory the Thais and Japanese had an agreement which allowed each of them to retain custody of any enemy personnel they captured.[146] Yet during his travels in Thailand, he happened to see some Australian prisoners being forced to work naked in the tropical sun by their Japanese guards. It was a pitiable sight, made worse by the impotence of the Thais to intervene and help them. Furthermore, in addition to the British, Dutch and Australian prisoners-of-war carrying out forced labour in Thailand, OSS had just learned that there were also some US sailors long believed killed in a naval battle in the Java Sea. Their discovery made OSS all the more anxious to press ahead with the liberation of Thailand.[147]

In pursuing their objective, OSS officers sent to Bangkok were impressed by Pridi's statesmanlike attitude. It was also apparent that he and the rest of the Seri Thai leadership were beginning to feel the strain of having to dissimulate with the Japanese all the time. The pressure grew throughout July as the Japanese strengthened their security measures.[148] Hence the Seri Thai leadership regretted all the more that in May the Allies had vetoed the idea of staging an uprising. Pridi still believed it would have been successful, whereas now it would be much more difficult for the Seri Thai to prove their loyalty by staging a full-scale attack on the Japanese.[149]

Another factor weighing heavily on Pridi was the declaration, issued on July 26 by the United States, China and Britain, vowing to deal a final blow to Japan unless it surrendered unconditionally. For Pridi the question was what fate awaited Thailand since it was still nominally allied to Japan. In particular, he was worried by the attitude of Britain, which had still given no public indication of its future policy towards Thailand. Here Pridi placed his faith in the British Labour Party, which had just inflicted a stunning electoral defeat on Churchill's Conservative Party with the help of a political manifesto including a pledge to end all forms of colonial domination.[150]

The Chinese too were now a source of anxiety to Pridi. Tai Li was reputed to have Thawil Udol and possibly other prominent Thais under his influence, as well as a force of about 1,500 Sino-Thais under training in Yunnan ready to infiltrate back into Thailand.[151] A Chinese army was also thought to have been invited to move into Laos via northern Thailand to take over the country in preference to either the Japanese or the

French.[152] Most worrying of all were the activities of the 93rd Chinese Army Division. Disregarding the unofficial ceasefire along the border, its forces were quietly moving into the Shan states to exploit the vacuum between the British and Thai armies. Pridi's concern that the Chinese might press on into northern Thailand was shared by the British and Americans, who both raised the matter in Chungking. In reply Chiang Kai-shek asserted that Thailand still came within his theatre of operations but that his troops had orders to attack only the Japanese and not the Thais. It was scant reassurance. Both the Western powers knew that the 93rd Division tended to be a law unto itself and subject only to the command of the local warlord in Yunnan.[153]

To add to Pridi's problems at the end of July, the Japanese suddenly announced that they had repulsed a British attempt to land troops at Phuket and sunk an aircraft-carrier in the process. In his dismay at the news, Pridi asked why he had not been forewarned of the British landings so the Seri Thai could provide assistance. Sinad too enquired what the armed forces could do to help. Force 136 was baffled, given the cancellation of Operation Roger. Still, while trying to find out what was happening off Phuket, Jacques asked both Pridi and Sinad to ensure that the reported landing attempt did not spark off any Thai action against the Japanese. It then transpired that the British navy preparing for the invasion of Malaya was carrying out a mine-sweeping operation in the Andaman Sea when it was unexpectedly attacked off Phuket. As usual, the Japanese exaggerated the size and nature of the engagement, although for the first (and last) time, *kamikaze* pilots were deployed west of the Straits of Malacca, causing the loss of a British minesweeper.

In conveying the information to Pridi, Force 136 suggested that he became more sceptical in future about Japanese reports.[154] Still, he was nervous two days later when, unusually, the Japanese ambassador requested a personal interview with him. Normally Japanese diplomats dealt only with Khuang or Prince Wan. The ambassador's purpose was to deliver a stern warning to the Regent himself about Thai connivance in the landing of Allied planes.[155]

In response to previous such protests, the Seri Thai had agreed that the Japanese could inspect the landing-strip at Pukio because it was simply a field and so remote that the Thai officer in charge had fobbed off the investigators with a hard-luck story of attacks by wild animals and the lack of locally available drinking water and food.[156] The clandestine airstrips constructed by Tiang's men in the north-east were a different matter. They were heavily defended in an area where well-trained and armed guerrillas were prepared to repel any intruders. Already there were indications of the Japanese massing troops for an attack, and the ambassador's protest to the regent was interpreted as a warning that unless the Thais became more amenable, fighting was bound to occur around Sakol Nakorn. Immediately Pridi ordered Tiang to lie low and not precipitate a Japanese attack.[157]

Still it seemed as if a major clash was inevitable and the Seri Thai could no longer be restrained from staging a nationwide uprising. Nicol Smith was hurried out of the country. All other Allied agents operating clandestinely in Thailand were instructed to take the utmost precautions for their own safety. Then on August 6 came news of an atomic bomb being dropped on Hiroshima.[158]

NOTES

1. *Magic*, Sep. 6 and Domei report of Aug. 27, 1944.
2. CSM, Aug. 12, 1944.
3. 892.01/8–744 and 892.01/8–2244 in RG59.
4. F3857/23/40 in FO 371/41845.
5. F3836/23/40 and file in ibid.
6. F4408/23/40 in ibid., and Gilchrist, p. 63.
7. Memo of Feb. 22, 1944, in 892.01/50 in RG59.
8. R.H. Smith, pp. 304ff, and Cruikshank, p. 88.
9. 892.01/9–1344 in RG59.
10. Nicol Smith, pp. 168ff; Bangkok Radio, Aug. 4, 1944; Adul in Suphote Dantrakul, p. 209.
11. Gilchrist, pp. 65ff, and Sanguan on Deng in 892.01/8–2144 in RG59.
12. Gilchrist, pp. 69ff.
13. F3941/23/40 in FO 371/41845 and Thorne, pp. 462ff.
14. FRUS (1944), V, pp. 1314ff.
15. Gilchrist, p. 87. The Foreign Office recalled that SOE action in Yugoslavia led to recognition of Tito and his communist partisans as against a rival royalist faction.
16. Text in WO 203/5186 (13).
17. Landing organised by Charn Bunnag, an official formerly responsible for cinemas and summarily dismissed by Pibul. Charn had shouted at him to stop driving through floods so fast and inconveniencing everybody nearby. Adul in Suphote Dantrakul, pp. 169ff, and Nai Chantana, pp. 261ff. Cover and protection for Operation Brillig was also provided by Pridi's naval friends and the customs service. Sangworn Suwannachip, p. 130.
18. Gilchrist, p. 81, and Kris Toshayananda, a participant in Brillig mission, in ibid., pp. 215ff.
19. F5720/23/40 and file in FO 371/41845; F269/54/40 in FO 371/46542; Gilchrist, pp. 85ff; Puey Ungpakorn in Suphote Dantrakul, p. 47. The idea that Seni and King Prajadhipok's relatives were primarily interested in restoring the

absolute monarchy is still used to discredit the Seri Thai. Ananta Pibulsongkram, III, p. 564.

20. Bangkok Radio, Aug. 25, Sep. 3, 6 and 9, Oct. 25, Nov. 11 and Dec. 14, 1944; Pin Chunhawan in Thak Chaloemtiarana (ed.), p. 570.
21. Netr Khemayothin, II, p. 44.
22. Bangkok Radio, Sep. 21 and 22, 1944. Text of amnesty in Prasert Patamasukhon, p. 443.
23. Pridi in Pramote Pungsunthorn, p. 71.
24. Bangkok Radio, Oct. 7, 1944; Batson (JSS 1974), p. 117; text in Prasert Patamasukhon, pp. 443ff.
25. 892.01/9–1344 in RG59.
26. Gilchrist, pp. 189ff.
27. Nicol Smith, p. 198; Nai Chantana, p. 259; Adul in Suphote Dantrakul, p. 214.
28. Adul claims he aided Songkiap and Songkim Sriboonruang, sons of Seow Hood Seng and brothers-in-law to Vilas, to escape to China after Japan's invasion of Thailand and that they subsequently sent various messages to him through infiltrators. Adul in Suphote Dantrakul, pp. 185 and 209ff.
29. Nicol Smith, pp. 181ff; 892.01/2–2245 and 892.01/3–1945 in RG59, although they differ slightly.
30. Nicol Smith, pp. 193ff.
31. 892.01/8–544 and 892.01/10–1844, and file in RG59, F2937/738/40 in FO 371/46561.
32. Adul in Suphote Dantrakul, p. 211, claiming that he arranged Karoon's return to Yunnan through a Chinese network he was exploiting to obtain intelligence.
33. This was Gen. Hsing Sen-Chou, Kuomintang Commissioner for Overseas Chinese Affairs in Thailand and Indo-China. XL14550 in RG226 (undated memo by a Thai who travelled to Yunnan with Thawil) and 892.01/2–845 in RG59.
34. XL14550 in RG226.
35. F5244/23/40 in FO 371/41845.
36. 892.01/10–1844 and file in RG59 and FRUS (1944), V, p. 1320.
37. 892.01/7–2744 and file in RG59.
38. 892.01/6–1244 in ibid. and F3881/23/40 in FO 371/41845.
39. Allen (1976), p. 39, and AL5199, pp. 19ff.
40. F6038/23/40 in FO 371/41845 and *Magic*, Dec. 5, 1944, and Jan. 3, 1945.
41. Assembly committee headed by Liang Chaiyakal. Bangkok Radio, Nov. 28, Dec. 7 and 8, 1944, and Prasert Patamasukhon, p. 450.
42. Bangkok Radio, Sep. 30, Oct. 12, 19 and 30, Dec. 13, 1944.
43. ibid., Dec. 7, 1944; Batson (JSS 1974), p. 119; *Magic*, Dec. 1 and 20, 1944.
44. Bangkok Radio, Dec. 7, 1944, and Sangworn Suwannachip, p. 131.
45. Aerial surveillance reports in WO 172/1745–1748.
46. Cruikshank, p. 33, and Gilchrist, p. 89.
47. ibid., pp. 51 and 95. Sangworn Suwannachip, p. 132, claims that Adul wanted to ensure that no arms went to people he could not control.
48. Gilchrist, p. 111, and account of Kris Toshayananda, ibid., pp. 217ff, and Nai Chantana, pp. 283ff.
49. Oune Sananikone, pp. 113ff, and Caply, *Guérilla au Laos*, pp. 222ff.
50. Gilchrist, p. 115, and Adul in Suphote Dantrakul, p. 228.
51. FRUS, 1944, V, p. 1314, and F4969/23/40 in FO 371/41845.

52. Mani named Evelyn Van Milligen, pre-war manager of the Bangkok branch of Bombay-Burmah Co. 892.00/1–1045. During the war Van Milligen worked in Delhi for ISLD, as MI6 was designated in the Far East.
53. FRUS, 1945, VI, p. 1242.
54. Nicol Smith, p. 201.
55. ibid., p. 199; Nai Chantana, p. 299; Gilchrist, p. 108; 892.01/2–2245 in RG59.
56. Thorne, p. 615, and R.H. Smith, p. 307.
57. Donovan submission to JCS, Feb. 24, 1945, in CCS 381 Thailand in RG218.
58. Konthi adopted the alias 'Suni Theparakse' to travel to Washington, and is so named in all reports. Konthi Suphamongkol, pp. 143ff, and NYHT, July 17, 1946.
59. 892.01/1–2445 in RG59.
60. FRUS 1945, VI, p. 1246.
61. Nicol Smith, pp. 198ff.
62. F738/738/40 in FO 371/46560.
63. Bangkok Radio, Jan. 9, 30 and 31 and Feb. 1, 1945; Prasert Patamasukhon, p. 417; *Magic*, Jan. 3 and 9, 1945.
64. F6038/23/40 in FO 371/41845.
65. A leading naval promoter, Luang Sangworn Yutthakit (as he was then known), spent 1936–8 in Japan liaising on the construction of gunboats and submarines for Siam. On his return he found many friends among the Japanese community in Bangkok, and according to his account they later helped him model his special security police on the *Kempei*. But after quarrelling with Pibul in 1943, he later linked up with the Seri Thai. Sangworn Suwannachip, pp. 130ff.
66. Nicol Smith, p. 200, and F1449/738/40 in FO 371/46560.
67. Gilchrist, p. 106, and F925/738/40 and file in FO 371/46560.
68. FO 371/35989 and Skinner, pp. 273ff.
69. AL 435, p. 20, and Joan and Clay Blair, *Return from the River Kwai*, describing background.
70. F1084/738/40 in FO 371/46560, WO 203/4340 (9a) and Gilchrist, pp. 97ff.
71. Direk, pp. 99 and 103.
72. Allen (1976), pp. 38ff, and AL 5199, pp. 18ff.
73. F1293/738/40 and file in FO 371/46560; WO 203/5186 (40 and 41); Cruikshank, p. 112.
74. This was Luang Chart Nakrop.
75. F1229/738/40 and file in FO 371/46560; Gilchrist, pp. 125ff; Direk, pp. 103ff; Ziegler, p. 329.
76. Domei report on Bangkok Radio, Mar. 10, 1945; Nakamura's testimony in Allen (1976), pp. 44ff, and F1610/738/40 in FO 371/46560.
77. 121834 in RG226 and *Magic*, Mar. 26, 1945.
78. F1229/738/40 in FO 371/46560.
79. AL 5199, p. 22, and Allen (1976), p. 40.
80. Bangkok Radio, Feb. 14, passim, 1945.
81. XL11154 in RG226.
82. *Magic*, Apr. 11, 1945, and cable of Mar. 29, 1945 in 711, Box 1 (Bangkok) RG84.
83. WO 203/4340 (42a) and Thawee Bunyaket in Netr Khemayothin, I, p. 19.
84. FRUS, 1945, VI, pp. 1246ff, and F1709/738/40 in FO 371/46560.

85. JPS 637/D of Mar. 26, 1945 and file in CCS 381 Thailand (Case 113/4) in RG218; FRUS, 1945, VI, p. 1260.
86. Nai Chantana, pp. 286ff.
87. Details in WO 203/5846 (2a) and WO 172/1786 report of Oct. 4, 1945.
88. Gilchrist, pp. 131ff.
89. 892.00/2–2245 in RG59 and account of Seri Thai finances in Direk, p. 355.
90. Magic of Apr. 24 and 30, 1945.
91. Nicol Smith, pp. 225ff; Nai Chantana, pp. 301ff; Thawee Bunyaket in Ray, p. 105.
92. Thawee Chullasap, pp. 70ff, and Adul in Suphote Dantrakul, p. 223.
93. Kirby, V, pp. 4ff, and Gilchrist, p. 151.
94. WO 203/4081 (74a), WO 203/4413 (6) and F2120/738/40 in FO 371/46560.
95. Gilchrist, pp. 104ff, and F925/738/40 in FO 371/46560.
96. Supra, p. 73.
97. Gilchrist, p. 129, and Puey in Pramote Pungsunthorn, pp. 33ff.
98. Prasert Patamasukhon, p. 459, and Bangkok Radio, May 10, 1945.
99. Batson (JSS 1974), p. 117.
100. F3490/738/40 in FO 371/46562, and Netr Khemayothin, II, pp. 109ff.
101. 892.01/4–245 in RG59 and F2332/738/40 in FO 371/46561.
102. Direk at Kandy, F1229/738/40 in FO 371/46560.
103. F3490/738/40 in FO 371/46562.
104. FO 371/46544 and 46545.
105. Puey in Direk, p. 141. After the Labour election victory, he tried to influence the new government through Professor Harold Laski of the London School of Economics.
106. Gilchrist, p. 130; Nai Chantana, p. 345; Tan Chin's account in F4973/4/40 in FO 371/54359.
108. Gilchrist, p. 178 and Nicol Smith, p. 291.
109. ibid., pp. 230ff; Nai Chantana, pp. 303ff; Thawee Bunyaket in Ray, p. 104; Jacques report in WO 203/4472 (117a) and Sangworn Suwannachip, p. 133.
110. *Magic*, Mar. 29 and May 16, 1945.
111. AL 5199, pp. 21ff, and Kirby, V, p. 292.
112. Nicol Smith, p. 242.
113. L57583 in RG226.
114. Allen (1976), pp. 39ff, and Tsuji's reputation in Bergamini, pp. 1406ff.
115. Kirby, V, pp. 4ff, and Gilchrist, pp. 174ff.
116. JCS 1304/2 in CCS 381 (Thailand) in RG218 and FRUS, 1945, VI, p. 1264.
117. Demand of May 15 in 892.515/3–2348 in RG59, documenting Thailand's financial transactions with Japan.
118. FRUS, 1945, VI, pp. 1269ff, F3161/738/40 in FO 371/46562 and WO 203/5168 (87).
119. ibid. and Nicol Smith, p. 231.
120. XL11155 in RG226.
121. F3490/738/40 in FO 371/46562.
122. AL5199, p. 26; Allen (1976), pp. 26ff; and Thawee Bunyaket in Direk, p. 120.
123. OPD 381 TS (Case 113/4) in RG165.
124. WO 203/5846 (2a and 3a).
125. ibid. and OPD 336 TS (FW122) in RG165.

126. WO 203/4472 (26ff).
127. Bangkok Radio, June 1 and 23, 1945.
128. Nicol Smith, p. 247; Thawee Bunyaket in Ray, pp. 102ff; Thawee Chullasap, pp. 188ff; and Khuang, loc. cit., p. 79.
129. *Magic*, May 29; June 1 and 9, 1945.
130. Bangkok Radio, June 25 and 26, 1945; Prasert Patamasukhon, pp. 461; and Pridi in Thak Chaloemtiarana (ed.), p. 392.
131. Thawee Chullasap, p. 176.
132. Nicol Smith, p. 228; F3942/738/40 in FO 371/46562; WO 203/4472 (65a).
133. Prasert Patamasukhon, p. 463, and *Magic*, June 19, and July 20, 1945.
134. 892.515/3-2348 with note of July 7, 1945, from Greater East Asia Ministry in Tokyo agreeing to repatriate the gold.
135. Allen (1976), pp. 46ff.
136. WO 203/4340 (73a).
137. WO 203/4472 (74a); WO 203/1876 (11); Nicol Smith, pp. 279ff (he misdates the raid).
138. Allen (1976), pp. 48ff.
139. WO 203/4472 (82a).
140. ibid. (87ff); Nai Chantana, p. 386; Oune Sananikone, p. 143; Allen (1976), p. 43; Khuang, loc. cit., p. 80, and Pridi in Pramote Pungsunthorn, p. 91.
141. Nicol Smith, p. 234; Adul in Suphote Dantrakul, p. 224; Netr Khemayothin.
142. ibid., p. 120, and Gilchrist, p. 120.
143. R.H. Smith, p. 310.
144. Nicol Smith, p. 291.
145. Thawee Chullasap, pp. 160ff, and Nicol Smith, pp. 214ff.
146. ibid., p. 223, and Thawee Bunyaket in Ray, p. 102.
147. Nicol Smith, pp. 220 and 249.
148. ibid., p. 298.
149. ibid., p. 232, and WO 203/4472 (117a).
150. F5021/738/40 in FO 371/46562 and Puey in Direk, p. 141.
151. L54685 in RG226 and 892.01/3-645 in RG59.
152. 892.002/3-2445 in RG59.
153. WO 203/4340 (61a); WO 203/4413 (25); F5120/738/40 in FO 371/46563; FRUS, 1945, China, VII, pp. 122 and 134; 892.01/3-2345 in RG59.
154. WO 203/4472 (103ff); Nicol Smith, p. 253; Kirby, V, p. 59.
155. Nicol Smith, p. 298.
156. ibid., p. 297; WO 203/4472 (110a); Thawee Chullasap, p. 178.
157. WO 203/4413(36); AL5199, pp. 24ff; *Magic* Aug. 8, 1945.
158. Nicol Smith, pp. 299ff.

14

THE PROBLEMS OF PEACE

The secrecy surrounding the development of the atomic bomb was such that even Mountbatten was not told of its existence and possible use against Japan till July when he went to the Potsdam Conference. There the three major powers were conferring, and several decisions had already been taken affecting the planning of future operations in South East Asia. To free the hands of General Macarthur, Supreme Commander in the Pacific, for an all-out drive against Japan, the theatre boundaries in East Asia were changed. In addition to its existing commitments, SEAC was assigned responsibility for the whole of the Netherlands East Indies and the South West Pacific area. At Potsdam the transfer of Thailand and southern Indo-China from the China theatre to SEAC was also agreed.

All these changes meant that Mountbatten became responsible for an immense area encompassing 1.5 million square miles and almost a million Japanese troops. His instructions were to defeat and disarm them while rescuing and repatriating everybody held captive by the Japanese. Beyond that, SEAC was expected to maintain order throughout the region, where the only country which had a functioning civilian administration was Thailand: consequently it was regarded as less problematical than anywhere else.[1]

Neither the French nor the Chinese participated in the Potsdam Conference, and both were angry when the Americans and British decided somewhat arbitrarily to split responsibility for Indo-China along the sixteenth parallel. Chiang Kai-shek protested that he would only agree to his theatre being curtailed if Thailand were partitioned as well. In other words he was demanding that Chinese troops move in and assume control of the whole of north and north-eastern Thailand down to a line extending roughly through Nakorn Sawan to Roi Et. The idea was immediately rejected by the Western Allies. Thai fears of the Chinese were by now well appreciated by the Americans as well as the British.[2]

Yet between themselves the Western powers still had policy differences over Thailand. As soon as the atomic bomb was dropped on Hiroshima, Mountbatten's political adviser pointed out that SEAC, as a joint Anglo-American command, would be in an awkward position if the war suddenly came to an end because, in contrast to the American view,

Thailand was still regarded in British eyes as an enemy country.[3] The dilemma was appreciated in London where at last it looked like being resolved. After months of discussion in a cabinet sub-committee, prolonged in part by the need for a final decision to be taken by Attlee's new government, it was agreed that Britain would not demand the formal surrender of Siam. Nor would it impose a peace treaty on Siam like other defeated enemy states. Instead it was proposed that Siam should acknowledge the error of Pibul's wartime policies and undertake to contribute towards international peace and economic rehabilitation in signing a document officially liquidating the state of war with Britain.

However, given the nature of wartime cooperation between the British dominions, they had to be consulted before the document could be put to the Siamese. Australia in particular was anxious to have a say in the matter, because opinion in certain quarters there was still bitter about what was regarded as Pibul's betrayal of the security of the entire South-West Pacific area in 1941. Apart from that, the British thought it politic to show the Americans the document they intended the Siamese to sign, although strictly speaking it was not necessary in the case of a bilateral arrangement between two sovereign states.[4]

While these consultations were underway, events on the ground moved fast. Coinciding with the dropping of the second atomic bomb on Nagasaki, the Soviet Union entered the war against Japan by attacking Manchuria. But in Thailand the Japanese still looked poised to attack the guerrilla bases near Sakol Nakorn, which aroused concern at SEAC about the Seri Thai seizing the opportunity to hit back and stage an uprising before it was too late.[5] The Japanese thought the same and held discussions in Bangkok on measures to defend themselves against a Thai attack. The outcome was an order sent to all Japanese commanders throughout Thailand on August 10 to regroup their forces in fortified positions and prepare for a siege. A bloody showdown seemed inevitable.[6]

Instead, and apparently unknown to anybody in Bangkok, the mood was even more desperate in Tokyo. There, on the evening of August 9, an imperial conference eventually and reluctantly decided to accept the Allies' ultimatum on the one condition that the sovereign prerogatives of the Emperor would not be prejudiced.[7] Before the Allies could reply, some officials in Tokyo were afraid that the military either at home or abroad might intervene to reverse Japan's decision to surrender. Hence, on August 10 Domei, the main Japanese news agency, was instructed to report the peace offer.[8] This evoked very mixed reactions in Bangkok the same evening. Colonel Tsuji wanted to fly off to Tokyo to find out what was happening. General Hamada, Chief of Staff to the Japanese army in Thailand, believed the Domei report to be false and ordered the closure of the news agency's Bangkok office. He also contemplated imposing controls on the Thai press to stop the news being published. The next morning General Nakamura, accompanied by Hamada, called on Khuang to register their disbelief in the reported surrender offer. At the same time, all Japanese forces in Thailand were ordered to continue fighting. Thai officials countered by telling the Bangkok press to go ahead and publish the Domei report.[9]

Because of the time differences between Tokyo, Washington, London and Moscow, news of the Allies' acceptance of Japan's offer did not reach East Asia until the evening of August 12. Meanwhile the Greater East Asia Ministry told the Japanese ambassador in Bangkok to inform the Thai government of the peace process and advise it to conduct its own negotiations independently with the Western Allies. Yet General Hamada, like some of the military in Tokyo, wanted to fight on. He continued to insist to Thai ministers that there could be no surrender. This placed the ambassador in an awkward position when he called on Khuang on the afternoon of August 12 to try to explain the situation. The impression he conveyed was of someone seeking help and advice. In reply, Khuang pointed out that the Japanese had not consulted him before contacting the Allies, and thus he was unable to suggest what they should do now. As for Thailand, it was a sovereign state and its prime minister asserted that it would make its own decisions in the light of the rapidly changing international situation.[10]

That was precisely what Pridi was doing behind the scenes. As a matter of urgency, he asked SEAC to drop leaflets informing Japanese troops in the field of the decision taken in Tokyo, and ordering them to stop fighting. He also offered to keep a watch on Allied prisoners-of-war to ensure that they did not suffer any last-minute acts of revenge from their Japanese captors.[11] But, naturally, he was even more anxious about the future of Thailand and its government.

When Khuang became prime minister in 1944, he had agreed with Pridi that he would simply head an interim administration until the Seri Thai could come out into the open and proclaim allegiance to the Allies. Now, a year later, that moment appeared finally to have arrived, and the Seri Thai leadership held a meeting with Khuang to discuss who should take over the premiership. The most suitable person seemed to be Seni, since he was the only prominent Thai who had never had any contact with the Japanese and hence was thought to be acceptable to the Allies as Thailand's post-war prime minister.[12]

Once the decision was taken, Pridi was quick to inform Mountbatten, and a message was sent through OSS channels to Washington requesting Seni to return home straight away to lead the country.[13] The invitation came as a complete surprise to many people, including Seni himself. His first reaction was that he lacked the experience necessary to be prime minister. Some American officials tended to agree; they believed it would be far better if Pridi took over. Similar views were expressed in London, but neither the British nor the Americans thought it right to intervene in the matter. As a result, and as Pridi insisted, Seni felt that he should set aside his misgivings and take over the premiership, but only on a temporary and transitional basis.[14] He was careful to explain his decision to the Americans, since he had earlier placed on record a statement disclaiming any political ambitions in heading the Seri Thai abroad.[15]

Meanwhile the drama of the Japanese surrender continued to unfold. In Tokyo, on August 14, the War Minister committed ritual suicide and a group of junior officers tried to seize power to prevent a statement by the Emperor from being broadcast.[16] In the same vein, Hamada in Bangkok was still talking of continuing the struggle. On the other hand, Nakamura said that he would obey the Emperor's orders, and asked the Thais to refrain from insulting the troops under his command once they laid down their arms. Having suffered such an abrupt loss of face, he warned that they might react with violence. Yet, there were parts of Thailand where Japanese units had already hoisted white flags. Simultaneously, some Thais who had collaborated with the Japanese decided to go into hiding.[17] Several Japanese officers resolved to follow a similar course rather than submit to whatever the Allies had in store for them. Before doing so, all the staff officers in Bangkok, led by Nakamura and Hamada, assembled for a final rite on August 15. Standing stiffly to attention in the fortified underground bunker at their headquarters, they listened, many of them with tears in their eyes, to the Emperor's broadcast ordering them to bear the unbearable and lay down their arms.[18]

In theory, the Japanese surrender left Thailand as the only country still at war with Britain and the United States. For the Americans, it was simply a formality, not so the British. However, at that historic juncture they decided to help Siam extricate itself from Pibul's unfortunate legacy. The cabinet in London told Mountbatten to send an immediate message to the Siamese Regent advising him to make a formal statement as soon as possible disavowing the declaration of war and the alliance with Japan. It was also suggested that the statement should include a pledge to return all the territory acquired by Siam since the outbreak of war in 1939 as well as an offer to place the Thai armed forces at the disposal of the Allies. At the same time Pridi should mention that the Western powers had stopped the Seri Thai from staging an uprising against the Japanese, as proposed in May. In return, Mountbatten promised Pridi that the British would renounce their right to demand the unconditional surrender of Siam. Moreover, the contribution of the Seri Thai would be taken into account when Britain set out its terms for liquidating the state of war with Siam.[19]

Like many other politically conscious Thais, Pridi was full of apprehension about British policy towards Thailand. After all, up till December 1941 Britain had had more political and economic influence in Thailand than any other foreign power. And given all the hostility and insults Pibul had subsequently directed at the British, Pridi – if no-one else – realised that they had good cause to exact retribution. Hence he was relieved by the tenor of Mountbatten's message and reacted swiftly.

On August 16, the Regent of Thailand issued a formal statement in the name of the King proclaiming the declaration of war null and void since it had always been contrary to the will of the Thai people and the constitution. That was coupled with a pledge of future Thai cooperation with the United Nations, including the return of those territories Thailand had acquired from Burma and Malaya.[20] The British, however, soon noticed that the statement made no reference to the territory acquired from Indo-China. There were other omissions too. When these were queried with Pridi, he replied that modesty forbade him to mention the messages he had exchanged with the Allies about the proposed Seri Thai uprising. Anyway, he still had to take the Japanese presence into account. He was equally worried about provoking the Thai armed forces by committing them publicly to cooperate with the Allies.[21] Instead Pridi wanted to get Thailand's anomalous position sorted out as soon as possible. He had already asked Seni to proceed to London immediately to conclude an agreement terminating the state of war with Britain,[22] but Seni's appointment as prime minister was not announced for fear of antagonising the Japanese.[23] Even so, on August 17 Khuang and his cabinet formally tendered their resignation to make way for a new administration.[24]

Some of the constraints on Thai freedom of action were appreciated by the Allies. They knew, for instance, that the Greater East Asia Ministry in Tokyo was still trying to protect Japan's friends and assets in Thailand. Moreover, the OSS team in Bangkok reported that some Japanese officers were openly threatening the Thais with talk of launching another war within twenty or thirty years to avenge their present defeat.[25] In the much nearer future, the British foresaw Thai political friction resurfacing. Jacques had already warned that the political prisoners released under the September 1944 amnesty were out to get their own back on Pibul and everybody associated with him. Force 136 was even more worried by growing rivalry and jealousy between the army and the Seri Thai guerrillas. For this reason SEAC was planning to send a special military mission to Bangkok to liaise with the Thai armed forces, while relations with the Seri Thai would continue to be maintained through Pridi.[26] He himself also asked OSS to exercise caution in publicising its contacts with the Seri Thai. He knew he still had to tread carefully with the Japanese as well as potential political opponents in Thailand.[27]

Nonetheless the Regent's peace declaration was publicly acknowledged in both Washington and London. On August 20, the US Secretary of State, James Byrnes, made a statement stressing American friendship for Thailand and a desire for future cooperation between their countries. The same day, the new British Foreign Secretary, Ernest Bevin, said in the course of his first speech to the House of Commons after assuming office that he hoped the state of war with Siam would soon be liquidated, especially in view of the contribution the Free Siamese had made to the Allied cause. It was the first time there had been any public reference in Britain to the Seri Thai, and it evoked considerable surprise.[28]

Even more surprising to the Allies was the way the *Bangkok Chronicle*, an English-language newspaper printed throughout the war under Japanese supervision, published the statements of Byrnes and Bevin. They were juxtaposed with an interview given by the Japanese ambassador to Thailand, thanking the Thai people for their cooperation during the war and expressing the hope that the two countries would continue to be as friendly as ever. Obviously Pridi was embarassed. The *Bangkok Chronicle* was quickly suppressed, only to re-appear several days later renamed *Democracy*, with a new editor but otherwise the same staff.

Such chameleon-like behaviour was typical of the way most Thais adjusted to post-war developments. Almost overnight, it seemed, widespread Thai antagonism towards the Japanese was transformed into feelings of sympathy for them in their defeat. The Japanese themselves played on the situation with a subtle mixture of threats and talk of the need for continuing Asian solidarity. Their efforts soon caused a split within the Thai ruling circle. In opposition to the tough policies Pridi wanted to introduce to bring Thailand into line with the United Nations, Khuang, backed up by Adul, argued against unduly antagonising the Japanese.[29] Perhaps they were swayed by Japanese attempts to live up to their promise in early July to repatriate some of the gold earmarked in Tokyo as a counterpart for their borrowings from Thailand. Even after the ceasefire, special arrangements were made to fly a consignment of gold bars from Japan to Saigon whence it was transported overland in a convoy of lorries to be deposited in safe custody in Bangkok.[30]

How much the Allies knew about these transactions is not clear. The agents they had infiltrated into Thailand were under instructions to remain in hiding until a formal agreement could be concluded for the Japanese to lay down their arms. Anyway Force 136 was very thin on the ground in Bangkok, whereas most members of the OSS liaison team were new to the subtleties of Thai and Asian politics.[31] For example, they urged Pridi to take immediate and firm action to arrest Thailand's war criminals, a move he knew would be highly controversial.[32] At the same time, these Americans forwarded Thai pleas for the Japanese in their midst to be disarmed by local forces in preference to Allied troops being sent in for the purpose. But if an Allied presence was inevitable, the Thais expressed the hope that it would be American – (and white) – rather than British. They also indicated that they would not welcome any of the Indian or, even less, African troops being deployed by SEAC. Lowest of all on the Thai list were the Chinese.[33]

The thought of allowing the Thais to disarm the Japanese did not even occur to Allied leaders. Like it or not, the Americans knew that forces from SEAC had to enter Thailand. But in Washington there was still concern because the State Department had just received full details of the terms on which the British were prepared to end the state of war with Thailand. They amounted to some sixty provisions ranging from demands for the renunciation of many of Pibul's policies to guarantees of future Siamese compliance with measures to ensure the security and prosperity of South East Asia as a whole. In perusing these provisions, what struck the Americans first was not so much the political and military undertakings Siam was required to make; rather their initial objections centred on British demands that Siam should comply with various international arrangements covering the export of vital commodities like tin, rubber and rice.[34]

Such complaints came as no surprise to the British. They knew the United States was more than ever committed to the principle of open-door trading policies. Obviously American businessmen wanted to take advantage of lucrative post-war markets opening up throughout the world, but in British eyes, opportunism also seemed to be involved. With the economies of all the countries of Europe, Britain included, devastated by the war, the Americans looked set to capture traditional European export markets at a time when nobody else was in a position to compete. The trend was already evident in the case of Thailand.

Seni and other Thais in the United States had long been involved in lobbying with various business interests anxious to obtain a stake in Thailand's post-war economy. For example, at an international civil aviation conference held in Chicago in 1944 Seni, acting apparently on his own initiative, signed an agreement to grant Pan American Airways landing rights at Don Muang. The British protested. In a global context they saw the move as part of an attempt by American airlines to monopolise international air traffic in the post-war world. By contrast, Seni saw the British protest as further evidence of their determination to undermine Thailand's independence.[35] That view was also incorporated in an American policy document drawn up in June 1945, which envisaged Thailand looking to the United States to protect its independence from both the British and Chinese, particularly in the economic sphere. Hence the Americans objected to Britain's proposals demanding the re-instatement of pre-war international arrangements relating to the export of Siam's tin and rubber.[36]

Anglo-American suspicions about Thailand's future were likewise evident at SEAC in Kandy, and it was there the British intended that the Siamese should sign an agreement liquidating the state of war. Pridi's suggestion that Seni undertake the task in London was not considered feasible. The British believed that he was too much out of touch with the situation on the ground to discuss the measures needed to restore Anglo-Siamese relations.[37]

First, however, Mountbatten needed a working agreement with the Thais covering the entry of his forces into Siam to disarm the Japanese. Hence he told Jacques to ask the regent to prepare to send a military mission to Kandy. Pridi did not demur. Only he indicated that the mission would include Thawee Bunyaket as well as military officers. He was anxious to dispel any impression that Thai officers had been summoned to take part in a surrender ceremony similar to those being arranged for the Japanese.[38]

It was, rather, the Americans who raised objections. Claiming that the atmosphere among the British at Kandy was so prejudiced against Thailand that any delegation sent from Bangkok was bound to be subject to unfair pressure, they demanded that the negotiations be held elsewhere. The Foreign Office refused since Mountbatten and his advisers had instructions to deal with the Siamese pragmatically and treat them as representatives of a friendly country. Indeed, the Supreme Commander publicly reprimanded British officers and even generals who referred to Siam as a "naughty nation" which needed to be punished. Furthermore, the Americans were informed that Britain had no intention of occupying Siam. SEAC was simply sending in the minimum number of troops necessary to disarm the Japanese and rescue Allied prisoners-of-war, and as soon as their task was completed, they would be withdrawn.

These reassurances had some effect in Washington,[39] but OSS, in strengthening its liaison team in Bangkok ostensibly to speed the repatriation of American prisoners-of-war, indicated that its main role was to stiffen the Thai will to resist British encroachments on the country's sovereignty. Some American diplomats were alarmed at the idea, and a stern warning was issued to OSS to steer clear of involvement in Thai politics or moves which might antagonise the British.[40]

In the days immediately following the end of the war, the situation in Siam was only one of many problems confronting SEAC. With little shipping and far fewer troops at his disposal than Macarthur who was in charge of occupying Japan, Mountbatten had to resolve how best to liberate virtually the whole of South East Asia. His top priority was Malaya, where sea-borne landings were already planned and getting underway. The British were also eager to re-establish their presence in Hong Kong as soon as possible to pre-empt any Chinese attempt to seize the colony. Because of the logistics involved in these operations, there were few resources to spare for Siam in the initial stages. About a week after the landings in Malaya, the despatch of an advance party of troops by air to Bangkok was envisaged.[41]

Meanwhile, SEAC broadcast orders to Japanese forces in Siam not to molest the local population. Likewise the Japanese were told to take care of the prisoners-of-war in their custody, especially since those in Thailand were estimated at about 28,000, more than anywhere else in South East Asia. The fear was that just as happened in the Philippines, Japanese guards might attempt to kill their captives rather than let them go free to tell of the brutality they had suffered. Ominous developments pointed in that direction. OSS and Force 136 officers in Thailand became aware that some camp inmates were being split up and dispersed to other locations, possibly in Indo-China. These moves were soon foiled. News of the Japanese surrender was quickly spread through the camps. The prisoners-of-war responded by hoisting clandestinely-made Allied flags and sending out search parties for food. They also despatched representatives to Bangkok in the hope of somehow getting in touch with the International Red Cross.[42] Pridi too was conscious of the plight of the prisoners-of-war, and offered to feed and care for them until relief teams could be sent in.

As it turned out, Pridi's proposal was opportune because SEAC's rescue plans suddenly came up against an unexpected hitch. On August 19 General Macarthur, who had been designated to receive the main Japanese surrender, summarily informed Mountbatten that no Allied troops could be moved into South East Asia till the end of the month, when representatives of the Emperor were due to participate in a formal ceremony symbolising a total ceasefire. Mountbatten was furious at the delay. Some of his troops were already at sea en route to Malaya. Since there was nothing he could do to reverse Macarthur's edict, they had to be recalled. Following on from there, the despatch of troops to Siam, as well as the departure of the Siamese military mission to Kandy, had to be postponed.[43]

Another cause for concern resulting from the delay was the action of the Chinese, who were overjoyed by Japan's defeat. In Bangkok, as elsewhere in South East Asia, these feelings were boosted by broadcasts from Chungking suggesting that Chinese troops would soon move in to disarm the Japanese and punish everybody who had collaborated with them. Some people could not wait that long. On August 16, the head of the Chinese Chamber of Commerce in Bangkok was savagely murdered in what was obviously a revenge killing by somebody who believed he had helped the Japanese. Pridi was worried by this event; he feared that the violence might spread and involve Thais as well.[44] In any case, he was still receiving reports of Chinese troops marauding in the Shan States and threatening to move into northern Thailand. Furthermore, the press in Chungking was insisting that a stern policy be adopted towards Thailand because it was a fascist country. Hence Chinese troops had a duty to disarm the Thai armed forces, as well as ensuring that war criminals were placed on trial, and that full rights were restored to the local Chinese community.

As well as alarming the Thais, such demands caused great concern to the Western powers. Chiang Kai-shek had still not agreed to the decision taken at Potsdam transferring Thailand to SEAC's theatre of responsibility. As a result he was subject to intense pressure from both the Americans and the British until he finally agreed to drop his demand that Chinese troops move into Thailand as far south as the sixteenth parallel. The decision was announced in a broadcast on August 24, when Chiang Kai-shek also appealed to Chinese in South East Asia to control their joy at Japan's defeat and not offend the local population.

The Western powers hoped that this broadcast would allay Thai anxiety and deflate the ebullience of the Chinese. But Chiang Kai-shek had little influence or control over the 93rd Division based in Yunnan where the local press continued to stress the Chinese army's right to move into Thailand in punishment for its collaboration with Japan.[45] If that happened, it looked like creating as many problems for SEAC as those emerging elsewhere in the region. During the hiatus imposed by Macarthur between the end of the war and the arrival of Allied troops in South East Asia, the Japanese encouraged Sukarno to proclaim the independence of Indonesia, and in Annam they stood by while Emperor Bao Dai abdicated to make way for Ho Chi Minh's declaration of Vietnam's independence.

To prevent any more such unforeseen developments happening in his theatre, Mountbatten decided to circumvent Macarthur's edict by establishing direct contact with Count Terauchi, the overall commander of Japan's southern army, who was still based in Saigon. Terauchi was instructed to send representatives to Rangoon. There on August 28, at the insistence of Mountbatten's Chief of Staff, the Japanese agreed that a local ceasefire should be proclaimed immediately throughout South East Asia for the sake of arranging an orderly transfer of power.[46]

As far as Thailand was concerned, the ceasefire enabled OSS and Force 136 officers to emerge from hiding and reveal their presence in the country for the first time. Their main concern was to rescue the prisoners-of-war. For OSS it was comparatively easy, since their officers found only about 300 Americans held captive in Thailand and quickly organised their departure.[47] Force 136, which sent in additional teams clandestinely after August 15, had far greater problems in coping with more than 20,000 British, Australian and Dutch prisoners who, even after the end of the war, were dying at a rate of fifteen a day through malnutrition and disease. In an even worse plight were the 100,000 and more Asian conscript labourers, many of them from Malaya, forced to work on the Death Railway.[48] When reports on the situation reached

SEAC, it was decided that as soon as Macarthur received Japan's formal
surrender and the way was open for Allied troops to enter Siam, hospital
equipment and medical staff had to be flown in immediately. In making
these arrangements, Mountbatten ordered Terauchi to instruct all the
officers under his command in Siam to place themselves at the disposal of
the regent.[49]

Since the formal resignation of Khuang's cabinet, Pridi had in any case
taken over most of the burden of administering Thailand. This was not
easy because, with the collapse of Japanese military authority, lawless-
ness was becoming widespread. In Bangkok, particularly, property
vacated by the Japanese was promptly looted. Pridi was especially
embarrassed by damage done to the British legation after the Japanese,
who had occupied it, moved out. This occurrence prompted concern in
Kandy for the safety of the medical personnel to be sent in, although the
Americans thought the British were deliberately exaggerating the
security problem as a pretext to move in more troops. Mountbatten
took no notice. As requested, Pridi was about to send a military mission
to Kandy to discuss the arrival of Allied forces. It left Bangkok on
September 1, but did not include Thawee Bunyaket. The day before
Macarthur presided over the formal surrender of Japan aboard the USS
Missouri in Tokyo Bay, Thawee was appointed interim prime minister of
Thailand pending Seni's return.[50]

The Thai mission to Kandy was headed by General Luang Senanarong, who was thought acceptable to the Allies because he was one of
the few senior Thai officers to have fought against the Japanese. On
December 8, 1941, he had led the opposition to their landing at Nakorn
Srithamarat,[51] an incident of which the British and Americans knew
little. Rather, they tended to pay more attention to other members of
the Thai mission like Netr Khemayothin, Thawee Chullasap and Puey
Ungpakorn, who were all well known to OSS and Force 136 as Seri
Thai liaison officers.

Yet, as a whole, the Thai mission impressed SEAC favourably with
the businesslike way it dealt with questions on Japanese troop deployment and ways of disarming them, which in Mountbatten's eyes
augured well. He saw the cooperative Siamese attitude in marked contrast to the problems emerging elsewhere in the region. So, with
advance parties of medical personnel already starting to fly into Don
Muang, the Supreme Commander wanted to ensure that everything
continued to proceed smoothly in Siam. Hence, at his daily staff meeting
on September 3, he proposed that an interim agreement be drafted for

him to sign the next afternoon with the Siamese, covering military and other arrangements to be made for the arrival of Allied forces. The task was assigned to Esler Dening, Mountbatten's political adviser, on the understanding it would not prejudice a subsequent formal agreement to liquidate the state of war with Siam.[52]

That evening, while the Thai mission was being entertained at a party hosted by OSS officers in Kandy, Dening sat down after dinner with several other members of Mountbatten's staff to draft an agreement as instructed. It amounted to roughly twenty clauses. Some dealt with the facilities to be made available to Allied forces on their arrival in Siam; others were measures to ensure that the Japanese and their residual Thai collaborators did not take advantage of the situation. There were also provisions designed to bring Siam into line with Allied controls on trade and shipping prevailing in the rest of the world. In other words, it was a standard military agreement modelled on those concluded in Europe as Allied forces entered German-occupied countries. Then in accordance with guidelines laid down by the Combined Food Boards in Washington, the officer on Mountbatten's staff responsible for food supplies added an annex with various provisions on the procurement of Siam's accumulated rice surplus to help alleviate the famine threatening various parts of the world.

The next morning, Dening handed a copy of the agreement and its annex to a member of the Thai mission. Apologising for the short notice, Dening expressed the hope that the Siamese would peruse the document before lunching with Mountbatten as planned, and participate in a signing ceremony afterwards. But half way through the morning, Puey phoned Dening's office to say that there were problems. According to his credentials, General Senanarong was not empowered to sign such an agreement.

In reality that was only half the story. The person to whom Dening had handed his draft was Thawee Thawetikul, the only civilian member of the mission. During the war, he had worked closely with Pridi and Direk part of the time in the trade section of the Foreign Ministry. As such he took strong objection to the economic clauses in the proposed agreement and particularly the annex concerning rice. When other members of the mission read what Dening had drafted simply as a provisional agreement to cover the period immediately after the entry of Allied forces to Siam, they construed it as a perfidious long-term British attempt to deprive their country of its sovereignty and independence. Hence their first reaction was to check with the Americans whether the

British proposals had the approval of the United States. Here Thawee Chullasap, who knew the OSS officers in Kandy well, volunteered his services. Hastening to their office, he found ready support for the view that Dening was involved in a devious British trick. Of all the Americans attached to SEAC, those in OSS were the most suspicious of British intentions; consequently they suggested that the Thais should raise the credentials issue to delay the signing and provide time for reference to be made back to Washington.[53]

Despite their anxiety over the agreement, all the Thais attended the lunch party arranged in their honour that day by Mountbatten at his private residence in Kandy. It was intended to be a special occasion symbolising a reconciliation between Britain and Siam. Throughout the war, for reasons of political protocol, Mountbatten had deliberately refrained from meeting any of the Seri Thai representatives visiting Kandy. Given the circumstances prevailing on September 4, the lunch took place in a fairly cordial atmosphere, marred only by a slight misunderstanding. General Senanarong arrived in full ceremonial dress and was clearly encumbered by his sword as he sat down to eat. Noticing the problem, Mountbatten told a servant to remove the sword at which General Senanarong blanched visibly. Apparently he thought he was being disarmed in a token gesture of surrender similar to that imposed on the Japanese. The General's fears surfaced again after the lunch when Mountbatten asked him to stay behind for a private discussion on the problems arising from the agreement. He believed he was being taken into custody by the Allied Supreme Commander.[54]

At that Mountbatten quickly convened a meeting of all his lunch guests, including the head of the OSS office in Kandy, who had been present, as well as the Thais. Then General Senanarong produced a copy of his credentials. Rather than imposing limitations on the type of agreement the Siamese were empowered to sign, Mountbatten thought they were so vaguely worded that they could be interpreted in any sense. Still, to save Siamese face, he proposed a compromise, namely that Dening's draft proposals should be separated into two agreements, one covering simply military matters and the other everything else. The redrafting was carried out by Dening working in concert with Thawee Thawetikul.

Once that was done, General Senanarong saw no objection to signing the first agreement dealing with issues concerning the entry of Allied forces to Siam. He also agreed to Mountbatten's suggestion that Thawee and several other members of the mission should fly back to

Bangkok straight away with the text of the second agreement to ascertain Pridi's views. The Thais were asked to move swiftly so that the signing could take place on September 7. The reason for the Supreme Commander's haste was his departure the next day with all his senior staff for Singapore to accept the formal surrender of the Japanese throughout South East Asia.[55]

Pridi, meanwhile, was forewarned of the return of Thawee Thawetikul carrying the draft of the second agreement. In a special message sent through Jacques, who continued to act as British liaison officer in Bangkok, Mountbatten explained to the Regent that, contrary to what the mission in Kandy apparently thought, the proposals put forward by Dening were only intended as an interim measure and Allied troops would not remain in Siam any longer than necessary to disarm the Japanese and rescue the prisoners-of-war.[56] As for the economic provisions, Pridi had been expecting something of the sort.

Seri Thai missions sent to Kandy and Washington before the end of the war had been intensely questioned about the state of the Siamese economy. As a result the Allies came to the conclusion that Thailand had suffered far less damage than its neighbours and would emerge from the war with a relatively healthy economy.[57] Indeed since most of Siam's pre-war gold and foreign currency reserves remained intact in London, the country was in theory much better off financially than Britain, which was heavily in debt to the United States.[58] Moreover, both the Western powers had been informed that Siam had an immediately exportable rice surplus of 2 million tons, which had accrued partly because of the increasing disruption of internal transport by Allied bombing. The shipping of exports had likewise become virtually impossible.

Besides, in February 1945 Force 136 had asked Pridi to deny rice to the Japanese and stockpile as much as possible for the Allies. The idea was to use the rice as counterpart payment for the arms being supplied to the Seri Thai. As for the rice thus acquired, the British envisaged its distribution according to the directions of the Combined Food Boards in Washington which were responsible for re-allocating certain staple foodstuffs on the basis of need. But the Americans did not like the idea, since they thought it would limit the freedom of US military procurement agencies to purchase rice in Bangkok as they wanted.[59]

The argument was still unresolved when the Japanese surrender revealed the extent of the rice shortage throughout East Asia. In these circumstances, the Americans suggested to Seri Thai representatives in

Washington that Thailand would earn itself a great deal of goodwill if it volunteered to make its surplus rice available to other countries suffering from food shortages.[60] A similar view was put to Seni when he called at the Foreign Office during the week he spent in London on his way home. Somewhat apprehensively, he replied that Siam had about 1.5 million tons of rice which could be placed at the disposal of the Allies.[61] Seni then informed Pridi by telegram of the commitment he had made. The interim premier, Thawee Bunyaket, was aghast, and protested that Thailand did not have such a rice surplus to give away. Pridi took a different view, suggesting that on humanitarian grounds alone Thailand should try to meet the commitment. In any case, he argued, the Thais were in no position to quibble; they might otherwise have to meet even harsher British demands.[62]

This remained Pridi's attitude when Thawee Thawetikul arrived back from Kandy late on September 5 with copies of the agreements Mountbatten wanted the Siamese to sign. By then the prime minister also thought it wiser for Thailand to comply with Allied demands. Just to make sure everybody else realised what was at stake, he rushed straight off with the agreements to the Assembly which happened to be in session that evening. Again dismay was expressed at the terms being imposed on Thailand, but eventually, and reluctantly, the Assembly voted to sign both agreements on the understanding that there was no other way out for the country.[63] Here the Thais were mistaken.

When OSS representatives in Kandy first saw the proposals Dening had put to the Thais, they soon set alarm bells ringing around the world. They alleged that Mountbatten was trying to impose long-term restrictions on Thailand's political and economic independence in the guise of an ultimatum decreed in the name of the Allies but in reality delivered behind the backs of the Americans.[64] These allegations let loose an international furore. From Washington the Joint Chiefs of Staff cabled to Mountbatten protesting that he had no right as an Allied Supreme Commander to give the Thais an ultimatum without first consulting the United States, and from Chungking Mountbatten's American deputy, General Wheeler, likewise signalled his disapproval.[65] In London there were also objections: some British officials thought that Dening had exceeded his terms of reference by including economic demands in a purely military agreement. They also feared that he might have spoiled the chance of securing a quick settlement with the Siamese ending the state of war.[66] Consequently, when the American ambassador in London was told to make representations at the highest level to stop

Mountbatten enforcing his ultimatum, there was no serious argument. At a midnight meeting on September 5 at 10 Downing Street, Attlee informed the American ambassador that Britain too had objections to the terms Mountbatten had put to the Siamese, and orders were already on their way to him to sign only the agreement dealing with military matters.[67]

These instructions did not stop Mountbatten from having a show-down with American officers in Kandy, including the head of OSS. He openly accused them of misrepresenting his position and pointed out that it was simply not true that he had delivered an ultimatum to the Siamese behind the backs of the Americans; at the same time as Dening had handed the proposed agreement to Thawee Thawetikul, a copy was given to the senior American general in Kandy. Mountbatten went on to claim that it was a unique situation, in which Siam was prepared to sign both agreements and make friends, but one of Britain's supposed allies was intervening to forbid the reconciliation.[68]

Pridi too was dismayed. After the effort to get the Assembly to approve both agreements, he considered it an affront that General Sena-narong was asked to sign only the one dealing with technical military matters. It seemed to him that Britain had scant respect for Siamese goodwill; worse still, without explaining why, Mountbatten told the regent to tear up the second agreement and forget about it. Later, when the British realised how hurt Pridi felt, they sought to reassure him that no snub had been intended. Nonetheless, the American intervention resulted in the suspension of further British negotiations with the Siamese until Mountbatten and his senior staff returned to Kandy after receiving the Japanese surrender in Singapore on September 12.[69]

Still the international tension arising from developments in Kandy had little effect on the arrival of Allied forces in Thailand. On September 3, an advance party of about 1,000 troops flew into Don Muang where the Japanese had been ordered to have liaison officers lined up ready to hand over control.[70] They were not there. Instead, the first British officers to arrive officially in Bangkok after the end of the war were greeted by a ceremonial Thai guard of honour. This both eased and complicated the task of Major-General Geoffrey Evans, who had been designated Commander, Allied Land Forces Siam. Coming straight from the rigours of the Burma campaign, he was not prepared for the apparently unwarlike atmosphere in Siam. His orders were to secure Don Muang before the landing of the main body of Allied troops and their supplies. From his temporary headquarters there, he insisted the

Japanese officers report to him to receive instructions on the disarming of the more than 100,000 of their troops scattered throughout Thailand. To assert his authority over them, General Evans issued orders on September 5 for all Japanese troops to remain in barracks. On the whole he was obeyed, although the Japanese left a powerful time-bomb at Don Muang to explode after they moved out.[71]

Another of General Evans' early preoccupations was the safety of Mountbatten's wife, Edwina. As Far Eastern representative of a British voluntary medical association, she made a flying visit to Thailand to see that everything possible was being done for the prisoners-of-war. Her visit to their camps along the Death Railway in early September created a sensation. It was the first time they had seen a white woman for more than three years. And no-one in Thailand had ever seen a jeep before. That was just one measure of how out of touch the Thais had become with developments elsewhere in the world during the war period. In the eyes of Pridi, however, the visit of Mountbatten's wife so soon after the end of the war constituted a token of British goodwill, and he was quick to lay on an official reception for her and General Evans.[72]

Such hospitality somewhat embarrassed the British. According to military regulations prevailing throughout the world, Allied troops entering an enemy country were subject to a ban on fraternisation with the local population. For obvious reasons the Thais failed to appreciate why such a ban should be applied to them, and many people in Bangkok hastened to lavish entertainment on the arriving Allied troops. Here too they had a surprise. Despite the pleas of the Seri Thai leadership for only *farang* troops to be sent to Thailand, most of the forces Mountbatten had at his disposal came from the Indian army. In fact General Evans was commander of its Seventh Division comprising mainly Sikhs and Gurkhas. Mountbatten sought to reassure Pridi that they were all highly disciplined,[73] but some incidents involving racial friction between Thais and Indians did occur.

Some Thais also objected to the way the British proceeded to carry out their designated tasks. For instance, the acting prime minister, Thawee Bunyaket, had to cope with a dispute over British medical officers, who were responsible for treating the prisoners-of-war, expropriating facilities at Chulalongkorn hospital where the administration was jealous of its own jurisdiction.[74] Similar incidents arose elsewhere as Allied forces sought to install themselves and get on with such work as clearing the minefields at the approaches to the Chao Phya and re-opening the port of Bangkok. Likewise there was public resentment at Allied planes using the open space at Sanam Luang as a temporary landing-ground to save the long trek in from Don Muang. In the eyes of some Thais, the British appeared just as peremptory as the Japanese, if not more so.[75]

Further resentment was caused by the British tendency to rely more on the cooperation of the Japanese armed forces than those of Thailand. True, Thai officers were included in discussions on disarming and concentrating Japanese troops before their eventual repatriation, but the overall view of the British military mission sent to Bangkok was that the Thais could provide little help in carrying out the task. Virtually the only transport the Thai army had at its disposal consisted of oxcarts, whereas the few naval ships and air force planes still in active use were antiquated compared to what the Allies had developed during the war.[76] On the other hand, British officers had learnt to respect Japanese military effectiveness and discipline, even though they hated it and suspected that many Japanese officers were not prepared to surrender.

These suspicions were well grounded. General Hamada chose to commit ritual suicide rather than surrender.[77] As for Colonel Tsuji, who had good reason to believe that he would be arrested as a war criminal, he had no intention of giving himself up. On the contrary, he was determined to continue the struggle against what he saw as the reassertion of Western domination over East Asia. Together with other like-minded Japanese, he managed to evade detection, disguised as a Buddhist monk and obtain help from Khuang as well as local Chinese in escaping across the Mekong into Laos en route eventually to Chungking.[78]

Another prominent figure who disappeared at the same time was Ebata Suriya, a Thai-Japanese businessman suspected of heading the Bangkok branch of the anti-Western Black Dragon Society.[79] Other less well-known Japanese managed to obtain false identity papers enabling them to stay on in Thailand incognito, and arrangements were made to transfer Japanese economic investments to Thai control until such time as their real owners felt safe to re-emerge. These developments resulted from plans long since drawn up by the Greater East Asia Ministry to protect and perpetuate Japanese influence and investments throughout the region, despite the way the war had ended.[80]

In fact, some Japanese officials assumed that the Western powers would simply demand the dismantling of their military empire in East Asia and business would otherwise continue as normal. Many Thais thought the same. On several occasions after August 15, Khuang reassured the Japanese ambassador in Bangkok that the friendly relations they had always maintained would not be affected by the change in Japan's international position. And Prince Wan was very apologetic on September 7 when he informed the ambassador that Thailand felt it necessary, as a result of talks with the Western powers in Kandy, to suspend although not break diplomatic relations with Japan.[81] On neither side was there any apparent feeling of guilt that their collaboration throughout the war had been to blame for the plight in which both countries now found themselves.

Such attitudes ran counter to the climate of international opinion. Throughout the rest of the world, there were widespread demands for the trial and punishment of those Germans and Japanese and their collaborators who had caused the war and committed atrocities during its course. Responding to this mood, Seni stated while still in Washington that Pibul would be arrested and tried as a war criminal. The idea was supported by the American press, which portrayed Pibul as a quisling and Japanese catspaw who had ignored and betrayed the wishes of the Thai people.[82]

Yet one of the clauses to which the Thais objected most in the agreement Mountbatten had proposed for their signature in Kandy concerned the detention of war criminals. As drafted, the agreement did not specify that these men were to be put on trial before an Allied War Crimes Tribunal, but that was the presumption in Bangkok. The Seri Thai leadership knew that the Americans had long since compiled a list of Thai war criminals. Konthi had been shown it during his visit to Washington as liaison officer and already protested that it was unjust to include people like Prince Wan who were officials simply carrying out orders. In July Nicol Smith had also questioned Pridi and Direk about Thai war criminals. If this was the American attitude, they thought the British were bound to be far more vengeful.[83]

Anyway, in an obvious move to pre-empt Allied attempts to take action against Thai war criminals, Pridi soon set up a commission in Bangkok to look into the issue. It was headed by Sanguan Tularaks, who had just returned home after spending a year as a liaison officer in Kandy. There he had told OSS that it was essential to discredit Pibul once and for all – otherwise he might make a political comeback. Apparently the Americans had little idea as yet that Sanguan himself was regarded as a notorious war profiteer before escaping to China, and was now bent on pursuing a personal vendetta against Pibul for stripping him of his Thai nationality and property. Indeed, on assuming his new position, Sanguan announced his intention of arresting hundreds of war criminals, with Pibul at the top of his list.[84]

Among the first to express alarm was, naturally, Pibul himself. He immediately sent a twenty-three-page letter to all Bangkok's newspaper editors in an effort to explain away his wartime policies as part of a vast and secret plan to fool and foil the Japanese. Now he complained that his intentions were now being deliberately distorted by his political enemies.[85] The same hurt tone imbued an interview he willingly gave to an OSS officer who wanted to question him on his wartime activities. The interview took place at Pibul's palatial home in Bang Khen on the outskirts of the capital, where he sought to impress his American visitor with the urbanity and personal charm that had long characterised his dealings with *farangs*. He claimed he could rebut any charges brought against him as a war criminal if only he were accorded a fair trial.[86] But at the same time he wrote privately to Pridi, pleading in the most abject terms for clemency. Pibul even went so far as to recall their student days together in Paris and apologise for any subsequent actions which might have been detrimental to Pridi's career. One incident that clearly preyed on his mind was the decision to sign the decree which led to Pridi's exile abroad as a communist back in 1933.[87]

For his part, Pridi was ostensibly more concerned with recent history, and the opportunities which now existed for moving towards a really democratic system of government. The idea was also on the minds of many other politicians. In July, even before the end of the war, the Assembly had voted to set up a committee to amend the constitution.[88] Above all, many members wanted to do away with the practice of having half the Assembly nominated by the government. If that was to happen, the amendment of the constitution needed to be duly authorised by the monarch. It would be very timely. On September 21, 1945, King Ananda was to celebrate his twentieth birthday, when, according to Thai custom, he came of age and assumed his full official duties. The prospect aroused a surge of loyal sentiment when it was discussed in the Assembly, and Pridi as regent sent a telegram to Switzerland suggesting that the young monarch return home as soon as possible.[89]

The war had barely touched the King's life. Together with his mother, elder sister and younger brother, he had continued to live in a modest villa in Lausanne and attend a local school and then university. Like most other children brought up in Switzerland, he also went skiing and skating in winter, while playing other open-air games in summer. The only official intrusion into his life had been an occasional visit from the Japanese ambassador in Berne; apparently the Japanese had thought it worthwhile attempting to curry favour with a young monarch who might be useful when the time came for his coronation.[90] The Americans, on the other hand, blocked various moves by Seni to involve the King in the Seri Thai, believing that it might attract too much publicity and provide the Japanese with a pretext for taking extreme counter-measures in Bangkok.[91]

After the war, however, President Truman sent a message congratulating the Thai King on attaining his majority, as did Pridi and Seni.[92] But in reply to the regent's request for him to return home, the King indicated that he wished to remain in Switzerland for at least another eighteen months to complete a course in law at the University of Lausanne. In the mean time, he was only prepared to visit Bangkok briefly.[93]

Seni, too, was slow to return home. After the message he sent from London about rice, nothing more was heard from him for the next two weeks, and Pridi asked SEAC to find out where he was.[94] The regent's anxiety was compounded by all the problems which remained to be sorted out in the aftermath of the war. The British were pressing for another delegation to be sent to Kandy to discuss an agreement liquidating the state of war, without which there could be no question of unfreezing Thailand's foreign reserves held in London and resuming trade. The Americans too had not yet agreed to resume diplomatic relations. Apparently they were waiting for Seni to take over the premiership. Another international problem looming ahead was the question of relations with the French. A message from Kandy indicated that they had a delegation waiting there to discuss the return of the territory Thailand had acquired from Indo-China in 1941.[95] The issue was such an obvious political minefield that the interim government preferred to leave it for Seni to deal with. Then there were the Chinese, who were insisting that it was high time for Thailand to make amends for Pibul's policies by allowing them to establish a diplomatic presence in Bangkok.

Given Seni's experience of dealing with the Allies, the interim government headed by Thawee Bunyaket obviously thought it better to leave all these problems for him to sort out. On the other hand, since he had been out of the country so long, the new Prime Minister had little knowledge of the internal political scene. That too might be an advantage in establishing a clean break with the past. Symbolic of this feeling

one of the few formal decisions taken by Thawee's government during
the seventeen days it held power was to decree that the country should
again be internationally known as Siam.[96] Hence, when Seni finally
returned to Bangkok on September 17, Siam appeared to be embarking
on a new era.

NOTES

1. Kirby, V, pp. 224ff, and Mountbatten, p. 181.
2. FRUS, 1945, VI, p. 1275, and F5020/738/40 in FO 371/47562.
3. F5115/296/40 in FO 371/46546.
4. FO 371/46545.
5. F5019/738/40 in FO 371/46562.
6. Allen (1976), p. 49, and Nai Chantana, p. 371.
7. Butow, *The Japanese Decision to Surrender*, pp. 159ff.
8. ibid., p. 186, and SEAC diary, Aug. 10, in WO 172/1776.
9. F5040/738/40 in FO 371/46563, and cable of Aug. 14 in 711.9 Box 1, Bangkok, RG84.
10. *Magic*, Aug. 14, 1945; WO 203/4472(138a); OSS R&A 3236 of Aug. 24, 1945; Nai Chantana, p. 374.
11. F5123/738/40 in FO 371/46563.
12. F5219/738/40 in ibid., and Thawee Bunyaket in Ray, p. 108.
13. F5050/738/40 in FO 371/46563 and 892.01/8–1345 in RG59.
14. 892.01/8–1645 in RG59; Phra Phisal Sukhumvit, *Chotmai Het kong Seri Thai*, p. 325, in contrast to Seni's claim in Ray, p. 161, about repeatedly refusing the premiership.
15. 892.01/8–2845 in RG59.
16. Butow, pp. 210ff.
17. Cable of Aug. 14 in 711.4 Box 1, Bangkok, RG84, and WO 203/4472 (136aff).
18. Allen (1976), p. 49.
19. F5115/296/40 in FO 371/46546 and FRUS, 1945, VI, p. 1278.
20. Text in Thak Chaloemtiarana (ed.), p. 459, and Prasert Patamasukhon, p. 465.
21. F5290/296/40 in FO 371/46546 and F5550/296/40 in FO 371/46547.
22. F5169/738/40 in FO 371/46563; 892.01/8–1745 in RG59; Seni, p. 4.
23. Cable of Aug. 25 in 711.4 Box 1, Bangkok, RG84.
24. Direk, p. 161.
25. *Magic*, Aug. 18, 20 and 22, and cables of Aug. 18 and 20 in 711.4 and 711.8 Box 1, Bangkok, RG84.
26. Report of Aug. 18 in WO 203/4419.
27. Cables in 711.9, Box 1, Bangkok, RG84.
28. FRUS, 1945, VI, p. 1280; F5646/296/40 in FO 371/46547; NYT, Aug. 20 and 21, 1945.
29. Cables of Aug. 21 and 23 in 711.9 Box 1, Bangkok, RG84.
30. 892.515/3–2349 including Japanese note of Aug. 25, 1945, covering delivery.
31. New OSS arrivals in Bangkok were James Thompson, Alexander Macdonald,

Edmund Taylor and Dillon Ripley. Their lack of knowledge is implied in XL22760 in FG226.

32. 711.9 in Box 1, Bangkok, RG84.
33. Cable of Aug. 20 in 711.4 in ibid.
34. FRUS, 1945, VI, p. 1290, and F5293/296/40 in FO 371/46546.
35. Thorne, pp. 390ff; Neher, *Prelude to Alliance: The Expansion of the American Economic Role in Thailand during the 1940s*, p. 505; Seni, p. 3; Seni in Ray, p. 156.
36. FRUS, 1945, VI, p. 568, and F5666/296/40 in FO 371/46547.
37. F5294/296/40 in FO 371/46546, and Seni, p. 4.
38. F5667/296/40 in FO 371/46547.
39. F5980/296/40 in ibid., and FRUS, 1945, VI, pp. 1282ff.
40. 892.01/8-2445 in RG59.
41. Mountbatten, p. 183.
42. Allen (1976), p. 51, and Cruikshank, pp. 239ff.
43. SAC meeting of Aug. 19 in WO 172/1777.
44. F5222/1197/40 and file in FO 371/46567; cable of Aug. 17 in 800, China, in Box 1, Bangkok, RG84; XL19078 in RG226 & WO 203/5576 (1).
45. WO 172/1777–1779.
46. Mountbatten, p. 184.
47. Cable of Aug. 30 in 711 Box 1, Bangkok, RG84, and SEAC Diary, Aug. 28, in WO 172/1779.
48. Gilchrist, pp. 233ff, and Allen (1976), p. 51.
49. WO 203/4472 (197a ff).
50. SAC meeting of Aug. 29 in WO 172/1779, and cable of Sep. 1 in 800 Box 1, Bangkok, RG84.
51. Puey in Direk, p. 141, and Netr Khemayothin, III, pp. 585ff.
52. WO 172/1781 entries for Sep. 3.
53. Dening letter of Sep. 7 in F6867/296/40 in FO 371/46550; Netr Khemayothin, III, pp. 588ff; Direk, pp. 164ff.
54. Ziegler, p. 329.
55. Netr Khemayothin, III, pp. 601ff, and entries for Sep. 4 in WO 172/1781.
56. WO 203/5579 (50).
57. FRUS, 1945, VI, p. 568.
58. ibid., p. 1309, and F6195/296/40 in FO 371/46548.
59. Correspondence in FO 371/46568 and 892.61317 in RG59.
60. FRUS, 1945, VI, p. 1282.
61. F6258/296/40 in FO 371/46548, although Seni later claimed to have made no such commitment. Seni in Ray, p. 162, and Seni, p. 6. Other discrepancies exist between Seni's accounts and official British records.
62. Thawee Bunyaket in Ray, p. 109.
63. Netr Khemayothin, III, pp. 628ff.
64. FRUS, 1945, VI, p. 1305.
65. F6572/296/40 in FO 371/46549 and entries for Sep. 6 in WO 172/1781.
66. F6362/296/40 in FO 371/46548.
67. FRUS, 1945, VI, pp. 1306ff, and F6645/296/40 in FO 371/46549.
68. F6593 and F6613/296/40 in ibid.
69. WO 203/4419 (Sep. 8 and 12).
70. WO 203/2214 (45).

71. WO 203/2309 (4a) and ops reports for Sep. 7, 10 and 12 in WO 172/1782–83.
72. Kirby, V, p. 294, and *Times*, Sep. 7, 1945.
73. WO 203/2214 (64).
74. Thawee Bunyaket in Ray, pp. 107ff.
75. Tsuji Masanobu, *Underground Escape*, p. 39.
76. Ops report for Sep. 16 in WO 172/1780.
77. Gilchrist, p. 230.
78. Allen (1976), pp. 56ff, quoting Tsuji's account.
79. WO 203/1783.
80. OSS R&A 3240 of Aug. 31, 1945.
81. *Magic* of Sep. 1, 6 and 12, 1945.
82. CSM July 14 and NYT, Aug. 21, 1945.
83. Konthi Suphamongkol, p. 151, and Nicol Smith, p. 261.
84. 143864 and XL23037 in RG226.
85. Pibul's letter in Thak Chaloemtiarana (ed.), pp. 348ff; 892.00/9–3045 in RG59; Ananta Pibulsongkram, III, pp. 623ff.
86. XL23034, XL24264 and XL24260 in RG226.
87. Text in Pramote Pungsunthorn, pp. 76ff.
88. Prasert Patamasukhon, p. 462.
89. ibid., p. 472, and text of telegram in Kruger, p. 57.
90. ibid., pp. 52ff, and FO 371/35987.
91. 892.01/5–1545ff in RG59.
92. 892.001/9–1945 in ibid.
93. Kruger, pp. 70ff, and NYT, Sep. 28, 1945.
94. WO 203/4472 (232a).
95. Cable of Sep. 14 in WO 203/4419.
96. Prasert Patamasukhon, p. 473, and NYT, Sep. 10, 1945. The decision also alleviated Anglo-American friction. Some Americans thought Britain deliberately perverse in using 'Siam' instead of 'Thailand'.

EPILOGUE

As the post-war history of Siam – or Thailand, as it again became in 1949 – has shown, most of the hopes of September 1945 did not materialise. To apportion blame would be invidious without going into a detailed study of the events which followed Seni's return to Bangkok on September 17.

Suffice it to say that immediately after taking over the premiership, he had to cope with a serious outbreak of rioting in the Chinese quarter of Bangkok. This led to the unprecedented establishment of diplomatic relations between Siam and China in January 1946. Meanwhile relations between Britain and Siam became much more fraught. Seni accepted the OSS view that Mountbatten had tried to impose long-term British domination – and even colonial rule – over Siam through the document General Senanarong was originally asked to sign in Kandy on September 4, 1945. Pridi, on the other hand, given his greater familiarity with SEAC and the role it was expected to play immediately after the war, was far less suspicious. Besides, he knew as a former Finance Minister how important it was to normalise relations with Britain – and for that matter with the United States – in order to unfreeze the country's foreign currency reserves held in London and New York and get trade going again. These differing perspectives between Seni and Pridi led to increasing strains in their relationship during the closing months of 1945. But eventually Seni found he could no longer count on US support in opposing Britain's terms for liquidating the state of war with Siam, and an agreement was signed on January 1, 1946. At the same time, the troops SEAC had sent to Siam to round up and disarm the Japanese in preparation for being repatriated had more or less completed their task and were starting to leave.

Siam's relations with France took much longer to normalise because of the problem of the lost territories. Only in October 1946, after France threatened to veto Siam's membership of the United Nations, were western Cambodia and the two Lao enclaves on the west bank of the Mekong returned to Indo-Chinese sovereignty. Then another problem arose. The Soviet Union too threatened to block Siam's entry to the new world body unless the anti-communist law dating back to 1933 was abrogated. That demand too had to be met so that Siam could finally be re-integrated into the prevailing international postwar community in early 1947.

Well before then, however, domestic politicking had cast a shadow over the hopes of creating a more democratic system of government in Siam. Within a month of assuming the premiership, Seni ran into opposition in the Assembly when he tried to introduce legislation to prosecute war criminals, including those responsible for imposing a form of dictatorship on the country. This immediately raised the hackles of Pibul's supporters. As a result, the Assembly, whose composition had remained basically unchanged since 1938, was dissolved on October 16, 1945, to pave the way for nationwide elections, and the next day Pibul, together with six of his henchmen, were detained as war criminals. At the same time it was announced that new moves were underway to amend the constitution. To put the seal on these developments the King agreed to return home on December 5, albeit for a brief visit, before resuming his studies in Switzerland. His arrival back in Bangkok nevertheless put an end to Pridi's regency, in acknowledgement of which he was accorded the title Senior Statesman.

The general elections held in early January 1946 also served as an acknowledgement of Pridi's popularity. Although political parties were still not officially allowed, a majority of the successful candidates won their seats on the premise that they supported Pridi and his ideas for constitutional reform as against military rule. The one exception was Bangkok, where several ex-political prisoners campaigned on the basis of opposition to thirteen years of domination by the Khana Ratsadorn, which included Pridi as well as Pibul. This group of Assemblymen, which crystallised a few months later into the Democrat Party, attracted the support of Seni and his more outspoken younger brother, the budding journalist Kukrit. More surprisingly Khuang, as ever ambivalent in his political manoeuvring, agreed to become leader of the Democrats, and with the tacit support of the army, which he pledged not to disband, he was selected for a second time as Prime Minister.

This unholy alliance did not last long. Khuang's government comprised various political reactionaries, some of whom had not held office since Phya Mano was overthrown in 1933, and proved incapable of coping with the problems of the post-war world. Within six weeks of taking office, it lost a vote in the Assembly relating to a measure to control inflation. As a result Pridi, who after relinquishing the prestigious position as Regent was reluctant to enter the political fray again, took up the gauntlet and immediately encountered a political minefield. In the interim between Khuang's departure from the premiership and Pridi's assumption of office, the Supreme Court decided to release Pibul and his colleagues on the grounds that the War Criminals' Act being retro-active was illegal.

Still, on becoming Prime Minister at the end of March 1946, Pridi immediately impressed at least the British and Americans with his energy and determination to get the economy running again and a new constitution adopted. Then tragedy struck. The young King Ananda, who had restored the popularity of the monarchy, was preparing to return to his studies in Switzerland with official visits to the United States and Britain en route, when he was found shot dead in bed at the Grand Palace on the morning of June 9, 1946.

The official communiqué announcing the news of his death, drawn up by several princes and by Pridi as Prime Minister, suggested that the cause had been an accident. The King and his younger brother Bhumipol, who immediately succeeded to the throne, were known to be fond of playing with guns. The Bangkok public refused to believe the thesis. Fanned by Seni and the Democrat Party, the rumour grew that Pridi or his Seri Thai supporters had assassinated the King for their own political purposes and possibly to establish a republic.

To ward off such criticism, Pridi appointed an official commission, which included several princes, to investigate the cause of the King's death, but it was to no avail in calming the mood in Bangkok. Consequently, in August 1946 Pridi – sickened by the bitter attacks on him – resigned the premiership and handed it over to Thamrong, the "golden tongue". With his special gift, he was thought capable of soothing public opinion and reuniting the disparate factions of the Khana Ratsadorn in opposition to the Democrats. The ploy proved successful for a time, despite increasing criticism of the government on the grounds of official corruption. Thamrong even managed to ward off a vote of no-confidence in the Assembly on this score in April 1947. But his triumph was short-lived. With the increasing re-emergence on the political scene of Pibul, the Democrats on the one hand and the military on the other continued to nag at the unresolved issue of who had been responsible for the King's death. This became the pretext for a military coup on November 7, 1947, which ousted Thamrong's government. Pridi was eventually helped to escape into exile through the good offices of the British and Americans.

Yet since the Western powers and most other governments refused to countenance another military regime headed by Pibul, he prevailed on Khuang and the Democrats to form a new government. They ostensibly had a common cause: the failure of the governments headed successively by Pridi and Thamrong to resolve the question of how King Ananda had met his death. It is a question which has remained unresolved, despite a prolonged trial and the execution in 1955 of three men, one of them a close friend of Pridi and the other two royal pages.

However, Khuang's third – and as it turned out his last government – was again short-lived. Once it had organised elections to prove its political legitimacy and gain international recognition, it was forced to resign in April 1948 during a confrontation with senior military officers, similar to that ten years earlier which had forced Phya Phahol to resign in favour of Pibul. Thus history repeated itself, except that Pibul was no longer his own master. This time he assumed the premiership subject to the acquiescence of various military officers, few of whom owed allegiance to the original Khana Ratsadorn oath. Consequently his hold on power was far less secure than during his previous period as premier. In fact, it was only due to his firmly anti-communist stance and, ironically, the support which this earned him from the Western powers that enabled Pibul to survive several more attempted coups before finally being toppled from power and forced into exile in 1957.

While that proved to be the end of the Khana Ratsadorn and its pretension to rule the country, Pibul's long tenure of power provided a precedent for future military rule. For many years it was sustained thanks to Cold War attitudes and the backing of the Western powers, which wanted to see a strong and stable regime in Thailand. Only when that consensus broke down in 1973 did some analysts of Thai politics begin to consider why the democratic hopes of August 1945 had failed to materialise. It is a process which still continues.

BIOGRAPHICAL NOTES

Aditya Dib-Abha Abhakorn, Phra Ong Chao, His Highness Prince
(1904-46)

Grandson of King Chulalongkorn (5th family). Educated in England and commissioned in Royal Navy. Appointed regent, 1935, and senior regent a few months later following suicide of Prince Oscar Anuvatana. Became close friend of Pibul and resigned from regency in 1944 rather than approve Khuang as prime minister. Married to Mom Kobkhaeow, née Visetkul, long regarded as a leader of fashion in Thailand and commissioned as Lt.-Col.in army, 1943.

Adul Detcharat, Police General Luang (1894-1969)

Son of British subject from Ceylon. Graduated from Military Academy, 1915, in same class as Pibul. Artillery officer. Member of junior army promoters' faction. Deputy Director-General of Police, 1933. Director-General of Police, 1935-45. First appointed to cabinet, 1935. Deputy premier, 1941-4. Member of Seri Thai leadership, codenamed "Pulao" by Force 136 and "Betty" by OSS. Army commander, July 1946. Retired from public life, Nov. 1947.

Ananta Mahidol, King Rama VIII (1925-46)

Born Heidelberg, Germany. Grandson of King Chulalongkorn and Queen Sawang. Son of Mahidol, Prince of Songkla (1892-1929) and Mom Sangwalya née Chakramol (b. 1900), later known as the Princess Mother. Ascended throne, 1935, but resided in Lausanne, Switzerland, till Dec. 1945, with a brief visit to Bangkok in 1938. Died in Bangkok of a gunshot wound in June 1946 and succeeded by younger brother Bhumipol Adulyadet.

Arthakit Kamchorn, Luang

Original name Klung Banomyong. Younger half-brother to Pridi. Civilian promoter. Joined Diplomatic Service, serving in Paris, Rome, Berne and Stockholm, Oct. 1944-7. Foreign Minister, May–Nov. 1947.

Bhumipol Adulyadet, King Rama IX

Born Boston, Massachusetts, 1927. Younger brother to King Ananda Mahidol. Succeeded to throne, June 1946.

Boripat, Chao Fa, His Celestial Highness Prince of Nakorn Sawan
(1877-1944)

Son of King Chulalongkorn and Queen Sukumala. Educated in Germany. Head of the Supreme Council, Minister of the Interior and heir-apparent to throne

367

during reign of King Prajadhipok. Forced into exile, June 1932; went to live in Bandung, Java. Father to Prince Chumpot.

Bovoradet Kridakorn, Mom Chao, His Serene Highness Prince (1877–1947)

Grandson of King Mongkut (1st family). Younger brother of Prince Charoonsak (Thai Minister, Paris, 1920–7) and elder brother of Prince Sitthiporn. Educated at Harrow and Woolwich Military Academy, England. Minister of War during reign of King Prajadhipok till resignation, 1931. Leader of abortive rebellion, Oct. 1933. Fled to exile in Indo-China.

Chai Pratipasen, Major-General (d. 1962)

Studied military science in France. Liaison officer, Franco-Thai joint committee, 1941. Member of Joint Thai-Japanese Military Commission, 1941–4. Military Secretary to Pibul and cabinet secretary. Youngest-ever Major-General in 1944. Disappeared from public life for fear of being branded as war criminal. Re-emerged 1947 to play a role in civil aviation.

Chamkad Balankura (d. 1943)

Educated Balliol College, Oxford. President of Sammakhi Samakom (Siamese Student Association in Britain), 1938–9, and wrote article critical of lack of democracy in Siam. Barred from official employment by Pibul. Worked as teacher at private school in Bangkok till Feb. 1943. Departed as secret envoy to China and died in Chungking.

Chula Chakrabongse, Phra Ong Chao, His Highness Prince (1908–63)

Grandson of King Chulalongkorn and Queen Saovabha. Son of Chakrabongse, Prince of Pitsanuloke (1883–1920) and Catherine Desnitsky. Educated Harrow and Trinity College, Cambridge. Excluded from succession to throne because of Russian mother. Resided in England with brief visits to Bangkok, 1931, 1937 and 1938. Manager for international motor-racing career of Prince Birabongse (1914–85). Author. Joined Home Guard in England during the Second World War. Married Elisabeth Hunter.

Chulalongkorn, King Rama V (1853–1910)

Son of King Mongkut and Queen Thepsirin. Ascended throne, 1868. Father of King Vajiravudh and King Prajadhipok. Had thirty-six male heirs.

Deng Gunatilaka

Official at Ministry of Foreign Affairs. Son of William Gunatilleke, a prominent Bangkok lawyer of Ceylonese origin and brother-in-law to Khuang. Accompanied Sanguan to China, Washington and Kandy, 1943–4.

Direk Chaiyanam (1905–67)

Studied law, Bangkok. Ministry of Justice, 1928–32. Civilian promoter. Secretary to delegation sent to London, 1934, to negotiate with King Prajadhipok. Cabinet secretary, 1935–40. Deputy Foreign Minister, July 1940–Aug. 1941. Foreign Minister, Aug.–Dec. 1941. Ambassador to Tokyo, Jan. 1942–July 1943. Foreign Minister, Sep. 1943–July 1944. Member of Seri Thai leadership, codenamed "Omar" by Force 136. Visited Kandy clandestinely, Feb. 1945. Minister of Finance, Aug. 1945–Jan. 1946. Foreign Minister, Apr. 1946–Feb. 1947. Ambassador to London, 1947–Feb. 1948. Ambassador to Bonn, 1959–65. Elder brother to Phairote Chaiyanam, Director-General of Government Propaganda, 1941–5.

Kad Songkram, General Luang (d. 1967)

Original name Pian Kengradomying. Attended Military Academy, Bangkok. Member of junior army promoters' faction. Injured in Bovoradet rebellion. Chief of Staff, Royal Thai Air Force, and injured in air crash. Director-General Customs and Excise, 1939. Cabinet minister, 1939–43. Escaped to China. Four children studying in United States, including son Karoon infiltrated back into Thailand by OSS. Leader of coup in 1947 and Deputy Defence Minister, 1948–50. Involved in financial scandal and exiled to Hong Kong.

Karb Kunjara, Colonel Mom Luang (d. 1987)

Appointed military attache in Washington, Aug. 1941. Chief liaison officer between OSS & Seri Thai 1942–4. Visited China Aug. 1943–Nov. 1944. Returned to Bangkok Feb. 1946. Appointed personal adviser to Pibul 1948.

Khuang Abhaiwongse (Luang Kowit Abhaiwongse) (1903–68)

Born Battambang, son of Phya Kanthatham, Thai governor of province till 1907, although the family continued to own large areas of land there and maintain influence till Jan. 1979. Studied electrical engineering at Lyon, France. Excluded from promoters' group in Paris because elder sister married to Prince Charoon, the Thai Minister there. Official in Department of Posts and Telegraphs, 1932, when recruited as civilian promoter. Cabinet minister, 1935–43. Travelled extensively abroad as Director-General of Telecommunications, 1938–40. Presided over ceremony in Battambang, July 1941, marking retrocession to Thailand. Brother-in-law of Poc Khun, a pro-Thai Cambodian propagandist known in Bangkok as Phra Phinit Piset. Minister of Communications, 1942. Minister of Commerce, 1942–3. Deputy Speaker of Assembly, June 1944. Prime Minister, Aug. 1944–5. Elected representative for Bangkok,

Jan. 1946. Prime Minister, Jan.–Mar. 1946. Leader of Democrat Party, Apr. 1946–68. Member of delegation to Washington to negotiate with French on Battambang with special visit to Paris, Aug. 1946–Jan. 1947. Prime Minister, Nov. 1947–Apr. 1948. Elected to Assembly, 1949 and 1957. Married to Lekha, née Gunatilleke.

Liang Chaiyakal (b. 1902)

Lawyer. Elected representative for Ubol in all elections, 1933–57. Responsible for exposing Crown Lands Scandal, 1937. Head of Assembly Committee on the economy, 1944. Member of Democrat Party, 1946. Split from Democrats and founded Peoples Party, 1947. Member of cabinet, Jan.–Mar. 1946, and Deputy Minister of Interior, 1948–51.

Mani Sanasen

Official at League of Nations. Attached to Thai Legation in Washington, 1941. Seri Thai liaison officer travelling to London and Kandy, 1942–4.

Manopakorn Nitthithada, Phya (1886–1948)

Sino-Thai. Educated in England. Lawyer. Judge in Supreme Court. Prime Minister and Finance Minister, June 1932–3. Exiled to Penang, July 1933, and died there.

Mongkut, King Rama IV (1804–68)

Ascended throne, 1851. Father of King Chulalongkorn.

Netr Khemayothin, Colonel (d. 1985)

Attended military staff college in France and Britain. Staff officer in Thai delegations visiting Saigon, Jan. 1941, and Tokyo, Feb.–May 1941, to negotiate ceasefire and treaty with French. Visited Stung Treng, July 1941, for territorial handover by French. Sent by Pibul to meet representatives of 93rd Division in Yunnan, Apr. 1944. Visited Kandy, May–July 1945, as liaison officer between Thai army and Force 136. Member of Thai military mission visiting Kandy, Sep. 1945. Involved in abortive staff officer coup, Oct. 1948, and temporarily detained. Cabinet minister, 1958.

Phahol Pholpayuhasena, Colonel Phya (1887–1947)

Original name Phot Phaholyothin. Military Academy, Bangkok. Attended military college in Germany, 1904–11 (classmate of Hermann Goering). Spent a year on attachment to Japanese army, 1920s. Deputy Director of Artillery, 1931–2. Leader of promoters. Army Commander, 1932–8. Prime Minister, June 1933–Dec. 1938. Given honorary title of "Elder Statesman", Dec.–1938, and made honorary major-general, Apr. 1939. Headed goodwill delegation to Tokyo, Apr. 1942. Refused premiership, July 1944. Cabinet minister, Aug. 1944–45. Armed Forces Commander, Aug. 1944–Mar 1946.

Pibul Songkram, Field-Marshal Luang (1897–1964)

Sino-Thai. Original name Plaek Kittasangka. Graduated from Military Academy, Bangkok, 1915. Artillery officer. Studied at French Artillery School, Fontainebleau, 1920–7. Joined promoters' group in Paris. Returned to Bangkok and appointed military staff instructor and royal equerry. Leader of junior army faction of promoters. Cabinet minister, 1932–44. Deputy Army Commander, June 1933–Jan. 1939. Minister of Defence, Oct. 1934–Aug. 1941. Prime Minister, Dec. 1938–July 1944. Minister of the Interior, 1938–41. Army Commander, Jan. 1939–Aug. 1944. Major-general, Apr. 1939. Minister of Foreign Affairs, July 1939–Aug. 1941. Supreme Commander, Oct. 1940–Mar. 1941. Lieutenant-General, June 1941. Field-Marshal, July 1941. Supreme Commander, Oct. 1941–Aug. 1944. Superior Adviser to Armed Forces, Aug. 1944–5. Detained as war criminal, Oct. 1945–Mar. 1946. Army Commander, Nov. 1947–May 1948. Prime Minister, Apr. 1948–Nov. 1957. Exiled and died in Japan. Married 1918 to La-iad, née Pantukrawi (1904–84). Eldest son Prasong studied at Dartmouth Naval College, England. Second son Ananta studied at Belgian military college and daughter Chirawat in France. All three children repatriated, July 1942. Third son Nit born 1941.

Prajadhipok, King Rama VII (1893–1941)

Son of King Chulalongkorn and Queen Saovabha. Younger brother of King Vajiravudh. Educated at Eton and Woolwich Military Academy. Commissioned in Royal Horse Artillery. Ascended throne, 1925. Left Siam on foreign tour and for medical treatment, Jan. 1934. Abdicated, Mar. 1935. Lived in England till death. Married cousin, Queen Rambhai Bharni. No children.

Prasat Pitthiyayuth, Colonel Phra

Original name Wan Chuthin. Studied at military college in Germany with Phya Phahol and Phya Song. Officer in Siamese military contingent sent to France, 1917. Director of General Staff School, Bangkok, 1932. Senior army promoter. Cabinet minister, 1932–June 1933. Accompanied Phya Song to Europe, 1933–4. Attached to Ministry of Defence, 1934–8. Thai minister to Berlin, 1939–45. Detained by Soviet army till Apr. 1946.

Prayoon Pamornmontri, Major-General (1897–1982)

Born Berlin. Son of Thai diplomat and German mother. Studied at Military Academy, Bangkok. Toured Europe, 1922–8. Joined promoters' group in Paris. Official at Post Office, 1932. Cabinet secretary, 1932–June 1933.

Suspected of involvement in Bovoradet rebellion, Oct. 1933. Consul in Saigon, 1934–6. Military secretary to Pibul. Attachment to German army, 1937–8. Head of Yuvachon, 1938–43. Cabinet minister, 1938–44. Visited Berlin, Sep. 1939. Deputy Minister of Education, Aug. 1940–4. Visited Berlin and Rome, Oct.–Dec. 1940. Visited Moscow, Jan. 1941, to establish diplomatic relations with Soviet Union. Member of Joint Thai-Japanese Military Commission, Dec. 1941–Aug. 1944. Detained as war criminal, Oct. 1945–Mar. 1946. Cabinet minister, Nov. 1951–Jun. 1952. Dropped out of public life.

Prem Purachatra, Phra Ong Chao, His Highness Prince (1915–81)

Son of Purachatra, Prince of Kampangphet (1882–36). Journalist and writer. Married Mom Ngarmchit, daughter of Phra Sarasat Pholkand.

Pridi Banomyong (Luang Pradit Manutharm) (1900–83)

Sino-Thai. Graduated in law, Bangkok. Studied in France, 1920–7. Doctorate in law and diploma in political economics at Sorbonne. Formed promoters' group in Paris. Official at Ministry of Justice, 1927–32. Mentor of Khana Ratsadorn. Cabinet minister, 1932–Mar. 1933. Member of constitutional drafting committee, 1932. Drafted National Economic Plan, Feb. 1933. Banished to France, Apr.–Sep. 1933. Cabinet minister, Sep.–Dec. 1933. Cleared of communist charges, Mar. 1934. Minister of Interior, Mar. 1934–Feb. 1936. World tour, 1935. Minister of Foreign Affairs, Feb. 1936–Dec. 1938. Minister of Finance, Dec. 1938–41. Regent, Dec. 1941–5. Sole regent from Aug. 1944. Leader of Seri Thai in Bangkok, codenamed "Ruth". Honorary title "Senior Statesman", Dec. 1945. Prime Minister, Mar.–Aug. 1946. World tour, Oct. 1946–Feb. 1947. Fled to exile, Nov. 1947. Involved in abortive Palace Rebellion, Feb. 1949. Lived in exile in China, 1949–70, and in Paris till death. Elder brother of Louis Banomyong, a banker, and Luang Arthakit Kamchorn, a diplomat. Married to Poonsuk, née na Pombejr. Four children.

Prom Yothi, General Luang (1896–1966)

Original name Mangkorn Polchiwin. Graduated from Military Academy, Bangkok, in same class as Pibul. Studied at military staff college in France and England. Member of junior army faction of promoters. Cabinet minister, 1938–44. Deputy Minister of Defence, Apr. 1939–Aug. 1941. Visited Indo-China and Japan, Aug.–Oct. 1940. Commander of Eastern Army fighting French, Oct. 1940–Mar, 1941. Minister of Defence, Aug.–Dec. 1941. Minister of Interior, Mar. 1942–3. Detained as war criminal, Oct. 1945–Mar. 1946. Minister of Education and Interior alternatively, Apr. 1948–Jun. 1952. Mayor of Bangkok.

Puey Ungpakorn, Dr (b. 1916)

Chinese born in Bangkok. Studied economics at University of Moral and Political Sciences. Studied for doctorate at London School of Economics. Joined Pioneer Corps, Aug. 1942. Commissioned in British army and joined Force 136, codenamed "Khem". Parachuted into Thailand, Apr. 1944. Imprisoned in Bangkok and established radio contact with Calcutta, Aug. 1944. Liaison officer for Force 136. Interpreter for Thai military mission visiting Kandy, Sep. 1945. Completed studies at London School of Economics, 1949. Official of Ministry of Finance, 1949–60. Governor of Bank of Thailand, 1959–71. Rector of Thammasat University, 1975–Oct. 1976. Fled to exile in London.

Radjwangsan, Admiral Phya (1886–1940)

Chief of Staff of Navy, 1932. Minister of Defence, 1932–Jun. 1933. Siamese Minister in Paris, 1936. Elder brother to Sindhu.

Rambhai Bharni, Queen (1904–84)

Daughter of Prince Svasti. Married cousin Prince Prajadhipok and became Queen Consort. Lived in England, 1934–49. Member of Free Siamese movement. Property restored and endowed a hospital in Chantaboon province. Sister of Prince Supha Svasti (Tan Chin).

Rangsit, Krom Khun His Highness Prince of Chainat (d. 1951)

Son of King Chulalongkorn (13th family). Studied in Germany. Guardian to King Ananda. Detained, Jan. 1939, and sentenced to death, commuted to life imprisonment. Released from prison, Sep. 1944, and royal ranks restored. Regent, June 1946–51. Married to German lady.

Ritthi Akaney, Colonel Phya (1889–1967)

Original name Sala Emsiri. Studied at Military Academy, Bangkok. Commander, First Artillery Regiment Royal Brigade of Guards, 1932. Member of senior army promoters' faction. Cabinet minister, 1932–June 1933. Minister of Agriculture, Feb. 1936–Sep. 1938. Exiled to Malaya, 1938–46.

Sakol Voravarn, Mom Chao His Serene Highness Prince

Grandson of King Mongkut (19th family). Adviser to Ministry of Interior, 1932. Supported Pridi's economic plan, 1933. Dubbed the "Red Prince". Adviser to Cooperative Party, 1946. Thai representative to Conciliation Commission on border with Indo-China, 1947. Elder brother of Prince Wan. Married to German lady.

Sanguan Tularaks (b. 1900)

Civilian promoter. Lectured on constitution, 1932. Director of penal colony for political prisoners. Director of State Tobacco Monopoly. Escaped to China, July 1943, with credentials from Pridi to set up Thai National Liberation Committee abroad. Fell under influence of General Tai Li. Transferred to Washington, Dec. 1943. OSS liaison officer in Kandy, Aug. 1944–5. Head of War Crimes Investigation Committee, Bangkok, Aug. 1945. Organised Sino-Thai movement, Sep. 1945. Ambassador to China, Oct. 1946–Nov. 1947. Lived in China for many years.

Sangworn Suwannakit, Admiral Luang (1901–73)

Original name Sangworn Suwannachip. Naval promoter. Lived in Japan, 1935–7 to oversee construction of gunboats and submarines for Thai navy. Cabinet minister, Dec. 1938–Oct. 1943. Commander of Sattahip naval base. Organised Special Security Police modelled on *Kempei*, Dec. 1943. Co-operated with Seri Thai, 1944–5. Provided sanctuary to Japanese suspected as war criminals. Director-General of Customs, Apr. 1946. Director-General of Police, 1947. Involved in abortive palace rebellion, Feb. 1949.

Sarasat Pholkand, Phra

Diplomat in Paris in 1920s. Won Calcutta sweepstake, 1927. Journalist advocating economic nationalism under pen-name "555". Minister of Economic Affairs, Mar.–Sep. 1934. Fled to Japan, Aug. 1935, and bought property in Manchukuo. Returned to Bangkok but fled to Japan again, Jan. 1939. Head of "Thai Room" in Tokyo and broadcaster of pro-Japanese propaganda. Returned to Bangkok, Mar. 1945. Detained as war criminal, Oct. 1945–Mar. 1946.

Sawang Srisavarinthira, Queen (1863–1955)

Daughter of King Mongkut and Chao Chom Piam. Royal consort to King Chulalongkorn, together with sisters Queen Sunanda (drowned 1881) and Queen Saovabha (1864–1919). Mother of Crown Prince Vajirunhis (1878–95) and Prince Mahidol. Queen Grandmother to King Ananda.

Sena Songkram, Major-General Phya

Original name Mom Rajawong Ee Nopawong. Commander First Army Corps. Wounded, June 24, 1932. Founder of Khana Chart, Jan. 1933. Joined Bovoradet rebellion, Oct. 1933. Fled to exile in Indo-China.

Senanarong, General Luang

Career military officer. Commanded forces opposed to Japanese landing in Nakorn Srithammarat, Dec. 8, 1941. Led military mission to Kandy, Sep. 1945.

Seni Pramoj, Mom Rajawong (b. 1902)

Great-grandson of King Rama II. Educated in England at Trent College and Oxford. Barrister-at-law, Grays Inn. Returned to Bangkok, 1929. Judge and lecturer in law, University of Moral and Political Science, till 1940. Minister in Washington, Apr. 1940–Aug. 1945. Leader of Seri Thai in United States. Prime Minister, Sep.–Jan. 1945. Foreign Minister, Sep. 1945–Mar. 1946. Minister of Justice, Nov. 1947–Apr. 1948. Leader of Democrat Party after death of Khuang, 1968. Prime Minister, Jan.–Mar. 1975, and Apr.–Oct. 1976. Elder brother of M.R. Kukrit Pramoj.

Seri Roengrit, Major-General Luang

Original name Charoon Ratanakul. Member of junior army promoters' faction. Director of State Railways. Cabinet minister, Dec. 1938–Aug. 1944. Deputy Commander Eastern Army, Oct. 1940–Mar. 1941. Commander Northern Army, Feb.–May 1942. Minister of Trade and Commerce, May 1942–July 1944. Detained as war criminal, Oct. 1945–Mar. 1946. Member of Assembly, May 1946–Nov. 1951. Father of Aram Ratanakul, a student in Switzerland who in 1944 married Princess Galyani, elder sister of King Ananda.

Sinad Yotharaks, Major-General Luang

Career military officer. Deputy army commander, Aug. 1944–5. Military representative in Seri Thai leadership, code-named "Champa" by Force 136. Minister of Defence, Aug.–Oct. 1945 and Nov. 1947–Apr. 1948. Member of Democrat Party.

Sindhu Songkramchai, Admiral Luang (1902–75)

Original name Sindhu Komolnawin. Studied at Danish naval school. Joined promoters' group in Paris. Naval staff instructor, 1932. Leader of naval promoters. Cabinet minister, 1932–Aug. 1945. Chief of Naval Staff, Aug. 1933–June 1951. Visited Japan and Italy, 1935–6. Minister of Education, Feb. 1935–Mar. 1942. Minister of Economic Affairs, Mar. 1942–July 1944. Minister of Defence, Aug. 1944–5. Dismissed from naval service after Manhattan Rebellion, June 1951.

Sitthiporn Kridakorn, Mom Chao His Serene Highness Prince (1883–1971)

Grandson of King Mongkut (1st family). Agricultural expert and government adviser. Detained as political prisoner, Oct. 1933–Sep. 1944. Minister of Agriculture, Feb.–Apr. 1948. Younger brother of Prince Bovoradet.

Song Suradej, Colonel Phya (1891–1944)

Half Vietnamese. Original name Thep Panthumsaen. Studied military science in Germany. Senior instructor at Military Academy, Bangkok, 1932. Member of senior army promoters' faction. Cabinet minister, 1932–June 1933. Deputy Army Commander and Director of Military Operations, 1932–June 1933. Study tour of Europe, Sep. 1933–June 1934. Tour of Burma, Oct. 1934–Jan. 1935. Tour of China, 1936. Head of military school in Chiengmai, 1936–Jan. 1939. Appointed to Defence Advisory Board and resigned, Aug.–Sep. 1938. Exiled to Indo-China, Jan. 1939, and lived in Saigon till death.

Srisith Songkram, Colonel Phya (d. 1933)

Classmate at Military Academy of Phya Phahol. Refused to join promoters. Offered to join new administration on afternoon of June 24, 1932, but excluded. Appointed Director of Military Operations, June 18, 1933, following resignation of Phya Song. Dismissed two days later. Plotted anti-government coup and joined Bovoradet rebellion as head of Ayuthya garrison. Killed in battle of Hin Lap.

Sri Visarn Vacha, Phya (1893–1968)

British citizen of Chinese origin. Under-Secretary in Ministry of Foreign Affairs before 1932. Advised King against introducing a constitution. Minister of Foreign Affairs, 1932–June 1933. Member of constitutional drafting committee, Oct. 1932. Minister of Finance, Jan.–Mar. 1946. Minister of Foreign Affairs, Nov. 1947–Apr. 1948. Government adviser, 1958–68.

Supha Chalasai, Luang (1895–1965)

Original name Bung Supha Chalasai. Naval promoter. Captained gunboat sent to collect King from Hua Hin, June 1932. Cabinet minister, Apr. 1933–Sep. 1945. Deputy Commander of Navy, Aug. 1933–Apr. 1934. Director of Physical Education in Ministry of Education, Apr. 1934–9. Minister of Interior, Aug. 1944–5. Member of Seri Thai leadership. Minister of Industry, Nov. 1947–Apr. 1948.

Suphasvasti Swasdiwat, Mom Chao His Serene Highness

Known as Tan Chin. Son of Prince Svasti and brother of Queen Rambhai. Educated in England and commissioned in British army. Suspected of involvement in Bovoradet rebellion. Departed to exile in England, Dec. 1933. Returned to service with British army, Aug. 1941. Recruited by SOE, codenamed "Major Arun". Sent to Chungking to meet Chamkad, July 1943. Infiltrated into Thailand, Apr. 1945, and worked with Seri Thai guerrilla group in Tak. Acted as liaison officer for British army in Bangkok, Sep.–Dec. 1945. Younger brother served with OSS, codenamed "Johnny".

Svasti, Prince (d. 1936)

Son of King Mongkut and Chao Chom Piam. Brother to three royal consorts of King Chulalongkorn, Queens Sunanda, Sawang and Saowabha. Father of Rambhai Bharni, Queen to King Prajadhipok. Controller of Privy Purse, 1925–33. Held controlling interest in *Bangkok Daily Mail* (closed down, Oct. 1933). Exiled to Penang, Dec. 1933.

Tasnai Niyomsuk, Captain Luang (d. 1933)

Original name Tasnai Mitrpakdi. Cavalry officer. Studied in France. Joined promoters' group in Paris. Declined cabinet position, June 1932. Accompanied Pridi to Singapore, Apr. 1933, as gesture of loyalty.

Thamrong Nawasawat, Admiral Luang (1901–88)

Original name Thawal Tharisawat. Studied at Naval Academy, Bangkok, and transferred to office of Naval Advocate-General for training as lawyer. Nicknamed Lin Thong ("Golden Tongue"). Naval promoter. Cabinet minister, Dec. 1933–Aug. 1944. Member of delegation to England to negotiate with King Prajadhipok, Nov. 1934. Minister of Interior, Feb. 1936–Dec. 1938. Minister of Justice, Dec. 1938–July 1944. Led goodwill mission to Burma, India and Australia, Sep.–Dec. 1940. Member of goodwill mission to Tokyo, Mar. 1942. Minister of Justice, Mar.–Aug. 1946. Founder of Constitutional Front Party, Apr. 1946. Prime Minister, Aug. 1946–Nov. 1947. Departed to temporary exile in Hong Kong and retired from public life into business.

Thanat Khoman, Dr (b. 1914)

Sino-Thai. Doctorate in law, Paris. Entered Diplomatic Service, 1940, and attached to Government Propaganda Bureau, Sep. 1940. Official in Battambang, July–Dec. 1941. First Secretary, Thai Embassy, Tokyo, Jan. 1942-3. Member of clandestine mission to Kandy, Feb. 1945. Chargé d'Affaires, Washington, 1946-7; Delhi, 1947-9. Ambassador in Washington, 1957-8. Foreign Minister, 1959-71. Head of Democrat Party, 1979-82. Deputy Prime Minister, 1980-2.

Thawee Bunyaket (1904–70)

Studied agricultural science in France. Joined promoters' group in Paris. Cabinet secretary, July 1939–Feb. 1943. Election as Assembly speaker aborted by Pibul, July 1943. Member of Seri Thai leadership. Minister of Education, Aug. 1944–5. Prime Minister, Sep. 1–17, 1945. Minister of Interior, Sep. 1945–Jan. 1946. Minister of Agriculture, Mar.–Aug. 1946. Lived in political exile in Penang, Oct. 1948–58. Vice-President and President of Constituent Assembly, 1958–68.

Thawee Chullasap, Air Chief Marshal (b. 1914)

Graduated from Military Academy, Bangkok, 1935, and jcined air force. Studied at Annapolis. Member of Thai military mission, Singapore, Oct. 1941. Attached to General Yamashita's staff, Malaya and Singapore, Dec. 1941–Mar. 1942. Visited Kandy, Mar.–June 1945, as liaison officer with US Air Force and OSS. Member, Thai military mission, Kandy, Sep. 1945. Air Attaché, Delhi, 1950. Chief of Air Staff, 1954. Deputy Chief of Defence Staff, 1957. Chief of Staff, Supreme Command, 1961–73. Minister of Communications, 1969–71. Minister of Agriculture, 1972–3. Visited Peking as head of Thai National Sports Committee, 1972–3. Deputy Prime Minister and Minister of Defence, Oct. 1973–Jan. 1976. Head of National Olympic Committee and elected representative for Mae Hongsorn.

Thawee Thawetikul (d. 1949)

Studied law in France. Diplomat in Tokyo, Jan. 1942–Aug. 1943. Head of Trade and Economic Section, Ministry of Foreign Affairs, Aug. 1943–5. Member of Thai military mission, Kandy, Sep. 1945. Head of Office for Enemy Alien Property, Oct. 1945. Shot dead after abortive palace rebellion.

Thawil Udol (d. 1949)

Elected representative for Roi Et, 1938–49. Escaped to China, Oct. 1944, as envoy from Pridi to Chiang Kai-shek. Cabinet minister, 1946–7. Murdered in police custody, Mar. 1949.

Thephatsadin, Major-General Phya (d. 1951)

Leader of Siamese military contingent to France, 1917. Pioneer of air transport in Siam. Elected representative for Bangkok, Nov. 1933, and Deputy Speaker of Assembly. Arrested for treason, Oct. 1934, but acquitted on appeal. Detained, Jan. 1939, and sentenced to death, commuted to life imprisonment. Two sons executed, Dec. 1939. Amnestied, Sep. 1944. Cabinet minister, Nov. 1948–Jan. 1951.

Thongin Buripat (d. 1949)

Lawyer. Elected representative for Ubol, 1933–49. Member of Seri Thai. Cabinet minister, Aug. 1945–Jan. 1946. Founder of Cooperative Party, Mar.

1946. Minister of Industry, Mar. 1946–Nov. 1947. Murdered in police custody, Mar. 1949.

Tiang Sirikhan (d. 1952)

Elected representative for Sakol Nakorn, Nov. 1938–52. Seri Thai guerrilla leader in north-east. Cabinet minister, Aug. 1945–Jan. 1946, and Aug. 1946–Apr. 1947. Member of Thai delegation to Conciliation Commission on border with Indo-China. Secretary-General of South East Asia League, Sep.–Nov. 1947. Disappeared, presumed murdered by police, 1952.

Vajiravudh, King Rama VI (1881–1925)

Son of King Chulalongkorn and Queen Saovabha. Ascended throne, 1910. No male heirs.

Vanich Pananond (d. 1944)

Sino-Thai businessman. Brother-in-law of Sindhu. Director of Fuel Oil Department of Ministry of Defence, Feb. 1937–Sep. 1940. Director of Thai Rice Company, Feb. 1939. Temporarily detained on charges of financial irregularity, Apr. 1940. Visited Tokyo, July–Sep. 1940. Director-General of Commerce, Nov. 1940–Dec. 1941. Member of Thai delegation to Tokyo to negotiate treaty with France, Jan.–May 1941. Attached to Ministry of Foreign Affairs, Aug. 1941. Investigated as a fifth columnist, Oct. 1941. Cabinet minister, Dec. 1941–Jan. 1944. Deputy Minister of Finance, Feb. 1942–4. Visited Tokyo, Mar.–June 1942, to negotiate devaluation of baht, financial loans and barter trade deals. Arrested on charges of gold speculation, Feb. 1944. Committed suicide in police custody.

Vichit Vadhakarn, Luang (1898–1962)

Original name Vichit Wattanaprida. Chinese in origin. Diplomat in Paris 1924–7. Married a French woman and subsequently divorced. Resigned from diplomatic service, Sep. 1932. Member of Khana Chart, Jan. 1933. Nominated member of Assembly, Sep. 1933. Director of Department of Fine Arts, 1933–41. Cabinet minister, 1937–Oct. 1943. Launched Pan-Thai movement, July 1938. Dubbed Goebbels of Thailand during irredentist campaign. Head of Government Broadcasting Committee, Oct. 1940. Visited Tokyo, Feb.–Mar. 1941, to participate in negotiations with French. Deputy Foreign Minister, Aug. 1941–Mar. 1942. Foreign Minister, Mar. 1942–Oct. 1943. Ambassador to Tokyo, Oct. 1943–Aug. 1945. Arrested by US forces, Tokyo, Sep. 1945. Repatriated to Bangkok, Dec. 1945, and detained as war criminal till Mar. 1946. Cabinet minister, Nov. 1951–Mar. 1952. Ambassador to Berne, 1954–9. Personal adviser to Prime Minister, 1959–62. Second wife a dancer, choreographer and lecturer at Silpakorn University.

Vilas Osatanond

Sino-Thai businessman. Married to daughter of Seow Hood Seng, representative of KMT in Bangkok and founder of Sriboonruang family. Civilian promoter. Thai Trade Commissioner, Hong Kong, 1937–9. Cabinet minister,
1939–Dec. 1941. Director-General, Government Propaganda, 1939–41. Director of various state enterprises. Visited Batavia and Singapore to negotiate for
oil, Apr.–May 1941. Following dismissal from cabinet in Dec. 1941, set up
various private business companies in partnership with Seri Roengrit and
Thamrong, and regarded as war profiteer. Brothers-in-law Songkim and
Songkiap fled to Yunnan, Jan. 1942, to work with KMT. Sister-in-law Songlan
organised clandestine KMT network in Bangkok. Stood for election in
Bangkok, Jan. 1946, but defeated by Khuang. Nominated member of Assembly, May 1946, and elected Speaker, May–Aug. 1946. Minister of Trade, Aug.
1946–Mar. 1947.

Wan Waityakorn Voravarn, Mom Chao His Serene Highness Prince
(1891–1976)

Grandson of King Mongkut (19th family), Younger brother of Prince Sakol.
Educated Marlborough and Balliol College, Oxford. Ecole Libre des Sciences
Politiques, Paris. Entered Diplomatic Service, 1918. Thai delegate to League of
Nations, 1926–30. Forced to resign from Diplomatic Service following divorce
and remarriage. Founded *Prachachart* newspaper (temporarily closed down Apr.
1933). Adviser to Ministry of Foreign Affairs and personal adviser to Prime
Minister, June 1933–Aug. 1945. Wrote newspaper articles under pen-name
"Warnwai", 1940–1. Head of Thai delegation visiting Tokyo to negotiate
treaty with French, Feb.–May 1941. Head of Thai delegation attending Greater
East Asia Conference, Tokyo, Nov. 1943. Member of constitutional drafting
committee, July 1945–May 1946. Nominated member of Assembly, May 1946.
Head of Thai delegation visiting Washington to negotiate retrocession of territory to Indo-China, Aug.–Dec. 1946. Ambassador to Washington and Thai
representative, United Nations, 1947–52. Elevated in royal rank and assumed
name "Prince Narathip". Foreign Minister, 1952–9. Thai representative to
Afro-Asia Conference, Bandung, 1955. President of UN General Assembly,
1956–7. Deputy Prime Minister, Jan. 1958–68.

BIBLIOGRAPHY

Unpublished documents

AL 435 (SEATIC 246). Burma-Siam Railway, Imperial War Museum (IWM), London.

AL 5192. Japanese Monograph on operations of 15th Army, IWM.

AL 5199. Japanese Monograph on operations in Thailand. IWM.

FO 371. Series of British Foreign Office correspondence, Public Records Office (PRO), Kew.

Magic Documents: Summaries and Transcripts of Japanese Top-Secret Diplomatic Communications, Jan. 1938–45 (Sanitised microfilm version prepared by University Publications of America, Inc.).

RG 59, State Department records, National Archives (NA), Washington.

RG 84. Boxes of correspondence from US mission in Bangkok, Washington National Records Centre (WNRC), Suitland.

RG 165 ABC files, Modern military records, NA.

RG 218. Joint Chiefs of Staff files. Modern military records, NA.

RG 226. OSS Research and Analysis reports. Modern military records, NA.

Testimonies to War Crimes Tribunal, Bangkok 1945, by Prince Aditya, Thawee Bunyaket and Police General Adul Detcharat although, since Adul's original is in manuscript, the text as published by Suphote Dantrakul is used as reference.

WO 172. Volumes of SEAC daily record, PRO.

WO 193. Records of Directorate of Military Operations, PRO.

WO 203. Series of SEAC correspondence, PRO.

WO 208. Records of Directorate of Military Intelligence, PRO.

Published documents

Buangraek Prachathipatai (The Beginnings of Democracy). Documents collected by Thai Journalists Association. Mitnara, Bangkok, 1973.

DBFP. Documents on British Foreign Policy, 2nd Series.

DGFP. Documents on German Foreign Policy.

FRUS. Foreign Relations of the United States, Far East Series.

Ike, Nobutake; *Japan's Decision for War* (Stanford 1967)

Prasert Patamasukhon: 42 Pi Ratasapha (Records of the National Assembly, 1932–74) (Chumnumchang, Bangkok 1974).

Thak Chaloemtiarana (ed.), *Thailand: Documents and Extracts 1932–57.* Bangkok: Social Science Association of Thailand, Bangkok, 1978.

Official histories and reports

Kirby, S. Woodburn, *The War against Japan* (5 vols.).

Mountbatten, Vice-Admiral, *Report to the Combined Chiefs of Staff by Supreme Commander SEA* London: HMSO, 1951.
OSS, *Japanese Domination of Thailand*. Washington, DC, 1943.
Woodward, Sir Llewellyn, *British Foreign Policy during the Second World War* (5 vols.).

Newspapers

Bangkok Post (BP).
Bangkok Times Weekly Mail, including translations from Thai press (BTWM).
Chicago Daily News.
Christian Science Monitor (CSM)
Daily Express.
Daily Telegraph (DT).
Democracy.
Manchester Guardian (MG).
New York Herald Tribune (NYHT).
New York Times (NYT).
Straits Times.
Syonon Shimbun.
Syonan Times.
Times.

Memoirs and personal accounts

Ananta Pibulsongram, *Chompol P. Pibulsongkram*, including selected cabinet records and personal correspondence (5 vols), Bangkok: Soon Karn Pim, 1975–7.
Baudouin, Paul, *The Private Diaries*. London, 1948.
Boulle, Pierre, *My Own River Kwai*. New York: Vanguard Press, 1967.
Caply, Michel, *Guérilla au Laos*. Paris, 1966.
Chula Chakrabongse, Prince, *Brought up in England*. London: G. T. Foulis, 1943.
——, *Lords of Life*. London: Alvin Redman, 1960.
——, *The Twain Have Met*. London: G.T. Foulis, 1956.
Churchill, Winston, *The Second World War*. 6 vols, London: Cassell, 1948–54.
Crosby, Josiah, *Siam at the Crossroads*. London, 1945.
Decoux, Admiral Jean, *A la barre de L'Indochine*. Paris, 1949.
Direk Chaiyanam, *Siam and World War II*. Including contributions by Thawee Bunyaket, Puey Ungpakorn, and Phra Phisal Sukhumvit (trans. J.G. Keyes). Bangkok: Social Science Association of Thailand, 1978.
Fujiwara, Iwaiki, *F Kikan*. Hong Kong: Heinemann Asia, 1983.
Galyani Wattana, Princess, *Chao Nai Lek: Yuvaksatri* (The young monarch). Bangkok, 1987.

Gilchrist, Andrew, *Bangkok Top Secret*. London, 1970.

Harn Songkram, General, *Anusorn* (Cremation volume of memoirs). Bangkok, 1962.

Hull, Cordell, *Memoirs* (2 vols).

Khuang Abhaiwongse, Address of Nov. 23, 1963, to Pedagogical Council (*Kurusapha*). Bangkok: Chumnum Chulalongkorn, Aug. 1969.

Konthi Suphamongkol *Karnvithesobai Kong Thai* (Thai Foreign Policy). Bangkok, 1984.

Macdonald, Alexander, *Bangkok Editor*. New York, 1949.

Miles, Milton, *A Different Kind of War*. New York, 1967.

Netr Khemayothin, *Chiwit Nai Pol* (Life of a General) and *Ngarn Taidin kong Pan Ek Yothi* (The Underground Work of Colonel Yothi), 3 vols. Bangkok: Kasembannakit, 1967.

Nicol Smith and Blake Clark, *Into Siam: Underground Kingdom*. New York: Bobbs Merrill, 1946.

Oune Chananikorn (Sananikone), *Kwamlang kong Karpajao* (My Past). Bangkok: Duangkamol, 1977.

Phinit Chonkadi, Phra, *Nithan Tamruaj*. (Cremation volume of memoirs). Bangkok, 1970.

Phaisal Traikuli, *Viraburut Niranam* (Unnamed Hero). Bangkok: Ruangsilp, 1979.

Phisal Sukhumvit, Phra, *Chotmaihet kong Seri Thai* (Account of a Seri Thai). Bangkok, 1979.

Pramote Pungsunthorn (ed.), *Bang Ruang kjeow kap Phraboromsanuwong nai Songkram Lok Ti Song* (Some matters relating to the Royal Family during the Second World War), including accounts by Mom Chaoying Aphasapha Tevakul, Puey Ungpakorn and Pridi Banomyong. Bangkok 1972.

Prayoon Pamornmontri, *Chiwit Ha Paendin* (My Life in Five Reigns). Bangkok, 1975.

Pridi Banomyong, *Ma vie mouvementée*. Paris, 1974.

Ray, Jayanta K., *Portraits of Thai Politics*, including the memoirs of Thawee Bunyaket, Seni Pramot and La-iad Pibulsongkram. Delhi: Orient Longman, 1972.

Sangworn Suwannachip, *Anusorn* (Cremation volume of personal memoirs). Bangkok: Chuan Pim, 1973.

Seni Pramoj, Mom Rajawong, *Chumnum Wannakhadi tang Karnmuang* (Collection of Political Speeches). Bangkok, 1968.

Sihanouk, Prince Norodom, *Souvenirs doux et amers*. Paris, 1981.

Smith, Malcolm, *A Physician at the Court of Siam*. London, 1957.

Suphote Dantrakul, *Pol Tamruaj Ek Adul Aduldecharat* (Cremation volume including testimony to War Crimes Tribunal and tributes by Puey Ungpakorn and La-iad Pibulsongkram). Bangkok, 1979.

Thawee Chullasap, *Chart Yoo Nua Sing Dai* (My Country Above All). Bangkok, 1974.

Tsuji, Masaobu, *Singapore: The Japanese Version*. London, 1962.
——, *Underground Escape*. Tokyo, 1952.
Vichit Vadhakarn, *Thailand's Case*. Bangkok, 1941.

Secondary sources

Allen, Louis, *Singapore, 1941–42*. London: Davis-Poynter, 1977.
——, *The End of the War in Asia*. London, 1976.
Batson, Benjamin, *Documents from the End of the Absolute Monarchy* (Cornell Data Paper, no. 96, July 1974).
——, *The End of the Absolute Monarchy in Siam*. Singapore: Oxford University Press, 1984.
——, "The Fall of the Pibul Government 1944", *Journal of Siam Society* (*JSS*), 62, 2 (July 1974).
Bergamini, David, *Japan's Imperial Conspiracy*. London, 1971.
Blair, Joan and Clay, *Return from the River Kwai*. London: Futura, 1980.
Boyle, Andrew, *The Climate of Treason*. (London, 1980).
Brimmel, J.H., *Communism in South East Asia*. London, 1959.
Butow, R.J., *Japan's Decision to Surrender*. Stanford, 1954.
Chai-anant Samutvanich, *14 Tula: Khana Rat kap Kobot Bovoradat* (14 October: The Khana Rat and the Bovoradet Rebellion). Bangkok, 1974.
Charivat Santaputra, *Thai Foreign Policy, 1932–46*. Bangkok, 1985.
Charnvit Kasetsiri, "The First Pibul Government and Its Involvement in World War II", *JSS*, 62, 2 (July 1974).
Coast, John, *Some Aspects of Siamese Politics*. New York: Institute of Pacific Relations, 1953.
Cruikshank, Charles, *SOE in the Far East*. Oxford University Press, 1983.
Darling, Frank C., *Thailand and the United States*. Washington, DC, 1965.
Duan Bunnag, *Tan Pridi, Rataburut Awuso* (Pridi, Senior Statesman). Bangkok, 1974.
Duncanson, Dennis, "Ho Chi Minh in Hong Kong, 1931–32", *China Quarterly*, 57 (Jan.–Mar. 1973).
Feis, Herbert, *The Road to Pearl Harbor*. Princeton, 1971.
Fistie, Pierre, *L'Evolution de la Thaïlande contemporaine*. Paris, 1967.
——, *Sous-développement et Utopie au Siam*. Paris, 1969.
Flood, E. Thadeus, "Japan's Relations with Thailand 1927–41" (unpubl. Ph.D. thesis, University of Washington, 1967).
Gaudel, André, *L'Indochine française en face du Japon*. Paris, 1947.
Huynh Kim Khanh, *The Vietnamese Communist Party*. Ithaca, NY: Cornell University Press, 1982.
Ingram, J.C., *Economic Change in Thailand since 1850*. Stanford, 1955.
Jones, F.C., *Japan's New Order in East Asia*. Oxford, 1954.
Kennedy, Malcolm, *Communism in Asia*. London, 1957.
Kruger, Rayne, *The Devil's Discus*. London: Cassell, 1964.

Kularb Saipradit, *Buanglang Karnpatiwat 2475* (Behind the 1932 Revolution). Reprinted by Burapha Deng, Bangkok, 1975.

Lacouture, Jean, *Ho Chi Minh*. Harmondsworth: Penguin, 1968.

Landon, Kenneth P., *Siam in Transition*. Chicago, 1939.

——, *The Chinese in Thailand*. London, 1941.

Lewin, Ronald, *The Other Ultra*. London, 1982.

Martin, James V., "Thai American Relations in World War II", *Journal of Asian Studies*, XXII, 4 (Aug. 1963).

Maclane, Charles B., *Soviet Strategies in South East Asia*. Princeton, 1966.

Morley, J.W. (ed.), *The Fateful Choice: Japan's Advance into South East Asia*. New York, 1980.

Nai Chantana (pseud.), *XO Group*. Bangkok: Progress Press, 1946.

Neher, Arlene, "Prelude to Alliance: The Expansion of the American Economic Role in Thailand during the 1940s". Unpubl. Ph.D. thesis, Northern Illinois University, 1980.

Riggs, Fred W., *Thailand: The Modernisation of a Bureaucratic Polity*. Honolulu: East West Centre, 1966.

Robertson, Eric, *The Japanese File*. Hong Kong: Heinemann Asia, 1979.

Sarasat Pholkand, Phra, *My Country, Thailand*. 2nd edn, Bangkok, 1950.

Sathuan Suphasophon, *Chiwit tang Karnmuang kong Pol Ek Phya Ritthi Akaney* (The Political Life of General Phya Ritthi Akaney). Bangkok, 1971.

Siri Premchit, *Chiwit lae Ngarn kong Pol Rua Tri Thawal Thamrong Nawasawat* (The Life and Work of Rear-Admiral Thawal Thamrong Nawasawat). Bangkok, 1978.

Sivaram, M., *The New Siam in the Making*. Bangkok, 1936.

Skinner, G.W., *Chinese Society in Thailand*. Ithaca, NY, 1957.

Smith, R. Harris, *OSS*. New York, 1972.

Sriphanon Singthong, *Sipsong Chompol Thai* (Twelve Thai Field-Marshals). Bangkok, 1963.

Tarling, Nicholas, "Atonement before Absolution", *JSS*, 66, 1 (Jan. 1978).

——, "Rice and Reconciliation", *JSS*.

——, *Thailand and the Japanese Presence, 1941–45*. Singapore: ISEAS, 1977.

Thamsook Numnonda, *Foon Adit* (Recovering the Past) Bangkok: Ruangsilp, 1979.

Thawatt Mokarapong, *History of the Thai Revolution*. Bangkok: Chalermnit, 1972.

Thompson, Virginia, *Thailand, the New Siam*. Institute of Pacific Relations, 1941.

Thorne, Christopher, *Allies of a Kind*. London: Hamish Hamilton, 1978.

Turton, Andrew (ed.), *Thailand, Roots of Conflict*. London, 1978.

Vella, Walter, *Chaiyo: The Role of King Vajiravudh in the Development of Thai Nationalism*. Honolulu, 1978.

——, *The Impact of the West on Government in Thailand*. Berkeley: University of California Press, 1955.

Wilson, David A., *Politics in Thailand*. Ithaca, NY, 1962.

Withet Korani (pseud.), *Hetkarn tang Karnmuang 43Pi haeng Rabop Prachathi-patai* (Political Events during 43 Years of the Democratic System). Bangkok, 1975.

Wohlstetter, R., *Pearl Harbor: Warning and Decision*. Stanford, 1962.

Wyatt, David L., *Thailand: A Short History*. New Haven, 1982.

Ziegler, Philip, *Mountbatten*. London: Collins, 1985.

INDEX